500
FABULOUS
CAKES
AND MORE

500

FABULOUS

CAKES

AND MORE

THE BEST-EVER FULLY ILLUSTRATED
CAKE AND BAKING BOOK

EDITOR: MARTHA DAY

BARNES & NOBLE BOOKS
NEW YORK

This edition published by Barnes & Noble Publishing, Inc., by
arrangement with Anness Publishing Limited

2005 Barnes & Noble Books

M 10 9 8 7 6 5 4 3 2 1

ISBN 0-7607-7228-2

Publisher: Joanna Lorenz
Managing Editor: Linda Fraser
Designer: Siân Keogh
Photographers: Karl Adamson, Edward Allwright, David Armstrong,
Steve Baxter, James Duncan, John Freeman, Michelle Garrett,
Amanda Heywood, Tim Hill, Don Last, Michael Michaels
Recipes: Alex Barker, Carole Clements, Roz Denny, Christine France,
Shirley Gill, Patricia Lousada, Norma MacMillan, Sue Maggs,
Janice Murfitt, Annie Nichols, Louise Pickford, Katherine Richmond,
Hilaire Walden, Steven Wheeler, Elizabeth Wolf-Cohen
Food for Photography: Carla Capalbo, Carole Handslip, Wendy Lee,
Sarah Maxwell, Angela Nilsen, Jane Stevenson, Liz Trigg and
Elizabeth Wolf-Cohen
Stylists: Madeleine Brehaut, Maria Kelly, Blake Minton,
Kirsty Rawlings, Fiona Tillett

Previously published as *500 Fabulous Cakes and Bakes*

Printed in Singapore

MEASUREMENTS:
Measurements have been provided in the following order:
metric, imperial and American cups. Do not mix units of
measurement within each recipe.
Size 3 (medium) eggs should be used unless otherwise stated.

CONTENTS

Introduction 6

Cookies and Bars 8

Teabreads, Buns and Muffins 40

Breads 68

Pies and Tarts 86

Cakes 112

Special Occasion Cakes 160

Children's Party Cakes 184

Novelty and Fantasy Cakes 210

Low Fat Baking 220

Basic Recipes 244

Index 254

Introduction

Baking is one of the most satisfying of all the culinary arts. It fills the house with the most wonderful aroma, gives ample reward for minimal effort and always meets with approval, especially from younger members of the family. Bake a batch of brownies, a fresh fruit pie, a crusty loaf of bread or a luxurious cake, and watch your rating rise!

This bonanza collection – five hundred of the finest recipes – is all you need to earn your champion baker's badge. It ranges from simple treats like drop pancakes and basic cookies to elaborate cakes for special celebrations. Each recipe carries a full color illustration of the finished bake, and the step-by-step instructions are so simple and straightforward that even a novice will find them easy to follow.

In fact, novice cooks often make the best bakers: preheating the oven in plenty of time, taking care to measure ingredients accurately and following recipe methods exactly. All these elements are important in baking, that demands more precision than many other types of cooking. With a soup or stew you can happily throw in extra ingredients or cheat a little when it comes to exact quantities, but the balance of ingredients, the temperature and the timing are all very important when you are baking a cake or pastry. It is worth reading the chosen recipe carefully before you begin, doing any advance preparation such as browning almonds or softening butter, then setting out the ingredients in the style of the TV cook.

Advice on lining pans is given in individual recipes. Wax paper is the traditional lining material, but nonstick parchment paper is even easier to use and gives excellent results. To line

the bottom of a pan, place it on the paper and draw around the outside edge, then cut out the shape. Grease the bottom of the pan with a dab of oil or butter to hold the paper in place, then fit it in the pan. Grease the paper (if using wax) and the sides of the pan.

Whether or not to grease pans used for pastry is a matter of choice. If the pastry is high in fat, such as piecrust, flaky or puff, it is not usually necessary; however, spills from fillings may stick. When in doubt, grease the pans lightly.

If you are a novice baker, start with some of the simpler recipes, such as Chocolate Chip Cookies, Chive and Potato Biscuits or a Quick-mix Sponge. Try some of the delectable breads, from a traditional Braided Loaf to the contemporary Saffron Focaccia.

You'll find every occasion amply catered for, from Valentine's Day through to a wedding. There are cakes for christenings, anniversaries and every possible birthday, from novelty teddies to telephones – including a mobile! For the family, the collection includes wonderful ways of keeping the cake tin and cookie barrel brimming with healthy snacks, including a selection for those with dietary restrictions. With vegans in view, there's a special chocolate cake and a Dundee cake, and an entire chapter is devoted to low fat cakes and bakes.

In this book, you will find a sweet or savory treat for every moment of the day, from breakfast Blueberry Muffins to a late-night slice of Pecan Tart. Tempted to embark on an immediate baking session? Go right ahead. Baking is a wonderfully therapeutic occupation – with sheer indulgence as the reward!

Farmhouse Cookies

Delightfully wholesome, these farmhouse cookies are ideal to serve with morning coffee.

Makes 18

¹/₂ cup butter or margarine, at room temperature
7 tablespoons light brown sugar
5 tablespoons crunchy peanut butter
1 egg
¹/₂ cup all-purpose flour
¹/₂ teaspoon baking powder
¹/₂ teaspoon ground cinnamon
¹/₄ teaspoon salt
1¹/₂ cups granola
¹/₂ cup raisins
¹/₂ cup chopped walnuts

1 Preheat the oven to 350°F. Grease a baking sheet.

2 Cream the butter or margarine and sugar until light and fluffy. Beat in the peanut butter and then beat in the egg.

3 Sift the flour, baking powder, cinnamon and salt over the peanut butter mixture and stir to blend. Stir in the granola, raisins and walnuts. Taste the mixture to see if it needs more sugar, as the sugar content of granola varies.

4 Drop rounded tablespoonfuls of the mixture onto the prepared baking sheet about 1 inch apart. Press gently with the back of a spoon to spread each mound into a circle.

5 Bake until lightly colored, about 15 minutes. With a metal spatula, transfer to a wire rack to cool. Store in an airtight container.

Crunchy Oatmeal Cookies

For nutty oatmeal cookies, substitute an equal quantity of chopped walnuts or pecans for the cereal.

Makes 14

³/₄ cup butter or margarine, at room temperature
³/₄ cup superfine sugar
1 egg yolk
1¹/₂ cups all-purpose flour
1 teaspoon baking soda
¹/₂ teaspoon salt
²/₃ cup rolled oats
²/₃ cup small crunchy nugget cereal

1 Cream the butter or margarine and sugar together until light and fluffy. Mix in the egg yolk.

2 Sift over the flour, baking soda and salt, then stir into the butter mixture. Add the oats and cereal and stir to blend. Chill for at least 20 minutes.

3 Preheat the oven to 375°F. Grease a baking sheet.

4 Roll the mixture into balls. Place them on the baking sheet and flatten with the base of a floured glass.

5 Bake until golden, about 10–12 minutes. Then with a metal spatula, transfer to a wire rack to cool. Store in an airtight container.

Apricot Yogurt Cookies

These cookies do not keep well, so it is best to eat them within two days, or to freeze them.

Makes 16

1½ cups all-purpose flour
1 teaspoon baking powder
1 teaspoon ground cinnamon
scant 1 cup rolled oats
½ cup light muscovado sugar
½ cup chopped ready-to-eat dried apricots
1 tablespoon slivered hazelnuts or almonds
scant ⅔ cup plain yogurt
3 tablespoons sunflower oil
raw sugar, to sprinkle

1 Preheat the oven to 375°F. Lightly oil a large baking sheet.

2 Sift together the flour, baking powder and cinnamon. Stir in the oats, sugar, apricots and nuts.

3 Beat together the yogurt and oil, then stir evenly into the mixture to make a firm dough. If necessary, add a little more yogurt.

4 Use your hands to roll the mixture into about 16 small balls, place on the baking sheet and flatten with a fork.

5 Sprinkle with raw sugar. Bake for 15–20 minutes, or until firm and golden brown. Transfer to a wire rack to cool. Store in an airtight container.

Oat and Apricot Clusters

You can change the ingredients according to what's in your pantry – try peanuts, pecans, raisins or dates.

Makes 12

4 tablespoons butter or margarine
4 tablespoons honey
½ cup medium oatmeal
¼ cup chopped ready-to-eat dried apricots
1 tablespoon banana chips
1 tablespoon dried coconut shreds
2–3 cups cornflakes or crispy cereal

1 Place the butter or margarine and honey in a small pan and warm over low heat, stirring until well blended.

2 Add the oatmeal, apricots, banana chips, coconut and cornflakes or crispy cereal and mix well.

3 Spoon the mixture into 12 paper muffin cases, piling it up roughly. Transfer to a baking sheet and chill until set and firm.

Oaty Coconut Cookies

The coconut gives these cookies both a wonderful texture and a great taste.

Makes 48

2 cups quick-cooking oats	1½ teaspoons vanilla
1½ cups dried coconut	extract
1 cup butter	1 cup all-purpose flour,
½ cup superfine sugar	sifted
¼ cup dark brown sugar	½ teaspoon baking soda
2 eggs	½ teaspoon salt
4 tablespoons milk	1 teaspoon ground
	cinnamon

1 Preheat the oven to 400°F. Spread the oats and coconut on a baking sheet. Bake for 8–10 minutes.

2 Cream the butter and sugars. Beat in the eggs, milk and vanilla. Fold in the dry ingredients. Add the oats and coconut. Drop spoonfuls of mixture onto two greased baking sheets. Bake for 8–10 minutes. Cool on a wire rack.

Crunchy Jumbles

For even crunchier cookies, add ½ cup walnuts, coarsely chopped, with the cereal and chocolate chips.

Makes 36

½ cup butter or	1¼ cups all-purpose
margarine, at room	flour, sifted
temperature	½ teaspoon baking soda
1 cup superfine sugar	¼ teaspoon salt
1 egg	2¼ cups crisped rice
1 teaspoon vanilla	cereal
extract	1 cup chocolate chips

1 Preheat the oven to 350°F. Grease two baking sheets. Cream the butter or margarine and sugar until fluffy. Add the egg and vanilla extract. Add the flour and baking soda and the salt, and fold in.

2 Add the cereal and chocolate chips and mix thoroughly. Drop spoonfuls 2 inches apart onto baking sheets and bake for 10–12 minutes. Transfer to a wire rack to cool.

Cinnamon-coated Cookies

Walnut cookies are rolled in a cinnamon and sugar mixture to give a delicate spicy flavor.

Makes 30

Preheat the oven to 375°F. Grease two baking sheets. Cream ½ cup butter, 1 cup sugar and 1 teaspoon vanilla extract. Beat in 2 eggs and ¼ cup milk. Sift over 3 cups all-purpose flour and 1 teaspoon baking soda. Stir in ½ cup chopped walnuts. Chill for 15 minutes, then roll into balls. Roll the balls in a sugar and cinnamon mixture. Bake for 10 minutes, then cool on a wire rack.

Ginger Cookies

So much tastier than store-bought varieties, these ginger cookies will disappear quickly, so make a large batch!

Makes 60

2¹/₂ cups all-purpose flour
1 teaspoon baking soda
1¹/₂ teaspoon ground ginger
¹/₄ teaspoon ground cinnamon
¹/₄ teaspoon ground cloves
¹/₂ cup butter or margarine, at room temperature
1³/₄ cups superfine sugar
1 egg, beaten
4 tablespoons molasses
1 teaspoon fresh lemon juice

1 Preheat the oven to 325°F. Lightly grease three to four baking sheets.

2 Sift the flour, baking soda and spices into a small bowl. Set aside.

3 Cream the butter or margarine and two-thirds of the sugar together. Stir in the egg, molasses and lemon juice. Add the flour mixture and mix in thoroughly with a wooden spoon to make a soft dough.

4 Shape the dough into ¾-inch balls. Roll the balls in the remaining sugar and place about 2 inches apart on the prepared baking sheets.

5 Bake until the cookies are just firm to the touch, about 12 minutes. With a metal spatula, transfer the cookies to a wire rack and let cool.

Cream Cheese Spirals

These cookies look so impressive and melt in the mouth, yet they are surprisingly easy to make.

Makes 32

1 cup butter, at room temperature
1 cup cream cheese
2 teaspoons superfine sugar
2 cups all-purpose flour
1 egg white, beaten with 1 tablespoon water, for glazing
superfine sugar, for sprinkling

For the filling
1 cup finely chopped walnuts
³/₄ cup light brown sugar
1 teaspoon ground cinnamon

1 Cream the butter, cream cheese and sugar until soft. Sift over the flour and mix until combined. Gather into a ball and divide in half. Flatten each half, wrap in wax paper and chill for 30 minutes. Meanwhile, mix all the filling ingredients together and set aside.

2 Preheat the oven to 375°F. Grease two baking sheets. Working with one half of the dough at a time, roll out thinly into an 11-inch circle. Using a dinner plate as a guide, trim the edges with a knife.

3 Brush the surface with the egg white glaze, and then sprinkle evenly with half the filling.

4 Cut the circle into 16 segments. Starting from the base of the triangles, roll up to form spirals.

5 Place on the baking sheets and brush with the remaining glaze. Sprinkle with superfine sugar. Bake until golden, about 15–20 minutes. Cool on a wire rack.

Italian Almond Biscotti

Serve biscotti after a meal, for dunking in sweet white wine, such as an Italian Vin Santo or a French Muscat.

Makes 48

1¾ cups whole
    unblanched almonds
scant 2 cups all-purpose
    flour
½ cup sugar
pinch of salt

pinch of saffron powder
½ teaspoon baking soda
2 eggs
1 egg white, lightly
    beaten

1   Preheat the oven to 375°F. Grease and flour two baking sheets.

2   Spread the almonds onto an ungreased baking sheet and bake until lightly browned, about 15 minutes. When cool, grind ½ cup of the almonds in a food processor, blender, or coffee grinder until pulverized. Coarsely chop the remaining almonds in two or three pieces each. Set aside.

3   Combine the flour, sugar, salt, saffron powder, baking soda and ground almonds in a bowl and mix to blend. Make a well in the center and add the eggs. Stir to form a rough dough. Transfer to a floured surface and knead until well blended. Knead in the chopped almonds.

4   Divide the dough into three equal parts. Roll into logs about 1 inch in diameter. Place on one of the prepared sheets, brush with the egg white and bake for 20 minutes. Remove from the oven. Lower the oven temperature to 275°F.

5   With a very sharp knife, cut into each log at an angle making ½-inch slices. Return the slices on the sheets to the oven and bake for 25 minutes. Transfer to a wire rack to cool.

Orange Cookies

These classic citrus-flavored cookies are ideal for a tasty treat at any time of the day.

Makes 30

½ cup butter, at room
    temperature
1 cup sugar
2 egg yolks
1 tablespoon fresh orange
    juice
grated rind of 1 large
    orange

1¾ cups all-purpose
    flour
1 tablespoon cornstarch
½ teaspoon salt
1 teaspoon baking
    powder

1   Cream the butter and sugar until light and fluffy. Add the yolks, orange juice and rind, and continue beating to blend.

2   In another bowl, sift together the flour, cornstarch, salt and baking powder. Add to the butter mixture and stir until it forms a dough. Wrap the dough in wax paper and chill for 2 hours.

3   Preheat the oven to 375°F. Grease two baking sheets. Roll spoonfuls of the dough into balls and place 1–2 inches apart on the baking sheets.

4   Press down with a fork to flatten. Bake until golden brown, about 8–10 minutes. Using a metal spatula, transfer to a wire rack to cool.

Raspberry Sandwich Cookies

These cookies can be stored in an airtight container with sheets of wax paper between the layers.

Makes 32

1 cup blanched almonds
1½ cups all-purpose
   flour
¾ cup butter, at room
   temperature
½ cup superfine sugar
grated rind of 1 lemon
1 teaspoon vanilla
   extract

1 egg white
¼ teaspoon salt
¼ cup slivered almonds
1 cup raspberry jam
1 tablespoon fresh lemon
   juice

1 Process the blanched almonds and 3 tablespoons flour in a food processor or blender until finely ground. Cream the butter and sugar together until light and fluffy. Stir in the lemon rind and vanilla. Add the ground almonds and remaining flour and mix well. Gather into a ball, wrap in wax paper, and chill for 1 hour.

2 Preheat the oven to 325°F. Line two baking sheets with wax paper. Divide the cookie mixture into four equal parts. Working with one section at a time, roll out to a thickness of ⅛-inch on a lightly floured surface. With a 2½-inch fluted pastry cutter, stamp out circles. Using a ¾-inch icing bag nozzle or pastry cutter, stamp out the centers from half the circles. Place the rings and circles 1 inch apart on the prepared baking sheets.

3 Whisk the egg white with the salt until just frothy. Chop the slivered almonds. Brush the cookie rings with the egg white, then sprinkle over the almonds. Bake until lightly browned, about 12–15 minutes. Cool for a few minutes on the baking sheets, then transfer to a wire rack.

4 In a saucepan, melt the jam with the lemon juice until it comes to a simmer. Brush the jam over the cookie circles and sandwich together with the rings.

Christmas Cookies

Decorate these delicious cookies with festive decorations or make them at any time of year.

Makes 30

¾ cup sweet butter, at
   room temperature
1½ cups superfine
   sugar
1 egg
1 egg yolk
1 teaspoon vanilla
   extract
grated rind of 1 lemon

¼ teaspoon salt
2½ cups all-purpose
   flour

**For decorating
(optional)**
colored fondant and
   small decorations

1 Preheat the oven to 350°F. With an electric mixer, cream the butter until soft. Add the sugar gradually and continue beating until light and fluffy. Using a wooden spoon, slowly mix in the whole egg and the egg yolk. Add the vanilla extract, lemon rind and salt. Stir to mix well. Add the flour and stir until blended. Gather the mixture into a ball, wrap in wax paper, and chill for 30 minutes.

2 On a floured surface, roll out the mixture about ⅛-inch thick. Stamp out shapes or rounds with cookie cutters. Bake until lightly colored, about 8 minutes. Transfer to a wire rack and let cool completely before icing and decorating, if wished.

Apricot Specials

Try other dried fruit, such as peaches or prunes, to vary the flavor of these special bars.

Makes 12
generous ¹/₂ cup light
  brown sugar
³/₄ cup all-purpose flour
6 tablespoons cold sweet
  butter, cut in pieces

1 cup water
grated rind of 1 lemon
generous ¹/₄ cup
  superfine sugar
2 teaspoons cornstarch
¹/₂ cup chopped walnuts

For the topping
generous ¹/₂ cup dried
  apricots

1   Preheat the oven to 350°F. In a mixing bowl, combine the brown sugar and flour. With a pastry blender, cut in the butter until the mixture resembles coarse bread crumbs.

2   Transfer to an 8-inch square baking pan and press level. Bake for 15 minutes. Remove from the oven but leave the oven on.

3   Meanwhile, for the topping, combine the apricots and water in a saucepan and simmer until soft; about 10 minutes. Strain the liquid and reserve. Chop the apricots.

4   Return the apricots to the saucepan and add the lemon rind, superfine sugar, cornstarch and 4 tablespoons of the soaking liquid. Cook for 1 minute.

5   Cool slightly before spreading the topping over the base. Sprinkle over the walnuts and bake for 20 minutes more. Cool in the pan before cutting into bars.

Brandy Snaps

You could serve these brandy snaps without the cream filling and eat with rich vanilla ice cream instead.

Makes 18
4 tablespoons butter, at
  room temperature
generous ¹/₂ cup
  superfine sugar
1 rounded tablespoon
  maple syrup
¹/₃ cup all-purpose flour

¹/₂ teaspoon ground
  ginger

For the filling
1 cup whipping cream
2 tablespoons brandy

1   Cream together the butter and sugar until light and fluffy, then beat in the maple syrup. Sift over the flour and ginger and mix together. Transfer the mixture to a work surface and knead until smooth. Cover and chill for 30 minutes.

2   Preheat the oven to 375°F. Grease a baking sheet. Working in batches of four, shape the mixture into walnut-size balls. Place well apart on the baking sheet and flatten slightly. Bake until golden and bubbling, about 10 minutes.

3   Remove from the oven and let cool for a few moments. Working quickly, slide a metal spatula under each one, turn over, and wrap around the handle of a wooden spoon (have four spoons ready). If they firm up too quickly, reheat for a few seconds to soften. When firm, slide the brandy snaps off and place on a wire rack to cool.

4   When all the brandy snaps are cool, prepare the filling. Whip the cream and brandy until soft peaks form. Pipe into each end of the brandy snaps just before serving.

Chocolate Pretzels

Pretzels come in many flavors – here is a chocolate version to bake and enjoy.

Makes 28

1¼ cups all-purpose flour	scant ⅔ cup sugar
¼ teaspoon salt	1 egg
6 tablespoons cocoa	1 egg white, lightly beaten, for glazing
½ cup butter, at room temperature	sugar crystals, for sprinkling

1 Sift together the flour, salt and cocoa. Set aside. Lightly grease two baking sheets. Cream the butter until light. Add the sugar and continue beating until light and fluffy. Beat in the egg. Add the dry ingredients and stir to blend. Gather the dough into a ball, place in plastic wrap and chill for 1 hour.

2 Roll the dough into 28 small balls. Chill the balls until needed. Preheat the oven to 375°F. Roll each ball into a rope about 10 inches long. With each rope, form a loop with the two ends facing you. Twist the ends and fold back onto the circle, pressing in to make a pretzel shape. Place on the prepared baking sheets.

3 Brush the pretzels with the egg white. Sprinkle sugar crystals over the tops and bake in the oven until firm, about 10–12 minutes. Transfer to a wire rack to cool.

Ginger Shapes

If your kids enjoy cooking with you, mixing and rolling the dough, or cutting out different shapes, this is the ideal recipe to let them practise on.

Makes 16

8 tablespoons brown sugar	1 tablespoon cocoa, sifted
½ cup soft margarine	2 teaspoons ground ginger
pinch of salt	a little milk
few drops vanilla extract	glacé icing and candied cherries, to decorate
1½ cups whole wheat flour	

1 Preheat the oven to 375°F Cream the sugar, margarine, salt and vanilla extract together until very soft and light.

2 Work in the flour, cocoa and ginger, adding a little milk, if necessary, to bind the mixture. Knead lightly on a floured surface until smooth.

3 Roll out the dough on a lightly floured surface to about 1¼-inch thick. Stamp out shapes using cookie cutters and place on baking sheets.

4 Bake the cookies for 10–15 minutes, let cool on the baking sheets until firm, then transfer to a wire rack to cool completely. Decorate with the icing and cherries.

Chocolate Macaroons

Roll one side of the macaroons in chopped nuts and bake nut-side up for a crunchier variation.

Makes 24

2 ounces semisweet
  chocolate, melted
1¹/₂ cups blanched
  almonds
1 cup superfine sugar
3 egg whites

¹/₂ teaspoon vanilla
  extract
¹/₄ teaspoon almond
  extract
confectioner's sugar, for
  dusting

1 Preheat the oven to 325°F. Line two baking sheets with wax paper, then grease. Grind the almonds in a food processor or blender. Transfer to a bowl, then blend in the sugar, egg whites, vanilla and almond extract. Stir in the chocolate. The mixture should just hold its shape; if it is too soft, chill for 15 minutes.

2 Shape the mixture into walnut-size balls. Place on the baking sheets and flatten slightly. Brush with water; dust with confectioner's sugar. Bake until just firm, 10–12 minutes. With a metal spatula, transfer to a wire rack to cool.

Chocolate-orange Sponge Drops

Light and crispy, with a marmalade filling, these sponge drops are truly decadent.

Makes 14–15

2 eggs
¹/₄ cup superfine sugar
¹/₂ teaspoon grated
  orange rind
¹/₂ cup all-purpose
  flour

4 tablespoons fine
  shred orange
  marmalade
1¹/₂ ounces semisweet
  chocolate, cut into
  small pieces

1 Preheat the oven to 400°F. Line three baking sheets with parchment paper. Put the eggs and sugar in a bowl over a pan of simmering water. Whisk until thick and pale. Remove from the pan and whisk until cool. Whisk in the orange rind. Sift the flour over and fold it in gently.

2 Put 28–30 dessert spoonfuls of the mixture on the baking sheets. Bake for 8 minutes, until golden. Cool slightly, then transfer to a wire rack. Sandwich pairs together with marmalade. Melt the chocolate, and drizzle over the drops.

Coconut Macaroons

Have a change from after-dinner mints, and serve these delicious coconut macaroons with coffee instead.

Makes 24

Preheat the oven to 350°F. Grease two baking sheets. Sift ¹/₃ cup all-purpose flour and 1¼ teaspoons salt into a bowl, then stir in 4 cups dried coconut. Pour in scant ¾ cup sweetened condensed milk. Add 1 teaspoon vanilla extract; stir from the center to a thick mixture. Drop tablespoonfuls of the mixture 1 inch apart on the baking sheets. Bake until golden brown, about 20 minutes. Cool on a wire rack.

Peanut Butter Cookies

For added crunchiness, stir in ½ cup peanuts, coarsely chopped, with the peanut butter.

Makes 24

1¼ cups all-purpose
   flour
½ teaspoon baking soda
½ teaspoon salt
½ cup butter, at room
   temperature
scant 1 cup light brown
   sugar

1 egg
1 teaspoon vanilla
   extract
scant 1¼ cups crunchy
   peanut butter

1 Sift together the flour, baking soda and salt and set aside. In another bowl, cream the butter and sugar together until light and fluffy.

2 In a third bowl, mix the egg and vanilla, then gradually beat into the butter mixture. Stir in the peanut butter and the chopped peanuts, if using, and blend thoroughly. Stir in the dry ingredients. Chill for 30 minutes, or until firm.

3 Preheat the oven to 350°. Grease two baking sheets. Spoon out rounded teaspoonfuls of the dough and roll into balls.

4 Place the balls on the baking sheets and press flat with a fork into circles about 2½ inches in diameter, making a crisscross pattern. Bake in the oven until lightly colored, about 12–15 minutes. Transfer to a wire rack to cool.

Chocolate Chip Cookies

A perennial favorite with all the family, these cookies contain walnuts as well as chocolate chips.

Makes 24

½ cup butter or
   margarine, at room
   temperature
scant ¼ cup superfine
   sugar
generous ½ cup dark
   brown sugar
1 egg

½ teaspoon vanilla
   extract
1½ cups all-purpose
   flour
½ teaspoon baking soda
¼ teaspoon salt
1 cup chocolate chips
½ cup walnuts, chopped

1 Preheat the oven to 350°F. Lightly grease two large baking sheets. With an electric mixer, cream the butter or margarine and both the sugars together until light and fluffy.

2 In another bowl, mix the egg and the vanilla extract, then gradually beat into the butter mixture. Sift over the flour, baking soda and salt, and stir. Add the chocolate chips and walnuts, and mix to combine well.

4 Place heaped teaspoonfuls of the dough 2 inches apart on the baking sheets. Bake in the oven until lightly colored, about 10–15 minutes. Transfer to a wire rack to cool.

Almond Tile Cookies

These cookies are named after the French roof tiles they so closely resemble.

Makes about 24

scant ¹/₂ cup whole
  blanched almonds,
  lightly toasted
¹/₃ cup superfine sugar
3 tablespoons sweet
  butter, softened

2 egg whites
¹/₂ teaspoon almond
  extract
¹/₃ cup all-purpose flour,
  sifted
¹/₂ cup slivered almonds

1 Preheat the oven to 400°F. Grease two baking sheets. Place the almonds and 2 tablespoons of the sugar in a blender or food processor and process until finely ground, but not pasty.

2 Beat the butter until creamy, add the remaining sugar and beat until light and fluffy. Gradually beat in the egg whites until the mixture is well blended, then beat in the almond extract. Sift the flour over the butter mixture and fold in, then fold in the almond mixture.

3 Drop tablespoonfuls of the mixture onto the baking sheets 6 inches apart. With the back of a wet spoon, spread each mound into a paper-thin 3-inch circle. Sprinkle with the slivered almonds.

4 Bake the cookies, one sheet at a time, for 5–6 minutes until the edges are golden and the centers still pale. Remove the baking sheet to a wire rack and, working quickly, use a metal spatula to loosen the edges of a cookie. Lift the cookie on the metal spatula and place over a rolling pin, then press down the sides of the cookie to curve it. Repeat with the remaining cookies, and let cool.

Brittany Butter Cookies

These little cookies are similar to shortbread, but richer in taste and texture.

Makes 18–20

6 egg yolks, lightly
  beaten
1 tablespoon milk
2 cups all-purpose flour
generous ³/₄ cup superfine
  sugar

scant 1 cup lightly salted
  butter at room
  temperature, cut into
  small pieces

1 Preheat the oven to 350°F. Lightly butter a large baking sheet. Mix 1 tablespoon of the egg yolks with the milk for a glaze. Set aside.

2 Sift the flour into a large bowl and make a central well. Add the egg yolks, sugar and butter and, using your fingertips, work the ingredients together until smooth and creamy. Gradually blend in the flour to form a smooth but slightly sticky dough.

3 Using floured hands, pat out the dough to ¹/₃ inch thick and cut out circles using a 3-inch cookie cutter. Transfer the circles to the baking sheet, brush with egg glaze, then score to create a lattice pattern.

4 Bake for 12–15 minutes until golden. Cool on the sheet on a wire rack for 15 minutes, then transfer to the wire rack to cool completely.

Ginger Florentines

These colorful, chewy cookies are delicious served with vanilla or other flavored ice cream.

Makes 30

4 tablespoons butter
$^1/_2$ cup superfine sugar
$^1/_4$ cup candied cherries, chopped
generous 1 tablespoon candied orange peel, chopped
$^1/_2$ cup slivered almonds
$^1/_2$ cup chopped walnuts
1 tablespoon candied ginger, chopped

2 tablespoons all-purpose flour
$^1/_2$ teaspoon ground ginger

To finish
2 ounces semisweet chocolate, melted
2 ounces white chocolate, melted

1 Preheat the oven to 350°F. Beat the butter and sugar together until light and fluffy. Thoroughly mix in all the remaining ingredients, except the melted semisweet and white chocolate.

2 Line some baking sheets with nonstick parchment paper. Put four small spoonfuls of the mixture onto each sheet, spacing them well apart to allow for spreading. Flatten the cookies and bake for 5 minutes.

3 Remove the cookies from the oven and flatten with a wet fork, shaping them into neat rounds. Return to the oven for about 3–4 minutes, until they are golden brown. Work in batches if necessary.

4 Let cool on the baking sheets for 2 minutes to firm up, and then transfer to a wire rack. When they are cold and firm, spread semisweet chocolate on the undersides of half the cookies and white chocolate on the undersides of the rest.

Christmas Shapes

These are great fun for kids to make as presents, and any shape of cookie cutter can be used.

Makes about 12

6 tablespoons butter
generous $^1/_2$ cup confectioner's sugar
finely grated rind of 1 small lemon
1 egg yolk
$1^1/_2$ cups all-purpose flour

pinch of salt

To decorate
2 egg yolks
red and green food coloring

1 Beat the butter, sugar and lemon rind together until pale and fluffy. Beat in the egg yolk, and then sift in the flour and the salt. Knead together to form a smooth dough. Wrap and chill for 30 minutes.

2 Preheat the oven to 375°F. On a lightly floured surface, roll out the dough to $^1/_8$-inch thick. Using a $2^1/_2$-inch fluted cutter, stamp out as many cookies as you can, with the cutter dipped in flour to prevent it from sticking to the dough.

3 Transfer the cookies onto lightly greased baking sheets. Mark the tops lightly with a 1-inch holly leaf cutter and use a $^1/_4$-inch plain icing bag nozzle for the berries. Chill for 10 minutes, until firm.

4 Meanwhile, put each egg yolk into a small cup. Mix red food coloring into one and green food coloring into the other. Using a small, clean paintbrush, carefully paint the colors onto the cookies. Bake for 10–12 minutes, or until they begin to color around the edges. Let them cool slightly on the baking sheets, then transfer to a wire rack.

Traditional Sugar Cookies

These lovely old-fashioned cookies would be ideal to serve at an elegant tea party.

Makes 36

3 cups all-purpose flour
1 teaspoon baking soda
2 teaspoons baking
   powder
$^{1}/_{4}$ teaspoon grated
   nutmeg
$^{1}/_{2}$ cup butter or
   margarine, at room
   temperature

generous 1 cup superfine
   sugar
$^{1}/_{2}$ teaspoon vanilla
   extract
1 egg
$^{1}/_{2}$ cup milk
colored or raw sugar, for
   sprinkling

1 Sift the flour, baking soda, baking powder and nutmeg into a small bowl. Set aside. Cream the butter or margarine, superfine sugar and vanilla extract together until the mixture is light and fluffy. Add the egg and beat to mix well.

2 Add the flour mixture alternately with the milk, stirring with a wooden spoon to make a soft dough. Place the dough in plastic film, and chill for 30 minutes.

3 Preheat the oven to 350°F. Roll out the dough on a lightly floured surface to a ⅛-inch thickness. Cut into circles with a cookie cutter.

4 Transfer the cookies to ungreased baking sheets. Sprinkle each one with sugar. Bake until golden, 10–12 minutes. With a metal spatula, transfer the cookies to a wire rack to cool.

Spicy Pepper Cookies

Despite the warm, complex flavor added by the spices, these light cookies are simple to make.

Makes 48

$^{3}/_{4}$ cup all-purpose flour
$^{1}/_{4}$ cup cornstarch
2 teaspoons baking
   powder
$^{1}/_{2}$ teaspoon ground
   cardamom
$^{1}/_{2}$ teaspoon ground
   cinnamon
$^{1}/_{2}$ teaspoon grated
   nutmeg
$^{1}/_{2}$ teaspoon ground
   ginger
$^{1}/_{2}$ teaspoon ground
   allspice
$^{1}/_{2}$ teaspoon salt

$^{1}/_{2}$ teaspoon freshly
   ground black pepper
1 cup butter or
   margarine, at room
   temperature
$^{1}/_{2}$ cup light brown sugar
$^{1}/_{2}$ teaspoon vanilla
   extract
1 teaspoon finely grated
   lemon rind
$^{1}/_{4}$ cup whipping cream
$^{3}/_{4}$ cup finely ground
   almonds
2 tablespoons
   confectioner's sugar

1 Preheat the oven to 350°F . Sift the flour, cornstarch, baking powder, spices, salt and pepper into a bowl.

2 Cream the butter or margarine and brown sugar until light and fluffy. Beat in the vanilla extract and lemon rind.

3 With the mixer on low speed, add the flour mixture alternately with the cream, beginning and ending with flour. Stir in the ground almonds.

4 Shape the dough into ¾-inch balls. Place them on ungreased baking sheets about 1 inch apart. Bake until golden brown underneath, about 15–20 minutes.

5 Let cool on the baking sheets for about 1 minute before transferring to a wire rack to cool completely. Before serving, sprinkle lightly with confectioner's sugar.

Marsala Cookies

These little yellow cookies come from the Veneto region of Italy, and Marsala wine enhances their regional appeal.

Makes about 48

½ cup golden raisins
½ cup finely ground
   yellow cornmeal
1½ cups all-purpose flour
1½ teaspoon baking
   powder
pinch of salt

1 cup butter
1 cup sugar
2 eggs
1 tablespoon Marsala or
   1 teaspoon vanilla
   extract

1 Soak the golden raisins in a small bowl of warm water for 15 minutes. Drain. Preheat the oven to 350°F. Sift the cornmeal and flour, the baking powder and the salt into a bowl.

2 Cream the butter and sugar together until light and fluffy. Beat in the eggs, one at a time. Beat in the Marsala or vanilla extract. Add the dry ingredients to the batter, beating until well blended. Stir in the golden raisins.

3 Drop heaped teaspoonfuls of batter onto a greased baking sheet in rows about 2 inches apart. Bake for 7–8 minutes, or until the cookies are golden brown at the edges. Transfer to a wire rack to cool.

Mexican Cinnamon Cookies

Pastelitos are traditional sweet shortbreads at weddings in Mexico, dusted in sugar to match the bride's dress.

Makes 20

½ cup butter
2 tablespoons superfine
   sugar
1 cup all-purpose flour
¼ cup cornstarch
¼ teaspoon ground
   cinnamon

2 tablespoons chopped
   mixed nuts
¼ cup confectioner's
   sugar, sifted

1 Preheat the oven to 325°F. Lightly grease a baking sheet. Place the butter and sugar in a bowl and beat until pale.

2 Sift in the all-purpose flour, cornstarch and cinnamon, and gradually work in with a wooden spoon until the mixture comes together. Knead lightly until completely smooth.

3 Take tablespoonfuls of the mixture, roll into 20 small balls and arrange on the baking sheet. Press a few chopped nuts into the top of each one and then flatten slightly.

4 Bake the cookies for about 30–35 minutes, until pale golden. Remove from the oven and, while they are still warm, toss them in the sifted confectioner's sugar. Let the cookies cool on a wire rack before serving.

Toasted Oat Meringues

Meringues needn't be plain. Try these oaty ones for a lovely crunchy change.

Makes 12

generous ¹/₂ cup rolled oats	¹/₄ teaspoon salt
	1¹/₂ teaspoons cornstarch
2 egg whites	³/₄ cup superfine sugar

1 Preheat the oven to 275°F. Spread the oats on a baking sheet and toast in the oven until golden, for about 10 minutes. Lower the heat to 250°F. Grease and flour a baking sheet.

2 Beat the egg whites and salt until they start to form soft peaks. Sift over the cornstarch and continue beating until the whites hold stiff peaks. Add half the sugar; whisk until glossy. Add the remaining sugar and fold in, then fold in the oats.

3 Place tablespoonfuls of the mixture onto the baking sheet and bake for 2 hours, then turn off the oven. Turn over the meringues, and let cool in the oven.

Meringues

Make these classic meringues as large or small as you like. Serve as a teatime treat or as an elegant dessert.

Makes about 24

4 egg whites	¹/₂ teaspoon vanilla or
¹/₄ teaspoon salt	almond extract
1¹/₄ cups superfine sugar	(optional)
	1 cup whipping cream

1 Preheat the oven to 225°F. Grease and flour two large baking sheets. Beat the egg whites and salt in a metal bowl. When they start to form soft peaks, add half the sugar and continue beating until the mixture holds stiff peaks.

2 With a large metal spoon, fold in the remaining sugar and vanilla or almond extract, if using. Pipe or spoon the meringue mixture onto the baking sheets. Bake for 2 hours, turn off the oven. Loosen the meringues, invert, and set in another place on the sheets to prevent sticking. Let cool in the oven. Whip the cream and use to fill the meringues.

Chewy Chocolate Cookies

If you have a weakness for chocolate, add ¹/₂ cup chocolate chips to the mixture with the nuts.

Makes 18

Preheat the oven to 350°F. Line two baking sheets with wax paper and grease. Using an electric mixer, beat 4 egg whites until frothy. Sift over 2 cups confectioner's sugar and 1 teaspoon coffee. Add 1 tablespoon water, beat on low speed to blend, then on high until thick. Fold in 1 cup chopped walnuts. Place generous spoonfuls of the mixture 1 inch apart on the sheets. Bake for 12–15 minutes. Transfer to a wire rack to cool.

Lavender Cookies

Instead of lavender you can use other flavorings, such as cinnamon, lemon, orange or mint.

Makes about 30
⅔ cup butter
½ cup sugar
1 egg, beaten
1 tablespoon dried
   lavender flowers

1½ cups self-rising flour
leaves and flowers,
   to decorate

1   Preheat the oven to 350°F. Grease two baking sheets. Cream the butter and sugar together, then stir in the egg. Mix in the lavender flowers and the flour.

2   Drop spoonfuls of the mixture onto the baking sheets. Bake for about 15–20 minutes, until the cookies are golden. Serve with some fresh leaves and flowers to decorate.

Chocolate Amaretti

As an alternative decoration, lightly press a few coffee sugar crystals on top of each cookie before baking.

Makes 24
scant 1 cup blanched,
   toasted whole almonds
½ cup superfine sugar
1 tablespoon cocoa
2 tablespoons
   confectioner's sugar

2 egg whites
pinch of cream of tartar
1 teaspoon almond
   extract
slivered almonds,
   to decorate

1   Preheat the oven to 325°F. Line a large baking sheet with nonstick parchment paper or foil. In a food processor fitted with a metal blade, process the toasted almonds with half the sugar until they are finely ground but not oily. Transfer to a bowl and sift in the cocoa and confectioner's sugar; stir to blend. Set aside.

2   Beat the egg whites and cream of tartar until stiff peaks form. Sprinkle in the remaining sugar 1 tablespoon at a time, beating well after each addition, and continue beating until the whites are glossy and stiff. Beat in the almond extract.

3   Sprinkle over the almond mixture and gently fold into the egg whites until just blended. Spoon the mixture into a large icing bag fitted with a plain ½-inch nozzle. Pipe 1½-inch rounds, 1 inch apart, on the baking sheet. Press a slivered almond into the center of each.

4   Bake the cookies for 12–15 minutes or until they appear crisp. Remove the baking sheet to a wire rack to cool for 10 minutes. With a metal metal spatula, transfer the cookies to the wire rack to cool completely.

Melting Moments

These cookies are very crisp and light – and they really do melt in your mouth.

Makes 16–20

3 tablespoons butter or margarine
5 tablespoons vegetable shortening
scant $^1/_2$ cup superfine sugar
$^1/_2$ egg, beaten

few drops of vanilla or almond extract
$1^1/_4$ cups self-rising flour
rolled oats, for coating
4–5 candied cherries, quartered, to decorate

1 Preheat the oven to 350°F. Beat together the butter or margarine, shortening and sugar, then gradually beat in the egg and vanilla or almond extract.

2 Stir the flour into the beaten mixture, with floured hands, then roll into 16–20 small balls. Spread the rolled oats on a sheet of wax paper and toss the balls in them to coat evenly.

3 Place the balls, spaced slightly apart, on two baking sheets, place a piece of cherry on top of each and bake for about 15–20 minutes, until lightly browned. Let the cookies cool on the sheets for 5 minutes before transferring to a wire rack to cool completely.

Easter Cookies

This is a seasonal recipe, but these cookies can be enjoyed at any time of the year.

Makes 16–18

$^1/_2$ cup butter or margarine
scant $^1/_2$ cup superfine sugar, plus extra for sprinkling
1 egg, separated
$1^3/_4$ cups all-purpose flour

$^1/_2$ teaspoon mixed spice
$^1/_2$ teaspoon ground cinnamon
4 tablespoons currants
1 tablespoon chopped candied peel
1–2 tablespoons milk

1 Preheat the oven to 400°F. Lightly grease two baking sheets. Cream together the butter or margarine and sugar until light and fluffy, then beat in the egg yolk.

2 Sift the flour and spices over the egg mixture, then fold in with the currants and peel, adding sufficient milk to make a fairly soft dough.

3 Turn the dough onto a floured surface, knead lightly until just smooth, then roll out using a floured rolling pin, to about a ¼-inch thickness. Cut the dough into circles using a 2-inch fluted cookie cutter. Transfer the circles to the baking sheets and bake for 10 minutes.

4 Beat the egg white, then brush over the cookies. Sprinkle with superfine sugar and return to the oven for 10 minutes more, until golden. Transfer to a wire rack to cool.

Shortbread

Once you have tasted this shortbread, you'll never buy a package from a store again.

Makes 8

generous ¹/₂ cup sweet
   butter, at room
   temperature
¹/₂ cup superfine sugar
1¹/₄ cups all-purpose
   flour

¹/₂ cup rice flour
¹/₄ teaspoon baking
   powder
¹/₄ teaspoon salt

1 Preheat the oven to 325°F. Lightly grease an 8-inch shallow round cake pan. Cream the butter and sugar together until light and fluffy. Sift over the flours, baking powder and salt, and mix well.

2 Press the mixture neatly into the prepared pan, smoothing the surface with the back of a spoon. Prick all over with a fork, then score into eight equal wedges.

3 Bake until golden, about 40–45 minutes. Let sit in the pan until cool enough to handle, then unmold and recut the wedges while still hot. Store in an airtight container.

Flapjacks

For a spicier version, add 1 teaspoon ground ginger to the melted butter.

Makes 8

¹/₄ cup butter
21 rounded tablespoons
   maple syrup
scant ¹/₂ cup dark brown
   sugar

generous 1 cup quick-
   cooking oats
¹/₄ teaspoon salt

1 Preheat the oven to 350°F. Line and grease an 8-inch shallow round cake pan. Place the butter, maple syrup and sugar in a pan over low heat. Cook, stirring, until melted and combined.

2 Remove from heat and add the oats and salt. Stir the mixture to blend. Spoon the mixture into the prepared pan and smooth the surface. Place in the center of the oven and bake until golden brown, 20–25 minutes. Let sit in the pan until cool enough to handle, then unmold and cut into wedges while still hot. Store in an airtight container.

Chocolate Delights

This method of making cookies makes sure they are all of a uniform size.

Makes 50

1 ounce semisweet
   chocolate
1 ounce bittersweet
   chocolate
2 cups all-purpose flour
1/2 teaspoon salt
1 cup sweet butter, at
   room temperature

generous 1 cup superfine
   sugar
2 eggs
1 teaspoon vanilla
   extract
1 cup finely chopped
   walnuts

1   Melt the chocolate in the top of a double boiler, or in a heat proof bowl set over a pan of gently simmering water. Set aside. In a bowl, sift together the flour and salt. Set aside.

2   Cream the butter until soft. Add the sugar and continue beating until the mixture is light and fluffy. Mix the eggs and vanilla extract, then gradually stir into the butter mixture. Stir in the chocolate, then the flour. Finally, stir in the nuts.

3   Divide the mixture into four equal parts, and roll each into a 2-inch diameter log. Wrap tightly in foil and chill or freeze until firm.

4   Preheat the oven to 375°F. Grease two baking sheets. With a sharp knife, cut the logs into ¼-inch slices. Place the circles on the baking sheets and bake until lightly colored, about 10 minutes. Using a metal spatula, transfer the cookies to a wire rack to cool.

Cinnamon Treats

Place these cookies in a heart-shape basket, as here, and serve them up with love.

Makes 50

generous 2 cups all-
   purpose flour
1/2 teaspoon salt
2 teaspoons ground
   cinnamon
1 cup sweet butter, at
   room temperature

generous 1 cup superfine
   sugar
2 eggs
1 teaspoon vanilla
   extract

1   Sift together the flour, salt and cinnamon into a bowl. Set aside.

2   Cream the butter until soft. Add the sugar and continue beating until the mixture is light and fluffy. Beat the eggs and vanilla extract together, then gradually stir into the butter mixture. Stir in the dry ingredients.

3   Divide the mixture into four equal parts, then roll each into a 2-inch diameter log. Wrap tightly in foil and chill or freeze until firm.

4   Preheat the oven to 375°F. Grease two baking sheets. With a sharp knife, cut the logs into ¼-inch slices. Place the rounds on the baking sheets and bake until lightly colored, about 10 minutes. Using a metal spatula, transfer to a wire rack to cool.

Chunky Chocolate Drops

Do not allow these cookies to cool completely on the baking sheet or they will break when you try to lift them.

Makes 18

6 ounces semisweet chocolate	1 cup pecans, toasted and coarsely chopped
1/2 cup sweet butter	1 cup semisweet chocolate chips
2 eggs	4 ounces fine quality white chocolate, chopped into 1/4-inch pieces
1/2 cup sugar	
1/4 cup light brown sugar	
1/3 cup all-purpose flour	
1/4 cup cocoa	
1 teaspoon baking powder	4 ounces fine quality milk chocolate, chopped into 1/4-inch pieces
2 teaspoons vanilla extract	
pinch of salt	

1 Preheat the oven to 325°F. Grease two large baking sheets. In a medium saucepan over low heat, melt the semisweet chocolate and butter until smooth, stirring frequently. Remove from the heat to cool slightly.

2 Beat the eggs and sugars for 2–3 minutes until pale and creamy. Gradually beat in the melted chocolate mixture. Beat in the flour, cocoa, baking powder, vanilla and salt, just to blend. Add the nuts, chocolate chips and chocolate pieces.

3 Drop 4–6 heaped tablespoonfuls of the mixture onto each baking sheet 4 inches apart and flatten each to a round about 3 inches. Bake for 8–10 minutes, until the tops are shiny and cracked and the edges look crisp.

4 Transfer the baking sheets to a wire rack to cool for about 2 minutes, until the cookies are just set, then transfer them to the wire rack to cool completely. Continue to bake in batches.

Chocolate Crackle-tops

These cookies are best eaten on the day they are baked, as they dry slightly on storage.

Makes 38

7 ounces semisweet chocolate, chopped	scant 2 cups all-purpose flour
7 tablespoons sweet butter	1/4 cup cocoa
1/2 cup superfine sugar	1/2 teaspoon baking powder
3 eggs	pinch of salt
1 teaspoon vanilla extract	1 1/2 cups confectioner's sugar, for coating

1 Heat the chocolate and butter over low heat until smooth, stirring frequently. Remove from the heat. Stir in the sugar, and continue stirring until dissolved. Add the eggs, one at a time, beating well after each addition; stir in the vanilla. In a separate bowl, sift together the flour, cocoa, baking powder and salt. Gradually stir into the chocolate mixture until just blended. Cover and chill for at least 1 hour.

2 Preheat the oven to 325°F. Grease two or three large baking sheets. Place the confectioner's sugar in a small, deep bowl. Using a teaspoon, scoop the dough into small balls and roll in your hands into 1 1/2-inch balls.

3 Drop the balls, one at a time, into the confectioner's sugar and roll until heavily coated. Remove each ball with a slotted spoon and tap against the bowl to remove any excess sugar. Place on the baking sheets 1 1/2 inches apart.

4 Bake the cookies for 10–15 minutes or until the tops feel slightly firm when touched with your fingertip. Remove the baking sheets to a wire rack for 2–3 minutes, then, with a metal spatula, transfer the cookies to the wire rack to cool.

Chocolate Chip Oat Cookies

Oat cookies are given a delicious lift by the inclusion of chocolate chips. Try caramel chips for a change, if you like.

Makes 60

1 cup all-purpose flour
$^1/_2$ teaspoon baking soda
$^1/_4$ teaspoon baking powder
$^1/_4$ teaspoon salt
$^1/_2$ cup butter or margarine, at room temperature
generous $^1/_2$ cup superfine sugar

generous $^1/_2$ cup light brown sugar
1 egg
$^1/_2$ teaspoon vanilla extract
scant $^1/_2$ cup rolled oats
1 cup semisweet chocolate chips

1 Preheat the oven to 350°F. Grease three or four baking sheets. Sift the flour, baking soda, baking powder and salt into a mixing bowl. Set aside.

2 With an electric mixer, cream the butter or margarine and the sugars together. Add the egg and vanilla, and beat until light and fluffy. Add the flour mixture and beat on low speed until thoroughly blended. Stir in the rolled oats and semisweet chocolate chips, mixing well with a wooden spoon. The dough should be crumbly.

3 Drop heaped teaspoonfuls onto the baking sheets, about 1 inch apart. Bake until just firm around the edges but still soft in the centers, about 15 minutes. With a metal spatula, transfer the cookies to a wire rack to cool.

Chocolate and Coconut Slices

These tasty family favorites are easier to slice if they are allowed to cool overnight.

Makes 24

2 cups crushed digestive cookies
$^1/_4$ cup superfine sugar
pinch of salt
$^1/_2$ cup butter or margarine, melted

$1^1/_2$ cups dried coconut
9 ounces semisweet chocolate chips
1 cup sweetened condensed milk
1 cup chopped walnuts

1 Preheat the oven to 350°F. In a bowl, combine the crushed cookies, sugar, salt and butter or margarine. Press the mixture over the bottom of an ungreased 13 x 9-inch baking dish.

2 Sprinkle the coconut over the cookie bottom, then sprinkle the chocolate chips over the top. Pour the condensed milk evenly over the chocolate. Sprinkle the walnuts on top. Bake for 30 minutes. Unmold onto a wire rack and let cool.

Nut Lace Wafers

Oatmeal Lace Rounds

To create a different taste, add some finely grated orange peel to these delicate cookies.

These rich, nutty cookies are very quick and simple to make and will be enjoyed by everyone.

Makes 18

scant *¹/₂ cup blanched almonds*
¹/₄ cup butter
¹/₃ cup all-purpose flour
¹/₂ cup superfine sugar
2 tablespoons heavy cream
¹/₂ teaspoon vanilla extract

1 Preheat the oven to 375°F. Lightly grease two baking sheets.

2 With a sharp knife, chop the almonds as finely as possible. Alternatively, use a food processor or blender to chop the nuts very finely.

3 Melt the butter in a saucepan over low heat. Remove from the heat and stir in the remaining ingredients and the finely chopped almonds.

4 Drop teaspoonfuls 2½ inches apart on the prepared sheets. Bake until golden, about 5 minutes. Cool on the baking sheets briefly, until the wafers are just stiff enough to remove. With a metal spatula, transfer to a wire rack to cool.

Makes 36

²/₃ cup butter or margarine
1¹/₄ cups quick-cooking porridge oats
³/₄ cup dark brown sugar
²/₃ cup superfine sugar
¹/₃ cup all-purpose flour
¹/₄ teaspoon salt
1 egg, lightly beaten
1 teaspoon vanilla extract
generous ¹/₂ cup pecans or walnuts, finely chopped

1 Preheat the oven to 350°F. Lightly grease two baking sheets.

2 Melt the butter or margarine in a saucepan over low heat. Set aside. In a mixing bowl, combine the oats, brown sugar, superfine sugar, flour and salt. Make a well in the center and add the butter or margarine, egg and vanilla. Mix until blended, then stir in the chopped nuts.

3 Drop rounded teaspoonfuls of the mixture about 2 inches apart on the prepared baking sheets. Bake in the oven until lightly browned on the edges and bubbling all over, about 5–8 minutes. Cool on the baking sheets for 2 minutes, then transfer to a wire rack to cool completely.

Nutty Chocolate Squares

These delicious squares are incredibly rich, so cut them smaller if you wish.

Makes 16

2 eggs
2 teaspoons vanilla
  extract
¹/₄ teaspoon salt
1¹/₂ cups pecans, coarsely
  chopped
¹/₂ cup all-purpose flour
¹/₄ cup superfine sugar

¹/₂ cup maple syrup
3 ounces semisweet
  chocolate, finely
  chopped
3 tablespoons butter
16 pecan halves, to
  decorate

1 Preheat the oven to 325°F. Line the bottom and sides of an 8-inch square baking pan with wax paper and lightly grease the paper.

2 Whisk together the eggs, vanilla and salt. In another bowl, mix together the chopped pecan and flour. Set both aside until needed.

3 In a saucepan, bring the sugar and maple syrup to a boil. Remove from the heat, stir in the chocolate and butter, and blend thoroughly with a wooden spoon. Mix in the beaten egg mixture, then fold in the pecan mixture.

4 Pour the mixture into the baking pan and bake until set, about 35 minutes. Cool in the pan for 10 minutes before unmolding. Cut into 2-inch squares and press pecan halves into the tops while warm. Cool on a wire rack.

Raisin Brownies

Cover these brownies with a light chocolate frosting for a truly decadent treat, if you wish.

Makes 16

¹/₂ cup butter or
  margarine
¹/₂ cup cocoa
2 eggs
generous 1 cup superfine
  sugar

1 teaspoon vanilla
  extract
¹/₃ cup all-purpose flour
³/₄ cup chopped walnuts
generous ¹/₂ cup raisins

1 Preheat the oven to 350°F. Line the bottom and sides of an 8-inch square baking pan with wax paper. Grease the paper.

2 Gently melt the butter or margarine in a small saucepan. Remove from the heat and stir in the cocoa. With an electric mixer, beat the eggs, sugar and vanilla together until light. Add the cocoa mixture and stir to blend.

3 Sift the flour over the cocoa mixture and gently fold in. Add the walnuts and raisins and scrape the mixture into the prepared baking tin.

4 Bake in the center of the oven for 30 minutes. Let cool in the pan before cutting into 2-inch squares and removing. The brownies should be soft and moist.

Chocolate Chip Brownies

A double dose of chocolate is incorporated into these melt-in-the-mouth brownies.

Makes 24

4 ounces semisweet
   chocolate
$1/2$ cup butter
3 eggs
1 cup sugar

$1/2$ teaspoon vanilla
   extract
pinch of salt
$1^1/4$ cups all-purpose
   flour
1 cup chocolate chips

1 Preheat the oven to 350°F. Line a 13 x 9-inch baking pan with wax paper and grease the paper.

2 Melt the chocolate and butter together in the top of a double boiler, or in a heat proof bowl set over a pan of gently simmering water.

3 Beat together the eggs, sugar, vanilla and salt. Stir in the chocolate mixture. Sift over the flour and fold in. Add the chocolate chips.

4 Pour the mixture into the baking pan and spread evenly. Bake until just set, about 30 minutes. The brownies should be slightly moist inside. Let cool in the tin.

5 To turn out, run a knife all around the edge and invert onto a baking sheet. Remove the paper. Place another sheet on top and invert again. Cut into bars for serving.

Marbled Brownies

Flavorsome and impressive in appearance, these fancy brownies are also great fun to make.

Makes 24

8 ounces semisweet
   chocolate
$1/3$ cup butter
4 eggs
$1^1/2$ cups sugar
$1^1/4$ cups all-purpose flour
$1/2$ teaspoon salt
1 teaspoon baking
   powder
2 teaspoons vanilla
   extract
1 cup walnuts, chopped

For the plain mixture
4 tablespoons butter, at
   room temperature
$3/4$ cup cream cheese
$1^1/2$ cups sugar
2 eggs
4 tablespoons all-purpose
   flour
1 teaspoon vanilla
   extract

1 Preheat the oven to 350°F. Line a 13 x 9-inch baking pan with wax paper and grease.

2 Melt the chocolate and butter over very low heat, stirring. Set aside to cool. Meanwhile, beat the eggs until light and fluffy. Gradually beat in the sugar. Sift over the flour, salt and baking powder and fold to combine.

3 Stir in the cooled chocolate mixture. Add the vanilla and nuts. Measure and set aside 2 cups of the chocolate mixture.

4 For the plain mixture, cream the butter and cream cheese with an electric mixer. Add the sugar and continue beating until blended. Beat in the eggs, flour and vanilla.

5 Spread the unmeasured chocolate mixture in the pan. Pour over the plain mixture. Drop spoonfuls of the reserved chocolate mixture on top.

6 With a metal spatula, swirl the mixtures to marble. Do not blend completely. Bake until just set, 35–40 minutes. Turn out when cool and cut into squares for serving.

Oatmeal and Date Brownies

These brownies are marvelous as a break-time treat. The secret of chewy, moist brownies is not to overcook them.

Makes 16

5 ounces semisweet
   chocolate
4 tablespoons butter
scant 1 cup quick-
   cooking porridge oats
3 tablespoons wheatgerm
$^1/_3$ cup milk powder
$^1/_2$ teaspoon baking
   powder

$^1/_2$ teaspoon salt
$^1/_2$ cup chopped walnuts
$^1/_3$ cup dates, chopped
$^1/_4$ cup molasses sugar
1 teaspoon vanilla
   extract
2 eggs, beaten

1 Break the chocolate into a heat proof bowl and add the butter. Place over a pan of simmering water and stir until completely melted.

2 Cool the chocolate, stirring occasionally. Preheat the oven to 350°F. Grease and line an 8-inch square cake pan.

3 Combine all the dry ingredients together in a bowl, then beat in the melted chocolate, vanilla and eggs. Pour the mixture into the cake pan, level the surface and bake in the oven for 20–25 minutes until firm around the edges yet still soft in the center.

4 Cool the brownies in the pan, then chill in the fridge. When they are more solid, turn them out of the pan and cut into 16 squares.

Banana Chocolate Brownies

Nuts traditionally give brownies their chewy texture. Here, oat bran is used instead, creating a wonderful alternative.

Makes 9

5 tablespoons cocoa
1 tablespoon superfine
   sugar
5 tablespoons milk
3 large bananas, mashed
1 cup light brown sugar

1 teaspoon vanilla
   extract
5 egg whites
$^3/_4$ cup self-rising flour
$^2/_3$ cup oat bran
confectioner's sugar, for
   dusting

1 Preheat the oven to 350°F. Line an 8-inch square cake pan with nonstick parchment paper.

2 Blend the cocoa and superfine sugar with the milk. Add the bananas, brown sugar and vanilla extract. Lightly beat the egg whites with a fork. Add the chocolate mixture and continue to beat well. Sift the flour over the mixture and fold in with the oat bran. Pour into the prepared pan.

3 Cook in the oven for 40 minutes, or until firm. Cool in the pan for 10 minutes, then turn out onto a wire rack. Cut into squares and dust with confectioner's sugar before serving.

White Chocolate Brownies

If you wish, hazelnuts can be substituted for the macadamia nuts in the topping.

Serves 12

1 cup all-purpose flour
½ teaspoon baking powder
pinch of salt
6 ounces fine quality white chocolate, chopped
½ cup superfine sugar
½ cup sweet butter, cut into pieces
2 eggs, lightly beaten

1 teaspoon vanilla extract
6 ounces semi-sweet chocolate chips

For the topping
7 ounces milk chocolate, chopped
1 cup unsalted macadamia nuts, chopped

1 Preheat the oven to 350°F. Grease a 9-inch springform pan. Sift together the flour, baking powder and salt, and set aside.

2 In a medium saucepan over moderate heat, melt the white chocolate, sugar and butter until smooth, stirring frequently. Cool slightly, then beat in the eggs and vanilla. Stir in the chocolate chips. Spread evenly in the prepared pan, smoothing the top.

3 Bake for 20–25 minutes until a toothpick inserted 2 inches from the side of the pan comes out clean. Remove from the oven to a heat proof surface, sprinkle chopped milk chocolate over the surface (avoid touching the side of pan) and return to the oven for 1 minute.

4 Remove from the oven and, using the back of a spoon, gently spread out the softened chocolate. Sprinkle with the macadamia nuts and gently press into the chocolate. Cool on a wire rack for 30 minutes; chill for 1 hour. Run a sharp knife around the side of the pan to loosen; then unclip and remove. Cut into thin wedges to serve.

Maple-Pecan Brownies

This recipe provides a delicious adaptation of the classic chocolate brownie.

Makes 12

½ cup butter, melted
½ cup light brown sugar
6 tablespoons maple syrup
2 eggs
1 cup self-rising flour

¾ cup pecans, chopped
⅔ cup semisweet chocolate chips
¼ cup sweet butter
12 pecan halves, to decorate

1 Preheat the oven to 350°F. Line and grease a 10 x 7-inch cake pan.

2 Beat together the melted butter, sugar, 4 tablespoons of the maple syrup, eggs and flour for 1 minute, or until smooth. Stir in the nuts and transfer to the cake pan. Smooth the surface and bake for 30 minutes, until risen and firm to the touch. Cool in the pan for 10 minutes, then transfer to a wire rack to cool completely.

3 Melt the chocolate chips, butter and remaining syrup over low heat. Cool slightly, then spread over the cake. Press in the pecan halves, let set for about 5 minutes, then cut into bars.

Chocolate Fudge Brownies

This is the classic recipe, but omit the frosting if you find it too rich.

Makes 12
³/₄ cup butter
6 tablespoons cocoa
2 eggs, lightly beaten
1 cup light brown sugar
¹/₂ teaspoon vanilla
  extract
1 cup chopped pecans
¹/₂ cup self-rising flour

For the frosting
4 ounces semisweet
  chocolate
2 tablespoons butter
1 tablespoon sour cream

1 Preheat the oven to 350°F. Grease, then line an 8-inch square shallow cake pan with wax paper. Melt the butter in a pan and stir in the cocoa. Set aside to cool.

2 Beat together the eggs, sugar and vanilla extract in a bowl, then stir in the cooled cocoa mixture with the nuts. Sift over the flour and fold into the mixture with a metal spoon.

3 Pour the mixture into the cake pan and bake in the oven for 30–35 minutes, until risen. Remove from the oven (the mixture will still be quite soft and wet, but it cooks further while cooling) and let cool in the pan.

4 To make the frosting, melt the chocolate and butter together in a pan and remove from the heat. Beat in the sour cream until smooth and glossy. Let cool slightly, and then spread over the top of the brownies. When set, cut into 12 pieces.

Fudge-glazed Chocolate Brownies

These brownies are just about irresistible, so hide them from friends – or make lots!

Makes 16
9 ounces bittersweet
  chocolate, chopped
1 ounce semisweet
  chocolate, chopped
¹/₂ cup sweet butter, cut
  into pieces
¹/₂ cup light brown sugar
¹/₄ cup sugar
2 eggs
1 tablespoon vanilla
  extract
¹/₂ cup all-purpose flour
1 cup pecans or walnuts,
  toasted and chopped
5 ounces white chocolate,
  chopped

pecan halves, to decorate
  (optional)

Fudgy chocolate glaze
6 ounces bittersweet
  chocolate, chopped
4 tablespoons sweet
  butter, cut into pieces
2 tablespoons maple
  syrup
2 teaspoons vanilla
  extract
1 teaspoon instant coffee

1 Preheat the oven to 350°F. Line an 8-inch square baking pan with foil, then grease the foil.

2 In a saucepan over low heat, melt the dark chocolates and butter. Remove from the heat and add the sugars. Stir for 2 minutes. Beat in the eggs and vanilla, then blend in the flour. Stir in the nuts and white chocolate. Pour into the pan. Bake for 20–25 minutes. Cool in the pan for 30 minutes then lift, using the foil, onto a wire rack to cool for 2 hours.

3 For the glaze, melt all the ingredients in a pan until smooth, stirring. Chill for 1 hour, then spread over the brownies. Chill until set, then cut into squares.

Chocolate Raspberry Macaroon Bars

Any seedless jam, such as strawberry or apricot, can be substituted for the raspberry in this recipe.

Makes 16–18

¹/₂ cup sweet butter, softened
¹/₂ cup confectioner's sugar
¹/₄ cup cocoa
pinch of salt
1 teaspoon almond extract
1¹/₄ cups all-purpose flour

For the topping
¹/₂ cup seedless raspberry jam

1 tablespoon raspberry flavor liqueur
1 cup milk chocolate chips
1¹/₂ cups finely ground almonds
4 egg whites
pinch of salt
1 cup superfine sugar
¹/₂ teaspoon almond extract
¹/₂ cup slivered almonds

1 Preheat the oven to 325°F. Line a 9 x 13-inch baking pan with foil, and grease. Beat together the butter, sugar, cocoa and salt until blended. Beat in the almond extract and flour to make a crumbly dough.

2 Turn the dough into the pan and smooth the surface. Prick with a fork. Bake for 20 minutes until just set. Remove from the oven and increase the temperature to 375°F. Combine the raspberry jam and liqueur. Spread over the cooked crust, then sprinkle with the chocolate chips.

3 In a food processor fitted with a metal blade, process the almonds, egg whites, salt, sugar and almond extract. Pour over the jam layer, spreading evenly. Sprinkle with slivered almonds.

4 Bake for 20–25 minutes, until the top is golden and puffed. Cool in the pan for 20 minutes. Carefully remove from the pan and cool completely. Peel off the foil and cut into bars.

Chewy Fruit Granola Slices

The apricots give these slices a wonderful chewy texture and the apple keeps them moist.

Makes 8

scant ¹/₂ cup ready-to-eat dried apricots, chopped
1 eating apple, cored and grated

1¹/₄ cups granola
²/₃ cup apple juice
1 tablespoon sunflower margarine

1 Preheat the oven to 375°F. Place all the ingredients in a large bowl and mix well.

2 Press the mixture into an 8-inch round nonstick sandwich pan and bake for 35–40 minutes, or until lightly browned and firm. Mark the bake into wedges and let cool in the pan.

Blueberry Streusel Slice

If you are short of time, use pre-made pastry for this delightful streusel.

Makes 30

8 ounces piecrust pastry
½ cup all-purpose flour
¼ teaspoon baking
　powder
3 tablespoons butter or
　margarine
2 tablespoons fresh white
　bread crumbs

⅓ cup light brown sugar
¼ teaspoon salt
4 tablespoons slivered or
　chopped almonds
4 tablespoons blackberry
　or bramble jelly
1 cup blueberries, fresh
　or frozen

1 Preheat the oven to 350°F. Roll out the pastry on a lightly floured surface and line a 7 x 11-inch jelly roll pan. Prick the bottom evenly with a fork.

2 Rub together the flour, baking powder, butter or margarine, bread crumbs, sugar and salt until really crumbly, then mix in the almonds.

3 Spread the pastry with the jelly, sprinkle with the blueberries, then cover evenly with the streusel topping, pressing down lightly. Bake for 30–40 minutes, reducing the temperature after 20 minutes to 325°F.

4 Remove from the oven when golden on the top and the pastry is cooked through. Cut into slices while still hot, then let cool.

Sticky Date and Apple Bars

If possible, allow this mixture to mature for 1–2 days before cutting – it will get stickier and even more delicious!

Makes 16

½ cup margarine
⅓ cup dark brown sugar
4 tablespoons maple
　syrup
¾ cup chopped dates
generous 1 cup rolled
　oats

1 cup whole wheat self-
　rising flour
2 eating apples, peeled,
　cored and grated
1–2 teaspoons lemon
　juice
20–25 walnut halves

1 Preheat the oven to 375°F. Line a 7–8-inch square or rectangular loose-based cake pan. In a large saucepan, heat the margarine, sugar, syrup and dates, stirring until the dates soften completely.

2 Gradually work in the oats, flour, apples and lemon juice until well mixed. Spoon into the pan and spread out evenly. Top with the walnut halves.

3 Bake for 30 minutes, then reduce the oven temperature to 325°F and bake for 10–20 minutes more, until firm to the touch and golden. Cut into squares or bars while still warm, or wrap in foil when nearly cold and keep for 1–2 days before eating.

Figgy Bars

Make sure you have napkins handy when you serve these deliciously sticky bars.

Makes 48

1¹/₂ cups dried figs
3 eggs
³/₄ cup superfine sugar
³/₄ cup all-purpose flour
1 teaspoon baking powder
¹/₂ teaspoon ground cinnamon
¹/₄ teaspoon ground cloves
¹/₄ teaspoon grated nutmeg
¹/₄ teaspoon salt
³/₄ cup finely chopped walnuts
2 tablespoons brandy or cognac
confectioner's sugar, for dusting

1 Preheat the oven to 325°F. Line a 12 x 8 x 1½-inch baking pan with wax paper and grease the paper.

2 With a sharp knife, chop the figs coarsely. Set aside. In a bowl, whisk the eggs and sugar until well blended. In another bowl, sift together the dry ingredients, then fold into the egg mixture in several batches.

3 Scrape the mixture into the baking pan and bake until the top is firm and brown, about 35–40 minutes. It should still be soft underneath.

4 Let cool in the pan for 5 minutes, then unmold and transfer to a sheet of wax paper lightly sprinkled with confectioner's sugar. Cut into bars.

Lemon Bars

A surprising amount of lemon juice goes into these bars, but you will appreciate why when you taste them.

Makes 36

¹/₂ cup confectioner's sugar
1¹/₂ cups all-purpose flour
¹/₂ teaspoon salt
³/₄ cup butter, cut in small pieces

For the topping
4 eggs
1¹/₂ cups superfine sugar
grated rind of 1 lemon
¹/₂ cup fresh lemon juice
³/₄ cup whipping cream
confectioner's sugar, for dusting

1 Preheat the oven to 325°F. Grease a 3 x 9-inch baking pan.

2 Sift the sugar, flour and salt into a bowl. With a pastry blender, cut in the butter until the mixture resembles coarse bread crumbs. Press the mixture into the bottom of the pan. Bake until golden brown, about 20 minutes.

3 Meanwhile, for the topping, whisk the eggs and sugar together until blended. Add the lemon rind and juice, and mix well.

4 Lightly whip the cream and fold into the egg mixture. Pour over the still warm bottom, return to the oven, and bake until set, about 40 minutes. Cool completely before cutting into bars. Dust with confectioner's sugar.

Spiced Raisin Bars

If you like raisins, these gloriously spicy bars are for you.
Omit the walnuts, if you prefer.

Makes 30

scant 1 cup all-purpose
   flour
1¹/₂ teaspoons baking
   powder
1 teaspoon ground
   cinnamon
¹/₂ teaspoon grated
   nutmeg
¹/₄ teaspoon ground
   cloves

¹/₄ teaspoon mixed spice
1¹/₂ cups raisins
¹/₂ cup butter or
   margarine, at room
   temperature
¹/₂ cup sugar
2 eggs
scant ¹/₂ cup molasses
¹/₂ cup walnuts, chopped

1 Preheat the oven to 350°F Line a 13 x 9-inch baking pan
with wax paper and grease the paper.

2 Sift together the flour, baking powder and spices. Place the
raisins in another bowl and toss with a few tablespoons of the
flour mixture.

3 With an electric mixer, cream the butter or margarine and
sugar together until light and fluffy. Beat in the eggs, one at a
time, then the molasses. Stir in the flour mixture, raisins and
walnuts.

4 Spread evenly in the baking pan. Bake until just set, about
15–18 minutes. Cool in the pan before cutting into bars.

Toffee Meringue Bars

Two delicious layers complement each other beautifully in
these easy-to-make bars.

Makes 12

4 tablespoons butter
scant 1¹/₄ cups dark
   brown sugar
1 egg
¹/₂ teaspoon vanilla
   extract
9 tablespoons all-purpose
   flour
¹/₂ teaspoon salt
¹/₄ teaspoon grated
   nutmeg

For the topping
1 egg white
¹/₄ teaspoon salt
1 tablespoon maple syrup
¹/₂ cup superfine sugar
¹/₂ cup walnuts, finely
   chopped

1 Combine the butter and brown sugar in a saucepan and
heat until bubbling. Set aside to cool.

2 Preheat the oven to 350°F. Line the bottom and sides of an
8-inch square cake pan with wax paper and grease the paper.

3 Beat the egg and vanilla into the cooled sugar mixture. Sift
over the flour, salt and nutmeg and fold in. Spread in the
bottom of the cake pan.

4 For the topping, beat the egg white with the salt until it
holds soft peaks. Beat in the maple syrup, then the sugar, and
continue beating until the mixture holds stiff peaks. Fold in
the nuts and spread on top. Bake for 30 minutes. Cut into bars
when completely cool.

Chocolate Walnut Bars

These double-decker bars should be stored in the fridge in an airtight container.

Makes 24

2/3 cup walnuts
generous 1/4 cup
superfine sugar
scant 1 cup all-purpose
flour, sifted
6 tablespoons cold sweet
butter, cut into pieces

For the topping
2 tablespoons sweet
butter

6 tablespoons water
1/4 cup cocoa
1/2 cup superfine sugar
1 teaspoon vanilla
extract
1/4 teaspoon salt
2 eggs
confectioner's sugar, for
dusting

1 Preheat the oven to 350°F. Grease the bottom and sides of an 8-inch square baking pan.

2 Grind the walnuts with a few tablespoons of the sugar in a food processor or blender. In a bowl, combine the ground walnuts, remaining sugar and flour. Rub in the butter until the mixture resembles coarse bread crumbs. Alternatively, use a food processor. Pat the walnut mixture evenly into the bottom of the baking pan. Bake for 25 minutes.

3 Meanwhile, for the topping, melt the butter with the water. Whisk in the cocoa and sugar. Remove from the heat, stir in the vanilla extract and salt, then cool for 5 minutes. Whisk in the eggs until blended. Pour the topping over the baked crust.

4 Return to the oven and bake until set, about 20 minutes. Set the pan on a wire rack to cool, then cut into bars and dust with confectioner's sugar.

Hazelnut Squares

These crunchy, nutty squares are made in a single bowl. What could be simpler?

Makes 9

2 ounces semisweet
chocolate
5 tablespoons butter or
margarine
generous 1 cup superfine
sugar
1/2 cup all-purpose flour

1/2 teaspoon baking
powder
2 eggs, beaten
1/2 teaspoon vanilla
extract
1 cup skinned hazelnuts,
coarsely chopped

1 Preheat the oven to 350°F. Grease an 8-inch square baking pan.

2 In a heat proof bowl set over a pan of barely simmering water, melt the chocolate and butter or margarine. Remove the bowl from the heat.

3 Add the sugar, flour, baking powder, eggs, vanilla and half of the hazelnuts to the melted mixture and stir well with a wooden spoon.

4 Pour the mixture into the prepared pan. Bake in the oven for 10 minutes, then sprinkle the reserved hazelnuts over the top. Return to the oven and continue baking until firm to the touch, about 25 minutes.

5 Cool in the tin, set on a wire rack for 10 minutes, then unmold onto the rack and cool completely. Cut into squares before serving.

Fruity Teabread

Serve this bread thinly sliced, toasted or plain, with butter or cream cheese and jam.

Makes one 9 x 5-inch loaf

2 cups all-purpose flour
generous ¹/₂ cup
    superfine sugar
1 tablespoon baking
    powder
¹/₂ teaspoon salt
grated rind of 1 large
    orange

generous ²/₃ cup fresh
    orange juice
2 eggs, lightly beaten
6 tablespoons butter or
    margarine, melted
1 cup fresh cranberries or
    bilberries
¹/₂ cup chopped walnuts

1 Preheat the oven to 350°F. Line a 9 x 5-inch loaf pan with wax paper and grease the paper.

2 Sift the flour, sugar, baking powder and salt into a mixing bowl. Then stir in the orange rind. Make a well in the center and add the fresh orange juice, eggs and melted butter or margarine. Stir from the center until the ingredients are blended; do not overmix. Add the berries and walnuts and stir until blended.

3 Transfer the mixture to the prepared pan and bake until a skewer inserted in the center of the loaf comes out clean, about 45–50 minutes. Let cool in the pan for 10 minutes before transferring to a wire rack to cool completely.

Date and Pecan Loaf

Walnuts may be used instead of pecans to make this luxurious teabread.

Makes one 9 x 5-inch loaf

1 cup chopped pitted
    dates
³/₄ cup boiling water
4 tablespoons sweet
    butter, at room
    temperature
¹/₃ cup dark brown sugar
¹/₄ cup superfine sugar
1 egg, at room
    temperature

2 tablespoons brandy
generous ¹/₄ cup all-
    purpose flour
2 teaspoons baking
    powder
¹/₂ teaspoon salt
³/₄ teaspoon freshly grated
    nutmeg
³/₄ cup coarsely chopped
    pecans

1 Place the dates in a bowl and pour over the boiling water. Set aside to cool. Preheat the oven to 350°F. Line a 9 x 5-inch loaf pan with wax paper and then grease the paper.

2 With an electric mixer, cream the butter and sugars until light and fluffy. Beat in the egg and brandy, then set aside.

3 Sift the flour, baking powder, salt and nutmeg together, at least three times. Fold the dry ingredients into the sugar mixture in three batches, alternating with the dates and water. Fold in the nuts.

4 Pour the mixture into the prepared pan and bake until a skewer inserted in the center comes out clean, 45–50 minutes. Let the loaf cool in the pan for 10 minutes before transferring to a wire rack to cool completely.

Banana Nut Loaf

A hearty and filling loaf, this would be ideal as a winter teatime treat.

Makes one 9 x 5-inch loaf

1/2 cup butter, at room temperature	*1/4 teaspoon salt*
generous 1/2 cup superfine sugar	*1 teaspoon ground cinnamon*
2 eggs, at room temperature	*1/2 cup whole wheat flour*
1 cup all-purpose flour	*3 large ripe bananas*
1 teaspoon baking soda	*1 teaspoon vanilla extract*
	1/2 cup chopped walnuts

1 Preheat the oven to 350°F. Line the bottom and sides of a 9 x 5-inch loaf pan with wax paper and grease the paper.

2 With an electric mixer, cream the butter and sugar together until light and fluffy. Add the eggs, one at a time, beating well after each addition.

3 Sift the all-purpose flour, baking soda, salt and cinnamon over the butter mixture and stir to blend. Then stir in the whole wheat flour.

4 With a fork, mash the bananas to a purée, then stir into the mixture. Stir in the vanilla and nuts.

5 Pour the mixture into the prepared pan and spread level. Bake until a skewer inserted in the center comes out clean, about 50–60 minutes. Let stand for 10 minutes before transferring to a wire rack to cool completely.

Apricot Nut Loaf

Apricots, raisins and walnuts combine to make a lovely light teabread.

Makes one 9 x 5-inch loaf

1/2 cup ready-to-eat dried apricots	*generous 2 cups all-purpose flour*
1 large orange	*2 teaspoons baking powder*
generous 1/2 cup raisins	*1/2 teaspoon salt*
2/3 cup superfine sugar	*1 teaspoon baking soda*
1/3 cup oil	*1/2 cup chopped walnuts*
2 eggs, lightly beaten	

1 Place the apricots in a bowl, cover with lukewarm water and let stand for 30 minutes. Preheat the oven to 350°F. Line a 9 x 5-inch loaf pan with wax paper and grease the paper.

2 With a vegetable peeler, remove the orange rind, leaving the pith. Chop the strips finely.

3 Drain the apricots and chop coarsely. Place in a bowl with the orange rind and raisins. Squeeze the peeled orange. Measure the juice and add enough hot water to obtain ¾ cup liquid. Add the orange juice mixture to the apricot mixture. Stir in the sugar, oil and eggs. Set aside.

4 In another bowl, sift together the flour, baking powder, salt and baking soda. Fold the flour mixture into the apricot mixture in three batches, then stir in the walnuts.

5 Spoon the mixture into the prepared pan and bake until a skewer inserted in the center of the loaf comes out clean, about 55–60 minutes. If the loaf browns too quickly, protect the top with a sheet of foil. Cool in the tin for 10 minutes, then transfer to a wire rack to cool completely.

Bilberry Teabread

A lovely crumbly topping helps to make this teabread extra special.

Makes 8 pieces

4 tablespoons butter or margarine, at room temperature
¾ cup superfine sugar
1 egg, at room temperature
½ cup milk
2 cups all-purpose flour
2 teaspoons baking powder
½ teaspoon salt

¾ cup fresh bilberries, or blueberries

For the topping
½ cup sugar
⅓ cup all-purpose flour
½ teaspoon ground cinnamon
4 tablespoons butter, cut into pieces

1 Preheat the oven to 375°F. Grease a 9-inch baking dish.

2 With an electric mixer, cream the butter or margarine with the sugar until light and fluffy. Add the egg, beat to combine, then mix in the milk until well blended.

3 Sift over the flour, baking powder and salt and stir just enough to blend the ingredients. Add the berries and stir. Transfer to the baking dish.

4 For the topping, place the sugar, flour, cinnamon and butter in a mixing bowl. Cut in with a pastry blender until the mixture resembles coarse bread crumbs. Sprinkle the topping over the mixture in the baking dish. Bake until a skewer inserted in the center comes out clean, about 45 minutes. Serve warm or cold.

Dried Fruit Loaf

Use any combination of dried fruit you like in this delicious teabread.

Makes one 9 x 5-inch loaf

2¾ cups mixed dried fruit, such as currants, raisins, chopped dried apricots and dried cherries
1¼ cups cold strong tea
generous 1 cup dark brown sugar
grated rind and juice of 1 small orange

grated rind and juice of 1 lemon
1 egg, lightly beaten
1¾ cups all-purpose flour
1 tablespoon baking powder
¼ teaspoon salt

1 In a bowl, mix the dried fruit with the cold tea and let soak overnight.

2 Preheat the oven to 350°F. Line the bottom and sides of a 9 x 5-inch loaf pan with wax paper and grease the paper.

3 Strain the fruit, reserving the liquid. In a bowl, combine the sugar, orange and lemon rind, and fruit. Pour the orange and lemon juice into a measuring cup; if the quantity is less than 1 cup, then top up with the soaking liquid. Stir the citrus juices and egg into the dried fruit mixture.

4 Sift the flour, baking powder and salt together into another bowl. Stir into the fruit mixture until blended.

5 Transfer to the pan and bake until a skewer inserted in the center comes out clean; about 1¼ hours. Let sit in the pan for 10 minutes before unmolding.

Corn Bread

Serve this bread as an accompaniment to a meal, with soup, or take it on a picnic.

Makes one 9 x 5-inch loaf

1 cup all-purpose flour
generous ¹/₄ cup
    superfine sugar
1 teaspoon salt
1 tablespoon baking
    powder
scant 1¹/₂ cups cornmeal
    or polenta

1¹/₂ cups milk
2 eggs
6 tablespoons butter,
    melted
¹/₂ cup margarine, melted

1 Preheat the oven to 400°F. Line a 9 x 5-inch loaf pan with wax paper and grease the paper.

2 Sift the flour, sugar, salt and baking powder into a mixing bowl. Add the cornmeal or polenta and stir to blend. Make a well in the center. Whisk together the milk, eggs, melted butter and margarine. Pour the mixture into the well. Stir until just blended; do not overmix.

3 Pour into the pan and bake until a skewer inserted in the center comes out clean, about 45 minutes. Serve hot or at room temperature.

Spicy Corn Bread

An interesting variation on basic corn bread; adjust the number of chilies used according to taste.

Makes 9 squares

3–4 whole canned chilies,
    drained
2 eggs
2 cups buttermilk
4 tablespoons butter,
    melted
¹/₂ cup all-purpose flour

1 teaspoon baking soda
2 teaspoons salt
scant 1¹/₂ cups cornmeal
    or polenta
2 cups corn, canned or
    frozen and defrosted

1 Preheat the oven to 400°F. Line the bottom and sides of a 9-inch square cake pan with wax paper. Grease the paper.

2 With a sharp knife, finely chop the canned chilies and set aside until needed.

3 In a large bowl, whisk the eggs until frothy, then whisk in the buttermilk. Add the melted butter.

4 Sift the flour, baking soda and salt together into another large bowl. Fold into the buttermilk mixture in three batches, then fold in the cornmeal or polenta in three batches. Finally, fold in the chilies and corn.

5 Pour the mixture into the pan and bake until a skewer inserted in the center comes out clean, about 25–30 minutes. Leave in the pan for 2–3 minutes before unmolding. Cut into squares and serve warm.

Sweet Sesame Loaf

Lemon and sesame seeds make a great partnership in this light teabread.

Makes one 9 x 5-inch loaf

6 tablespoons sesame
  seeds
2¹/₂ cups all-purpose
  flour
2¹/₂ teaspoons baking
  powder
1 teaspoon salt
4 tablespoons butter or
  margarine, at room
  temperature

scant ²/₃ cup sugar
2 eggs, at room
  temperature
grated rind of 1 lemon
1¹/₂ cups milk

1 Preheat the oven to 350°F. Line a 9 x 5-inch loaf pan with wax paper and then grease the paper.

2 Reserve 2 tablespoons of the sesame seeds. Spread the rest on a baking sheet and bake in the oven until lightly toasted, about 10 minutes.

3 Sift the flour, baking powder and salt into a bowl. Stir in the toasted sesame seeds and set aside.

4 Cream the butter or margarine and sugar together until light and fluffy. Beat in the eggs, then stir in the lemon rind and milk. Pour the milk mixture over the dry ingredients and fold in with a large metal spoon until just blended.

5 Pour into the pan and sprinkle over the reserved sesame seeds. Bake until a skewer inserted in the center comes out clean, about 1 hour. Cool in the pan for 10 minutes. Turn out onto a wire rack to cool completely.

Cardamom and Saffron Tea Loaf

An aromatic sweet bread ideal for an afternoon snack, or lightly toasted for breakfast.

Makes one 2-pound loaf

generous pinch of saffron
  strands
3 cups lukewarm milk
2 tablespoons butter
8 cups all-purpose bread
  flour
2 envelopes fast-rising
  dried yeast

3 tablespoons superfine
  sugar
6 cardamom pods, split
  open and seeds
  extracted
scant ³/₄ cup raisins
2 tablespoons honey
1 egg, beaten

1 Crush the saffron straight into a cup containing a little of the warm milk and leave to infuse for 5 minutes. Rub the butter into the flour, then mix in the yeast, sugar, cardamom seeds and raisins.

2 Beat the remaining milk with the honey and egg, then mix this into the flour, along with the saffron milk and strands, to form a firm dough. Turn out the dough and knead it on a lightly floured surface for 5 minutes.

3 Return the dough to the mixing bowl, cover with oiled plastic wrap and let sit in a warm place until doubled in size.

4 Preheat the oven to 400°F. Grease 2-pound loaf pan. Turn the dough out onto a floured surface, punch down, knead for 3 minutes, then shape into a fat roll and fit into the pan. Cover with a sheet of lightly oiled plastic wrap and let stand in a warm place until the dough begins to rise again.

5 Bake the loaf for 25 minutes until golden brown and firm on top. Turn out onto a wire rack, and as it cools brush the top with honey.

Zucchini Teabread

Like carrots, zucchini are a vegetable that work well in baking, adding moistness and lightness to the bread.

Makes one 9 x 5-inch loaf

4 tablespoons butter	1 teaspoon salt
3 eggs	1 teaspoon ground
1 cup vegetable oil	cinnamon
1½ cups sugar	1 teaspoon grated
2 unpeeled zucchini,	nutmeg
grated	¼ teaspoon ground
2½ cups all-purpose	cloves
flour	1 cup chopped walnuts
2 teaspoons baking soda	
1 teaspoon baking	
powder	

1 Preheat the oven to 350°F. Line the bottom and sides of a 9 x 5-inch loaf pan with wax paper and grease the paper.

2 In a saucepan, melt the butter over low heat. Set aside until needed.

3 With an electric mixer, beat the eggs and oil together until thick. Beat in the sugar, then stir in the melted butter and the zucchini. Set aside.

4 In another bowl, sift all the dry ingredients together three times. Carefully fold into the zucchini mixture. Fold in the chopped walnuts.

5 Pour into the pan and bake until a skewer inserted in the center comes out clean, about 60–70 minutes. Let stand for 10 minutes before turning out onto a wire rack to cool.

Mango Teabread

A delicious teabread with an exotic slant – baked with juicy, ripe mango.

Makes two 9 x 5-inch loaves

2½ cups all-purpose	1½ cups sugar
flour	½ cup vegetable oil
2 teaspoons baking soda	1 large ripe mango,
2 teaspoons ground	peeled and chopped
cinnamon	generous 1½ cups dried
½ teaspoon salt	coconut
½ cup margarine, at	½ cup raisins
room temperature	
3 eggs, at room	
temperature	

1 Preheat the oven to 350°F. Line the bottom and sides of two 9 x 5-inch loaf pans with wax paper and grease the paper.

2 Sift together the flour, baking soda, cinnamon and salt. Set aside until needed.

3 Cream the margarine until soft. Beat in the eggs and sugar until light and fluffy. Beat in the oil.

4 Fold the dry ingredients into the creamed ingredients in three batches, then fold in the mango, two-thirds of the coconut and the raisins.

5 Spoon the batter into the pans. Sprinkle over the remaining coconut. Bake until a skewer inserted in the center comes out clean, about 50–60 minutes. Let stand for 10 minutes before turning out onto a wire rack to cool.

Cornsticks

If you don't have a cornstick mold, use éclair pans or a muffin tray and reduce the cooking time by 10 minutes.

Makes 6

1 egg
1/2 cup milk
1 tablespoon vegetable oil
scant 1 cup cornmeal or polenta

1/2 cup all-purpose flour
2 teaspoons baking powder
3 tablespoons superfine sugar

1 Preheat the oven to 375°F. Grease a cast-iron cornstick mold.

2 Beat the egg in a small bowl. Stir in the milk and vegetable oil, and set aside.

3 In a mixing bowl, stir together the cornmeal or polenta, flour, baking powder and sugar. Pour in the egg mixture and stir with a wooden spoon to combine.

4 Spoon the mixture into the prepared mold. Bake until a skewer inserted in the center of a cornstick comes out clean, about 25 minutes. Cool in the mold on a wire rack for 10 minutes before unmolding.

Savory Corn Bread

For a spicy bread, stir 1/2 tablespoon chopped fresh chilies into the mixture with the cheese and corn.

Makes 9

2 eggs, lightly beaten
1 cup buttermilk
1 cup all-purpose flour
scant 1 cup cornmeal or polenta
2 teaspoons baking powder

1/2 teaspoon salt
1 tablespoon superfine sugar
1 cup Cheddar cheese, grated
1 1/3 cups corn, fresh, or frozen and defrosted

1 Preheat the oven to 400°F. Grease a 9-inch square baking pan.

2 Combine the eggs and buttermilk in a small bowl and whisk until well mixed. Set aside.

3 In another bowl, stir together the flour, cornmeal or polenta, baking powder, salt and sugar. Add the egg mixture and stir with a wooden spoon to combine. Stir in the cheese and corn.

4 Pour the mixture into the baking pan. Bake until a skewer inserted in the center comes out clean, about 25 minutes. Unmold the bread onto a wire rack and let cool. Cut into squares before serving.

Herb Popovers

Popovers are delicious when flavored with herbs, and are good served as a snack or appetizer.

Makes 12

3 eggs
1 cup milk
2 tablespoons butter, melted
¾ cup all-purpose flour
¼ teaspoon salt
1 small sprig each mixed fresh herbs, such as chives, tarragon, dill and parsley

1 Preheat the oven to 425°F. Grease 12 small ramekins or individual baking cups.

2 With an electric mixer, beat the eggs until blended. Beat in the milk and melted butter. Sift together the flour and salt, then beat into the egg mixture to combine thoroughly.

3 Strip the herb leaves from the stems and chop finely. Mix together and measure out 2 tablespoons. Stir the measured herbs into the batter.

4 Half-fill the prepared ramekins or baking cups. Bake until golden; 25–30 minutes. Do not open the oven door during baking time or the popovers may collapse. For drier popovers, pierce each one with a knife after 30 minutes baking time and then bake for 5 minutes more. Serve the herb popovers hot.

Cheese Popovers

Serve these popovers simply as an accompaniment to a meal, or make a filling and serve them as an appetizer.

Makes 12

3 eggs
1 cup milk
2 tablespoons butter, melted
¾ cup all-purpose flour
¼ teaspoon salt
¼ teaspoon paprika
⅓ cup freshly grated Parmesan cheese

1 Preheat the oven to 425°F. Grease 12 small ramekins or individual baking cups.

2 With an electric mixer, beat the eggs until blended. Beat in the milk and melted butter. Sift together the flour, salt and paprika, then beat into the egg mixture. Add the Parmesan cheese and stir in.

3 Half-fill the prepared cups and bake until golden, about 25–30 minutes. Do not open the oven door or the popovers may collapse. For drier popovers, pierce each one with a knife after about 30 minutes baking time and then bake for 5 minutes more. Serve hot.

Sweet Potato and Raisin Bread

Serve buttered slices of this subtly-spiced loaf at coffee or tea time.

Makes one 2-pound loaf

3 cups all-purpose flour
2 teaspoons baking
  powder
½ teaspoon salt
1 teaspoon ground
  cinnamon
½ teaspoon grated
  nutmeg

1 pound mashed cooked
  sweet potato
3½ oz light brown sugar
½ cup butter or
  margarine, melted and
  cooled
3 eggs, beaten
generous ½ cup raisins

1 Preheat the oven to 350°F. Grease a 2-pound loaf pan.

2 Sift the flour, baking powder, salt, cinnamon, and nutmeg into a small bowl. Set aside.

3 With an electric mixer, beat the mashed sweet potato with the sugar, butter or margarine, and eggs until well mixed.

4 Add the flour mixture and the raisins. Stir with a wooden spoon until the flour is just mixed in.

5 Transfer the batter to the prepared pan. Bake until a skewer inserted in the center of the loaf comes out clean, about 1–1¼ hours.

6 Let the bread cool in the pan on a wire rack for 15 minutes, then unmold onto the wire rack and let cool completely.

Lemon and Walnut Teabread

Beaten egg whites give this citrus-flavor loaf a lovely light and crumbly texture.

Makes one 9 x 5-inch loaf

½ cup butter or
  margarine, at room
  temperature
½ cup sugar
2 eggs, at room
  temperature, separated
grated rind of 2 lemons
2 tablespoons lemon juice

scant 2 cups all-purpose
  flour
2 teaspoons baking
  powder
½ cup milk
½ cup chopped walnuts
¼ teaspoon salt

1 Preheat the oven to 350°F. Line a 9 x 5-inch loaf pan with wax paper and grease the paper.

2 Cream the butter or margarine with the sugar until light and fluffy. Beat in the egg yolks. Add the lemon rind and juice and stir until blended. Set aside.

3 In another bowl, sift together the flour and baking powder three times. Fold into the butter mixture in three batches, alternating with the milk. Fold in the walnuts. Set aside.

4 Beat the egg whites and salt until stiff peaks form. Fold a large spoonful of the egg whites into the walnut mixture to lighten it. Fold in the remaining egg whites carefully until the mixture is just blended.

5 Pour the batter into the prepared pan and bake until a skewer inserted in the center of the loaf comes out clean, about 45–50 minutes. Cool in the pan for 5 minutes before turning out onto a wire rack to cool completely.

Date and Nut Maltloaf

Choose any type of nut you like to include in this very rich and fruit-packed teabread.

Makes two 1-pound loaves

2 cups all-purpose bread
    flour
2 cups plain whole wheat
    bread flour
1 teaspoon salt
6 tablespoons brown
    sugar
1 envelope fast-rising
    dried yeast
4 tablespoons butter or
    margarine

1 tablespoon molasses
4 tablespoons malt
    extract
1 cup lukewarm milk
½ cup chopped dates
½ cup chopped nuts
generous ½ cup golden
    raisins
generous ½ cup raisins
2 tablespoons honey, to
    glaze

1 Sift the flours and salt into a large bowl, then add the wheat flakes from the strainer. Stir in the sugar and yeast.

2 Put the butter or margarine in a small pan with the molasses and malt extract. Stir over low heat until melted. Let cool, then combine with the milk.

3 Stir the milk mixture into the dry ingredients and knead thoroughly for 15 minutes until the dough is elastic.

4 Knead in the fruits and nuts. Transfer the dough to an oiled bowl, cover with plastic wrap and let sit in a warm place for about 1½ hours, until the dough has doubled in size.

5 Grease two 1-pound loaf pans. Knock back the dough and knead lightly. Divide in half, form into loaves and place in the pans. Cover and let sit in a warm place for 30 minutes, until risen. Meanwhile, preheat the oven to 375°F.

6 Bake for 35–40 minutes, until well risen. Cool on a wire rack. Brush with honey while warm.

Orange Wheatloaf

Perfect just with butter as a breakfast teabread and lovely for banana sandwiches.

Makes one 1-pound loaf

2¼ cups whole wheat all-
    purpose flour
½ teaspoon salt
2 tablespoons butter
2 tablespoons light
    brown sugar

½ envelope fast-rising
    dried yeast
grated rind and juice of
    ½ orange

1 Sift the flour into a large bowl and return any wheat flakes from the strainer. Add the salt, and rub in the butter lightly with your fingertips.

2 Stir in the sugar, yeast and orange rind. Pour the orange juice into a measuring cup and use hot water to make up to scant 1 cup (the liquid should not be more than hand hot).

3 Stir the liquid into the flour and mix to a soft ball of dough. Knead gently on a lightly floured surface until quite smooth and elastic.

4 Place the dough in a greased 1-pound loaf pan and let sit in a warm place until nearly doubled in size. Preheat the oven to 425°F.

5 Bake the bread for 30–35 minutes, or until it sounds hollow when tapped underneath. Turn out of the pan and cool on a wire rack.

Orange and Honey Teabread

Honey gives a special flavor to this teabread. Serve just with a scraping of butter.

Makes one 9 x 5-inch loaf

scant 3¹/₂ cups all-
   purpose flour
2¹/₂ teaspoons baking
   powder
¹/₂ teaspoon baking soda
¹/₂ teaspoon salt
2 tablespoons margarine
1 cup honey

1 egg, at room
   temperature, lightly
   beaten
1¹/₂ tablespoons grated
   orange rind
³/₄ cup freshly squeezed
   orange juice
1 cup chopped walnuts

1 Preheat the oven to 325°F. Line the bottom and sides of a 9 x 5-inch loaf pan with wax paper and grease the paper.

2 Sift the flour, baking powder, baking soda and salt together in a bowl.

3 Cream the margarine until soft. Stir in the honey until blended, then stir in the egg. Add the orange rind and stir to combine thoroughly.

4 Fold the flour mixture into the honey and egg mixture in three batches, alternating with the orange juice. Stir in the chopped walnuts.

5 Pour into the prepared pan and bake in the oven until a skewer inserted in the center comes out clean, about 60–70 minutes. Let sit for 10 minutes before turning out onto a wire rack to cool completely.

Apple Loaf

Ring the changes with this loaf by using different nuts and dried fruit.

Makes one 9 x 5-inch loaf

1 egg
1 cup bottled or
   homemade apple sauce
4 tablespoons butter or
   margarine, melted
scant ³/₄ cup dark brown
   sugar
scant ¹/₄ cup superfine
   sugar
2¹/₂ cups all-purpose
   flour

2 teaspoons baking
   powder
¹/₂ teaspoon baking soda
¹/₂ teaspoon salt
1 teaspoon ground
   cinnamon
¹/₂ teaspoon grated
   nutmeg
¹/₂ cup currants or raisins
¹/₂ cup pecans or
   walnuts, chopped

1 Preheat the oven to 350°F. Line the bottom and sides of a 9 x 5-inch loaf pan with wax paper and grease the paper.

2 Break the egg into a bowl and beat lightly. Stir in the apple sauce, butter or margarine and both sugars. Set aside.

3 In another bowl, sift together the flour, baking powder, baking soda, salt, cinnamon and nutmeg. Fold the dry ingredients, including the currants or raisins and the nuts, into the apple sauce mixture in three batches.

4 Pour into the prepared pan and bake in the oven until a skewer inserted in the center of the loaf comes out clean, about 1 hour. Let stand in the pan for 10 minutes, then turn out onto a wire rack to cool completely.

Fruit and Brazil Nut Teabread

Mashed bananas are a classic ingredient in teabreads, and help to create a moist texture.

Makes one 9 x 5-inch loaf

2 cups all-purpose flour
2 teaspoons baking
  powder
1 teaspoon mixed spice
½ cup butter, diced
¾ cup light brown sugar
2 eggs, lightly beaten
2 tablespoons milk
2 tablespoons dark rum
2 bananas, peeled and
  mashed

½ cup dried figs, chopped
½ cup brazil nuts,
  chopped

To decorate
8 whole brazil nuts
4 whole dried figs, halved
2 tablespoons apricot jam
1 teaspoon dark rum

1 Preheat the oven to 350°F. Grease and line the bottom of a 9 x 5-inch loaf pan. Sift the flour, baking powder and mixed spice into a bowl. Rub in the butter until the mixture resembles fine bread crumbs. Stir in the sugar.

2 Make a well in the center and work in the eggs, milk and rum until combined. Stir in the remaining ingredients and transfer to the loaf pan.

3 Press the whole brazil nuts and halved figs gently into the mixture, to form an attractive pattern. Bake for 1¼ hours, or until a skewer inserted in the center comes out clean. Cool in the pan for 10 minutes, then transfer to a wire rack.

4 Heat the jam and rum together in a small saucepan. Increase the heat and boil for 1 minute. Remove from the heat and pass through a fine strainer. Cool the glaze slightly, brush over the warm cake, and let cool completely.

Glazed Banana Spiced Loaf

The lemony glaze perfectly sets off the flavors in this banana teabread.

Makes one 9 x 5-inch loaf

½ cup butter, at room
  temperature
generous ⅔ cup superfine
  sugar
2 eggs, at room
  temperature
scant 2 cups all-purpose
  flour
1 teaspoon salt
1 teaspoon baking soda
½ teaspoon grated
  nutmeg
¼ teaspoon mixed spice

¼ teaspoon ground
  cloves
¾ cup sour cream
1 large ripe banana,
  mashed
1 teaspoon vanilla
  extract

For the glaze
1 cup confectioner's
  sugar
1–2 tablespoons lemon
  juice

1 Preheat the oven to 350°F. Line a 9 x 5-inch loaf pan with wax paper and grease the paper.

2 Cream the butter and sugar until light and fluffy. Add the eggs, one at a time, beating well after each addition.

3 Sift together the flour, salt, baking soda, nutmeg, mixed spice and cloves. Add to the butter mixture and stir to combine well. Add the sour cream, banana and vanilla and mix to just blend. Pour into the prepared pan.

4 Bake until the top springs back when touched lightly, about 45–50 minutes. Cool in the pan for 10 minutes. Turn out onto a wire rack.

5 For the glaze, combine the confectioner's sugar and lemon juice, then stir until smooth. Place the cooled loaf on a rack set over a baking sheet. Pour the glaze over and let set.

Banana Bread

For a change, add ½–¾ cup chopped walnuts with the dry ingredients or pecans.

Makes one 8½ x 4½-inch loaf

1¾ cups all-purpose flour
2¼ teaspoons baking powder
½ teaspoon salt
¾ teaspoon ground cinnamon (optional)
4 tablespoons wheatgerm
5 tablespoons butter, at room temperature

generous ½ cup superfine sugar
¾ teaspoon grated lemon rind
3 ripe bananas, mashed
2 eggs, beaten

1 Preheat the oven to 350°F. Grease and flour an 8½ x 4½-inch loaf pan.

2 Sift the flour, baking powder, salt and cinnamon, if using, into a bowl. Stir in the wheatgerm.

3 In another bowl, combine the butter with the superfine sugar and grated lemon rind. Beat thoroughly until the mixture is light and fluffy.

4 Add the mashed bananas and eggs, and mix well. Add the dry ingredients and blend quickly and evenly.

5 Spoon into the loaf pan. Bake for 50–60 minutes or until a wooden skewer inserted in the center comes out clean. Cool in the pan for 5 minutes, then turn out onto a wire rack to cool completely.

Banana Orange Loaf

For the best banana flavor and a really good, moist texture, make sure the bananas are ripe for this cake.

Makes one 9 x 5-inch loaf

generous ⅔ cup whole wheat all-purpose flour
generous ¾ cup all-purpose flour
1 teaspoon baking powder
1 teaspoon ground mixed spice
3 tablespoons slivered hazelnuts, toasted

2 large ripe bananas
1 egg
2 tablespoons sunflower oil
2 tablespoons honey
finely grated rind and juice of 1 small orange
4 orange slices, halved
2 teaspoons confectioner's sugar

1 Preheat the oven to 350°F. Brush a 9 x 5-inch loaf pan with oil and line the bottom with nonstick parchment paper.

2 Sift the flours with the baking powder and spice into a large bowl, adding any bran that is caught in the strainer. Stir the hazelnuts into the dry ingredients.

3 Peel and mash the bananas. Beat in the egg, oil, honey and the orange rind and juice. Stir evenly into the dry ingredients.

4 Spoon into the prepared pan and smooth the top. Bake for 40–45 minutes, or until firm and golden brown. Turn out onto a wire rack to cool.

5 Sprinkle the orange slices with the confectioner's sugar and broil until golden. Use to decorate the cake.

Marmalade Teabread

If you prefer, leave the top of the loaf plain and serve sliced and lightly buttered instead.

Makes one 8½ x 4½-inch loaf

1¾ cups all-purpose flour	4 tablespoons chunky
1 teaspoon baking	orange marmalade
powder	1 egg, beaten
1¼ teaspoon ground	about 3 tablespoons milk
cinnamon	4 tablespoons glacé icing
7 tablespoons butter or	and shreds of orange
margarine	and lemon rind,
⅓ cup light brown sugar	to decorate

1 Preheat the oven to 325°F. Butter an 8½ x 4½-inch loaf pan, then line the bottom with wax paper. Grease the paper.

2 Sift the flour, baking powder and cinnamon together, toss in the butter or margarine, then rub in until the mixture resembles coarse bread crumbs. Stir in the sugar.

3 In a separate bowl, mix together the marmalade, egg and most of the milk, then stir into the flour mixture to make a soft dropping consistency, adding more milk, if necessary.

4 Transfer the mixture to the pan and bake for 1¼ hours, or until firm to the touch. Let the cake cool for 5 minutes, then turn onto a wire rack, peel off the lining paper, and let cool.

5 Drizzle the icing over the top of the cake and decorate with the orange and lemon rind.

Cherry Marmalade Muffins

Purists say you should never serve a muffin cold, so enjoy these fresh from the oven.

Makes 12

2 cups self-rising flour	2 tablespoons orange
1 teaspoon ground mixed	marmalade
spice	⅔ cup milk
scant ½ cup superfine	4 tablespoons sunflower
sugar	margarine
½ cup candied cherries,	marmalade, to glaze
quartered	

1 Preheat the oven to 400°F. Lightly grease 12 deep muffin cups with oil.

2 Sift together the flour and spice, then stir in the sugar and candied cherries.

3 Mix the marmalade with the milk and beat into the dry ingredients with the margarine. Spoon into the greased cups. Bake for 20–25 minutes, until golden brown and firm. Turn out onto a wire rack and brush the tops of the muffins with warmed marmalade.

Spiced Date and Walnut Cake

Nuts and dates are a classic flavor combination. Use pecans instead of walnuts, if you wish.

Makes one 2-pound cake

2³/₄ cups whole wheat
    self-rising flour
2 teaspoons mixed spice
generous ³/₄ cup chopped
    dates
¹/₂ cup chopped walnuts
4 tablespoons sunflower
    oil

³/₄ cup dark muscovado
    sugar
1¹/₄ cups milk
walnut halves, to
    decorate

1 Preheat the oven to 350°F. Line a 2-pound loaf pan with wax paper and grease the paper.

2 Sift together the flour and spice, adding back any bran from the strainer. Stir in the dates and walnuts.

3 Mix the oil, sugar and milk, then stir evenly into the dry ingredients. Spoon into the loaf pan and arrange the walnut halves on top.

4 Bake the cake in the oven for about 45–50 minutes, or until golden brown and firm. Turn out the cake, remove the lining paper, and let cool on a wire rack.

Prune and Peel Rock Buns

The fruit content of these buns gives them plenty of flavor – and they're a low fat option, too!

Makes 12

2 cups all-purpose flour
2 teaspoons baking
    powder
¹/₂ cup raw sugar
¹/₂ cup chopped ready-to-
    eat dried prunes

¹/₃ cup chopped mixed
    candied peel
finely grated rind of
    1 lemon
¹/₄ cup sunflower oil
5 tablespoons skim milk

1 Preheat the oven to 400°F. Lightly oil a large baking sheet. Sift together the flour and baking powder, then stir in the sugar, prunes, peel and lemon rind.

2 Mix the oil and milk, then stir into the mixture, to make a dough which just binds together.

3 Spoon into rocky heaps on the baking sheet and bake for 20 minutes, until golden. Let cool on a wire rack.

Raisin Bran Buns

Serve these buns warm or at room temperature, on their own, with butter, or with cream cheese.

Makes 15

4 tablespoons butter or margarine
⅓ cup all-purpose flour
½ cup whole wheat flour
1½ teaspoons baking soda
¼ teaspoon salt
1 teaspoon ground cinnamon
generous 1 cup bran
generous ½ cup raisins
scant ½ cup dark brown sugar
¼ cup superfine sugar
1 egg
1 cup buttermilk
juice of ½ lemon

1 Preheat the oven to 400°F. Lightly grease 15 muffin cups. Put the butter or margarine in a saucepan and melt over gentle heat. Set aside.

2 In a mixing bowl, sift together the flours, baking soda, salt and cinnamon. Add the bran, raisins and sugars and then stir until blended.

3 In another bowl, mix together the egg, buttermilk, lemon juice and melted butter. Add the buttermilk mixture to the dry ingredients and stir in lightly and quickly until just moistened. Do not mix until smooth.

4 Spoon the mixture into the prepared muffin cups, filling them almost to the top. Half-fill any empty cups with water. Bake until golden, about 15–20 minutes. Remove to a wire rack to cool slightly, or serve immediately.

Raspberry Crumble Buns

The crumble topping adds an unusual twist to these lovely fruit buns.

Makes 12

1½ cups all-purpose flour
¼ cup superfine sugar
scant ⅓ cup light brown sugar
2 teaspoons baking powder
¼ teaspoon salt
1 teaspoon ground cinnamon
½ cup butter, melted
1 egg
½ cup milk
¾ cup fresh raspberries
grated rind of 1 lemon

For the crumble topping

¼ cup finely chopped pecans or walnuts
⅓ cup dark brown sugar
3 tablespoons all-purpose flour
1 teaspoon ground cinnamon
3 tablespoons butter, melted

1 Preheat the oven to 350°F. Lightly grease 12 muffin cups or use 12 paper cases. Sift the flour into a bowl. Add the sugars, baking powder, salt and cinnamon, and stir to blend.

2 Make a well in the center. Place the butter, egg and milk in the well and mix until just combined. Stir in the raspberries and lemon rind. Spoon the mixture into the prepared cups, filling them almost to the top.

3 For the crumble topping, mix the nuts, dark brown sugar, flour and cinnamon in a bowl. Add the melted butter and stir to blend.

4 Spoon some of the crumble over each bun. Bake until browned, about 25 minutes. Transfer to a wire rack to cool slightly. Serve warm.

Banana and Pecan Muffins

As a variation on this recipe, substitute an equal quantity of walnuts for the pecans.

Makes 8

1¼ cups all-purpose flour
1½ teaspoons baking powder
4 tablespoons butter or margarine, at room temperature
¾ cup superfine sugar
1 egg
1 teaspoon vanilla extract
3 bananas, mashed
½ cup pecans, chopped
5 tablespoons milk

1 Preheat the oven to 375°F. Lightly grease eight deep muffin cups. Sift the flour and baking powder into a bowl. Set aside.

2 With an electric mixer, cream the butter or margarine and sugar together. Add the egg and vanilla and beat until fluffy. Mix in the banana.

3 Add the pecans. With the mixer on low speed, beat in the flour mixture alternately with the milk.

4 Spoon the mixture into the prepared muffin cups, filling them two-thirds full. Bake until golden brown and a skewer inserted into the center of a muffin comes out clean, about 20–25 minutes.

5 Let the muffins cool in the cups on a wire rack for about 10 minutes. To loosen, run a knife gently around each muffin and unmold onto the wire rack. Let cool 10 minutes more before serving.

Blueberry and Cinnamon Muffins

These moist and "moreish" muffins appeal equally to adults and children.

Makes 8

1 cup all-purpose flour
1 tablespoon baking powder
pinch of salt
¼ cup light brown sugar
1 egg
¾ cup milk
3 tablespoons vegetable oil
2 teaspoons ground cinnamon
⅔ cup fresh or frozen and defrosted blueberries

1 Preheat the oven to 375°F. Lightly grease eight deep muffin cups.

2 With an electric mixer, beat the first eight ingredients together until smooth. Fold in the blueberries.

3 Spoon the mixture into the muffin cups, filling them two-thirds full. Bake until a skewer inserted in the center of a muffin comes out clean, about 25 minutes.

4 Let the muffins cool in the cups on a wire rack for about 10 minutes, then unmold them onto the wire rack and allow to cool completely. Serve slightly warm.

Carrot Buns

Carrots give these buns a lovely moist consistency, and a delightful taste too.

Makes 12

*3/4 cup margarine, at
   room temperature
generous 1/2 cup dark
   brown sugar
1 egg, at room
   temperature
1 tablespoon water
1 1/2 cups grated carrots
1 1/4 cups all-purpose
   flour*

*1 teaspoon baking
   powder
1/2 teaspoon baking soda
1 teaspoon ground
   cinnamon
1/4 teaspoon grated
   nutmeg
1/2 teaspoon salt*

1 Preheat the oven to 350°F. Grease a 12-cup muffin tray or use paper cases.

2 With an electric mixer, cream the margarine and sugar until light and fluffy. Beat in the egg and water, then stir in the carrots.

3 Sift over the flour, baking powder, baking soda, cinnamon, nutmeg and salt. Stir to blend.

4 Spoon the mixture into the prepared muffin tray, filling the cups almost to the top. Bake until the tops spring back when touched lightly, about 35 minutes. Let stand for about 10 minutes in the tray before transferring to a wire rack to cool completely.

Dried Cherry Buns

Dried cherries have a wonderful tart flavor, quite unlike candied cherries.

Makes 16

*1 cup plain yogurt
3/4 cup dried cherries
1/2 cup butter, at room
   temperature
generous 3/4 cup superfine
   sugar
2 eggs, at room
   temperature*

*1 teaspoon vanilla
   extract
generous 1 3/4 cups all-
   purpose flour
2 teaspoons baking
   powder
1 teaspoon baking soda
1/4 teaspoon salt*

1 In a mixing bowl, combine the yogurt and cherries. Cover and let stand for 30 minutes. Preheat the oven to 350°F. Grease 16 muffin cups or use paper cases.

2 With an electric mixer, cream the butter and sugar together until light and fluffy. Add the eggs, one at a time, beating well after each addition. Add the vanilla and the cherry mixture and stir to blend. Set aside.

3 In another bowl, sift together the flour, baking powder, baking soda and salt. Fold into the cherry mixture in three batches.

4 Fill the prepared cups two-thirds full. For even baking, half-fill any empty cups with water. Bake until the tops spring back when touched lightly, about 20 minutes. Transfer to a wire rack to cool completely.

Chelsea Buns

A traditional English recipe, Chelsea buns enjoy wide popularity elsewhere in the world.

Makes 12

2 cups white bread flour
1/2 teaspoon salt
3 tablespoons sweet
   butter
1 1/2 teaspoons fast-rising
   dried yeast
1/2 cup milk

1 egg, beaten
1/2 cup mixed dried fruit
2 1/2 tablespoons chopped
   mixed candied peel
1/3 cup light brown sugar
honey, to glaze

1 Preheat the oven to 375°F. Grease a 7-inch square pan. Sift together the flour and salt; rub in 2 tablespoons of the butter.

2 Stir in the yeast and make a central well. Slowly add the milk and egg, stirring, then beat until the dough leaves the sides of the bowl clean.

3 Knead the dough until smooth. Place in an oiled bowl, cover and set aside until doubled in size. Transfer to a floured surface and roll it out to a rectangle 12 x 9 inches.

4 Mix the dried fruits, peel and sugar. Melt the remaining butter and brush over the dough. Sprinkle the fruit mixture, over the top leaving a 1-inch border. Roll up the dough from a long side. Seal the edges, then cut into 12 slices.

5 Place the slices, cut-sides up, in the greased pan. Cover and set aside until doubled in size. Bake for 30 minutes, until a rich golden brown. Brush with honey and let cool slightly in the pan before turning out.

Sticky Nut Buns

These buns will be popular, so save time by making double the recipe and freezing half for another occasion.

Makes 12

generous 2/3 cup
   lukewarm milk
1 tablespoon fast-rising
   dried yeast
2 tablespoons superfine
   sugar
4 cups white bread flour
1 teaspoon salt
1/2 cup cold butter, cut
   into small pieces
2 eggs, lightly beaten
finely grated rind of 1
   lemon

For the topping and filling
1 3/4 cups dark brown
   sugar
5 tablespoons butter
1/2 cup water
3/4 cup chopped pecans or
   walnuts
3 tablespoons superfine
   sugar
2 teaspoons ground
   cinnamon
generous 1 cup raisins

1 Preheat the oven to 350°F. Mix the milk, yeast and sugar and leave until frothy. Combine the flour and salt, and rub in the butter. Add the yeast mixture, eggs and lemon rind. Stir to a rough dough. Knead until smooth, then return to the bowl, cover and let stand until doubled in size.

2 Cook the brown sugar, butter and water in a heavy-bottomed saucepan until syrupy, about 10 minutes. Place 1 tablespoon syrup in the bottom of 12 1/2-inch muffin cups. Sprinkle a thin layer of nuts in each, reserving the remainder.

3 Punch down the dough; roll out to an 18 x 12-inch rectangle. Combine the superfine sugar, cinnamon, raisins and reserved nuts. Sprinkle over the dough. Roll up tightly from a long edge and cut into 1-inch rounds. Place in the muffin cups, cut-sides up. Let rise for 30 minutes.

4 Bake until golden, about 25 minutes. Invert the pans onto a baking sheet, let stand for 5 minutes, then remove the pans. Cool on a wire rack, sticky-sides up.

Oatmeal Buttermilk Muffins

Makes 12

1 cup rolled oats
1 cup buttermilk
1/2 cup butter, at room
temperature
1/2 cup dark brown sugar,
firmly packed
1 egg, at room
temperature

1 cup all-purpose flour
1 teaspoon baking
powder
1/4 teaspoon baking soda
1/4 cup raisins

1 In a bowl, combine the oats and buttermilk and let soak for 1 hour.

2 Grease a 12-cup muffin pan or use paper cases.

3 Preheat the oven to 400°F. With an electric mixer, cream the butter and sugar until light and fluffy. Beat in the egg.

4 In another bowl, sift together the flour, baking powder, baking soda, and salt. Stir into the butter mixture, alternating with the oat mixture. Fold in the raisins. Do not overmix.

5 Fill the prepared cups two-thirds full. Bake until a cake tester inserted in the center comes out clean, 20–25 minutes. Transfer to a rack to cool.

Pumpkin Muffins

Makes 14

2/3 cup butter or
margarine, at room
temperature
3/4 cup dark brown sugar
1/3 cup molasses
1 egg, at room
temperature, beaten
1 cup cooked or canned
pumpkin

1 3/4 cups all-purpose flour
1/4 teaspoon salt
1 teaspoon baking soda
1 teaspoon ground
cinnamon
1 teaspoon grated
nutmeg
1/4 cup currants or raisins

1 Preheat the oven to 400°F. Grease 14 muffin cups or use paper cases.

2 With an electric mixer, cream the butter or margarine. Add the sugar and molasses and beat until light and fluffy.

3 Add the egg and pumpkin and stir until well blended.

4 Sift over the flour, salt, baking soda, cinnamon, and nutmeg. Fold just enough to blend; do not overmix.

5 Fold in the currants or raisins.

6 Spoon the batter into the prepared muffin cups, filling them three-quarters full.

7 Bake for 12–15 minutes until the tops spring back when touched lightly. Serve warm or cold.

Blueberry Muffins

Hot blueberry muffins with a hint of vanilla are a favorite for breakfast, brunch or tea.

Makes 12

3 cups all-purpose flour
2 teaspoons baking
  powder
$^1/_4$ teaspoon salt
$^1/_2$ cup superfine sugar
2 eggs, beaten

$1^1/_4$ cups milk
$^1/_2$ cup butter, melted
1 teaspoon vanilla
  extract
$1^1/_2$ cups blueberries

1 Preheat the oven to 400°F. Grease a 12-cup muffin pan.

2 Sift the flour, baking powder and salt into a large mixing bowl and stir in the sugar.

3 Place the eggs, milk, butter and vanilla extract in a separate bowl and whisk together well.

4 Fold the egg mixture into the dry ingredients with a metal spoon, then gently stir in the blueberries.

5 Spoon the mixture into the muffin cups, filling them to just below the top. Place the muffin pan on the top shelf of the oven and bake for 20–25 minutes, until the muffins are well risen and lightly browned. Let the muffins stand in the pan for about 5 minutes, and then turn them out onto a wire rack to cool. Serve warm or cold.

Apple and Cranberry Muffins

Not too sweet, but good and spicy, these muffins will be a favorite with family and friends.

Makes 12

4 tablespoons butter
1 egg
$^1/_2$ cup superfine sugar
grated rind of 1 orange
$^1/_2$ cup fresh orange juice
$1^1/_4$ cups all-purpose flour
1 teaspoon baking powder
$^1/_2$ teaspoon baking soda
1 teaspoon ground
  cinnamon
$^1/_2$ teaspoon grated
  nutmeg

$^1/_2$ teaspoon mixed spice
$^1/_4$ teaspoon ground
  ginger
$^1/_4$ teaspoon salt
1–2 eating apples
$1^1/_2$ cups cranberries
$^1/_2$ cup chopped walnuts
confectioner's sugar, for
  dusting (optional)

1 Preheat the oven to 350°F. Grease a 12-cup muffin pan or use paper cases. Melt the butter over gentle heat. Let cool.

2 Place the egg in a mixing bowl and whisk lightly. Add the melted butter and whisk to combine, then add the sugar, orange rind and juice. Whisk to blend.

3 In a large bowl, sift together the flour, baking powder, baking soda, spices and salt. Quarter, core and peel the apples. With a sharp knife, chop coarsely.

4 Make a well in the center of the dry ingredients and pour in the egg mixture. With a spoon, stir until just blended. Add the apples, cranberries and walnuts and stir to blend.

5 Fill the cups three-quarters full and bake until the the tops spring back when touched lightly, about 25–30 minutes. Transfer to a wire rack to cool. Dust with confectioner's sugar before serving, if liked.

Yogurt and Honey Muffins

For a more substantial texture, fold in ½ cup chopped walnuts with the flour.

Makes 12

4 tablespoons butter	¼ cup lemon juice
5 tablespoons honey	¼ cup all-purpose flour
1 cup plain yogurt	½ cup whole wheat flour
1 large egg, at room temperature	1½ teaspoon baking soda
grated rind of 1 lemon	¼ teaspoon grated nutmeg

1 Preheat the oven to 375°F. Grease a 12-cup muffin pan or use paper cases.

2 In a saucepan, melt the butter and honey. Remove from the heat and set aside to cool slightly.

3 In a bowl, whisk together the yogurt, egg, lemon rind and juice. Add the butter and honey mixture. Set aside.

4 In another bowl, sift together the dry ingredients. Fold them into the yogurt mixture to blend.

5 Fill the prepared cups two-thirds full. Bake until the tops spring back when touched lightly, about 20–25 minutes. Cool in the pan for 5 minutes before turning out. Serve warm or at room temperature.

Prune Muffins

Prunes bring a delightful moisture to these tasty and wholesome muffins.

Makes 12

1 egg	2 teaspoons baking powder
1 cup milk	½ teaspoon salt
½ cup vegetable oil	¼ teaspoon grated nutmeg
scant ¼ cup superfine sugar	½ cup cooked pitted prunes, chopped
2 tablespoons dark brown sugar	
2½ cups all-purpose flour	

1 Preheat the oven to 400°F. Grease a 12-cup muffin pan or use paper cases.

2 Break the egg into a mixing bowl and beat with a fork. Beat in the milk and oil. Stir in the sugars and set aside.

3 Sift the flour, baking powder, salt and nutmeg into a mixing bowl. Make a well in the center, pour in the egg mixture and stir until moistened. Do not overmix; the batter should be slightly lumpy. Finally, fold in the prunes.

4 Fill the prepared cups two-thirds full. Bake until golden brown, about 20 minutes. Let stand for 10 minutes before turning out. Serve warm or at room temperature.

Crunchy Granola Muffins

The granola in these muffins gives them an unusual texture and makes them ideal to serve for breakfast.

Makes 10

1¼ cups all-purpose flour
2½ teaspoon baking
   powder
2 tablespoons superfine
   sugar
1½ cups toasted oat
   cereal with raisins

1 cup milk
4 tablespoons butter,
   melted, or corn oil
1 egg, beaten

1 Preheat the oven to 400°F. Grease 10 cups of a muffin pan or use paper cases.

2 Sift the flour, baking powder and sugar together into a large bowl. Add the oat cereal and stir to blend.

3 In a separate bowl, combine the milk, melted butter or corn oil and the beaten egg. Add to the dry ingredients. Stir until moistened, but do not overmix.

4 Spoon the mixture into the cups, leaving room for the muffins to rise. Half-fill any empty cups with water. Bake in the oven for 20 minutes, or until golden brown. Transfer to a wire rack to cool.

Raspberry Muffins

If you are using frozen raspberries, work quickly as the cold berries make the mixture solidify.

Makes 12

1 cup self-rising flour
1 cup whole wheat self-
   rising flour
3 tablespoons superfine
   sugar
½ teaspoon salt
2 eggs, beaten

scant 1 cup milk
4 tablespoons butter,
   melted
1 cup raspberries, fresh
   or frozen (defrosted for
   less than 30 minutes)

1 Preheat the oven to 375°F. Lightly grease a 12-cup muffin pan, or use paper cases. Sift the dry ingredients together, then add any wheat flakes left in the strainer.

2 Beat the eggs, milk and melted butter together and stir into the dry ingredients to make a thick batter.

3 Stir the raspberries in gently. If you mix too much, the raspberries begin to disintegrate and color the dough. Spoon into the cups or paper cases.

4 Bake for 30 minutes, until well risen and just firm. Let cool in the pan placed on a wire rack. Serve warm or cool.

Biscuits

Traditionally, biscuits should be served with butter, clotted or whipped cream and jam.

Makes 10–12
2 cups all-purpose flour
1 tablespoon baking
   powder
4 tablespoons butter,
   diced
1 egg, beaten
5 tablespoons milk
1 beaten egg, to glaze

1 Preheat the oven to 425°F. Lightly butter a baking sheet. Sift the flour and baking powder, then rub in the butter.

2 Make a well in the center of the flour mixture, add the egg and milk and mix to a soft dough using a round-bladed knife.

3 Turn out the biscuit dough onto a floured surface, and knead very lightly until smooth.

4 Roll out the dough to about a ¾-inch thickness and cut into 10 or 12 circles using a 2-inch plain or fluted cutter dipped in flour.

5 Transfer to the baking sheet, brush with egg, then bake for about 8 minutes, until risen and golden. Cool slightly on a wire rack before serving.

Drop Pancakes

If you place the cooked pancakes in a folded dish towel they will stay soft and moist.

Makes 8–10
1 cup all-purpose flour
1 teaspoon baking soda
1 teaspoon cream of
   tartar
2 tablespoons butter,
   diced
1 egg, beaten
²⁄₃ cup milk

1 Lightly grease a griddle or heavy-bottomed frying pan, then preheat it.

2 Sift the flour, baking soda and cream of tartar together, then rub in the butter until the mixture resembles bread crumbs. Make a well in the center, then stir in the egg and sufficient milk to give the consistency of heavy cream.

3 Drop spoonfuls of the mixture, spaced slightly apart, onto the griddle or frying pan. Cook over steady heat for 2–3 minutes, until bubbles rise to the surface and burst.

4 Turn the pancakes over and cook for 2–3 minutes more, until golden underneath. Serve warm with butter and honey.

Whole Wheat Biscuits

Split these wholesome biscuits in two with a fork while still warm and spread with butter and jam, if liked.

Makes 16

¾ cup cold butter
3 cups whole wheat flour
1¼ cups all-purpose flour
2 tablespoons sugar
½ teaspoon salt
2½ teaspoons baking soda
2 eggs
3¾ cups buttermilk
¼ cup raisins

1 Preheat the oven to 400°F. Grease and flour a large baking sheet.

2 Cut the butter into small pieces. Combine all the dry ingredients in a bowl. Add the butter and rub in until the mixture resembles coarse bread crumbs. Set aside.

3 In another bowl, whisk together the eggs and buttermilk. Set aside 2 tablespoons for glazing, then stir the remaining egg mixture into the dry ingredients until it just holds together. Stir in the raisins.

4 Roll out the dough to about ¾-inch thickness. Stamp out circles with a biscuit cutter. Place on the baking sheet and brush with the glaze.

5 Bake until golden, about 12–15 minutes. Allow to cool slightly before serving.

Orange and Raisin Biscuits

Split these biscuits when cool and toast them under a preheated broiler. Butter them while still hot.

Makes 16

2½ cups all-purpose flour
1½ teaspoons baking powder
generous ¼ cup sugar
½ teaspoon salt
5 tablespoons butter, diced
5 tablespoons margarine, diced
grated rind of 1 large orange
scant ½ cup raisins
½ cup buttermilk
milk, to glaze

1 Preheat the oven to 425°F. Grease and flour a large baking sheet.

2 Combine the dry ingredients in a large bowl. Add the butter and margarine and rub in until the mixture resembles coarse bread crumbs.

3 Add the orange rind and raisins. Gradually stir in the buttermilk to form a soft dough. Roll out the dough to about a ¾-inch thickness. Stamp out circles with a biscuit cutter. Place on the baking sheet and brush the tops with milk.

4 Bake until golden, about 12–15 minutes. Serve hot or warm, with butter, or whipped or clotted cream and jam.

Cheese and Chive Biscuits

Feta cheese makes an excellent substitute for butter in these tangy savory biscuits.

Makes 9

1 cup self-rising flour
1 cup whole wheat self-
   rising flour
½ teaspoon salt
3 ounces feta cheese
1 tablespoon chopped
   fresh chives

⅔ cup milk, plus extra to
   glaze
¼ teaspoon cayenne
   pepper

1 Preheat the oven to 400°F. Sift the flours and salt into a mixing bowl. Add any bran left in the strainer.

2 Crumble the feta cheese and rub into the dry ingredients. Stir in the chives, then add the milk and mix to a soft dough.

3 Turn out onto a floured surface and lightly knead until smooth. Roll out to a ¾-inch thickness and stamp out biscuits with a 2½-inch biscuit cutter.

4 Transfer the biscuits to a nonstick baking sheet. Brush with milk, then sprinkle over the cayenne pepper. Bake in the oven for 15 minutes, or until golden brown. Serve warm or cold.

Sunflower Golden Raisin Biscuits

Sunflower seeds give these wholesome fruit biscuits an interesting flavor and appealing texture.

Makes 10–12

2 cups self-rising flour
1 teaspoon baking
   powder
2 tablespoons soft
   sunflower margarine
2 tablespoons golden
   superfine sugar

scant ½ cup golden
   raisins
2 tablespoons sunflower
   seeds
½ cup plain yogurt
about 2–3 tablespoons
   skim milk

1 Preheat the oven to 450°F. Lightly oil a baking sheet. Sift the flour and baking powder into a bowl and rub in the margarine evenly.

2 Stir in the sugar, golden raisins and half the sunflower seeds, then mix in the yogurt, with just enough milk to make a fairly soft, but not sticky, dough.

3 Roll out on a lightly floured surface to about a ¾-inch thickness. Cut into 2½-inch flower shapes or rounds with a biscuit cutter and lift onto the baking sheet.

4 Brush with milk and sprinkle with the reserved sunflower seeds, then bake for 10–12 minutes, until well risen and golden brown. Cool the biscuits on a wire rack. Serve split and spread with jam or low fat spread.

Buttermilk Biscuits

If time is short, drop heaped tablespoonfuls of the mixture onto the baking sheet.

Makes 10
2 cups all-purpose flour
1 teaspoon baking
   powder
½ teaspoon baking soda
1 teaspoon salt
4 tablespoons butter or
   margarine, chilled
¾ cup buttermilk

1 Preheat the oven to 425°F. Sift the flour, baking powder, baking soda and salt into a mixing bowl. Cut in the butter or margarine with a fork until the mixture resembles coarse bread crumbs.

2 Add the buttermilk and mix until well combined to form a soft dough. Turn the dough onto a lightly floured surface and knead for about 30 seconds.

3 Roll out the dough to a ½-inch thickness. Use a floured 2½-inch pastry cutter to cut out rounds. Transfer the rounds to a baking sheet and bake until golden brown, about 10–12 minutes. Serve hot with butter and honey.

Date Oven Biscuits

To get light, well-risen biscuits, don't handle the dough too much or roll it out too thinly.

Makes 12
2 cups self-rising flour
pinch of salt
4 tablespoons butter
¼ cup superfine sugar
⅓ cup chopped dates
⅔ cup milk
1 beaten egg, to glaze

1 Preheat the oven to 450°F. Sift the flour and salt into a bowl and, using a pastry blender or your fingers, rub in the butter until the mixture resembles fine bread crumbs. Add the sugar and chopped dates, and stir to blend.

2 Make a well in the center of the dry ingredients and add the milk. Stir with a fork until the mixture comes together in a fairly soft dough.

3 Turn the dough out onto a lightly floured surface and knead gently for 30 seconds. Roll it out to a ¾-inch thickness. Cut out circles with a biscuit cutter. Arrange them, not touching, on an ungreased baking sheet, then glaze with the beaten egg.

4 Bake in the oven for 8–10 minutes, or until well risen and golden brown. Using a metal spatula, transfer the biscuits to a wire rack to cool completely.

Cheese and Marjoram Biscuits

A great success for a hearty tea. With savory toppings, these biscuits can make a good basis for a light lunch.

Makes 18

1 cup whole wheat flour
1 cup self-rising flour
pinch of salt
3 tablespoons butter
¼ teaspoon dry mustard
2 teaspoons dried marjoram
½–¾ cup finely grated Cheddar cheese
½ cup milk, or as required
½ cup pecans or walnuts, chopped

1 Gently sift the two flours into a bowl and add the salt. Cut the butter into small pieces, and rub into the flour until the mixture resembles fine bread crumbs.

2 Add the mustard, marjoram and grated cheese, and mix in sufficient milk to make a soft dough. Knead the dough lightly.

3 Preheat the oven to 425°F. Lightly grease two or three baking sheets. Roll out the dough on a floured surface to about a ¾-inch thickness and cut it out with a 2-inch square biscuit cutter. Place the biscuits, slightly apart, on the baking sheets.

4 Brush the biscuits with a little milk and then sprinkle the chopped pecans or walnuts over the top. Bake for about 12 minutes. Serve warm, spread with butter.

Dill and Potato Cakes

The inclusion of dill in these potato cakes makes them quite irresistible.

Makes 10

2 cups self-rising flour
3 tablespoons butter, softened
pinch of salt
1 tablespoon finely chopped fresh dill
scant 1 cup mashed potato, freshly made
2–3 tablespoons milk

1 Preheat the oven to 450°F. Grease a baking sheet. Sift the flour into a bowl and add the butter, salt and dill. Mix in the mashed potato and enough milk to make a soft, pliable dough.

2 Roll out the dough on a well-floured surface until fairly thin. Cut into circles with a 3-inch biscuit cutter.

3 Place the potato cakes on the baking sheet, and bake for 20–25 minutes until risen and golden.

White Bread

There is nothing quite like the smell and taste of home-baked bread, eaten while still warm.

Makes two 9 x 5-inch loaves

¼ cup lukewarm water	*2 tablespoons butter or*
1 tablespoon active dried	*margarine, at room*
yeast	*temperature*
2 tablespoons sugar	*2 teaspoons salt*
2 cups lukewarm milk	*about 8 cups bread flour*

1 Combine the water, yeast and 1 tablespoon of the sugar in a measuring cup and let stand for 15 minutes until frothy.

2 Pour the milk into a large bowl. Add the remaining sugar, butter or margarine, and salt. Stir in the yeast mixture, then stir in the flour, 1¼ cups at a time, to make a stiff dough.

3 Transfer the dough to a floured surface. Knead the dough until it is smooth and elastic, then place it in a large greased bowl, cover with a plastic bag, and let rise in a warm place until doubled in volume, about 2–3 hours.

4 Grease two 9 x 5-inch loaf pans. Punch down the dough and divide in half. Form into loaf shapes and place in the pans, seam-sides down. Cover and let rise again until almost doubled in volume, about 45 minutes. Meanwhile, preheat the oven to 375°F.

5 Bake until firm and brown, about 45–50 minutes. Turn out and tap the bottom of a loaf: if it sounds hollow, the loaf is done. If necessary, return to the oven and bake for a few minutes longer. Turn out and cool on a wire rack.

Multigrain Bread

Try different flours, such as rye, cornmeal, buckwheat or barley to replace the wheatgerm and the soy flour.

Makes two 8½ x 4½-inch loaves

1 tablespoon active dried	*2 tablespoons honey*
yeast	*2 eggs, lightly beaten*
¼ cup lukewarm water	*1 ounce wheatgerm*
¾ cup rolled oats	*1½ cups soy flour*
2 cups milk	*scant 2½ cups whole*
2 teaspoons salt	*wheat flour*
¼ cup oil	*about 4 cups bread flour*
⅓ cup light brown sugar	

1 Combine the yeast and water, stir, and let stand for 15 minutes to dissolve. Place the oats in a large bowl. Scald the milk, then pour over the rolled oats. Stir in the salt, oil, sugar and honey. Let stand until lukewarm.

2 Stir in the yeast mixture, eggs, wheatgerm, soy and whole wheat flours. Gradually stir in enough bread flour to obtain a rough dough. Transfer the dough to a floured surface and knead, adding flour, if necessary, until smooth and elastic. Return to a clean bowl, cover and let rise in a warm place until doubled in volume, about 2½ hours.

3 Grease two 8½ x 4½-inch loaf pans. Punch down the risen dough and knead briefly. Then divide the dough into quarters. Roll each quarter into a cylinder 1½ inches thick. Twist together two cylinders and place in a pan; repeat for the remaining cylinders. Cover and let rise until doubled in volume again, about 1 hour. Preheat the oven to 375°F.

4 Bake until the bottoms sound hollow when tapped lightly, about 45–50 minutes. Turn out and cool on a wire rack.

Braided Loaf

It doesn't take much effort to turn an ordinary dough mix into this work of art.

Makes one loaf

1 tablespoon active dried
   yeast
1 teaspoon honey
1 cup lukewarm milk
4 tablespoons butter,
   melted

3¾ cups bread flour
1 teaspoon salt
1 egg, lightly beaten
1 egg yolk, beaten with
   1 teaspoon milk,
   to glaze

1 Combine the yeast, honey, milk and butter. Stir and let stand for 15 minutes to dissolve.

2 In a large bowl, mix together the flour and salt. Make a central well and add the yeast mixture and egg. With a wooden spoon, stir from the center, gradually incorporating the flour, to obtain a rough dough.

3 Transfer to a floured surface and knead until smooth and elastic. Place in a clean bowl, cover and let rise in a warm place until doubled in volume, about 1½ hours.

4 Grease a baking sheet. Punch down the dough and divide into three equal pieces. Roll each piece into a long thin strip. Begin braiding with the center strip, tucking in the ends. Cover loosely and let rise in a warm place for 30 minutes. Preheat the oven to 375°F.

5 Brush the bread with the egg and milk glaze and bake until golden, about 40–45 minutes. Turn out onto a wire rack to cool.

Oatmeal Bread

A healthy, rustic-looking bread made with rolled oats as well as flour.

Makes two loaves

2 cups milk
2 tablespoons butter
4 tablespoons dark brown
   sugar
2 teaspoons salt
1 tablespoon active dried
   yeast

¼ cup lukewarm water
4 cups rolled oats
6–8 cups strong white
   flour

1 Scald the milk. Remove from the heat and stir in the butter, brown sugar and salt. Let stand until lukewarm.

2 Combine the yeast and warm water in a large bowl and let stand until frothy. Stir in the milk mixture. Add 3 cups of the oats and enough flour to obtain a soft dough.

3 Transfer to a floured surface and knead until smooth and elastic. Place in a greased bowl, cover with a plastic bag, and let stand until doubled in volume, about 2–3 hours.

4 Grease a large baking sheet. Transfer the dough to a lightly floured surface and divide in half. Shape into rounds. Place on the baking sheet, cover with a dish towel and let rise until doubled in volume, about 1 hour. Preheat the oven to 400°F.

5 Score the tops and sprinkle with the remaining oats. Bake until the bottoms sound hollow when tapped, about 45–50 minutes. Turn out onto wire racks to cool.

Country Bread

A filling bread made with a mixture of whole wheat and white flour.

Makes two loaves

scant 2½ cups whole
   wheat flour
3 cups all-purpose flour
1¼ cups bread flour
4 teaspoons salt
4 tablespoons butter, at
   room temperature
2 cups lukewarm milk

For the starter
1 tablespoon active dried
   yeast
1 cup lukewarm water
1¼ cups all-purpose flour
¼ teaspoon superfine
   sugar

1 Combine all the starter ingredients in a bowl. Cover and let stand in a warm place for 2–3 hours.

2 Place the flours, salt and butter in a food processor or blender and process just until blended, about 1–2 minutes. Stir together the milk and starter, then slowly pour into the processor or blender, with the motor running, until the mixture forms a dough. Knead until smooth.

3 Place in an ungreased bowl, cover with a plastic bag, and let rise in a warm place until doubled in size, about 1½ hours. Knead again, then return to the bowl and let stand until tripled in size, about 1½ hours.

4 Grease a baking sheet. Divide the dough in half. Cut off one-third of the dough from each half and shape into four balls. Top each large ball with a small ball and press the center with the handle of a wooden spoon to secure. Cover with a plastic bag, slash the top, and let rise. Preheat the oven to 400°F.

5 Dust the loaves with flour and bake until browned and the bottoms sound hollow when tapped, 45–50 minutes. Cool on a wire rack.

Whole Wheat Rolls

To add interest when serving, make these individual rolls into different shapes, if you like.

Makes 12

2 tablespoons active dried
   yeast
¼ cup lukewarm water
1 teaspoon superfine
   sugar
¾ cup lukewarm
   buttermilk
¼ teaspoon baking soda

1 teaspoon salt
3 tablespoons butter, at
   room temperature
scant 1½ cups whole
   wheat flour
1¼ cups all-purpose flour
1 beaten egg, to glaze

1 In a large bowl, combine the yeast, water and sugar. Stir, and let stand for 15 minutes to dissolve.

2 Add the buttermilk, baking soda, salt and butter and stir to blend. Stir in the whole wheat flour. Add just enough of the all-purpose flour to obtain a rough dough.

3 Knead on a floured surface until smooth. Divide into three equal parts. Roll each into a cylinder, then cut in four.

4 Grease a baking sheet. Form the pieces into torpedo shapes, place on the baking sheet, cover and let stand in a warm place until doubled in size. Preheat the oven to 400°F.

5 Brush the rolls with the egg. Bake until firm, about 15–20 minutes. Let cool on a wire rack.

Whole Wheat Bread

A simple wholesome bread to be enjoyed by the whole family at any time.

Makes one 9 x 5-inch loaf

generous 4 cups whole
   wheat flour
2 teaspoons salt
4 teaspoons active dried
   yeast

1¾ cups lukewarm water
2 tablespoons honey
2 tablespoons oil
1½ ounces wheatgerm
milk, to glaze

1 Warm the flour and salt in a bowl in the oven at its lowest setting for 10 minutes. Meanwhile, combine the yeast with half of the water and let dissolve.

2 Make a central well in the flour. Pour in the yeast mixture, the remaining water, honey, oil and wheatgerm. Stir from the center until smooth.

3 Grease a 9 x 5-inch loaf pan. Knead the dough just enough to shape into a loaf. Put it in the pan and cover with a plastic bag. Let stand in a warm place until the dough is about 1 inch higher than the pan rim, about 1 hour. Preheat the oven to 400°F.

4 Brush the loaf with milk, and bake until the bottom sounds hollow when tapped, about 35–40 minutes. Cool on a wire rack.

Two-tone Bread

A tasty, malty bread that, when cut, reveals an attractive swirled interior.

Makes two 12-ounce loaves

1½ tablespoons active
   dried yeast
½ cup warm water
generous ¼ cup superfine
   sugar
6 cups white bread flour
½ tablespoon salt

2½ cups warm milk
5 tablespoons butter or
   margarine, melted and
   cooled
3 tablespoons molasses
2 cups whole wheat bread
   flour

1 Dissolve the yeast in the water with 1 teaspoon of the sugar. Sift 3 cups of the white bread flour, the salt and remaining sugar. Make a well in the center and add the yeast, milk and butter or margarine. Mix in gradually to form a smooth soft batter.

2 Divide the batter into two bowls. To one bowl, add 2½ cups of the bread flour and mix together to a soft dough. Knead until smooth. Shape into a ball, put into a greased bowl and rotate to grease all over. Cover with plastic wrap.

3 Mix the molasses and whole wheat flour into the second bowl. Add enough of the remaining white bread flour to make a soft dough. Knead until smooth. Shape into a ball, put in a greased bowl and cover. Let the doughs rise in a warm place for about 1 hour, until doubled in size. Grease two 8½ x 4½-inch loaf pans. Preheat the oven to 425°F.

4 Punch down the dough and divide each ball in half. Roll out half of the light dough to a 12 x 8-inch rectangle. Roll out half of the dark dough to the same size. Set the dark dough rectangle on the light one. Roll up tightly from a short side. Set in a loaf pan. Repeat. Cover the pans and let the dough rise until doubled in size. Bake for 30–35 minutes.

Pleated Rolls

Fancy homemade rolls show that every care has been taken to make a welcoming dinner party.

Makes 48 rolls

1 tablespoon active dried yeast	2 teaspoons salt
2 cups lukewarm milk	2 eggs
½ cup margarine	scant 7–8 cups bread flour
4 tablespoons sugar	4 tablespoons butter

1 Combine the yeast and ½ cup milk in a large bowl. Stir and let stand for 15 minutes to dissolve. Scald the remaining milk, let cool for 5 minutes, then beat in the margarine, sugar, salt and eggs. Let stand until lukewarm.

2 Pour the milk mixture into the yeast mixture. Stir in half the flour with a wooden spoon. Add the remaining flour, 1¼ cups at a time, to obtain a rough dough.

3 Transfer the dough to a floured surface, knead until elastic. Place in a clean bowl, cover with a plastic bag and let rise in a warm place until doubled in volume.

4 In a saucepan, melt the butter and set aside. Lightly grease two baking sheets. Punch down the dough and divide into four equal pieces. Roll each piece into a 12 x 8-inch rectangle, about ¼ inch thick.

5 Cut each of the rectangles into four long strips, then cut each strip into three 4 x 2-inch rectangles. Brush each rectangle with melted butter, then fold the rectangles in half, so that the top extends about ½ inch over the bottom.

6 Place the rectangles slightly overlapping on the baking sheet, with the longer sides facing up. Cover and chill for 30 minutes. Preheat the oven to 350°F. Bake until golden, 18–20 minutes. Cool slightly before serving.

Cheese Bread

This flavored bread is ideal to serve with hot soup for a hearty lunch snack.

Makes one 9 x 5-inch loaf

1 tablespoon active dried yeast	3¾ cups bread flour
1 cup lukewarm milk	2 teaspoons salt
2 tablespoons butter	scant 1 cup grated aged Cheddar cheese

1 Combine the yeast and milk. Stir and let stand for 15 minutes to dissolve. Meanwhile, melt the butter, let cool, then add to the yeast mixture.

2 Mix the flour and salt together in a large bowl. Make a central well and pour in the yeast mixture. With a wooden spoon, stir from the center to obtain a rough dough. If the dough seems too dry, add 2–3 tablespoons water.

3 Transfer to a floured surface and knead until smooth and elastic. Return to the bowl, cover and let rise in a warm place until doubled in volume, about 2–3 hours.

4 Grease a 9 x 5-inch loaf pan. Punch down the dough and knead in the cheese to distribute it evenly. Twist the dough, form into a loaf shape and place in the pan, tucking the ends under. Let stand in a warm place until the dough rises above the rim of the pan. Preheat the oven to 400°F.

5 Bake the bread for 15 minutes, then lower the oven heat to 375°F and bake until the bottom sounds hollow when tapped, about 30 minutes more.

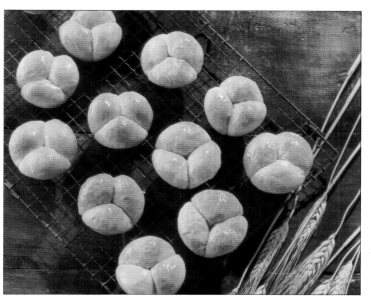

Poppyseed Knots

The poppyseeds look attractive and add a slightly nutty flavor to these rolls.

Makes 12

1¼ cups lukewarm milk
4 tablespoons butter, at
   room temperature
1 teaspoon superfine
   sugar
2 teaspoons active dry
   yeast
1 egg yolk

2 teaspoons salt
4–4½ cups all-purpose
   flour
1 egg beaten with
   2 teaspoons of water,
   to glaze
poppyseeds, for
   sprinkling

1 In a large bowl, stir together the milk, butter, sugar and yeast. Let stand for 15 minutes to dissolve. Stir in the egg yolk, salt and 2½ cups of the flour. Add half the remaining flour and stir to obtain a soft dough.

2 Transfer to a floured surface and knead, adding flour, if necessary, until smooth and elastic. Place in a bowl, cover and let stand in a warm place until the dough doubles in volume, about 1½–2 hours.

3 Grease a baking sheet. Punch down the dough with your fist and cut into 12 pieces the size of golf balls. Roll each piece into a rope, twist to form a knot and place 1 inch apart on the sheet. Cover loosely and let rise in a warm place until doubled in volume, about 1–1½ hours.

4 Preheat the oven to 350°F. Brush the knots with the egg glaze and sprinkle over the poppyseeds. Bake until the tops are lightly browned, about 30 minutes. Cool slightly on a wire rack before serving.

Clover Leaf Rolls

For a witty touch, make one "lucky four-leaf clover" in the batch.

Makes 24

1¼ cups milk
2 tablespoons superfine
   sugar
4 tablespoons butter, at
   room temperature
2 teaspoons active dried
   yeast

1 egg
2 teaspoons salt
4–5 cups all-purpose
   flour
melted butter, to glaze

1 Heat the milk to lukewarm, pour into a large bowl and stir in the sugar, butter and yeast. Let stand for 15 minutes. Stir in the egg and salt. Gradually stir in 4½ cups of the flour. Add just enough extra to obtain a rough dough. Knead until smooth. Place in a greased bowl, cover and let stand in a warm place until doubled in size, about 1½ hours.

2 Grease two 12-cup muffin trays. Punch down the dough, and make 72 equal-size balls.

3 Place three balls, in one layer, in each muffin cup. Cover loosely and let rise in a warm place until doubled in size, about 1½ hours. Preheat the oven to 400°F.

4 Brush the rolls with glaze. Bake until lightly browned, about 20 minutes. Cool slightly on a wire rack before serving.

French Bread

For a taste of France at the breakfast table, or serve with French cheeses for a supper snack.

Makes 2 loaves

1 tablespoon active dried yeast
2 cups lukewarm water
1 tablespoon salt

3½–4 cups all-purpose flour
semolina or flour, for sprinkling

1 In a large bowl, combine the yeast and water, stir, and let stand for 15 minutes. Stir in the salt.

2 Add the flour, 1¼ cups at a time, to obtain a smooth dough. Knead for 5 minutes.

3 Shape into a ball, place in a greased bowl and cover with a plastic bag. Let rise in a warm place until doubled in size, about 2–4 hours.

4 On a lightly floured surface, shape into two long loaves. Place on a baking sheet sprinkled with semolina or flour and let rise for 5 minutes.

5 Score the tops diagonally with a sharp knife. Brush with water and place in a cold oven. Place a pan of boiling water on the base of the oven and set the oven to 400°F. Bake until crusty and golden, about 40 minutes. Cool on a wire rack.

Croissants

Enjoy breakfast Continental-style with these melt-in-your-mouth croissants.

Makes 18

1 tablespoon active dried yeast
1⅓ cups lukewarm milk
2 teaspoons superfine sugar
1½ teaspoons salt

4 cups all-purpose flour
1 cup cold sweet butter
1 egg, beaten with 2 teaspoons water, to glaze

1 In an electric mixer bowl, stir together the yeast and milk. Let stand for about 15 minutes. Stir in the sugar, salt and about 1¼ cups of the flour.

2 Using a dough hook, slowly add the remaining flour. Beat on high speed until the dough pulls away from the sides of the bowl. Cover and let rise in a warm place until doubled in size, about 1½ hours. Knead until smooth, wrap in wax paper and chill for 15 minutes.

3 Roll out the butter between two sheets of wax paper to make two 6 x 4-inch rectangles. Roll out the dough to 12 x 8 inches. Interleave the butter with the dough. With a short side facing you, roll it out again to 12 x 8 inches. Fold in thirds again, wrap and chill for 30 minutes. Repeat the procedure twice, then chill for 2 hours.

4 Roll out the dough to a rectangle about ⅛ inch thick. Trim the sides. Cut into 18 equal-size triangles. Roll up from base to point. Place point-down on baking sheets and form crescents. Cover and let rise in a warm place until more than doubled in size, about 1–1½ hours. Preheat the oven to 475°F.

5 Brush with egg and bake for 2 minutes. Lower the heat to 375°F and bake until golden, about 10–12 minutes. Serve warm.

Individual Brioches

These buttery rolls with their distinctive topknots are delicious served with jam at coffee time.

Makes 8

1 tablespoon active dried
  yeast
1 tablespoon superfine
  sugar
2 tablespoons warm milk
2 eggs
1¾ cups all-purpose flour

½ teaspoon salt
6 tablespoons butter, cut
  into six pieces, at
  room temperature
1 egg yolk, beaten with
  2 teaspoons water,
  to glaze

1 Butter eight individual brioche or muffin cups. Put the yeast and sugar in a small bowl, add the milk and stir until dissolved. Let stand for 5 minutes, then beat in the eggs.

2 Put the flour and salt into a food processor or blender, then, with the machine running, slowly pour in the yeast mixture. Scrape down the sides and process until the dough forms a ball. Add the butter and pulse to blend.

3 Transfer the dough to a buttered bowl and cover with a dish towel. Let rise in a warm place for 1 hour, then punch down.

4 Shape three-quarters of the dough into eight balls and put into the pans. Shape the last quarter into eight small balls, make a depression in the top of each large ball and set a small ball into it.

5 Let rise in a warm place for 30 minutes. Preheat the oven to 400°F.

6 Brush the brioches with the egg glaze. Bake for about 15–18 minutes, until golden brown. Transfer to a wire rack and let cool completely.

Dinner Milk Rolls

Making bread especially for your dinner guests is not only a wonderful gesture, but it is also quite easy to do.

Makes 12–16

6 cups bread flour
2 teaspoons salt
2 tablespoons butter
1 envelope fast-rising
  dried yeast
1¾ cups lukewarm milk

cold milk, to glaze
poppy, sesame and
  sunflower seeds, or sea
  salt flakes, for
  sprinkling

1 Sift together the flour and salt into a large bowl. Work in the butter, then stir in the yeast. Mix to a firm dough with the milk (you may not need it all).

2 Knead the dough for 5 minutes, then return to the bowl, cover with oiled plastic wrap and let rise until doubled.

3 Grease a baking sheet. Punch down the dough and knead again, then divide into 12–16 pieces and make into shapes of your choice. Place on the baking sheet, glaze the tops with milk, and sprinkle over your chosen seeds or sea salt flakes.

4 Let rise again. Meanwhile, preheat the oven to 450°F. Bake the rolls for 12 minutes or until golden brown and cooked. Cool on a wire rack. Eat the same day – they will not keep.

Dill Bread

Tasty herb breads such as this are expensive to buy pre-made – if they can be found at all.

Makes two loaves

4 teaspoons active dried yeast	1 large bunch dill, finely chopped
2 cups lukewarm water	2 eggs, lightly beaten
2 tablespoons sugar	⅔ cup cottage cheese
scant 9½ cups bread flour	4 teaspoons salt
½ onion, chopped	milk, to glaze
4 tablespoons oil	

1 Mix together the yeast, water and sugar in a large bowl and let stand for 15 minutes to dissolve. Stir in about half of the flour. Cover and let rise in a warm place for 45 minutes.

2 In a frying pan, cook the onion in 1 tablespoon of the oil until soft. Set aside to cool, then stir into the yeast mixture. Stir the dill, eggs, cottage cheese, salt and the remaining oil into the yeast. Gradually add the remaining flour until the dough is too stiff to stir.

3 Transfer to a floured surface and knead until smooth and elastic. Place in a bowl, cover and let rise until doubled in volume, about 1–1½ hours.

4 Grease a large baking sheet. Cut the dough in half and shape into two rounds. Place on the sheet and let rise in a warm place for 30 minutes. Preheat the oven to 375°F.

5 Score the tops, brush with the milk to glaze and bake until browned, about 50 minutes. Transfer to a wire rack to cool.

Spiral Herb Bread

When you slice this unusual loaf, its herbal secret is revealed inside.

Makes two 9 x 5-inch loaves

2 tablespoons active dried yeast	1 bunch scallions, chopped
2½ cups lukewarm water	1 garlic clove, finely chopped
3¾ cups bread flour	salt and freshly ground black pepper
generous 3½ cups whole wheat flour	1 egg, lightly beaten
1 tablespoon salt	milk, for glazing
2 tablespoons butter	
1 large bunch parsley, finely chopped	

1 Combine the yeast and ¼ cup of the water, stir and let stand for 15 minutes to dissolve.

2 Combine the flours and salt in a large bowl. Make a central well and pour in the yeast mixture and the remaining water. With a wooden spoon, stir to a rough dough. Transfer to a floured surface; knead until smooth. Return to the bowl, cover with a plastic bag, and let stand until doubled in size.

3 Meanwhile, combine the butter, parsley, scallions and garlic in a large frying pan. Cook over low heat, stirring, until softened. Season and set aside.

4 Grease two 9 x 5-inch loaf pans. When the dough has risen, cut in half and roll each half into a 14 x 9-inch rectangle . Brush with the beaten egg and spread with the herb mixture. Roll up to enclose the filling, pinch the short ends to seal. Place in the pans, seam-sides down. Cover, let stand in a warm place until the dough rises above the pan rims.

5 Preheat the oven to 375°F. Brush the loaves with milk and bake until the bottoms sound hollow when tapped, about 55 minutes. Cool on a wire rack.

Sesame Seed Bread

This delicious bread breaks into individual rolls. It is ideal for entertaining.

Makes one 9-inch loaf

2 teaspoons active dried
   yeast
1¼ cups lukewarm water
1¾ cups all-purpose flour
scant 1½ cups whole
   wheat flour

2 teaspoons salt
5 tablespoons toasted
   sesame seeds
milk, to glaze
2 tablespoons sesame
   seeds, for sprinkling

1 Combine the yeast and 5 tablespoons of the water and let dissolve. Mix the flours and salt in a large bowl. Make a central well and pour in the yeast and water. Stir from the center to obtain a rough dough.

2 Transfer to a floured surface and knead until smooth and elastic. Return to the bowl and cover with a plastic bag. Let stand in a warm place until the dough has doubled in size, about 1½–2 hours.

3 Grease a 9-inch round cake pan. Punch down the dough and knead in the sesame seeds. Divide the dough into 16 balls and place in the pan. Cover with a plastic bag and let stand in a warm place until risen above the rim. Preheat the oven to 425°F.

4 Brush the loaf with milk and sprinkle with the sesame seeds. Bake for 15 minutes. Lower the heat to 375°F and bake until the bottom sounds hollow when tapped, about 30 minutes. Cool on a wire rack.

Rye Bread

To bring out the flavor of the caraway seeds, toast them lightly in the oven first.

Makes one loaf

scant 1½ cups rye flour
2 cups boiling water
½ cup molasses
5 tablespoons butter, cut
   into pieces
1 tablespoon salt
2 tablespoons caraway
   seeds

1 tablespoon active dried
   yeast
½ cup lukewarm water
about 7½ cups all-
   purpose flour
semolina or flour, for
   dusting

1 Mix the rye flour, boiling water, molasses, butter, salt and caraway seeds in a large bowl. Let cool.

2 In another bowl, mix the yeast and lukewarm water and let dissolve. Stir into the rye flour mixture. Stir in just enough all-purpose flour to obtain a stiff dough. If it becomes too stiff, stir with your hands. Transfer to a floured surface and knead thoroughly until the dough is no longer sticky and is smooth and shiny.

3 Place in a greased bowl, cover with a plastic bag, and let stand in a warm place until doubled in volume. Punch down the dough, cover, and let rise again for 30 minutes.

4 Preheat the oven to 350°F. Dust a baking sheet with semolina or flour.

5 Shape the dough into a ball. Place on the sheet and score several times across the top. Bake until the bottom sounds hollow when tapped, about 40 minutes. Cool on a wire rack.

Rosemary Focaccia

Italian flat bread is easy to make using a package mix. Additions include olives and sun-dried tomatoes.

Makes two loaves

1-pound package white
  bread mix
4 tablespoons extra
  virgin olive oil
2 teaspoons dried
  rosemary, crushed
8 sun-dried tomatoes,
  chopped

12 black olives, pitted
  and chopped
scant 1 cup lukewarm
  water
sea salt flakes, for
  sprinkling

1 Combine the bread mix with half the oil, the rosemary, tomatoes, olives and water to form a firm dough.

2 Knead the dough on a lightly floured surface for about 5 minutes. Return to the mixing bowl and cover with a piece of oiled plastic wrap. Let the dough rise in a warm place until doubled in size. Meanwhile, lightly grease two baking sheets and preheat the oven to 425°F.

3 Punch down the dough and knead again. Divide into two, and shape into flat rounds. Place on the baking sheet, and make indentations with your fingertips. Trickle over the remaining olive oil and sprinkle with sea salt flakes.

4 Bake the focaccia for 12–15 minutes until golden brown and cooked. Turn out onto wire racks to cool. This bread is best eaten slightly warm.

Saffron Focaccia

A dazzling yellow bread that is both light in texture and distinctive in flavor.

Makes one loaf

pinch of saffron strands
⅔ cup boiling water
2 cups all-purpose flour
½ teaspoon salt
1 teaspoon fast-rising
  dried yeast
1 tablespoon olive oil

For the topping
2 garlic cloves, sliced
1 red onion, cut into thin
  wedges
rosemary sprigs
12 black olives, pitted
  and coarsely chopped
1 tablespoon olive oil

1 Place the saffron in a heat proof pitcher and pour in the boiling water. Infuse until lukewarm.

2 Place the flour, salt, yeast and olive oil in a food processor or blender. Turn it on and gradually add the saffron and its liquid. Process until the dough forms a ball.

3 Turn onto a floured surface; knead for 10–15 minutes. Place in a bowl, cover and let rise until doubled in size, about 30–40 minutes.

4 Punch down the dough and roll into an oval shape about ½ inch thick. Place on a lightly greased baking sheet and let rise for 30 minutes. Preheat the oven to 400°F.

5 With your fingers, press indentations over the surface of the bread.

6 Cover with the topping ingredients, brush lightly with olive oil, and bake for 25 minutes or until the loaf sounds hollow when tapped on the bottom. Let cool on a wire rack.

Rosemary Bread

Sliced thinly, this herb bread is delicious with cheese or soup for a light meal.

Makes one 9 x 5-inch loaf

*1 envelope fast-rising
   dried yeast
1¼ cups whole wheat
   flour
1½ cups self-rising flour
2 tablespoons butter
¼ cup warm water
1 cup milk, at room
   temperature
1 tablespoon sugar
1 teaspoon salt*

*1 tablespoon sesame
   seeds
1 tablespoon dried
   chopped onion
1 tablespoon fresh
   rosemary leaves
1 cup cubed Cheddar
   cheese
rosemary leaves and
   coarse salt, to decorate*

1 Mix the yeast with the flours in a large mixing bowl. Melt the butter. Then stir the warm water, milk, sugar, butter, salt, sesame seeds, onion and rosemary into the flour. Knead thoroughly until quite smooth.

2 Flatten the dough, then add the cheese cubes. Knead them in until they are well combined.

3 Place the dough into a clean bowl greased with a little melted butter. Cover with a dish towel and put in a warm place for 1½ hours, or until the dough has doubled in size.

4 Grease a 9 x 5-inch loaf pan with butter. Punch down the dough and shape into a loaf. Place in the pan, cover with the dish towel and leave for about 1 hour until doubled in size. Preheat the oven to 375°F.

5 Bake for 30 minutes. Cover the loaf with foil for the last 5–10 minutes of baking. Turn the bread out onto a wire rack to cool. Garnish with some rosemary leaves and coarse salt sprinkled on top.

Potato Bread

Don't add butter or milk to the potatoes when you mash them, or the dough will be too sticky.

Makes two 9 x 5-inch loaves

*4 teaspoons active dried
   yeast
1 cup lukewarm milk
8oz potatoes, boiled
   (reserve 1 cup of the
   cooking liquid)*

*2 tablespoons oil
4 teaspoons salt
3½–4 cups all-purpose
   flour*

1 Combine the yeast and milk in a large bowl and let dissolve, about 15 minutes. Meanwhile, mash the potatoes.

2 Add the potatoes, oil and salt to the yeast mixture and mix well. Stir in the reserved cooking water, then stir in the flour, in six separate batches, to form a stiff dough. Knead until smooth, return to the bowl, cover, and let stand in a warm place until doubled in size, about 1–1½ hours. Punch down, then let rise again for 40 minutes.

3 Grease two 9 x 5-inch loaf pans. Roll the dough into 20 small balls. Place two rows of balls in each pan. Let stand until the dough has risen above the rims of the pans.

4 Preheat the oven to 400°F. Bake the dough for 10 minutes, then lower the heat to 375°F. Bake until the bottoms of the loaves sound hollow when tapped, about 40 minutes. Cool on a wire rack.

Irish Soda Bread

Easy to make, this distinctive bread goes well with soup, cheese and traditional, rustic-style dishes.

Makes one loaf
2½ cups all-purpose flour
1 cup whole wheat flour
1 teaspoon baking soda
1 teaspoon salt
2 tablespoons butter or margarine, at room temperature

1¼ cups buttermilk
1 tablespoon all-purpose flour, for dusting

1 Preheat the oven to 400°F. Grease a baking sheet. Sift together the flours, baking soda and salt. Make a central well and add the butter or margarine and buttermilk. Working from the center, stir to combine the ingredients until a soft dough is formed.

2 With floured hands, gather the dough into a ball. Knead for 3 minutes. Shape the dough into a large round.

3 Place on the baking sheet. Cut a cross in the top with a sharp knife and dust with the flour. Bake until brown, about 40–50 minutes. Transfer to a wire rack to cool.

Sage Soda Bread

This wonderful loaf, quite unlike bread made with yeast, has a velvety texture and a powerful sage aroma.

Makes one loaf
⅔ cups whole wheat flour
1 cup bread flour
½ teaspoon salt
1 teaspoon baking soda

2 tablespoons grated fresh sage
1¼–1¾ cups buttermilk

1 Preheat the oven to 425°F. Sift the dry ingredients into a bowl. Stir in the sage and add enough buttermilk to make a soft dough.

2 Shape the dough into a round loaf and place on a lightly greased baking sheet.

3 Cut a deep cross in the top. Bake in the oven for about 40 minutes, or until the loaf is well risen and sounds hollow when tapped on the bottom. Let cool on a wire rack.

Breadsticks

If liked, use other seeds, such as poppy or caraway, in these sticks.

Makes 18–20

1 tablespoon active dried yeast
1¼ cups lukewarm water
scant 4 cups all-purpose flour
2 teaspoons salt
1 teaspoon superfine sugar
2 tablespoons olive oil
1 egg, beaten, to glaze
10 tablespoons sesame seeds, toasted
coarse salt, for sprinkling

1 Combine the yeast and water, stir and let stand for about 15 minutes. Place the flour, salt, sugar and olive oil in a food processor or blender. With the motor running, slowly pour in the yeast mixture and process until the dough forms a ball.

2 Knead until smooth. Place in a bowl, cover and let rise in a warm place for 45 minutes. Grease two baking sheets.

3 Roll the dough into 18–20 12-inch sticks. Place on the baking sheets, brush with egg then sprinkle with sesame seeds and coarse salt. Let rise, uncovered, for 20 minutes. Preheat the oven to 400°F.

4 Bake until golden, about 15 minutes. Turn off the heat but let stand in the oven for 5 minutes more. Serve warm or cool.

Tomato Breadsticks

Once you've tried this simple recipe, you'll never buy manufactured breadsticks again.

Makes 16

2 cups all-purpose flour
½ teaspoon salt
½ tablespoon fast-rising dried yeast
1 teaspoon honey
1 teaspoon olive oil
⅔ cup warm water
6 halves sun-dried tomatoes in olive oil, drained and chopped
1 tablespoon milk
2 teaspoons poppyseeds

1 Place the flour, salt and yeast in a food processor or blender. Add the honey and olive oil and, with the machine running, gradually pour in the water until the dough starts to cling together (you may not need all the water). Process for 1 minute more.

2 Turn out the dough onto a floured surface and knead for 3–4 minutes, until springy and smooth. Knead in the sun-dried tomatoes. Form into a ball and place in a lightly oiled bowl. Let rise for 5 minutes. Preheat the oven to 300°F.

3 Divide the dough into 16 pieces and roll each piece into a 11 x ½-inch stick. Place on a lightly greased baking sheet and let rise in a warm place for 15 minutes.

4 Brush the sticks with milk and sprinkle with poppy seeds. Bake for 30 minutes. Let cool on a wire rack.

Walnut Bread

This rich bread could be served at a dinner party with the cheese course, or with a country-style lunch.

Makes one loaf

3 cups whole wheat flour
1¼ cups bread flour
2½ teaspoons salt
2¼ cups lukewarm water
1 tablespoon honey
1 tablespoon active dried yeast
1 cup walnut pieces, plus more to decorate
1 beaten egg, to glaze

1 Combine the flours and salt in a large bowl. Make a well in the center and add 1 cup of the water, the honey and the yeast. Set aside until the mixture is frothy.

2 Add the remaining water. With a wooden spoon, stir from the center, incorporating flour with each turn, to obtain a smooth dough. Add more flour if the dough is too sticky and use your hands if the dough becomes too stiff to stir.

3 Transfer to a floured board and knead, adding flour, if necessary, until the dough is smooth and elastic. Place in a greased bowl and roll the dough around in the bowl to coat thoroughly on all sides. Cover with a plastic bag and let stand in a warm place until doubled in volume. Punch down the dough and knead in the walnuts evenly.

4 Grease a baking sheet. Shape the dough into a round loaf and place on the baking sheet. Press in walnut pieces to decorate the top. Cover loosely with a damp cloth and let rise in a warm place until doubled in size, 25–30 minutes. Preheat the oven to 425°F.

5 With a sharp knife, score the top. Brush with the beaten egg. Bake for 15 minutes. Lower the heat to 375°F and bake until the bottom sounds hollow when tapped, about 40 minutes. Cool on a rack.

Pecan Rye Bread

A tasty homespun loaf that recalls the old folk cooking of the United States.

Makes two 8½ x 4½-inch loaves

1½ tablespoons active dried yeast
2¾ cups lukewarm water
6 cups bread flour
5 cups rye flour
2 tablespoons salt
1 tablespoon honey
2 teaspoons caraway seeds, (optional)
8 tablespoons butter, at room temperature
2 cups pecans, chopped

1 Combine the yeast and ½ cup of the water. Stir and let stand for 15 minutes to dissolve. In the bowl of an electric mixer, combine the flours, salt, honey, caraway seeds and butter. With the dough hook, mix on low speed until blended.

2 Add the yeast mixture and the remaining water, and mix on medium speed until the dough forms a ball. Transfer to a floured surface and knead in the pecans.

3 Return the dough to a bowl, cover with a plastic bag and let stand in a warm place until doubled, about 2 hours. Grease two 8½ x 4½-inch loaf pans. Punch down the risen dough.

4 Divide the dough in half and form into loaves. Place in the pans, seam-sides down. Dust the tops with flour. Cover with plastic bags and let rise in a warm place until doubled in volume, about 1 hour.

5 Preheat the oven to 375°F. Bake until the bottoms sound hollow when tapped, 45–50 minutes. Transfer to wire racks to cool completely.

Prune Bread

Makes 1 loaf

1 cup dried prunes	1 teaspoon pepper
1 tablespoon fast-rising dried yeast	2 tablespoons butter, at room temperature
⅔ cup whole wheat flour	⅔ cup buttermilk
3–4 cups bread flour	½ cup walnuts, chopped
½ teaspoon baking soda	milk, for glazing
1 teaspoon salt	

1 Simmer the prunes in water to cover until soft, or soak overnight. Drain, reserving 4 tablespoons of the soaking liquid. Pit and chop the prunes.

2 Combine the yeast and the reserved prune liquid, stir and let stand for 15 minutes to dissolve.

3 In a large bowl, stir together the flours, baking soda, salt and pepper. Make a well in the center.

4 Add the prunes, butter, and buttermilk. Pour in the yeast mixture. With a wooden spoon, stir from the center, folding in more flour with each turn, to obtain a rough dough.

5 Transfer to a floured surface and knead until smooth and elastic. Return to the bowl, cover with a plastic bag and let rise in a warm place until doubled in volume, for about 1½ hours. Grease a baking sheet.

6 Punch down the dough, then knead in the walnuts. Shape the dough into a long, cylindrical loaf. Place on the baking sheet, cover loosely, and let rise in a warm place for about 45 minutes. Preheat the oven to 425°F.

7 With a sharp knife, score the top. Brush with milk and bake for 15 minutes. Lower to 375°F and bake for 35 minutes more, until the bottom sounds hollow. Cool.

Zucchini Crown Bread

Adding grated zucchini and cheese to a loaf mixture will keep it tasting fresher for longer.

Serves 8

3 cups coarsely grated zucchini	freshly ground black pepper
salt, for sprinkling	2 tablespoons olive oil
5 cups all-purpose flour	lukewarm water, to mix
2 envelopes fast-rising dried yeast	milk, to glaze
4 tablespoons freshly grated Parmesan cheese	sesame seeds, to garnish

1 Spoon the zucchini into a colander, sprinkling them lightly with salt. Drain for 30 minutes, then dry with paper towels.

2 Mix the flour, yeast and Parmesan together and season with black pepper. Stir in the oil and zucchini, and add enough lukewarm water to make a firm dough.

3 Knead the dough on a lightly floured surface until smooth, then return to the mixing bowl, cover it with oiled plastic wrap and let rise in a warm place, until doubled in size.

4 Meanwhile, grease and line a 9-inch round sandwich pan. Preheat the oven to 400°F.

5 Punch down the dough, and knead it lightly. Break into eight balls, roll each one and arrange them, touching, in the pan. Brush the tops with milk and sprinkle the sesame seeds over the top.

6 Let rise again, then bake for 25 minutes or until golden brown. Cool in the pan, then turn out onto a wire rack.

Raisin Bread

Makes 2 loaves

1 tablespoon fast-rising
   dried yeast
1¾ cups lukewarm milk
1 cup raisins
4 tablespoons currants
1 tablespoon sherry or
   brandy
½ teaspoon grated
   nutmeg

grated rind of 1 large
   orange
7 tablespoons sugar
1 tablespoon salt
8 tablespoons butter,
   melted
about 4½ cups bread flour
1 egg beaten with
   1 tablespoon cream

1 Stir the yeast with ½ cup of the milk and let stand for
15 minutes to dissolve. Mix the raisins, currants, sherry or
brandy, nutmeg and orange rind together.

2 In another bowl, mix the remaining milk, sugar, salt and
half the butter. Add the yeast mixture. With a wooden spoon,
stir in half the flour, 1¼ cups at a time, until blended. Add the
remaining flour as needed for a stiff dough.

3 Transfer to a floured surface and knead until smooth and
elastic. Place in a greased bowl, cover and let rise in a warm
place until doubled in volume, about 2½ hours.

4 Punch down the dough, return to the bowl, cover and let
rise in a warm place for 30 minutes. Grease two 8½ x 4½-inch
bread pans. Divide the dough in half and roll each half into a
20 x 7-inch rectangle.

5 Brush the rectangles with the remaining melted butter.
Sprinkle over the raisin mixture, then roll up tightly, tucking
in the ends slightly as you roll. Place in the prepared pans,
cover, and let rise until almost doubled in volume. Preheat the
oven to 400°F.

6 Brush the loaves with the egg and milk. Bake for
20 minutes. Lower the temperature to 350°F and bake until
golden, 25–30 minutes more. Cool on racks.

Coconut Bread

**This bread is delicious served with a cup of hot chocolate
or a glass of fruit punch.**

Makes 1 loaf

¾ cup butter
⅔ cup raw sugar
2 cups self-rising flour
scant 2 cups all-purpose
   flour
4 ounces dried coconut
1 teaspoon mixed spice
2 teaspoons vanilla
   extract

1 tablespoon rum
2 eggs
about ⅔ cup milk
1 tablespoon superfine
   sugar, blended with
   2 tablespoons water,
   to glaze

1 Preheat the oven to 350°F. Grease two 1-pound loaf pans.

2 Place the butter and sugar in a large bowl and sift in the
flour. Work the ingredients together with your fingertips until
the mixture resembles fine bread crumbs.

3 Add the coconut, mixed spice, vanilla, rum, eggs and milk
and mix together well with your hands. If the mixture is too
dry, moisten with milk. Knead on a floured board until firm
and pliable.

4 Halve the mixture and place in the prepared loaf pans.
Glaze with sugared water and bake for 1 hour until the loaves
are cooked. Test with a skewer; the loaves are ready when the
skewer comes out clean.

Danish Wreath

Serves 10–12

1 teaspoon fast-rising
    dried yeast
¾ cup milk
4 tablespoons sugar
4 cups strong white flour
½ teaspoon salt
½ teaspoon vanilla
    extract
1 egg, beaten
½ cup blocks sweet butter
1 egg yolk beaten with
    2 teaspoons water

1 cup confectioner's
    sugar

For the filling

generous 1 cup dark
    brown sugar
1 teaspoon ground
    cinnamon
½ cup walnuts or pecans,
    plus extra

1 Mix the yeast, milk and ½ teaspoons of the sugar. Let stand for 15 minutes to dissolve. Mix the flour, sugar and salt. Make a well and add the yeast, vanilla and egg to make a rough dough. Knead until smooth, wrap and chill.

2 Roll the butter to form two 6 x 4-inch rectangles. Roll the dough to a 12 x 8-inch rectangle. Place one butter rectangle in the center. Fold the bottom third of dough over and seal the edge. Place the other butter rectangle on top and cover with the top third of the dough.

3 Roll the dough into a 12 x 8-inch rectangle. Fold into thirds. Wrap and chill for 30 minutes. Repeat twice more. After the third fold, chill for 1–2 hours. Grease a baking sheet.

4 Roll out the dough to a 25 x 6-inch strip. Mix the filling ingredients and spread over, leaving a ½-inch edge. Roll the dough into a cylinder, place on the sheet in a circle and seal the edges. Cover and let rise for 45 minutes. Preheat the oven to 400°F.

5 Slash the top every 2 inches, cutting ½inch deep. Brush with the egg and milk. Bake for 35–40 minutes until golden. Cool. To serve, mix the confectioner's sugar with some water, then drizzle over the wreath. Sprinkle with some nuts.

Kugelhopf

A traditional round molded bread from Germany, flavored with kirsch or brandy.

Makes one ring loaf

¾ cup raisins
1 tablespoon kirsch or
    brandy
1 tablespoon fast-rising
    dried yeast
½ cup lukewarm water
½ cup sweet butter, at
    room temperature
½ cup sugar
3 eggs, at room
    temperature
grated rind of 1 lemon

1 teaspoon salt
½ teaspoon vanilla
    extract
3¾ cups bread flour
½ cup milk
¼ cup slivered almonds
generous ½ cup whole
    blanched almonds,
    chopped
confectioner's sugar, for
    dusting

1 Combine the raisins and kirsch or brandy in a bowl. Combine the yeast and water, stir and let stand for 15 minutes.

2 Cream the butter and sugar until thick and fluffy. Beat in the eggs, one at a time. Add the lemon rind, salt and vanilla. Stir in the yeast mixture. Add the flour, alternating with the milk, until well blended. Cover and let rise in a warm place until doubled in volume, about 2 hours.

3 Grease a 11¼-cup kugelhopf mold, then sprinkle the slivered almonds evenly over the bottom. Work the raisins and chopped almonds into the dough, then spoon into the mold. Cover with a plastic bag, and let rise in a warm place until the dough almost reaches the top of the pan, about 1 hour. Preheat the oven to 350°F.

4 Bake until golden brown, about 45 minutes. If the top browns too quickly, cover with foil. Cool in the pan for 15 minutes, then turn out onto a wire rack. Dust the top lightly with confectioner's sugar.

Open Apple Pie

If using eating apples for this pie, make sure they are firm-fleshed rather than soft.

Serves 8

3–3½ pounds tart eating
  or cooking apples
scant ¼ cup sugar
2 teaspoons ground
  cinnamon
grated rind and juice of 1
  lemon
2 tablespoons butter,
  diced
2–3 tablespoons honey, to
  glaze

For the pastry

2½ cups all-purpose flour
½ teaspoon salt
½ cup butter, cut into
  pieces
4½ tablespoons vegetable
  fat or shortening, cut
  into pieces
5–6 tablespoons iced
  water

1 For the pastry, sift the flour and salt into a bowl. Add the butter and fat and rub in until the mixture resembles coarse bread crumbs. Stir in just enough water to bind the dough. Gather into a ball, wrap and chill for at least 20 minutes.

2 Preheat the oven to 400°F. Place a baking sheet in the oven.

3 Peel, core and slice the apples. Combine with the sugar, cinnamon, lemon rind and juice.

4 Roll out the pastry to a 12-inch circle. Use to line a 9-inch pie dish, leaving an overhanging edge. Fill with the apples. Fold in the edges and crimp loosely. Dot the apples with diced butter.

5 Bake on the hot baking sheet until the pastry is golden and the apples are tender, about 45 minutes.

6 Melt the honey in a saucepan and brush over the apples to glaze. Serve warm or at room temperature.

Apple and Cranberry Lattice Pie

Serves 8

grated rind of 1 orange
3 tablespoons orange
  juice
2 large cooking apples
1⅓ cups cranberries
½ cup raisins
4 tablespoons walnuts,
  chopped
generous 1 cup superfine
  sugar
½ cup dark brown sugar
2 tablespoons all-purpose
  flour

For the crust

2½ cups all-purpose flour
½ teaspoon salt
6 tablespoons cold butter,
  cut into pieces
½ cup cold vegetable fat
  or shortening, cut into
  pieces
4–8 tablespoons iced
  water

1 For the crust, sift the flour and salt, add the butter and fat and rub in well. Stir in enough water to bind the dough. Form into two equal balls, wrap and chill for at least 20 minutes.

2 Put the orange rind and juice into a bowl. Peel and core the apples and grate into the bowl. Stir in the cranberries, raisins, walnuts, all except 1 tablespoon of the superfine sugar, the brown sugar and flour. Place a baking sheet in the oven and preheat to 400°F.

3 Roll out one ball of dough about ⅛ inch thick. Transfer to a 9-inch pie plate and trim. Spoon the cranberry and apple mixture into the case.

4 Roll out the remaining dough to a circle about 11 inches in diameter. With a serrated pastry wheel, cut the dough into ten strips, ¾ inch wide. Place five strips horizontally across the top of the tart at 1-inch intervals. Weave in five vertical strips and trim. Sprinkle the top with sugar.

5 Bake for 20 minutes. Reduce the heat to 350°F and bake until the crust is golden and the filling is bubbling, about 15 minutes more.

Peach Leaf Pie

Serves 8

2½ pounds ripe peaches	**For the pastry**
juice of 1 lemon	2½ cups all-purpose flour
½ cup sugar	¾ teaspoon salt
3 tablespoons cornstarch	½ cup cold butter, cut
¼ teaspoon grated	into pieces
nutmeg	4½ tablespoons cold
½ teaspoon ground	vegetable fat or
cinnamon	shortening, cut into
2 tablespoons butter,	pieces
diced	5–6 tablespoons iced
	water
	1 egg beaten with
	1 tablespoon water

1 Make the pastry as described for Open Apple Pie on page 86. Gather into two balls, one slightly larger than the other. Wrap and chill for at least 20 minutes. Place a baking sheet in the oven and preheat to 425°F.

2 Drop the peaches into boiling water for 20 seconds, then transfer to a bowl of cold water. When cool, peel off the skins. Slice the flesh and combine with the lemon juice, sugar, cornstarch and spices. Set aside.

3 Roll out the larger dough ball to ⅛ inch thick. Use to line a 9-inch pie dish. Chill. Roll out the remaining dough to ¼ inch thick. Cut out leaves 3 inches long. Mark veins. With the scraps, roll a few balls.

4 Brush the pastry case with egg glaze. Add the peaches and dot with the butter. To assemble, start from the outside edge and cover the peaches with a ring of leaves. Place a second, staggered ring above. Continue until covered. Place the balls in the center. Brush with glaze.

5 Bake on the hot baking sheet for 10 minutes. Lower the heat to 350°F and bake for 35–40 minutes more.

Walnut and Pear Lattice Pie

For a cut-out lattice top, roll out the pastry into a circle. Use a small pastry cutter to cut out shapes in a pattern.

Serves 6–8

1 pound piecrust pastry	4 tablespoons chopped
2 pounds pears, peeled,	walnuts
cored and thinly sliced	½ teaspoon ground
4 tablespoons superfine	cinnamon
sugar	½ cup confectioner's
2 tablespoons all-purpose	sugar
flour	1 tablespoon lemon juice
½ teaspoon grated lemon	about 2 teaspoons cold
rind	water
scant ¼ cup raisins or	
golden raisins	

1 Preheat the oven to 375°F. Roll out half of the pastry and use it to line a 9-inch pan that is about 2 inches deep.

2 Combine the pears, superfine sugar, flour and lemon rind. Toss to coat the fruit. Mix in the raisins, nuts and cinnamon. Put the filling into the pastry case and spread it evenly.

3 Roll out the remaining pastry and use to make a lattice top. Bake the pie for 55 minutes, or until the pastry is golden brown on top.

4 Combine the confectioner's sugar, lemon juice and water in a bowl and stir until smooth. Remove the pie from the oven. Drizzle the glaze evenly over the top, on the pastry and filling. Let the pie cool in its pan on a wire rack.

Lemon Meringue Pie

A classic dish whose popularity never seems to wane.

Serves 8

8 ounces piecrust pastry
grated rind and juice of
  1 large lemon
1 cup plus 1 tablespoon
  cold water
generous ½ cup superfine
  sugar, plus
  6 tablespoons extra

2 tablespoons butter
3 tablespoons cornstarch
3 eggs, separated
pinch of salt
pinch of cream of tartar

1 Line a 9-inch pie dish with the pastry, folding under a ½-inch overhang. Crimp the edge and chill for 20 minutes.

2 Preheat the oven to 400°F. Prick the pastry case, line with wax paper and fill with baking beans. Bake for 12 minutes. Remove the paper and beans and bake until golden, 6–8 minutes more.

3 In a saucepan, combine the lemon rind and juice with 1 cup of the water, generous ½ cup of the sugar, and the butter. Bring to a boil.

4 Meanwhile, dissolve the cornstarch in the remaining water. Add the egg yolks. Beat into the lemon mixture, return to a boil and whisk until thick, about 5 minutes. Cover the surface with wax paper and let cool.

5 For the meringue, beat the egg whites with the salt and cream of tartar until stiff peaks form. Add the remaining sugar and beat until glossy.

6 Spoon the lemon mixture into the pastry case. Spoon the meringue on top, sealing it with the pastry rim. Bake until golden, 12–15 minutes.

Blueberry Pie

Serve this tangy blueberry pie with crème fraîche or heavy cream.

Serves 6–8

1 pound piecrust pastry
5 cups blueberries
generous ⅔ cup superfine
  sugar
3 tablespoons all-purpose
  flour
1 teaspoon grated orange
  rind

¼ teaspoon grated
  nutmeg
2 tablespoons orange
  juice
1 teaspoon lemon juice

1 Preheat the oven to 375°F. On a lightly floured surface, roll out half of the pastry and use it to line a 9-inch pan that is 2 inches deep.

2 Combine the blueberries, ¾ cup of the sugar, the flour, orange rind and nutmeg. Toss the mixture gently to coat all the fruit.

3 Pour the blueberry mixture into the pastry case and spread evenly. Sprinkle over the citrus juices.

4 Roll out the remaining pastry and cover the pie. Cut out small decorative shapes from the top. Use to decorate the pastry, and finish the edge.

5 Brush the top with water and sprinkle with the remaining superfine sugar. Bake for 45 minutes, or until the pastry is golden brown. Serve warm or at room temperature.

Creamy Banana Pie

Do not prepare the topping for this pie too soon before serving, or the banana slices will discolor.

Serves 6

2¼ cups ginger cookies, finely crushed
5 tablespoons butter or margarine, melted
½ teaspoon grated nutmeg or ground cinnamon
1 ripe banana, mashed
1½ cups cream cheese, at room temperature

generous 3 tablespoons thick plain yogurt or sour cream
3 tablespoons dark rum or 1 teaspoon vanilla extract

For the topping
1 cup whipping cream
3–4 bananas

1 Preheat the oven to 375°F. For the crust, combine the crushed cookies, butter or margarine and spice. Mix thoroughly with a wooden spoon.

2 Press the biscuit mixture into a 9-inch pie dish, building up thick sides with a neat edge. Bake for 5 minutes, then let cool.

3 Beat the mashed bananas with the cream cheese. Fold in the yogurt or sour cream and rum or vanilla. Spread the filling in the biscuit case. Chill for at least 4 hours or preferably overnight.

4 For the topping, whip the cream until soft peaks form. Spread on the pie filling. Slice the bananas and arrange on top in a decorative pattern.

Red Berry Sponge Tart

When soft berry fruits are in season, serve this delicious tart warm with scoops of vanilla ice cream.

Serves 4

4 cups soft berry fruits, such as raspberries, blackberries, black currants, red currants, strawberries and blueberries
2 eggs

¼ cup superfine sugar, plus extra to taste (optional)
1 tablespoon flour
¾ cup ground almonds
vanilla ice cream, to serve

1 Preheat the oven to 375°F. Grease and line a 9-inch pie dish with wax paper. Sprinkle the fruit in the bottom of the dish with a little sugar if the fruits are tart.

2 Beat the eggs and sugar together for about 3–4 minutes, or until they leave a thick trail across the surface.

3 Mix the flour and almonds, then fold into the egg mixture with a metal spatula, retaining as much air as possible.

4 Spread the mixture on top of the fruit base and bake in the preheated oven for 15 minutes. Turn out onto a serving plate.

De Luxe Mincemeat Tart

Serves 8

2 cups all-purpose flour
2 teaspoons ground
    cinnamon
½ cup walnuts, finely
    ground
½ cup butter
4 tablespoons superfine
    sugar, plus extra for
    dusting
1 egg
2 drops vanilla extract
1 tablespoons cold water

For the mincemeat

2 eating apples, peeled,
    cored and grated
generous 1½ cups raisins
½ cup ready-to-eat dried
    apricots, chopped

½ cup ready-to-eat dried
    figs or prunes,
    chopped
8 ounces green grapes,
    halved and seeded
½ cup chopped almonds
finely grated rind of
    1 lemon
2 tablespoons lemon juice
2 tablespoons brandy or
    port
¼ teaspoon mixed spice
generous ½ cup light
    brown sugar
2 tablespoons butter,
    melted

1 Process the flour, cinnamon, nuts and butter in a food
processor or blender to make fine crumbs. Turn into a bowl
and stir in the sugar. Beat the egg with the vanilla and water
and stir into the dry ingredients. Form a soft dough, knead
until smooth, wrap and chill for 30 minutes.

2 Mix the mincemeat ingredients together. Use two-thirds of
the pastry to line a 9-inch, loose-based quiche pan. Push the
pastry well into the edges, then trim. Fill with the mincemeat.

3 Roll out the remaining pastry and cut into ½-inch strips.
Arrange the strips in a lattice over the top of the pastry, wet
the joins and press them together. Chill for 30 minutes.

4 Preheat a baking sheet in the oven at 375°F. Brush the
pastry with water and dust with superfine sugar. Bake the tart
on the baking sheet for 30–40 minutes. Cool in the pan on a
wire rack for 15 minutes. Then remove the pan.

Crunchy Apple and Almond Flan

**Don't put sugar with the apples as this produces too much
liquid. The sweetness is in the pastry and topping.**

Serves 8

6 tablespoons butter
1½ cups all-purpose flour
4 tablespoons ground
    almonds
2 tablespoons superfine
    sugar
1 egg yolk
1 tablespoon cold water
¼ teaspoon almond
    extract
6–7 cooking apples
2 tablespoons raisins

For the topping

1 cup all-purpose flour
¼ teaspoon ground mixed
    spice
4 tablespoons butter, cut
    in small cubes
4 tablespoons raw sugar
½ cup slivered almonds

1 To make the pastry, rub the butter into the flour until it
resembles bread crumbs. Stir in the almonds and sugar.
Whisk the egg yolk, water and almond extract together and
mix into the dry ingredients to form a soft dough. Knead until
smooth, wrap, and let rest for 20 minutes.

2 For the topping, sift the flour and spice into a bowl and
work in the butter. Stir in the sugar and almonds. Roll out the
pastry and use to line a 9-inch, loose-based quiche pan. Trim
the top and chill for 15 minutes.

3 Preheat a baking sheet in the oven at 375°F. Peel, core and
slice the apples thinly. Arrange in the flan in overlapping,
concentric circles, doming the center. Sprinkle with raisins.

4 Cover with the topping mixture, pressing it on lightly.
Bake on the hot baking sheet for 25–30 minutes, or until the
top is golden brown and the apples are tender (test them with
a fine skewer). Let the flan cool in the pan for 10 minutes
before serving.

Rhubarb and Cherry Pie

**The unusual partnership of rhubarb and cherries works
well in this pie.**

Serves 8

1 pound rhubarb, cut
   into 1-inch pieces
1 pound canned pitted
   tart red or black
   cherries, drained
scant 1½ cups superfine
   sugar
3 tablespoons quick-
   cooking tapioca

For the pastry
2½ cups all-purpose flour
1 teaspoon salt
6 tablespoons cold butter,
   cut in pieces
4 tablespoons cold
   vegetable fat or
   shortening, cut in
   pieces
¼–½ cup iced water
milk, for glazing

1 For the pastry, sift the flour and salt into a bowl. Add the
butter and fat and rub in until the mixture resembles coarse
bread crumbs. Stir in enough water to bind. Form into two
balls, wrap and chill for 20 minutes.

2 Preheat a baking sheet in the oven at 400°F. Roll out one
pastry ball and use to line a 9-inch pie dish, leaving a
½-inch overhang.

3 Mix together the filling ingredients and spoon into the
pastry case.

4 Roll out the remaining pastry, cut out four leaf shapes, and
use to cover the pie leaving a ¾-inch overhang. Fold this
under the pastry base and flute. Roll small balls from the
scraps, mark veins in the leaves and use to decorate the pie.

5 Glaze the top and bake on the baking sheet until golden,
40–50 minutes.

Festive Apple Pie

Serves 8

9 cooking apples
2 tablespoons all-purpose
   flour
generous ½ cup superfine
   sugar
1½ tablespoons fresh
   lemon juice
½ teaspoon ground
   cinnamon
½ teaspoon mixed spice
¼ teaspoon ground
   ginger
¼ teaspoon grated
   nutmeg

¼ teaspoon salt
4 tablespoons butter,
   diced

For the pastry
2½ cups all-purpose flour
1 teaspoon salt
6 tablespoons cold butter,
   cut in pieces
4 tablespoons cold
   vegetable fat or
   shortening, cut in
   pieces
¼–½ cup iced water

1 For the pastry, sift the flour and salt into a bowl. Add the
butter and fat, and rub in until the mixture resembles coarse
bread crumbs. Stir in just enough water to bind. Form two
balls, wrap and chill for 20 minutes.

2 Roll out one ball and use to line a 9-inch pie dish. Preheat a
baking sheet in the oven at 425°F.

3 Peel, core and slice the apples. Toss with the flour, sugar,
lemon juice, spices and salt. Spoon into the pastry case and
dot with butter.

4 Roll out the remaining pastry. Place on top of the pie and
trim to leave a ¾-inch overhang. Fold this under the pastry
case and press to seal. Crimp the edge. Form the scraps into
leaf shapes and balls. Arrange on the pie and cut steam vents.

5 Bake on the baking sheet for 10 minutes. Reduce the heat
to 350°F and bake for 40 minutes, until golden.

Black Bottom Pie

Serves 8

2 teaspoons gelatin
3 tablespoons cold water
2 eggs, separated
¾ cup superfine sugar
2 tablespoons cornstarch
½ teaspoon salt
2 cups milk
2 ounces semisweet
    chocolate, finely
    chopped
2 tablespoons rum

¼ teaspoon cream of
    tartar
chocolate curls, to
    decorate

For the crust
2 cups ginger cookies,
    crushed
5 tablespoons butter,
    melted

1 Preheat the oven to 350°F. Mix the crushed ginger cookies and melted butter. Press evenly over the base and side of a 9-inch pie plate. Bake for 6 minutes. Sprinkle the gelatin over the water and let soften.

2 Beat the egg yolks in a large mixing bowl and set aside. In a saucepan, combine half the sugar, the cornstarch and salt. Gradually stir in the milk. Boil for 1 minute, stirring constantly. Whisk the hot milk mixture into the yolks, pour back into the saucepan and return to a boil, whisking. Cook for 1 minute, still whisking. Remove from the heat.

3 Pour 8 ounces of the custard mixture into a bowl. Add the chopped chocolate and stir until melted. Stir in half the rum and pour into the pie crust. Whisk the softened gelatin into the plain custard until dissolved, then stir in the remaining rum. Set the pan in cold water to reach room temperature.

4 Beat the egg whites and cream of tartar until they peak stiffly. Add the remaining sugar gradually, beating thoroughly after each addition. Fold the custard into the egg whites, then spoon over the chocolate mixture in the pie crust. Chill until set, about 2 hours. Decorate with chocolate curls.

Pumpkin Pie

A North American classic, this pie is traditionally served at Thanksgiving.

Serves 8

scant ½ cup pecans,
    chopped
9 ounces puréed
    pumpkin
2 cups light cream
¾ cup light brown sugar
¼ teaspoon salt
1 teaspoon ground
    cinnamon
½ teaspoon ground
    ginger
¼ teaspoon ground cloves

¼ teaspoon grated
    nutmeg
2 eggs

For the pastry
1⅓ cups all-purpose flour
½ teaspoon salt
½ cup vegetable fat or
    shortening
2–3 tablespoons iced
    water

1 Preheat the oven to 425°F. For the pastry, sift the flour and salt into a mixing bowl. Rub in the fat until the mixture resembles coarse bread crumbs. Sprinkle in enough water to form the mixture into a ball.

2 Roll out the pastry to a ¼inch thickness. Use to line a 9-inch pie dish. Trim and flute the edge. Sprinkle the chopped pecans over the case.

3 Beat together the pumpkin, cream, sugar, salt, spices and eggs. Pour the pumpkin mixture into the pastry case.

4 Bake for 10 minutes, then reduce the heat to 350°F and continue baking until the filling is set, about 45 minutes. Let the pie cool in the dish, set on a wire rack.

Chocolate Nut Tart

This is a sophisticated tart – strictly for grown-ups!

Serves 6–8

8 ounces sweet piecrust
  pastry
1¾ cups dry amaretti
  cookies
⅔ cup blanched almonds
½ cup blanched
  hazelnuts
3 tablespoons sugar

7 ounces semisweet
  chocolate
3 tablespoons milk
4 tablespoons butter
3 tablespoons amaretto
  liqueur or brandy
2 tablespoons light cream

1   Grease a shallow loose-based 10-inch quiche pan. Roll out the pastry and use to line the pan. Trim the edge, prick the base with a fork and chill for 30 minutes.

2   Grind the amaretti cookies in a blender or food processor. Turn into a mixing bowl.

3   Set eight whole almonds aside and place the rest in the food processor or blender with the hazelnuts and sugar. Grind to a medium texture. Add the nuts to the amaretti, and mix well.

4   Preheat the oven to 375°F. In the top of a double boiler, melt the chocolate with the milk and butter. Stir until smooth.

5   Pour the chocolate mixture into the dry ingredients, and mix well. Add the liqueur or brandy and cream.

6   Spread the filling evenly in the pastry case. Bake for 35 minutes, or until the crust is golden brown and the filling has puffed up and is beginning to darken. Let cool to room temperature. Split the reserved almonds in half and use to decorate the tart.

Pecan Tartlets

These delightful individual tartlets make an elegant dinner party dessert.

Makes six 4-inch tartlets

1 pound piecrust pastry
1 cup pecan halves
3 eggs, beaten
2 tablespoons butter,
  melted
1¼ cups maple syrup

½ teaspoon vanilla
  extract
generous ½ cup superfine
  sugar
1 tablespoon all-purpose
  flour

1   Preheat the oven to 350°F. Roll out the pastry and use to line six 4-inch tartlet pans. Divide the pecan halves between the pastry cases.

2   Combine the eggs with the butter, and add the syrup and vanilla extract. Sift over the superfine sugar and flour, and blend. Fill the pastry cases with the mixture and let stand until the nuts rise to the surface.

3   Bake for 35–40 minutes, until a skewer inserted in the center comes out clean. Cool in the pans for 15 minutes, then turn out onto a wire rack.

Pear and Hazelnut Flan

A delicious flan for Sunday lunch. Grind the hazelnuts yourself, if you prefer, or use ground almonds instead.

Serves 6–8

1 cup all-purpose flour	4 tablespoons superfine
¾ cup whole wheat flour	sugar
½ cup sunflower	4 tablespoons butter,
margarine	softened
3 tablespoons cold water	2 eggs, beaten
	3 tablespoons raspberry
For the filling	jam
½ cup self-rising flour	14-ounce can pears in
1 cup ground hazelnuts	natural juice
1 teaspoon vanilla	few chopped hazelnuts, to
extract	decorate

1 For the pastry, stir the flours together, then work in the margarine until the mixture resembles fine bread crumbs. Mix to a firm dough with the water.

2 Roll out the dough and use to line a 9–10-inch pastry dish, pressing it up the sides after trimming, so the pastry sits a little above the dish. Prick the base, line with wax paper and fill with baking beans. Chill for 30 minutes.

3 Preheat the oven to 400°F. Place the dish on a baking sheet and bake blind for 20 minutes. Remove the paper and beans after 15 minutes.

4 Beat all the filling ingredients together except for the jam and pears. If it is too thick, stir in some of the pear juice. Reduce the oven temperature to 350°F. Spread the jam on the pastry case and spoon over the filling.

5 Drain the pears and arrange them, cut-side down, in the filling. Sprinkle the nuts over the top. Bake for 30 minutes until risen, firm and golden brown.

Latticed Peaches

This elegant dessert may be prepared using canned peach halves when fresh peaches are out of season.

Serves 6
For the pastry

1 cup all-purpose flour	3 tablespoons ground
3 tablespoons butter or	almonds
sunflower margarine	2 tablespoons plain
3 tablespoons plain	yogurt
yogurt	finely grated rind of
2 tablespoons orange	1 small orange
juice	¼ teaspoon almond
milk, to glaze	extract

For the sauce
1 ripe peach
3 tablespoons orange
juice

For the filling
3 ripe peaches

1 Lightly grease a baking sheet. Sift the flour into a bowl and rub in the butter or margarine. Stir in the yogurt and orange juice to make a firm dough. Roll out half the pastry thinly and stamp out six rounds with a 3-inch cookie cutter.

2 Skin the peaches, halve and remove the pits. Mix together the almonds, yogurt, orange rind and almond extract. Spoon into the hollows of each peach half and place, cut-side down, on the pastry rounds.

3 Roll out the remaining pastry thinly and cut into thin strips. Arrange the strips over the peaches to form a lattice, brushing with milk to secure firmly. Trim the ends. Chill for 30 minutes. Preheat the oven to 400°F. Brush with milk and bake for 15–18 minutes, until golden brown.

4 For the sauce, skin the peach and halve it to remove the pit. Place the flesh in a food processor or blender, with the orange juice, and liquidize until smooth. Serve the peaches hot, with the peach sauce spooned around.

Surprise Fruit Tarts

These delicious and simple little tarts are the perfect summer treat.

Serves 6

4 large or 8 small sheets frozen and defrosted filo pastry
5 tablespoons butter or margarine, melted
1 cup whipping cream
3 tablespoons strawberry jam
1 tablespoon Cointreau or other orange-flavor liqueur
1 cup seedless black grapes, halved

1 cup seedless white grapes, halved
5 ounces fresh pineapple, cubed, or drained canned pineapple chunks
⅔ cup raspberries
2 tablespoons confectioner's sugar
6 sprigs fresh mint, to decorate

1   Preheat the oven to 350°F. Grease six cups of a muffin tray. Stack the filo sheets and cut with a sharp knife or scissors into 24 4½-inch squares.

2   Lay four squares of pastry in each of the six greased cups. Press the pastry firmly into the cups, rotating slightly to make star-shaped baskets. Brush the pastry baskets lightly with butter or margarine. Bake until the pastry is crisp and golden, 5–7 minutes. Cool on a wire rack.

3   In a bowl, lightly whip the cream until soft peaks form. Gently fold the strawberry jam and Cointreau into the cream.

4   Just before serving, spoon a little of the cream mixture into each pastry basket. Top with the fruit. Sprinkle with confectioner's sugar and decorate each basket with a small sprig of mint.

Truffle Filo Tarts

The cups can be prepared a day ahead and stored in an air-tight container.

Makes 24 cups

3–6 sheets fresh or defrosted frozen filo pastry, depending on size
3 tablespoons sweet butter, melted
sugar, for sprinkling
lemon rind, to decorate

Truffle mixture
1 cup heavy cream
8 ounces bittersweet or semisweet chocolate, chopped
4 tablespoons sweet butter, cut into pieces
2 tablespoons brandy

1   Prepare the truffle mixture. In a saucepan over medium heat, bring the cream to a boil. Remove from the heat and add the chocolate, stirring until melted. Beat in the butter and add the brandy. Strain into a bowl and chill for 1 hour.

2   Preheat the oven to 400°F. Grease a muffin tray with 24 1½-inch cups. Cut each filo sheet into 2½-inch squares. Cover with a damp dish towel.

3   Keeping the filo sheets covered, place one square on a work surface. Brush lightly with melted butter, turn over and brush the other side. Sprinkle with a pinch of sugar. Butter another square and place it over the first at an angle. Sprinkle with sugar. Butter a third square and place over the first two, unevenly, so the corners form an uneven edge. Press the layered square into the tray. Continue to fill the tray.

4   Bake the filo cups for 4–6 minutes, until golden. Cool for 10 minutes on a wire rack in the tray. Remove from the tray and cool completely.

5   Stir the chocolate mixture, which should be just thick enough to pipe. Spoon the mixture into an icing bag fitted with a medium star nozzle and pipe a swirl into each cup. Decorate with lemon rind.

Apple Strudel

Premade filo pastry makes a good substitute for paper-thin strudel pastry in this classic Austrian dish.

Serves 10–12

generous ½ cup raisins
2 tablespoons brandy
5 eating apples
3 large cooking apples
generous ½ cup dark
*   brown sugar*
1 teaspoon ground
*   cinnamon*
grated rind and juice of
*   1 lemon*

½ cup dry bread crumbs
½ cup chopped pecans or
*   walnuts*
12 sheets defrosted frozen
*   filo pastry*
¾ cup butter, melted
confectioner's sugar, for
*   dusting*

1 Soak the raisins in the brandy for 15 minutes.

2 Peel, core and thinly slice the apples. Combine with the rest of the filling ingredients, reserving half the bread crumbs.

3 Preheat the oven to 375°F. Grease two baking sheets. Unfold the filo pastry and cover with a dish towel. One by one, butter and stack the sheets to make a six-sheet pile.

4 Sprinkle half the reserved bread crumbs over the last sheet and spoon half the apple mixture at the bottom edge. Roll up from this edge, jelly roll style. Place on a baking sheet, seam-side down and fold under the ends to seal. Repeat to make a second strudel. Brush both with butter.

5 Bake in the oven for 45 minutes, cool slightly, then dust with confectioner's sugar.

Cherry Strudel

A refreshing variation on traditional apple strudel. Serve with whipped cream, if you like.

Serves 8

1¼ cups fresh bread
*   crumbs*
¾ cup butter, melted
1 cup sugar
1 tablespoon ground
*   cinnamon*
1 teaspoon grated lemon
*   rind*

2 cups sour cherries,
*   pitted*
8 sheets filo pastry
confectioner's sugar, for
*   dusting*

1 In a frying pan, fry the bread crumbs in 5 tablespoons of the butter until golden. Set aside.

2 In a large mixing bowl, toss together the sugar, cinnamon and lemon rind. Stir in the cherries.

3 Preheat the oven to 375°F. Grease a baking sheet. Unfold the filo sheets. Keep the unused sheets covered with damp paper towels. Lift off one sheet and place on a piece of wax paper. Brush the pastry with butter. Sprinkle an eighth of the bread crumbs over the surface.

4 Lay a second sheet of filo pastry on top, brush with butter and sprinkle with bread crumbs. Continue until you have used up all the pastry.

5 Spoon the cherry mixture at the bottom edge of the strip. Starting at the cherry-filled end, roll up the dough jelly roll style. Use the paper to flip the strudel onto the baking sheet, seam-side down. Carefully fold under the ends to seal. Brush the top with melted butter.

6 Bake the strudel for 45 minutes. Cool slightly, then dust with a fine layer of confectioner's sugar.

Strawberry Tart

This tart is best assembled just before serving, but you can bake the pastry case and make the filling ahead.

Serves 6

12 ounces rough-puff or
  puff pastry
1 cup cream cheese
grated rind of ½ orange
2 tablespoons orange
  liqueur or juice

3–4 tablespoons
  confectioner's sugar,
  plus extra for dusting
  (optional)
4 cups ripe strawberries,
  hulled

1 Preheat the oven to 400°F. Roll out the pastry to about a ⅛-inch thickness and use to line an 11 x 4-inch rectangular flan pan. Trim the edges, then chill for 30 minutes.

2 Prick the bottom of the pastry all over. Line with foil, fill with baking beans and bake for 15 minutes. Remove the foil and beans and bake for 10 minutes, until the pastry is browned. Gently press down on the pastry base to deflate, then let cool on a wire rack.

3 Beat together the cheese, orange rind, orange liqueur or juice and confectioner's sugar to taste. Spread the cheese filling in the pastry case. Halve the strawberries and arrange them on top of the filling. Dust with confectioner's sugar, if you like.

Alsatian Plum Tart

Fruit and custard tarts, similar to a fruit quiche, are typical in Alsace. Sometimes they have a yeast dough base instead of pastry. You can use other seasonal fruits in this tart, or a mixture of fruit.

Serves 6–8

1 pound ripe plums,
  halved and pitted
2 tablespoons kirsch or
  plum brandy
12 ounces piecrust or
  sweet piecrust pastry
2 tablespoons seedless
  raspberry jam

For the custard filling
2 eggs
4 tablespoons
  confectioner's sugar
¾ cup heavy cream
grated rind of ½ lemon
¼ teaspoon vanilla extract

1 Preheat the oven to 400°F. Mix the plums with the kirsch or brandy and set aside for about 30 minutes.

2 Roll out the pastry thinly and use to line a 9-inch pie dish. Prick the pastry case all over and line with foil. Add a layer of baking beans and bake for 15 minutes until slightly dry and set. Remove the foil and the baking beans.

3 Brush the bottom of the pastry case with a thin layer of jam, then bake for 5 minutes more. Remove the pastry case from the oven and transfer to a wire rack. Reduce the oven temperature to 350°F.

4 To make the custard filling, beat the eggs and sugar until well combined, then beat in the cream, lemon rind, vanilla and any juice from the plums.

5 Arrange the plums, cut-side down, in the pastry case and pour over the custard mixture. Bake for about 30–35 minutes until a knife inserted in the center comes out clean. Serve the tart warm or at room temperature.

Almond Mincemeat Tartlets

Makes 36

2½ cups all-purpose flour
¾ cup confectioner's
   sugar
1 teaspoon ground
   cinnamon
¾ cup butter
½ cup ground almonds
1 egg yolk
3 tablespoons milk
1-pound bottle
   mincemeat
1 tablespoon brandy or
   rum

For the lemon filling

½ cup butter or
   margarine
½ cup superfine sugar
1½ cups self-rising flour
2 large eggs
finely grated rind of
   1 large lemon

For the lemon icing

1 cup confectioner's
   sugar
1 tablespoon lemon juice

1 Sift the flour, sugar and cinnamon into a bowl and work in the butter until it resembles bread crumbs. Add the ground almonds and bind with the egg yolk and milk to a soft, pliable dough. Knead until smooth, wrap and chill for 30 minutes.

2 Preheat the oven to 375°F. On a lightly floured surface, roll out the pastry and cut out 36 fluted rounds with a pastry cutter. Mix the mincemeat with the brandy or rum and put a small teaspoonful in the bottom of each pastry case. Chill.

3 For the lemon sponge filling, whisk the butter or margarine, sugar, flour, eggs and lemon rind together until smooth. Spoon on top of the mincemeat, dividing it evenly, and level the tops. Bake for 20–30 minutes, or until golden brown and springy to the touch. Remove and let cool on a wire rack.

4 For the lemon icing, sift the confectioner's sugar and mix with the lemon juice to a smooth coating consistency. Spoon into an icing bag and drizzle a zigzag pattern over each tart. If you're short of time, simply dust the tartlets with confectioner's sugar.

Mince Pies with Orange Pastry

Homemade mince pies are so much nicer than store-bought, especially with this flavorsome pastry.

Makes 18

2 cups all-purpose flour
scant ⅓ cup
   confectioner's sugar
2 teaspoons ground
   cinnamon
generous 1 cup butter

grated rind of 1 orange
4 tablespoons iced water
1½ cups mincemeat
1 egg, beaten, to glaze
confectioner's sugar, for
   dusting

1 Sift together the flour, confectioner's sugar and cinnamon. Work in the butter until it resembles fine bread crumbs. Stir in the grated orange rind.

2 Mix to a firm dough with the water. Knead lightly, then roll out to a ¼ inch thickness. Using a 2½-inch round cookie cutter, stamp out 18 circles, then stamp out 18 smaller 2-inch circles.

3 Line two muffin trays with the larger circles. Place a small spoonful of mincemeat into each pastry case and top with the smaller pastry circles, pressing the edges to seal.

4 Glaze the tops with egg and chill for 30 minutes. Preheat the oven to 400°F.

5 Bake for 15–20 minutes, or until golden brown. Remove to wire racks. Serve just warm, dusted with sugar.

Candied Fruit Pie

Use half digestive and half ginger cookies for the crust, if you prefer.

Serves 10

1 tablespoon rum	chocolate curls, to
4 tablespoons mixed	decorate
candied fruit, chopped	
2 cups milk	**For the crust**
4 teaspoons gelatin	2 cups digestive cookies,
½ cup sugar	crushed
½ teaspoon salt	5 tablespoons butter,
3 eggs, separated	melted
1 cup whipping cream,	1 tablespoon sugar
whipped	

1 Mix the digestive cookies, butter and sugar. Press evenly over the bottom and sides of a 9-inch pie plate. Chill.

2 Stir together the rum and candied fruit. Set aside. Pour ½ cup of the milk into a small bowl. Sprinkle over the gelatin and let stand for 5 minutes to soften.

3 In the top of a double boiler, combine 4 tablespoons of the sugar, the remaining milk and salt. Stir in the gelatin mixture. Cook, stirring, until the gelatin dissolves. Whisk in the egg yolks and cook, stirring, until thick enough to coat the spoon. Pour the custard over the candied fruit mixture, set in a bowl of iced water.

4 Beat the egg whites until they peak softly. Add the remaining sugar and beat just to blend. Fold a large dollop of the egg whites into the cooled gelatin mixture. Pour into the remaining egg whites and fold together. Fold in the cream.

5 Pour into the pie crust and chill until firm. Decorate with chocolate curls.

Chocolate Chiffon Pie

As the name suggests, this is a wonderfully smooth and light-textured pie.

Serves 8

7 ounces semisweet	whipped cream and
chocolate, chopped	chocolate curls, to
1 cup milk	decorate
1 tablespoon gelatin	
1 cup sugar	**For the crust**
2 extra-large eggs,	2⅓ cups digestive
separated	cookies, crushed
1 teaspoon vanilla	6 tablespoons butter,
extract	melted
¼ teaspoon salt	
1½ cups whipping cream,	
whipped	

1 Place a baking sheet in the oven and preheat to 350°F. Mix the cookies and butter together and press over the bottom and sides of a 9-inch pie plate. Bake for 8 minutes.

2 Grate the chocolate in a blender or food processor. Place the milk in the top of a double boiler. Sprinkle over the gelatin and let stand for 5 minutes to soften.

3 In the top of a double boiler, put 6 tablespoons sugar, the chocolate and egg yolks. Stir until dissolved. Add the vanilla. Place the top in a bowl of ice and stir until the mixture reaches room temperature. Remove from the ice.

4 Beat the egg whites and salt until they peak softly. Add the remaining sugar and beat just to blend. Fold a dollop of egg whites into the chocolate mixture, then pour back into the whites and fold in.

5 Fold in the cream and pour into the pie crust. Freeze until just set, about 5 minutes, then chill for 3–4 hours. Decorate with whipped cream and chocolate curls.

Chocolate Pear Tart

Chocolate and pears have a natural affinity, well used in this luxurious dessert.

Serves 8

4 ounces semisweet
   chocolate, grated
3 large firm, ripe pears
1 egg
1 egg yolk
½ cup light cream
½ teaspoon vanilla
   extract
3 tablespoons superfine
   sugar

For the pastry

1¼ cups all-purpose flour
¼ teaspoon salt
2 tablespoons sugar
½ cup cold sweet butter,
   cut into pieces
1 egg yolk
1 tablespoon lemon juice

1 For the pastry, sift the flour and salt into a bowl. Add the sugar and butter. Rub in until the mixture resembles coarse bread crumbs. Stir in the egg yolk and lemon juice. Form a ball, wrap, and chill for 20 minutes.

2 Preheat the oven to 400°F. Roll out the pastry and use to line a 10-inch pie dish.

3 Sprinkle the pastry case with the grated chocolate.

4 Peel, halve and core the pears. Cut in thin slices crosswise, then fan out slightly. Transfer the pears to the tart using a metal spatula and arrange like wheel spokes.

5 Whisk together the egg and egg yolk, cream and vanilla. Ladle over the pears and sprinkle with sugar.

6 Bake on a baking sheet for 10 minutes. Reduce the heat to 350°F and cook until the custard is set and the pears begin to caramelize, about 20 minutes more. Serve while still warm.

Pear and Apple Crumble Pie

You could use just one fruit in this pie if you prefer.

Serves 8

3 firm pears
4 cooking apples
scant 1 cup superfine
   sugar
2 tablespoons cornstarch
¼ teaspoon salt
grated rind of 1 lemon
2 tablespoons fresh lemon
   juice
generous ½ cup raisins
¾ cup all-purpose flour
1 teaspoon ground
   cinnamon

6 tablespoons cold butter,
   cut in pieces

For the pastry

1¼ cups all-purpose flour
½ teaspoon salt
5 tablespoons cold
   vegetable fat or
   shortening, cut in
   pieces
2 tablespoons iced water

1 For the pastry, sift the flour and salt into a bowl. Add the fat and work in until the mixture resembles bread crumbs. Stir in enough water to bind. Form into a ball, roll out, and use to line a 9-inch pie dish, leaving a ½-inch overhang. Fold this under for double thickness. Flute the edge, then chill.

2 Preheat a baking sheet at 450°F. Peel, core and slice the fruit. Combine in a bowl with one-third of the sugar, the cornstarch, salt, lemon rind and juice, and raisins.

3 For the crumble topping, combine the remaining sugar, flour, cinnamon and butter in a bowl. Rub in until the mixture resembles coarse bread crumbs.

4 Spoon the filling into the pastry case. Sprinkle the crumbs over the top.

5 Bake on the baking sheet for 10 minutes, then reduce the heat to 350°F. Cover the pie loosely with foil and bake until browned, 35–40 minutes more.

Chocolate Lemon Tart

The unusual chocolate pastry complements the lemon filling superbly in this rich tart.

Serves 8–10

1¼ cups superfine sugar
6 eggs
grated rind of 2 lemons
generous ⅔ cup fresh lemon juice
generous ⅔ cup whipping cream
chocolate curls, to decorate

For the pastry
generous 1½ cups all-purpose flour
2 tablespoons cocoa
4 tablespoons confectioner's sugar
½ teaspoon salt
½ cup butter or margarine
1 tablespoon water

1 Grease a 10-inch pie dish. For the pastry, sift the flour, cocoa, confectioner's sugar and salt into a bowl. Set aside.

2 Melt the butter or margarine and water over low heat. Pour over the flour mixture and stir until the dough is smooth.

3 Press the dough evenly over the base and sides of the dish. Chill while preparing the filling.

4 Preheat a baking sheet in the oven at 375°F. Whisk the sugar and eggs until the sugar is dissolved. Add the lemon rind and juice and mix well. Add the cream.

5 Pour the filling into the pastry case and bake on the hot baking sheet until the filling is set, 20–25 minutes. Cool on a wire rack, then decorate with chocolate curls.

Kiwi Ricotta Cheese Tart

A delicious filling in a rich pastry case creates an elegant dinner party dessert.

Serves 8

½ cup blanched almonds, ground
½ cup sugar
4 cups ricotta cheese
1 cup whipping cream
1 egg and 3 egg yolks
1 tablespoon all-purpose flour
pinch of salt
2 tablespoons rum
grated rind of 1 lemon
2 tablespoons lemon juice
2 tablespoons honey

5 kiwi fruit

For the pastry
1¼ cups all-purpose flour
1 tablespoon sugar
½ teaspoon each salt and baking powder
6 tablespoons butter, cut into pieces
1 egg yolk
3–4 tablespoons whipping cream

1 For the pastry, mix the flour, sugar, salt and baking powder. Add the butter and work in. Mix in the egg yolk and cream to bind the pastry. Wrap and chill for 30 minutes.

2 Preheat the oven to 425°F. On a lightly floured surface, roll out the dough to a ⅛-inch thickness and line a 9-inch springform pan. Prick the pastry all over with a fork. Line with crumpled wax paper and fill with dried beans. Bake for 10 minutes. Remove the paper and beans and bake for another 6–8 minutes until golden. Reduce oven to 350°F.

3 Mix the almonds with 1 tablespoon of the sugar. Beat the ricotta until creamy, then add the cream, egg, yolks, remaining sugar, flour, salt, rum, lemon rind and 2 tablespoons lemon juice. Beat, add the almonds and mix.

4 Pour into pastry case and bake for 1 hour, until golden. Cool and chill. Mix the honey and remaining lemon juice. Halve the kiwis lengthwise, then slice. Arrange them over the tart and brush with the honey glaze.

Lime Tart

Use lemons instead of limes, with yellow food coloring, if you prefer.

Serves 8

3 large egg yolks
14-ounce can sweetened
    condensed milk
1 tablespoon grated lime
    rind
½ cup fresh lime juice
green food coloring
    (optional)

½ cup whipping cream

For the base
1⅓ cups crushed
    digestive cookies
5 tablespoons butter or
    margarine, melted

1 Preheat the oven to 350°F. For the base, place the crushed cookies in a bowl, add the butter or margarine and mix.

2 Press the mixture evenly over the bottom and sides of a 9-inch pie dish. Bake for 8 minutes, then cool.

3 Beat the yolks until thick. Beat in the milk, lime rind and juice and coloring, if using. Pour into the pastry case and chill until set, about 4 hours.

4 To serve, whip the cream. Pipe a lattice pattern on top, or spoon dollops around the edge.

Fruit Tartlets

You could make one large fruit tart for an elegant dessert, if you like.

Makes 8

¾ cup redcurrant jelly
1 tablespoon fresh lemon
    juice
¾ cup whipping cream
1½ pounds fresh fruit,
    such as strawberries,
    raspberries, kiwi fruit,
    peaches, grapes or
    currants, peeled and
    sliced as necessary

For the pastry
generous ½ cup cold
    butter, cut in pieces
scant ½ cup dark brown
    sugar
3 tablespoons cocoa
1¾ cups all-purpose flour
1 egg white

1 For the pastry, melt the butter, brown sugar and cocoa over low heat. Remove from the heat and sift over the flour. Stir, then add enough egg white to bind. Form into a ball, wrap, and chill for 30 minutes.

2 Grease eight 3-inch tartlet pans. Roll out the pastry between two sheets of wax paper. Stamp out eight 4-inch rounds with a fluted cookie cutter.

3 Line the tartlet pans and prick the pastry with a fork. Chill for 15 minutes. Preheat the oven to 350°F.

4 Bake the pastry cases until firm, 20–25 minutes. Cool, then turn out.

5 Melt the jelly with the lemon juice. Brush over the tartlet cases. Whip the cream and spread thinly in the tartlet cases. Arrange the fruit on top. Brush with the jelly glaze and serve.

Chocolate Cheesecake Tart

You can just use digestive cookies for the bottom of this tart, if you prefer.

Serves 8

1½ cups cream cheese	**For the base**
4 tablespoons whipping cream	1 cup crushed digestive cookies
generous 1 cup superfine sugar	scant 1 cup crushed amaretti cookies
½ cup cocoa	6 tablespoons butter, melted
½ teaspoon ground cinnamon	
3 eggs	
whipped cream and chocolate curls, to decorate	

1 Preheat a baking sheet in the oven at 350°F. For the base, mix the crushed cookies and butter in a bowl. Press the mixture over the bottom and sides of a 9-inch pie dish. Bake for 8 minutes. Let cool. Keep the oven on.

2 Beat the cream cheese and cream together until smooth. Beat in the sugar, cocoa and cinnamon until blended.

3 Add the eggs, one at a time, beating just enough to blend.

4 Pour into the cookie base and bake on the baking sheet for 25–30 minutes. The filling will sink down as it cools. Decorate with whipped cream and chocolate curls.

Frozen Strawberry Tart

For a frozen raspberry tart, use raspberries in place of the strawberries.

Serves 8

1 cup cream cheese	**For the base**
1 cup sour cream	1⅓ cups crushed digestive cookies
5 cups frozen strawberries, defrosted and sliced	1 tablespoon superfine sugar
	5 tablespoons butter, melted

1 For the base, mix together the cookies, sugar and butter. Press the mixture over the bottom and sides of a 9-inch pie dish. Freeze until firm.

2 Blend together the cream cheese and sour cream. Reserve 6 tablespoons of the strawberries. Add the rest to the cream cheese mixture.

3 Pour the filling into the cookie base and freeze until firm, about 6–8 hours. To serve, spoon some of the reserved strawberries on top.

Treacle Tart

A very rich dessert, popular with all the family.

Serves 4–6
¾ cup maple syrup
1½ cups fresh white
    bread crumbs
grated rind of 1 lemon
2 tablespoons fresh lemon
    juice

For the pastry
1½ cups all-purpose flour
½ teaspoon salt
6 tablespoons cold butter,
    cut in pieces
3 tablespoons cold
    margarine, cut in
    pieces
3–4 tablespoons iced
    water

1 For the pastry, sift together the flour and salt, add the fats and work in until the mixture resembles coarse bread crumbs. Stir in enough water to bind. Form into a ball, wrap and chill for 20 minutes.

2 Roll out the pastry and use to line an 8-inch pie dish. Chill for 20 minutes. Reserve the pastry trimmings.

3 Preheat a baking sheet in the oven at 400°F. In a saucepan, warm the syrup until thin and runny. Stir in the bread crumbs and lemon rind. Let stand for 10 minutes, then stir in the lemon juice. Spread in the pastry case.

4 Roll out the pastry trimmings and cut into 12 thin strips. Lay six strips on the filling, then lay the other six at an angle over them to form a lattice.

5 Bake on the baking sheet for 10 minutes. Lower the heat to 375°F. Bake until golden, about 15 minutes more. Serve warm or cold.

Almond Syrup Tart

Serves 6
1½ cups fresh white
    bread crumbs
1 cup maple syrup
finely grated rind of
    ½ lemon
2 teaspoons lemon juice
9-inch pastry case, made
    with basic, nut or rich
    piecrust pastry

4 tablespoons slivered
    almonds
milk, to glaze (optional)
cream, custard, ice
    cream, to serve

1 Preheat the oven to 400°F. Combine the bread crumbs with the syrup and the lemon rind and juice.

2 Spoon into the pastry case and spread out evenly. Sprinkle the slivered almonds evenly over the top.

3 Brush the pastry with milk to glaze, if you like. Bake for 25–30 minutes, until the pastry and filling are golden brown.

4 Transfer to a wire rack to cool. Serve warm or cold, with cream, custard or ice cream.

Tarte Tatin

A special *tarte tatin* pan is ideal, but an oven proof frying pan can be used quite successfully.

Serves 8–10
½ pound puff or piecrust pastry
10–12 large Golden Delicious apples
½ cup butter, cut into pieces
½ cup superfine sugar
½ teaspoon ground cinnamon
crème fraîche or whipped cream, to serve

1 On a lightly floured surface, roll out the pastry to a an 11-inch round less than ¼ inch thick. Transfer to a lightly floured baking sheet and chill.

2 Peel, halve and core the apples, sprinkle with lemon juice.

3 In a 10-inch *tarte tatin* pan or ovenproof frying pan, cook the butter, sugar and cinnamon until the butter has melted and the sugar has dissolved. Cook for 6–8 minutes until the mixture is a medium caramel color. Remove from the heat and arrange the apple halves, standing on edge, in the pan.

4 Return the pan to the heat and simmer for 20–25 minutes until the apples are tender and colored. Remove from the heat and cool slightly.

5 Preheat the oven to 450°F. Place the pastry over the apples and tuck the edges inside the pan around the apples. Pierce the pastry in two or three places, then bake for 25–30 minutes until the pastry is golden and the filling is bubbling. Cool in the pan for 10–15 minutes.

6 To serve, run a sharp knife around the edge of the pan to loosen the pastry. Cover with a serving plate and carefully invert the pan and plate together. It is best to do this over a sink in case any caramel drips. Lift off the pan and loosen any apples that stick with a metal spatula. Serve the tart warm with crème fraîche or whipped cream.

Rich Chocolate Pie

A delicious pie generously decorated with chocolate curls.

Serves 8
3 ounces semisweet chocolate
4 tablespoons butter or margarine
3 tablespoons maple syrup
3 eggs, beaten
⅔ cup superfine sugar
1 teaspoon vanilla extract
4 ounces milk chocolate
2 cups whipping cream

For the pastry
1⅓ cups all-purpose flour
½ teaspoon salt
½ cup vegetable fat or shortening
2–3 tablespoons iced water

1 Preheat the oven to 425°F. For the pastry, sift the flour and salt into a bowl. Work in the fat until the mixture resembles coarse bread crumbs. Add water until the pastry forms a ball.

2 Roll out the pastry and use to line an 8–9-inch quiche pan. Flute the edge. Prick the bottom and sides of the pastry case with a fork. Bake until lightly browned, 10–15 minutes. Cool in the pan on a wire rack.

3 Reduce the oven temperature to 350°F. In the top of a double boiler, melt the semisweet chocolate, butter or margarine and syrup. Remove from the heat and stir in the eggs, sugar and vanilla. Pour the chocolate mixture into the pastry case. Bake until the filling is set, 35–40 minutes. Cool in the pan on a wire rack.

4 For the decoration, use the heat of your hands to soften the milk chocolate slightly. Use a swivel-headed vegetable peeler to shave off short, wide curls. Chill until needed.

5 Before serving, lightly whip the cream until soft peaks form. Spread the cream over the surface of the chocolate filling. Decorate with the milk chocolate curls.

Red Berry Tart with Lemon Cream

This tart is best filled just before serving so the pastry remains mouth-wateringly crisp.

Serves 6–8

1¼ cups all-purpose flour
4 tablespoons cornstarch
scant ⅓ cup confectioner's sugar
7 tablespoons butter
1 teaspoon vanilla extract
2 egg yolks, beaten

For the filling

scant 1 cup cream cheese, softened
3 tablespoons lemon curd
grated rind and juice of 1 lemon
confectioner's sugar, to taste (optional)
2 cups mixed red berry fruits
3 tablespoons redcurrant jelly

1 Sift the flour, cornstarch and confectioner's sugar together. Rub in the butter until the mixture resembles bread crumbs.

2 Beat the vanilla into the egg yolks, then stir into the flour mixture to make a firm dough. Add cold water if necessary.

3 Roll out the pastry and use it to line a 9-inch round quiche pan. Trim the edges. Prick the pastry and let rest in the fridge for 30 minutes.

4 Preheat the oven to 400°F. Line the tart with wax paper and fill with baking beans. Place on a baking sheet and bake for 20 minutes, removing the paper and beans after 15 minutes. Let cool, then remove the pastry case from the quiche pan.

5 Cream the cheese, lemon curd and lemon rind and juice, adding confectioner's sugar, if you wish. Spread the mixture into the base of the tart. Top with the fruits.

6 Warm the redcurrant jelly and trickle over the fruits just before serving.

Peach Tart with Almond Cream

Serves 8–10

1 cup blanched almonds
2 tablespoons all-purpose flour
scant ¼ cup sweet butter
1 cup, plus 2 tablespoons superfine sugar
1 egg, plus 1 egg yolk
¼ teaspoon vanilla extract, or 2 teaspoons rum
4 large ripe peaches, peeled

For the pastry

generous 1½ cups all-purpose flour
½ teaspoon salt
scant ¼ cup cold sweet butter, diced
1 egg yolk
2–3 tablespoons iced water

1 Sift the flour and salt into a bowl. Rub in the butter until the mixture resembles coarse bread crumbs. Stir in the egg yolk and enough water to bind the pastry. Gather into a ball, wrap and chill for at least 20 minutes. Preheat a baking sheet in the center of a 400°F oven.

2 Roll out the pastry ⅛ inch thick. Transfer to a 10-inch pie dish. Trim the edge, prick with a fork and chill.

3 Grind the almonds with the flour. With an electric mixer, cream the butter and scant ¾ cup of the sugar until light and fluffy. Gradually beat in the egg and yolk. Stir in the almonds and vanilla or rum. Spread in the pastry case.

4 Halve the peaches and remove the pits. Cut crosswise in thin slices and arrange on top of the almond cream like the spokes of a wheel. Keep the slices of each peach-half together. Fan out by pressing down gently at a slight angle.

5 Bake until the pastry browns, 10–15 minutes. Lower the heat to 350°F and bake until the almond cream sets, about 15 minutes more. 10 minutes before the end of the cooking time, sprinkle with the remaining sugar.

Pear and Almond Cream Tart

This tart is equally successful made with nectarines, peaches, apricots or apples.

Serves 6

12 ounces piecrust or sweet piecrust pastry	**For the filling**
3 firm pears	generous ½ cup blanched whole almonds
lemon juice	4 tablespoons superfine sugar
1 tablespoon peach brandy or cold water	5 tablespoons butter
4 tablespoons peach jam, strained	1 egg, plus 1 egg white
	few drops almond extract

1 Roll out the pastry and use to line a 9-inch quiche pan. Chill. For the filling, put the almonds and sugar in a food processor or blender and process until finely ground but not pasty. Add the butter and process until creamy, then add the egg, egg white and almond extract and mix well.

2 Preheat a baking sheet in the oven at 375°F. Peel the pears, halve them, remove the cores and rub with lemon juice. Put the pear halves, cut-side down, on a board and slice thinly crosswise, keeping the slices together.

3 Pour the filling into the pastry case. Slide a metal spatula under one pear half and press the top to fan out the slices. Transfer to the tart, placing the fruit on the filling like spokes of a wheel.

4 Bake the tart on the baking sheet for 50–55 minutes, until the filling is set and well browned. Cool on a wire rack.

5 Heat the brandy or water with the jam. Brush over the top of the hot tart to glaze. Serve at room temperature.

Lemon Tart

This tart, a classic of France, has a refreshing tangy flavor.

Serves 8–10

12 ounces piecrust or sweet piecrust pastry	½ cup superfine sugar
grated rind of 2–3 lemons	4 tablespoons crème fraîche or heavy cream
⅔ cup freshly squeezed lemon juice	4 eggs, plus 3 egg yolks
	confectioner's sugar, for dusting

1 Preheat the oven to 375°F. Roll out the pastry and use to line a 9-inch quiche pan. Prick the pastry, line with foil and fill with baking beans. Bake for 15 minutes, or until the edges are dry. Remove the foil and beans, and bake for 5–7 minutes more, until golden.

2 Beat together the lemon rind, juice and sugar, then gradually add the crème fraîche or cream and beat until well blended. Beat in the eggs, one at a time, then beat in the yolks.

3 Pour the filling into the baked pastry case. Bake for about 15–20 minutes, until the filling is set. If the pastry begins to brown too much, cover the edges with foil. Let cool. Dust with confectioner's sugar before serving.

Maple Walnut Tart

Makes sure you use 100 per cent pure maple syrup in this decadent tart.

Serves 8

3 eggs
¼ teaspoon salt
4 tablespoons superfine
  sugar
4 tablespoons butter,
  melted
1 cup pure maple syrup
1 cup chopped walnuts
whipped cream, to
  decorate

For the pastry
9 tablespoons all-purpose
  flour
½ cup whole wheat flour
¼ teaspoon salt
4 tablespoons cold butter,
  cut in pieces
3 tablespoons cold
  vegetable fat or
  shortening, cut in
  pieces
1 egg yolk

1 For the pastry, mix the flours and salt in a bowl. Add the fats and rub in until the mixture resembles coarse bread crumbs. Stir in the egg yolk and 2–3 tablespoons iced water to bind. Form into a ball, wrap and chill for 20 minutes.

2 Preheat the oven to 425°F. Roll out the pastry and use to line a 9-inch pie dish. Use the trimmings to stamp out heart shapes. Arrange on the pastry case rim with a little water.

3 Prick the pastry base, line with wax paper and fill with baking beans. Bake for 10 minutes. Remove the paper and beans and bake until golden, 3–6 minutes more.

4 Whisk together the eggs, salt and sugar. Stir in the butter and maple syrup. Set the pastry case on a baking sheet. Pour in the filling, then sprinkle with the nuts.

5 Bake until just set, about 35 minutes. Cool on a wire rack. Decorate with piped whipped cream.

Pecan Tart

Serve this tart warm, accompanied by ice cream or whipped cream, if you wish.

Serves 8

3 eggs
pinch of salt
generous 1 cup dark
  brown sugar
½ cup maple syrup
2 tablespoons fresh lemon
  juice
6 tablespoons butter,
  melted
1¼ cups chopped pecans
½ cup pecan halves

For the pastry
1½ cups all-purpose flour
1 tablespoon superfine
  sugar
1 teaspoon baking
  powder
½ teaspoon salt
6 tablespoons cold sweet
  butter, cut in pieces
1 egg yolk
3–4 tablespoons
  whipping cream

1 For the pastry, sift together the flour, sugar, baking powder and salt. Add the butter and rub in until the mixture resembles coarse bread crumbs.

2 Blend the egg yolk and whipping cream, then stir into the flour mixture.

3 Form the pastry into a ball, then roll out and use to line a 9-inch pie dish. Flute the edge and chill for 20 minutes.

4 Preheat a baking sheet in the oven at 400°F. Lightly whisk the eggs and salt. Mix in the sugar, syrup, lemon juice and butter. Stir in the chopped nuts.

5 Pour into the pastry case and arrange the pecan halves in concentric circles on top.

6 Bake on the baking sheet for 10 minutes. Reduce the heat to 325°F and bake for 25 minutes more.

Velvety Mocha Tart

A creamy, smooth filling tops a dark, light-textured base in this wondrous dessert.

Serves 8

2 teaspoons instant
　espresso coffee
2 tablespoons hot water
6 ounces semisweet
　chocolate
1 ounce bittersweet
　chocolate
1½ cups whipping cream,
　slightly warmed
½ cup whipped cream, to
　decorate

chocolate-coated coffee
　beans, to decorate

For the base
2½ cups crushed
　chocolate wafers
2 tablespoons superfine
　sugar
5 tablespoons butter,
　melted

1 Combine the base ingredients. Press the mixture over the bottom and sides of a 9-inch pie dish. Chill.

2 Dissolve the coffee in the water. Set aside.

3 Melt the chocolates in the top of a double boiler. Set the bottom of the pan in cold water to cool.

4 Whip the cream until light and fluffy. Add the coffee and whip until the cream just holds its shape.

5 When the chocolate is at room temperature, fold it gently into the cream.

6 Pour into the cookie base and chill until firm. Decorate with piped whipped cream and chocolate-coated coffee beans just before serving.

Coconut Cream Tart

Serves 8

5 ounces dried coconut
¾ cup superfine sugar
4 tablespoons cornstarch
¼ teaspoon salt
2½ cups milk
¼ cup whipping cream
2 egg yolks
2 tablespoons unsalted
　butter
2 teaspoons vanilla
　extract

For the pastry
1¼ cups all-purpose flour
¼ teaspoon salt
3 tablespoons cold butter,
　cut in pieces
3 tablespoons cold
　vegetable fat or
　shortening
2–3 tablespoons iced
　water

1 Sift the flour and salt into a bowl, add the fats and work in until it resembles coarse bread crumbs. With a fork, stir in just enough water to bind the pastry. Gather into a ball, wrap and chill for 20 minutes. Preheat the oven to 425°F.

2 Roll out the pastry ⅛ inch thick. Line a 9-inch pie dish. Trim and flute the edges, prick the base, line with crumpled wax paper and fill with baking beans. Bake for 10–12 minutes. Remove the paper and beans, reduce heat to 350°F and bake until brown, 10–15 minutes.

3 Spread 2 ounces of the coconut on a baking sheet and toast in the oven until golden, 6–8 minutes.

4 Put the sugar, cornstarch and salt in a saucepan. In a bowl, whisk the milk, cream and yolks together. Add the egg mixture to the saucepan.

5 Cook over low heat, stirring, until the mixture comes to a boil. Boil for 1 minute, then remove from the heat. Add the butter, vanilla and remaining coconut.

6 Pour into the pre-baked pastry case. When cool, sprinkle toasted coconut in a ring in the center.

Orange Tart

If you like oranges, this is the dessert for you!

Serves 8

1 cup sugar
1 cup fresh orange juice,
    strained
2 large navel oranges
scant 1 cup whole
    blanched almonds
4 tablespoons butter
1 egg
1 tablespoon all-purpose
    flour
3 tablespoons apricot jam

For the pastry

scant 2 cups all-purpose
    flour
½ teaspoon salt
4 tablespoons cold butter,
    cut into pieces
3 tablespoons cold
    margarine, cut into
    pieces
3–4 tablespoons iced
    water

1 For the pastry, sift the flour and salt into a bowl. Add the butter and margarine and work in until the mixture resembles coarse bread crumbs. Stir in just enough water to bind the dough. Wrap and chill for 20 minutes. Roll out the pastry to a ¼-inch thickness. Use to line an 8-inch quiche pan. Trim and chill until needed.

2 In a saucepan, combine ¾ cup of the sugar and the orange juice and boil until thick and syrupy. Cut the unpeeled oranges into ¼-inch slices. Add to the syrup. Simmer gently for 10 minutes. Put on a wire rack to dry. When cool, cut in half. Reserve the syrup. Place a baking sheet in the oven and heat to 400°F.

3 Grind the almonds finely in a blender or food processor. Cream the butter and remaining sugar until light and fluffy. Beat in the egg and 2 tablespoons of the orange syrup. Stir in the almonds and flour.

4 Melt the jam over low heat, then brush over the pastry case. Pour in the almond mixture. Bake on the baking sheet until set, about 20 minutes, then cool. Arrange overlapping orange slices on top. Boil the remaining syrup until thick and brush on top to glaze.

Raspberry Tart

A luscious tart with a custard topped with juicy berries.

Serves 8

4 egg yolks
generous 4 tablespoons
    superfine sugar
3 tablespoons all-purpose
    flour
1¼ cups milk
¼ teaspoon salt
½ teaspoon vanilla
    extract
2⅔ cups fresh raspberries
5 tablespoons redcurrant
    jelly
1 tablespoon orange juice

For the pastry

1⅔ cups all-purpose flour
½ teaspoon baking
    powder
¼ teaspoon salt
1 tablespoon sugar
grated rind of ½ orange
6 tablespoons cold butter,
    cut in pieces
1 egg yolk
3–4 tablespoons
    whipping cream

1 For the pastry, sift the flour, baking powder and salt into a bowl. Stir in the sugar and orange rind. Add the butter and work in until the mixture resembles bread crumbs. Stir in the egg yolk and cream to bind. Form into a ball, wrap and chill.

2 For the filling, beat the egg yolks and sugar until thick and creamy. Gradually stir in the flour. Bring the milk and salt just to a boil, then remove from the heat. Whisk into the egg yolk mixture, return to the pan and continue whisking over moderately high heat until just bubbling. Cook for 3 minutes to thicken. Transfer to a bowl. Stir in the vanilla, then cover with wax paper.

3 Preheat the oven to 400°F. Roll out the pastry and line a 10-inch pie dish. Prick the base, line with wax paper and fill with baking beans. Bake for 15 minutes. Remove the paper and beans, and bake until golden, 6–8 minutes more. Cool.

4 Spread an even layer of the custard filling in the pastry case and arrange the raspberries on top. Melt the jelly and orange juice in a pan and brush on top to glaze.

Lattice Berry Pie

Choose any berries you like for this handsome pie.

Serves 8

about 4 cups berries, such as bilberries, blueberries and black currants	**For the pastry**
	2½ cups all-purpose flour
	¾ teaspoon salt
generous ½ cup superfine sugar	½ cup cold butter, diced
3 tablespoons cornstarch	3 tablespoons cold vegetable fat or shortening, diced
2 tablespoons fresh lemon juice	5–6 tablespoons iced water
2 tablespoons butter, diced	1 egg, beaten with 1 tablespoon water, for glazing

1 For the pastry, sift the flour and salt into a bowl. Add the butter and fat and work in until the mixture resembles coarse bread crumbs. Stir in just enough water to bind. Form into two balls, wrap and chill for 20 minutes. Roll out one ball and use to line a 9-inch pie dish, leaving a ½-inch overhang. Brush the base with egg.

2 Mix all the filling ingredients together, except the butter (reserve a few berries for decoration). Spoon into the pastry case and dot with the butter. Brush egg around the pastry rim.

3 Preheat a baking sheet at 425°F. Roll out the remaining pastry on a baking sheet lined with wax paper. With a serrated pastry wheel, make 24 thin strips. Use the scraps to cut out leaf shapes, and mark veins. Weave the strips in a close lattice and transfer to the pie. Seal the edges and trim. Arrange the leaves around the rim. Brush with egg and bake for 10 minutes.

4 Reduce the heat to 350°F and bake for 40–45 minutes more. Decorate with berries.

Plum Pie

Treat someone special with this lightly spiced plum pie.

Serves 8

2 pounds red or purple plums	**For the pastry**
grated rind of 1 lemon	2½ cups all-purpose flour
1 tablespoon fresh lemon juice	1 teaspoon salt
1–1¼ cups superfine sugar	6 tablespoons cold butter, diced
3 tablespoons quick-cooking tapioca	4 tablespoons cold vegetable fat or shortening, diced
¼ teaspoon salt	¼–½ cup iced water
½ teaspoon ground cinnamon	milk, for glazing
¼ teaspoon grated nutmeg	

1 For the pastry, sift the flour and salt into a bowl. Add the butter and fat and work in until the mixture resembles coarse bread crumbs. Stir in just enough water to bind the pastry. Form into two balls, wrap and chill for 20 minutes.

2 Preheat a baking sheet in the oven at 425°F. Roll out a pastry ball and use to line a 9-inch pie dish.

3 Halve and pit the plums, and chop coarsely. Mix all the filling ingredients together, then transfer to the pastry case.

4 Roll out the remaining pastry, place on a baking sheet lined with wax paper, and stamp out four hearts. Transfer the pastry lid to the pie using the paper.

5 Trim to leave a ¾-inch overhang. Fold this under the pastry base and pinch to seal. Arrange the hearts on top. Brush with milk and bake for 15 minutes. Reduce the heat to 350°F and bake for 30–35 minutes more.

Dorset Apple Cake

Serve this fruity apple cake warm, and spread with butter, if liked.

Makes one 7-inch round cake

2 large cooking apples, peeled, cored and chopped
juice of ½ lemon
2 cups all-purpose flour
1½ teaspoons baking powder
½ cup butter, diced

scant 1 cup light brown sugar
1 egg, beaten
about 2–3 tablespoons milk, to mix
½ teaspoon ground cinnamon

1 Preheat the oven to 350°F. Grease and line a 7-inch round cake pan.

2 Toss the apple with the lemon juice and set aside. Sift the flour and baking powder together, then work in the butter, until the mixture resembles bread crumbs.

3 Stir in ¾ cup of the brown sugar, the apple and the egg, and mix well, adding sufficient milk to make a soft dropping consistency.

4 Transfer the dough to the prepared pan. In a bowl, mix together the remaining sugar and the cinnamon. Sprinkle over the cake mixture, then bake for 45–50 minutes, until golden. Let cool in the pan for 10 minutes, then transfer to a wire rack.

Parkin

The flavor of this cake will improve if it is stored in an air-tight container for several days or a week before serving.

Makes 16–20 squares

1¼ cups milk
5 tablespoons maple syrup
4 tablespoons molasses
½ cup butter or margarine, diced
scant ¼ cup dark brown sugar

4 cups all-purpose flour
½ teaspoon baking soda
1¼ teaspoons ground ginger
4 cups medium oatmeal
1 egg, beaten
confectioner's sugar, for dusting

1 Preheat the oven to 350°F. Grease and line the bottom of an 8-inch square cake pan.

2 Gently heat together the milk, syrup, molasses, butter or margarine and sugar, stirring until smooth. Do not allow the mixture to boil.

3 Stir together the flour, baking soda, ginger and oatmeal. Make a well in the center, pour in the egg, then slowly pour in the warmed mixture, stirring to make a smooth batter.

4 Pour the cake batter into the pan and bake for about 45 minutes, until firm to the touch. Cool slightly in the pan, then cool completely on a wire rack. Cut into squares and dust with confectioner's sugar.

Banana Ginger Parkin

Parkin keeps well and really improves with keeping. Store it in a covered container for up to two months.

Makes 16–20 squares

scant 2 cups all-purpose
  flour
2 teaspoons baking soda
2 teaspoons ground
  ginger
1¼ cups medium oatmeal
4 tablespoons dark
  muscovado sugar
6 tablespoons sunflower
  margarine

3 tablespoons maple
  syrup
1 egg, beaten
3 ripe bananas, mashed
¾ cup confectioner's
  sugar
preserved ginger, to
  decorate (optional)

1 Preheat the oven to 325°F. Grease and line the bottom and sides of a 7 x 11-inch cake pan.

2 Sift together the flour, baking soda and ginger, then stir in the oatmeal. Melt the sugar, margarine and syrup in a saucepan, then stir into the flour mixture. Beat in the egg and mashed bananas.

3 Spoon into the pan and bake for about 1 hour, or until firm to the touch. Allow to cool in the pan, then turn out and cut into squares.

4 Sift the confectioner's sugar into a bowl and stir in just enough water to make a smooth, runny icing. Drizzle the icing over each square and top with a piece of preserved ginger, if you like.

Gooseberry Cake

This cake is delicious served warm with whipped cream.

Makes one 7-inch square cake

½ cup butter
1⅓ cups self-rising flour
1 teaspoon baking
  powder
2 eggs, beaten
generous ½ cup superfine
  sugar
1–2 teaspoons rose water

pinch of freshly grated
  nutmeg
4-ounce bottle
  gooseberries in syrup,
  drained, juice reserved
superfine sugar, to
  decorate
whipped cream, to serve

1 Preheat the oven to 350°F. Grease a 7-inch square cake pan, line the bottom and sides with wax paper and grease the paper. Gently melt the butter, then transfer to a mixing bowl and let cool.

2 Sift together the flour and baking powder and add to the butter. Beat in the eggs, one at a time, the sugar, rose water and grated nutmeg, to make a smooth batter.

3 Mix in 1–2 tablespoons of the reserved gooseberry juice, then pour half of the batter mixture into the prepared pan. Sprinkle the gooseberries over the top and pour over the remaining batter mixture.

4 Bake for about 45 minutes, or until a skewer inserted into the center of the cake comes out clean.

5 Let rest in the pan for 5 minutes, then turn out onto a wire rack, peel off the lining paper and let cool for 5 minutes more. Dredge with sugar and serve immediately with whipped cream, or let the cake cool completely before decorating.

Crunchy-topped Sponge Loaf

This light sponge makes a perfect teatime treat.

Makes one 1-pound loaf

scant 1 cup butter,
    softened
finely grated rind of
    1 lemon
5 tablespoons superfine
    sugar
3 eggs
¾ cup all-purpose flour,
    sifted

1¼ cups self-rising flour,
    sifted

For the topping
3 tablespoons honey
¾ cup mixed candied peel
½ cup slivered almonds

1 Preheat the oven to 350°F. Grease and line a 1-pound loaf pan with wax paper. Grease the paper.

2 Beat together the butter, lemon rind and sugar until light and fluffy. Blend in the eggs, one at a time.

3 Sift together the flours, then stir into the egg mixture. Fill the loaf pan.

4 Bake for 45 minutes, or until a skewer inserted into the center comes out clean. Let stand in the pan for 5 minutes.

5 Turn the loaf out onto a wire rack, peel off the lining paper and let cool.

6 For the topping, melt the honey with the candied peel and almonds. Remove from the heat, stir briefly, then spread over the cake top. Cool before serving.

Irish Whiskey Cake

Other whiskies could be used in this cake.

Makes one 9 x 5-inch cake

1½ cups chopped walnuts
generous ½ cup raisins,
    chopped
scant ½ cup currants
1 cup all-purpose flour
1 teaspoon baking
    powder
¼ teaspoon salt
½ cup butter
scant 1½ cups superfine
    sugar

3 eggs, separated, at
    room temperature
1 teaspoon grated
    nutmeg
½ teaspoon ground
    cinnamon
5 tablespoons Irish
    whiskey
confectioner's sugar, for
    dusting

1 Preheat the oven to 325°F. Line the bottom and grease a 9 x 5-inch loaf pan. Mix the nuts and dried fruit with 2 tablespoons of the flour and set aside. Sift together the remaining flour, baking powder and salt.

2 Cream the butter and sugar until light and fluffy. Beat in the egg yolks.

3 Mix the nutmeg, cinnamon and whiskey. Fold into the butter mixture, alternating with the flour mixture.

4 Beat the egg whites until stiff. Fold into the whiskey mixture until just blended. Fold in the walnut mixture.

5 Fill the loaf pan and bake until a skewer inserted in the center comes out clean, about 1 hour. Cool in the pan. To serve, dust with confectioner's sugar over a template.

Fall Dessert Cake

Greengages, plums or semi-dried prunes are delicious in this recipe.

Serves 6−8

½ cup butter, softened
5 tablespoons superfine
 sugar
3 eggs, beaten
¾ cup ground hazelnuts
1¼ cups shelled pecans,
 chopped
½ cup all-purpose flour
1 teaspoon baking
 powder

½ teaspoon salt
3 cups pitted plums,
 greengages or semi-
 dried prunes
4 tablespoons lime
 marmalade
1 tablespoon lime juice
2 tablespoons blanched
 almonds, chopped, to
 decorate

1 Preheat the oven to 350°F. Grease a 9-inch round, fluted tart pan.

2 Beat the butter and sugar until light and fluffy. Gradually beat in the eggs, alternating with the ground hazelnuts.

3 Stir in the pecans, then sift and fold in the flour, baking powder and salt. Spoon into the tart pan.

4 Bake for 45 minutes, or until a skewer inserted into the center comes out clean.

5 Arrange the fruit on the base. Return to the oven and bake for 10–15 minutes, until the fruit has softened. Transfer to a wire rack to cool, then turn out.

6 Warm the marmalade and lime juice gently. Brush over the fruit, then sprinkle with the almonds. Let set, then chill before serving.

Apple Crumble Cake

In the fall, use windfall apples. Served warm with thick cream or custard, this cake doubles as a dessert.

Serves 8−10
For the topping
⅔ cup self-rising flour
½ teaspoon ground
 cinnamon
3 tablespoons butter
2 tablespoons superfine
 sugar

1 cup self-rising flour,
 sifted
2 cooking apples, peeled,
 cored and sliced
4 tablespoons golden
 raisins

For the base
4 tablespoons butter,
 softened
6 tablespoons superfine
 sugar
1 egg, beaten

To decorate
1 red dessert apple, cored,
 thinly sliced and
 tossed in lemon juice
2 tablespoons superfine
 sugar, sifted
pinch of ground
 cinnamon

1 Preheat the oven 350°F. Grease a deep 7-inch springform pan, line the bottom with wax paper and grease the paper.

2 To make the topping, sift the flour and cinnamon into a mixing bowl. Work the butter into the flour until it resembles bread crumbs, then stir in the sugar. Set aside.

3 To make the base, put the butter, sugar, egg and flour into a bowl and beat for 1–2 minutes until smooth. Spoon into the prepared pan.

4 Mix together the apple slices and golden raisins and spread them evenly over the top. Sprinkle with the topping.

5 Bake in the center of the oven for about 1 hour. Cool in the pan for 10 minutes before turning out onto a wire rack and peeling off the lining paper. Serve warm or cool, decorated with slices of red dessert apple and superfine sugar and cinnamon sprinkled over the top.

Light Fruit Cake

For the best flavor, wrap this cake in foil and store for a week before cutting.

Makes two 9 x 5-inch cakes

1 cup prunes
1⅓ cups dates
1 cup currants
generous 1½ cups golden
   raisins
1 cup dry white wine
1 cup rum
3 cups all-purpose flour
2 teaspoons baking
   powder
1 teaspoon ground
   cinnamon

½ teaspoon grated
   nutmeg
1 cup butter, at room
   temperature
scant 1¼ cups superfine
   sugar
4 eggs, lightly beaten
1 teaspoon vanilla
   extract

1 Pit the prunes and dates and chop finely. Place in a bowl with the currants and golden raisins. Stir in the wine and rum and let stand, covered, for 2 days. Stir occasionally.

2 Preheat the oven to 300°F with a tray of hot water in the bottom. Line two 9 x 5-inch loaf pans with wax paper and grease the paper.

3 Sift together the flour, baking powder, ground cinnamon and grated nutmeg.

4 Cream the butter and sugar together until light and fluffy. Gradually add the eggs and vanilla. Fold in the flour mixture in three batches. Fold in the dried fruit mixture and its liquid.

5 Divide the mixture between the pans and bake until a skewer inserted in the center comes out clean, about 1½ hours. Stand for 20 minutes, then unmold onto a wire rack.

Rich Fruit Cake

Makes one 9 x 3-inch cake

½ cup currants
generous 1 cup raisins
½ cup golden raisins
4 tablespoons candied
   cherries, halved
3 tablespoons sweet
   sherry
¾ cup butter
scant 1 cup dark brown
   sugar
2 eggs, at room
   temperature
1¾ cups all-purpose flour
2 teaspoons baking
   powder

2 teaspoons each ground
   ginger, allspice, and
   cinnamon
1 tablespoon maple syrup
1 tablespoon milk
5 tablespoons cut mixed
   candied peel
1 cup chopped walnuts

For the decoration
½ cup orange marmalade
candied citrus fruit slices
candied cherries

1 A day in advance, mix the dried fruit and cherries in a bowl. Stir in the sherry, cover and soak overnight.

2 Preheat the oven to 300°F. Line and grease the bottom and sides of a 9 x 3-inch springform pan with wax paper. Place a tray of hot water on the bottom of the oven.

3 Cream the butter and sugar. Beat in the eggs, 1 at a time. Sift the flour, baking powder and spices together three times. Fold into the butter mixture in three batches. Fold in the syrup, milk, dried fruit and liquid, candied peel and nuts.

4 Spoon into the pan, spreading out so there is a slight depression in the center. Bake for about 2½–3 hours. Cover with foil when the top is golden to prevent over-browning. Cool in the pan on a rack.

5 Melt the marmalade over low heat, then brush over the top of the cake. Decorate with the candied citrus fruit slices and cherries.

Creole Christmas Cake

Makes one 9-inch cake

3 cups raisins
1 cup currants
¾ cup golden raisins
½ cup non-soak prunes, chopped
1 cup candied orange peel, chopped
1 cup chopped walnuts
4 tablespoons dark brown sugar
1 teaspoon vanilla extract
1 teaspoon ground cinnamon
¼ teaspoon each ground nutmeg and cloves
1 teaspoon salt

4 tablespoons each rum, brandy and whisky

For the second stage
2 cups all-purpose flour
1 teaspoon baking powder
1 cup raw sugar
1 cup butter
4 eggs, beaten

For the topping
¾ cup apricot jam, strained
pecan halves and candied kumquat slices, to decorate

1 Put the first set of ingredients into a pan, mix and heat gently. Simmer over low heat for 15 minutes. Remove from the heat and cool. Transfer to a lidded jar and let stand in the fridge for 7 days, stirring at least once a day.

2 Preheat the oven to 275°F. Line a 9-inch round cake pan with a double thickness of nonstick parchment paper and grease it well. Beat the flour, baking powder, sugar and butter together until smooth, then gradually beat in the eggs until the mixture is well blended and smooth.

3 Fold in the fruit mixture and stir well to mix. Spoon the mixture into the pan, level the surface and bake in the center of the oven for 3 hours. Cover with foil and bake for 1 hour, until the cake feels springy. Cool on a wire rack, then remove from the pan. Wrap in foil. The cake will keep well for 1 year.

4 To decorate , heat the jam with 2 tablespoons water and brush half over the cake. Arrange the nuts and fruit over the cake and brush with the remaining apricot glaze.

Light Jeweled Fruit Cake

If you want to cover this cake with marzipan and icing, omit the almond decoration.

Makes one 8-inch round or 7-inch square cake

½ cup currants
¾ cup golden raisins
1 cup mixed candied cherries, quartered
½ cup mixed candied peel, finely chopped
2 tablespoons rum, brandy or sherry
1 cup butter
generous 1 cup superfine sugar
finely grated rind of 1 orange

grated rind of 1 lemon
4 eggs
½ cup chopped almonds
5 tablespoons ground almonds
2 cups all-purpose flour

To decorate
5 tablespoons whole blanched almonds (optional)
1 tablespoon apricot jam

1 A day in advance, soak the currants, golden raisins, candied cherries and peel in the rum, brandy or sherry, cover and let soak overnight.

2 Grease and line either an 8-inch round cake pan or a 7-inch square cake pan with a double thickness of wax paper. Preheat the oven to 325°F. Beat the butter, sugar and orange and lemon rinds together until light and fluffy. Beat in the eggs, one at a time. Mix in the chopped almonds, ground almonds, soaked fruits (with the liquid) and the flour. Spoon into the cake pan and level the top. Bake for 30 minutes.

3 Arrange the almonds, if using, on top of the cake (do not press them into the cake or they will sink during cooking). Return the cake to the oven and cook for 1½–2 hours, or until the center is firm to the touch.

4 Let the cake cool in the pan for 30 minutes, then turn it out in its paper onto a wire rack. When cold, wrap foil over the paper and store in a cool place. To finish, warm, then strain the jam and use to glaze the cake.

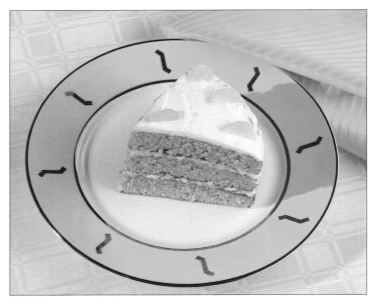

Angel Cake

This heavenly cake tastes simply divine!

Makes one 10-inch cake

generous 1 cup sifted all-
purpose flour
2 tablespoons cornstarch
1½ cups superfine sugar
10–11 egg whites
1¼ teaspoon cream of
tartar

¼ teaspoon salt
1 teaspoon vanilla
extract
¼ teaspoon almond
extract
confectioner's sugar, to
decorate

1 Preheat the oven to 325°F. Sift the flours before measuring, then sift them four times together with ½ cup of the sugar.

2 Beat the egg whites until foamy. Sift over the cream of tartar and salt and continue to beat until the egg whites form soft peaks.

3 Add the remaining sugar in three batches, beating well after each addition. Stir in the vanilla and almond extracts. Fold in the flour mixture in two batches.

4 Transfer to an ungreased 10-inch cake pan and bake until just browned on top, about 1 hour.

5 Turn the pan upside-down onto a wire rack and cool for 1 hour. Then invert onto a serving plate. Lay a star-shaped template on top of the cake, sift over some confectioner's sugar and remove the template.

Spice Cake with Ginger Frosting

A rich three-layer cake with a creamy ginger frosting.

Makes one 8-inch round cake

1¼ cups milk
2 tablespoons maple
syrup
2 teaspoons vanilla
extract
¾ cup chopped walnuts
¾ cup butter, at room
temperature
1½ cups sugar
1 whole egg, plus 3 egg
yolks
2½ cups all-purpose flour
1 tablespoon baking
powder
1 teaspoon grated
nutmeg
1 teaspoon ground
cinnamon

½ teaspoon ground cloves
¼ teaspoon ground
ginger
¼ teaspoon mixed spice
preserved ginger pieces,
to decorate

For the frosting

¾ cup cream cheese
2 tablespoons sweet
butter
1⅓ cups confectioner's
sugar
2 tablespoons finely
chopped preserved
ginger
2 tablespoons syrup from
preserved ginger

1 Preheat the oven to 350°F. Line and grease the bottom and sides of three 8-inch cake pans with wax paper. In a bowl, combine the milk, maple syrup, vanilla and walnuts.

2 Cream the butter and sugar until light and fluffy. Beat in the egg and egg yolks. Add the milk mixture and stir well. Sift together the flour, baking powder and spices three times. Add to the butter mixture in four batches, folding in carefully.

3 Divide the cake mixture between the pans. Bake until the cakes spring back when touched lightly, about 25 minutes. Let stand in the pans for 5 minutes, then cool on a wire rack.

4 For the frosting, combine all the ingredients and beat until smooth. Spread the frosting between the layers and over the top. Decorate with pieces of preserved ginger.

Lemon Coconut Layer Cake

Makes one 8-inch round cake

8 eggs
scant 2 cups superfine
    sugar
1 tablespoon grated
    orange rind
grated rind of 2 lemons
juice of 1 lemon
1¼ cups sweetened,
    shredded coconut
1¼ cups all-purpose
    flour, sifted with
    ¼ teaspoon salt
2 tablespoons cornstarch

1 cup water
6 tablespoons butter

For the frosting
½ cup sweet butter
1 cup confectioner's
    sugar
grated rind of 1 lemon
6–8 tablespoons lemon
    juice
2 cups sweetened
    shredded coconut

1 Preheat the oven to 350°F. Line and grease the bottom and sides of three 8-inch cake pans with wax paper.

2 Place 6 of the eggs in a bowl set over hot water and beat until frothy. Beat in ¾ cup sugar until the mixture doubles in volume. Remove from the heat. Fold in the orange rind, half the lemon rind, 1 tablespoon of the lemon juice and the coconut. Sift over the flour mixture and fold in well.

3 Divide the mixture between the cake pans. Bake until the cakes pull away from the sides of the pans, 25–30 minutes. Let stand in the pans for 5 minutes, then cool on a wire rack.

4 Blend the cornstarch with cold water to dissolve. Whisk in the remaining eggs until blended. In a pan, mix the remaining lemon rind and juice, water, remaining sugar and butter. Bring to a boil. Whisk in the cornstarch, and return to a boil. Whisk until thick. Remove and cover with plastic wrap.

5 Cream the butter and sugar. Stir in the lemon rind and enough lemon juice to obtain a spreadable consistency. Sandwich the cake layers with the lemon custard. Spread the frosting over the top and sides. Cover with the coconut.

Lemon Yogurt Ring

The glaze gives this dessert a refreshing finishing touch.

Serves 12

1 cup butter, at room
    temperature
1½ cups superfine sugar
4 eggs, separated
2 teaspoons grated lemon
    rind
6 tablespoons lemon juice
1 cup plain yogurt
2½ cups all-purpose flour
2 teaspoons baking
    powder

1 teaspoon baking soda
½ teaspoon salt

For the glaze
1 cup confectioner's
    sugar
2 tablespoons lemon juice
3–4 tablespoons plain
    yogurt

1 Preheat the oven to 350°F. Grease a 12½-cup *bundt* or fluted tube pan and dust with flour.

2 Cream the butter and sugar until light and fluffy. Add the egg yolks, one at a time, beating well after each addition. Add the lemon rind, juice and yogurt and stir .

3 Sift together the flour, baking powder and baking soda. In another bowl, beat the egg whites and salt until they hold stiff peaks.

4 Fold the dry ingredients into the butter mixture, then fold in a dollop of egg whites. Fold in the remaining whites.

5 Pour into the pan and bake until a skewer inserted in the center comes out clean, about 50 minutes. Let stand in the pan for 15 minutes, then turn out and cool on a wire rack.

6 For the glaze, sift the confectioner's sugar into a bowl. Stir in the lemon juice and just enough of the plain yogurt to make a smooth glaze.

7 Set the cooled cake on the wire rack over a sheet of wax paper. Pour over the glaze and let set.

Carrot Cake with Geranium Cheese

Makes one 9 x 5-inch cake

1 cup self-rising flour
1 teaspoon baking soda
½ teaspoon ground
   cinnamon
½ teaspoon ground cloves
generous 1 cup brown
   sugar
generous 1½ cups grated
   carrots
1 cup golden raisins
½ cup finely chopped
   preserved ginger
generous 1 cup pecans
⅔ cup sunflower oil
2 eggs, lightly beaten

For the topping

2–3 lemon-scented
   geranium leaves
2 cups confectioner's
   sugar
generous 4 tablespoons
   cream cheese
generous 2 tablespoons
   softened butter
1 teaspoon grated lemon
   rind

1 For the topping, put the geranium leaves, torn into small pieces, in a small bowl and mix with the confectioner's sugar. Let stand in a warm place overnight for the sugar to take up the scent.

2 For the cake, sift the flour, baking soda and spices together. Add the sugar, carrots, golden raisins, ginger and pecans. Stir well, then add the oil and beaten eggs. Mix with an electric mixer for 5 minutes.

3 Preheat the oven to 350°F. Then grease a 9 x 5-inch loaf pan, line the bottom with wax paper, and grease the paper. Pour the mixture into the pan and bake for about 1 hour. Remove the cake from the oven, let stand for a few minutes, and then cool on a wire rack.

4 Meanwhile, make the cream cheese topping. Remove the pieces of geranium leaf from the confectioner's sugar and discard. Place the cream cheese, butter and lemon rind in a bowl. Using an electric mixer, gradually add the confectioner's sugar, beating well until smooth. Spread over the top of the cooled cake.

Carrot and Zucchini Cake

If you can't resist the lure of a slice of iced cake, you'll love this spiced sponge with its delicious creamy topping.

Makes one 7-inch square cake

1 carrot
1 zucchini
3 eggs, separated
¾ cup light brown sugar
2 tablespoons ground
   almonds
finely grated rind of
   1 orange
1¼ cups self-rising whole
   wheat flour
1 teaspoon ground
   cinnamon

1 teaspoon confectioner's
   sugar, for dusting
fondant carrots and
   zucchini, to decorate

For the topping

¾ cup low fat cream
   cheese
1 teaspoon honey

1 Preheat the oven to 350°F. Line a 7-inch square pan with nonstick parchment paper. Coarsely grate the carrot and zucchini.

2 Put the egg yolks, sugar, ground almonds and orange rind into a bowl and whisk until very thick and light. Sift together the flour and cinnamon and fold into the mixture together with the grated vegetables. Add any bran left in the strainer.

3 Whisk the egg whites until stiff and carefully fold them in, a half at a time. Spoon into the pan. Bake in the oven for 1 hour, covering the top with foil after 40 minutes. Let cool in the pan for 5 minutes, then turn out onto a wire rack and remove the lining paper.

4 For the topping, beat together the cheese and honey and spread over the cake. Dust with confectioner's sugar and decorate with fondant carrots and zucchini.

Banana Coconut Cake

Slightly overripe bananas are best for this perfect morning cake.

Makes one 7-inch square cake

½ cup butter, softened
generous ½ cup superfine
  sugar
2 eggs
1 cup self-rising flour
½ cup all-purpose flour
1 teaspoon baking soda
½ cup milk
2 large bananas, peeled
  and mashed

1½ cups dried coconut,
  toasted

For the topping

2 tablespoons butter
2 tablespoons honey
2 cups shredded coconut

1 Preheat the oven to 375°F. Grease a deep 7-inch square cake pan, line with wax paper and grease the paper.

2 Beat the butter and sugar until smooth and creamy. Beat in the eggs, one at a time. Sift together the flours and baking soda, sift half into the butter mixture and stir to mix.

3 Combine the milk and mashed banana and beat half into the egg mixture. Stir in the remaining flour and banana mixtures and toasted coconut. Transfer to the cake pan and smooth the surface.

4 Bake for 1 hour, or until a skewer inserted into the center of the cake comes out clean. Let stand in the pan for about 5 minutes, then turn out onto a wire rack, peel off the paper and cool.

5 For the topping, gently melt the butter and honey. Stir in the shredded coconut and cook, stirring, for 5 minutes or until lightly browned. Remove from the heat and let cool slightly. Spoon the topping over the cake and let cool.

St Clement's Cake

A tangy orange-and-lemon cake makes a spectacular centerpiece when decorated with fruits and flowers.

Makes one 9-inch ring cake

¾ cup butter
⅓ cup light brown sugar
3 eggs, separated
grated rind and juice of
  1 orange and 1 lemon
1¼ cups self-rising flour
6 tablespoons superfine
  sugar
2 tablespoons ground
  almonds

1½ cups heavy cream
1 tablespoon Grand
  Marnier
16 candied orange and
  lemon slices, silver
  dragées, sugared
  almonds and fresh
  flowers, to decorate

1 Preheat the oven to 350°F. Grease and flour a 3¾-cup ring mold.

2 Cream half the butter and all of the brown sugar until pale and light. Beat in the egg yolks, orange rind and juice and fold in ⅔ cup flour.

3 Cream the remaining butter and superfine sugar. Stir in the lemon rind and juice and fold in the remaining flour and ground almonds. Whisk the egg whites until stiff, and fold in.

4 Spoon the two mixtures alternately into the prepared pan. Using a skewer or small spoon, swirl through the mixture to create a marbled effect. Bake for 45–50 minutes until risen, and a skewer inserted in the cake comes out clean. Cool in the pan for 10 minutes then transfer to a wire rack to cool.

5 Whip the cream and Grand Marnier together until lightly thickened. Spread over the cake and swirl a pattern over the icing with a metal spatula. Decorate the ring with the candied fruits, dragées and sugared almonds to resemble a jeweled crown. Arrange a few fresh flowers in the center.

Apple Cake

Makes one ring cake

6–7 apples, peeled, cored
and quartered
generous 2½ cups
superfine sugar
1 tablespoon water
3 cups all-purpose flour
1¾ teaspoon baking soda
1 teaspoon ground
cinnamon
1 teaspoon ground cloves
generous 1 cup raisins
1¼ cups chopped walnuts

1 cup butter or
margarine, at room
temperature
1 teaspoon vanilla
extract

For the icing

1 cup confectioner's
sugar
¼ teaspoon vanilla
extract
2 – 3 tablespoons milk

1 Put the apples, 4 tablespoons of the sugar and the water in a saucepan and bring to a boil. Simmer for 25 minutes, stirring occasionally to break up any lumps. Let cool. Preheat the oven to 325°F. Grease and flour a 7½-cup tube pan.

2 Sift the flour, baking soda and spices into a bowl. Remove 2 tablespoons of the mixture to another bowl and toss with the raisins and 1 cup of the walnuts.

3 Cream the butter or margarine and remaining sugar together until light and fluffy. Fold in the apple mixture gently. Fold the flour mixture into the apple mixture. Stir in the vanilla and the raisin and walnut mixture. Pour into the tube pan. Bake until a skewer inserted in the center comes out clean, about 1½ hours. Cool completely in the pan on a wire rack, then unmold onto the rack.

4 For the icing, put the sugar in a bowl and stir in the vanilla and 1 tablespoon milk. Add more milk until the icing is smooth and has a thick pouring consistency. Transfer the cake to a serving plate and drizzle the icing on top. Sprinkle with the remaining nuts. Allow the icing to set.

Chocolate Amaretto Marquise

This light-as-air marquise is perfect for a special occasion, served with Amaretto cream.

Makes one heart-shape cake

1 tablespoon sunflower
oil
7–8 amaretti cookies,
crushed
2 tablespoons unblanched
almonds, toasted and
finely chopped
1 pound semisweet
chocolate, broken into
pieces
5 tablespoons Amaretto
liqueur

5 tablespoons maple
syrup
2 cups heavy cream
cocoa, to dust

For the Amaretto cream

1½ cups whipping or
heavy cream
2–3 tablespoons
Amaretto liqueur

1 Lightly oil a 9-inch heart-shape or springform cake pan. Line the base with nonstick parchment paper and oil the paper. Mix the crushed amaretti cookies with the chopped almonds. Sprinkle evenly over the bottom of the pan.

2 Place the chocolate, Amaretto liqueur and maple syrup in a saucepan over very low heat. Stir frequently until the chocolate is melted and the mixture is smooth. Let cool for 6–8 minutes, until the mixture just feels warm.

3 Beat the cream until it just begins to hold its shape. Stir a large spoonful into the chocolate mixture, then quickly add the remaining cream and gently fold into the chocolate mixture. Pour into the prepared pan and tap the pan gently on the work surface to release any large air bubbles. Cover the pan with plastic wrap and chill overnight.

4 To unmold, run a thin-bladed sharp knife under hot water and dry carefully. Run the knife around the edge of the pan to loosen, place a serving plate over the pan, then invert to unmold. Carefully peel off the paper then dust with cocoa. Whip the cream and liqueur and serve separately.

Tangy Lemon Cake

The lemon syrup forms a crusty topping when completely cooled. Let stand in the pan until ready to serve.

Makes one 2-pound loaf

¾ cup butter
scant 1 cup superfine
   sugar
3 eggs, beaten
1½ cups self-rising flour
grated rind of 1 orange
grated rind of 1 lemon

For the syrup
generous ½ cup
   superfine sugar
juice of 2 lemons

1 Preheat the oven to 350°F. Grease a 2-pound loaf pan.

2 Beat the butter and sugar together until light and fluffy, then gradually beat in the eggs. Fold in the flour and the orange and lemon rinds.

3 Turn the cake mixture into the cake pan and bake for 1¼–1½ hours, until set in the center, risen and golden. Remove the cake from the oven, but let stand in the pan.

4 To make the syrup, gently heat the sugar in the lemon juice until melted, then boil for 15 seconds. Pour the syrup over the cake in the pan and let cool.

Pineapple and Apricot Cake

This is not a long-keeping cake, but it does freeze, well-wrapped in wax paper and then foil.

Makes one 7-inch square or 8-inch round cake

¾ cup sweet butter
generous ¾ cup superfine
   sugar
3 eggs, beaten
few drops vanilla extract
2 cups all-purpose flour
¼ teaspoon salt
1½ teaspoons baking
   powder
1¾ cups ready-to-eat
   dried apricots,
   chopped

½ cup each chopped
   candied ginger and
   candied pineapple
grated rind and juice of
   ½ orange
grated rind and juice of
   ½ lemon
a little milk

1 Preheat the oven to 350°F. Double line a 7-inch square or an 8-inch round cake pan. Cream the butter and sugar together until light and fluffy.

2 Gradually beat in the eggs with the vanilla extract, beating well after each addition. Sift together the flour, salt and baking powder, add a little with the last of the egg, then fold in the rest.

3 Gently fold in the apricots, ginger and pineapple and the fruit rinds, then add sufficient fruit juice and milk to give a fairly soft dropping consistency.

4 Spoon into the cake pan and smooth the top with a wet spoon. Bake for 20 minutes, then reduce the oven temperature to 325°F and bake for 1½–2 hours more, or until firm to the touch and a skewer comes out of the center clean. Let the cake cool completely in the pan. Wrap in fresh paper before storing in an airtight container.

Sour Cream Crumble Cake

The consistency of this cake, with its two layers of crumble, is sublime.

Makes one 9-inch square cake

½ cup butter, at room
    temperature
scant ¾ cup superfine
    sugar
3 eggs
scant 2 cups all-purpose
    flour
1 teaspoon baking soda
1 teaspoon baking
    powder
1 cup sour cream

For the topping
1 cup dark brown sugar
2 teaspoons ground
    cinnamon
1 cup finely chopped
    walnuts
4 tablespoons cold butter,
    cut into pieces

1 Preheat the oven to 350°F. Line the bottom of a 9-inch square cake pan with wax paper and grease the paper and sides.

2 For the topping, place the brown sugar, cinnamon and walnuts in a bowl. Mix, then add the butter and work in until the mixture resembles bread crumbs.

3 To make the cake, cream the butter until soft. Add the sugar and beat until light and fluffy. Add the eggs, one at a time, beating well after each addition.

4 In another bowl, sift the flour, baking soda and baking powder together three times. Fold the dry ingredients into the butter mixture in three batches, alternating with the sour cream. Fold until blended after each addition.

5 Pour half of the batter into the prepared pan and sprinkle over half of the topping. Pour the remaining batter on top and sprinkle over the remaining topping. Bake until browned, 60–70 minutes. Let stand in the pan for 5 minutes, then turn out and cool on a wire rack.

Plum Crumble Cake

This cake can also be made with the same quantity of apricots or cherries.

Serves 8–10

generous ½ cup butter or
    margarine, at room
    temperature
¾ cup superfine sugar
4 eggs, at room
    temperature
1½ teaspoons vanilla
    extract
1¼ cups all-purpose flour
1 teaspoon baking
    powder
1½ pounds red plums,
    halved and pitted

For the topping
1 cup all-purpose flour
generous ¾ cup light
    brown sugar
1½ teaspoons ground
    cinnamon
6 tablespoons butter, cut
    in pieces

1 Preheat the oven to 350°F. Using wax paper, line a 10 x 2-inch pan and grease the paper. For the topping, combine the flour, brown sugar and cinnamon in a bowl. Add the butter and work in until it resembles coarse bread crumbs.

2 Cream the butter or margarine and sugar until light and fluffy. Beat in the eggs, one at a time. Stir in the vanilla. In three batches, sift, then fold in the flour and baking powder.

3 Pour the mixture into the pan. Arrange the plums on top and sprinkle with the topping.

4 Bake until a skewer inserted in the center comes out clean, about 45 minutes. Cool in the pan.

5 To serve, run a knife around the inside edge and invert onto a plate. Invert again onto a serving plate so the topping is uppermost.

Pineapple Upside-down Cake

For an apricot cake, replace the pineapple slices with 1¾ cups dried ready-to-eat apricots.

Makes one 10-inch round cake

½ cup butter
generous 1 cup dark
   brown sugar
1 pound canned
   pineapple slices,
   drained
4 eggs, separated

grated rind of 1 lemon
pinch of salt
generous ½ cup superfine
   sugar
¾ cup all-purpose flour
1 teaspoon baking
   powder

1 Preheat the oven to 350°F. Melt the butter in a 10-inch ovenproof cast-iron frying pan. Then reserve 1 tablespoon butter. Add the brown sugar to the pan and stir to blend. Place the pineapple on top in one layer. Set aside.

2 Whisk together the egg yolks, reserved butter and lemon rind until well blended. Set aside.

3 Beat the egg whites and salt until stiff. Gradually fold in the superfine sugar, then the egg yolk mixture.

4 Sift the flour and baking powder together. Carefully fold into the egg mixture in three batches.

5 Pour the mixture over the pineapple. Bake until a skewer inserted in the center comes out clean, about 30 minutes.

6 While still hot, invert onto a serving plate. Serve either hot or cold.

Upside-down Pear and Ginger Cake

This light, spicy sponge, topped with glossy baked fruit and ginger, makes an excellent dessert.

Serves 6–8

2-pound can pear halves,
   drained
8 tablespoons finely
   chopped preserved
   ginger
8 tablespoons ginger
   syrup from the jar

1½ cups self-rising flour
½ teaspoon baking
   powder
1 teaspoon ground ginger
1 cup light brown sugar
¾ cup butter, softened
3 eggs, lightly beaten

1 Preheat the oven to 350°F. Line the bottom and grease a deep 8-inch round cake pan.

2 Fill the hollow in each pear with half the chopped preserved ginger. Arrange, flat-sides down, in the bottom of the cake pan, then spoon over half the ginger syrup.

3 Sift together the flour, baking powder and ground ginger. Stir in the sugar and butter, add the eggs and beat until creamy, 1–2 minutes.

4 Spoon the mixture into the cake pan. Bake in the oven for 50 minutes, or until a skewer inserted in the center of the cake comes out clean. Let the cake stand in the pan for 5 minutes. Turn out onto a wire rack, peel off the lining paper and let cool completely.

5 Add the reserved ginger to the pear halves and drizzle over the remaining syrup.

Cranberry and Apple Ring

Tangy cranberries add an unusual flavor to this cake which is best eaten very fresh.

Makes one ring cake

2 cups self-rising flour
1 teaspoon ground
  cinnamon
½ cup light muscovado
  sugar
1 eating apple, cored and
  diced

¾ cup fresh or frozen
  cranberries
4 tablespoons sunflower
  oil
⅔ cup apple juice
cranberry jelly and apple
  slices, to decorate

1 Preheat the oven to 350°F. Lightly grease a 4-cup ring pan with oil.

2 Sift together the flour and ground cinnamon, then stir in the muscovado sugar.

3 Toss together the diced apple and cranberries. Stir into the dry ingredients, then add the oil and apple juice and beat together well.

4 Spoon the mixture into the prepared ring pan and bake for 35–40 minutes, or until the cake is firm to the touch. Turn out and let cool completely on a wire rack.

5 To serve, drizzle warmed cranberry jelly over the cake and decorate with apple slices.

Greek Honey and Lemon Cake

A wonderfully moist and tangy cake, you could ice it once cooked, if you wished.

Makes one 7½-inch square cake

3 tablespoons sunflower
  margarine
4 tablespoons honey
finely grated rind and
  juice of 1 lemon
⅔ cup milk
1¼ cups all-purpose flour

1½ teaspoons baking
  powder
½ teaspoon grated
  nutmeg
¼ cup semolina
2 egg whites
2 teaspoons sesame seeds

1 Preheat the oven to 400°F. Lightly oil and line the bottom of a 7½-inch square deep cake pan.

2 Place the margarine and 3 tablespoons of the honey in a saucepan and heat gently until melted. Reserve 1 tablespoon lemon juice, then stir in the rest with the lemon rind and milk.

3 Sift together the flour, baking powder and nutmeg, then beat in with the semolina. Whisk the egg whites until they form soft peaks, then fold evenly into the mixture.

4 Spoon into the cake pan and sprinkle with sesame seeds. Bake for 25–30 minutes, until golden brown. Mix the reserved honey and lemon juice and drizzle over the cake while warm. Cool in the pan, then cut into fingers to serve.

Pear and Cardamom Spice Cake

Fresh pears and cardamoms – a classic combination – are used together in this moist fruit and nut cake.

Makes one 8-inch round cake

½ cup butter
generous ½ cup superfine sugar
2 eggs, lightly beaten
2 cups all-purpose flour
1 tablespoon baking powder
2 tablespoons milk
crushed seeds from 2 cardamom pods

½ cup walnuts, chopped
1 tablespoon poppy seeds
1¼ pounds dessert pears, peeled, cored and thinly sliced
3 walnut halves, to decorate
honey, to glaze

1 Preheat the oven to 350°F. Grease and line the bottom of an 8-inch round, loose-based cake pan.

2 Cream the butter and sugar until pale and light. Gradually beat in the eggs. Sift over the flour and baking powder and fold in with the milk.

3 Stir in the cardamom seeds, chopped nuts and poppy seeds. Reserve one-third of the pear slices, and chop the rest. Fold into the creamed mixture.

4 Transfer to the cake pan. Smooth the surface, making a small dip in the center. Place the walnut halves in the center of the cake and fan the reserved pear slices around the walnuts, covering the cake mixture. Bake for 1¼–1½ hours, or until a skewer inserted in the center comes out clean.

5 Remove the cake from the oven and brush with the honey. Let stand in the pan for 20 minutes, then transfer to a wire rack to cool before serving.

Spiced Honey Nut Cake

A combination of ground pistachios and bread crumbs replaces flour in this recipe, resulting in a light, moist sponge cake.

Makes one 8-inch square cake

generous ½ cup superfine sugar
4 eggs, separated
grated rind and juice of 1 lemon
generous 1 cup ground pistachios
scant 1 cup dried bread crumbs

For the glaze
1 lemon
6 tablespoons honey
1 cinnamon stick
1 tablespoon brandy

1 Preheat the oven to 350°F. Grease and line the bottom of an 8-inch square cake pan.

2 Beat the sugar, egg yolks, lemon rind and juice together until pale and creamy. Fold in 1 cup of the ground pistachios and the bread crumbs.

3 Whisk the egg whites until stiff and fold into the creamed mixture. Transfer to the cake pan and bake for 15 minutes, until risen and springy to the touch. Cool in the pan for 10 minutes, then transfer to a wire rack.

4 For the syrup, peel the lemon and cut the rind into very thin strips. Squeeze the juice into a small pan and add the honey and cinnamon stick. Bring to a boil, add the shredded rind, and simmer fast for 1 minute. Cool slightly and stir in the brandy.

5 Place the cake on a serving plate, prick all over with a skewer, and pour over the cooled syrup, lemon shreds and cinnamon stick. Sprinkle over the reserved pistachios.

Clare's American Carrot Cake

Makes one 8-inch round cake

1 cup corn oil
1¼ cups granulated
   sugar
3 eggs
1½ cups all-purpose flour
1½ teaspoons baking
   powder
1½ teaspoons baking soda
¼ teaspoon salt
1½ teaspoons ground
   cinnamon
good pinch of grated
   nutmeg
¼ teaspoon ground
   ginger
1 cup chopped walnuts

generous 1½ cups finely
   grated carrots
1 teaspoon vanilla
   extract
2 tablespoons sour cream
8 tiny marzipan carrots,
   to decorate

For the frosting

1 cup full fat cream
   cheese
2 tablespoons butter,
   softened
2 cups confectioner's
   sugar, sifted

1 Preheat the oven to 350°F. Grease and line the bottom of two 8-inch loose-based round cake pans.

2 Put the corn oil and sugar into a bowl and beat well. Add the eggs, one at a time, and beat thoroughly. Sift the flour, baking powder, baking soda, salt, cinnamon, nutmeg and ginger into the bowl and beat well. Fold in the chopped walnuts and grated carrots and stir in the vanilla extract and sour cream.

3 Divide the mixture between the cake pans and bake in the center of the oven for about 65 minutes, or until a skewer inserted into the center of the cakes comes out clean. Let cool in the pans on a wire rack before turning out.

4 Beat all the frosting ingredients together until smooth. Sandwich the cakes together with a little frosting. Spread the remaining frosting over the top and sides of the cake. Just before serving, decorate with the marzipan carrots.

Passion Cake

This cake is associated with Passion Sunday. The carrot and banana give it a rich, moist texture.

Makes one 8-inch round cake

1¾ cups self-rising flour
2 teaspoons baking
   powder
1 teaspoon cinnamon
½ teaspoon freshly grated
   nutmeg
10 tablespoons butter,
   softened, or sunflower
   margarine
¾ cup brown sugar
grated rind of 1 lemon
2 eggs, beaten
2 carrots, coarsely grated
1 ripe banana, mashed
¾ cup raisins

½ cup chopped walnuts
   or pecans
2 tablespoons milk
6–8 walnuts, halved, to
   decorate
coffee crystal sugar, to
   decorate

For the frosting

scant 1 cup cream cheese,
   softened
scant ⅓ cup
   confectioner's sugar
juice of 1 lemon
grated rind of 1 orange

1 Preheat the oven to 350°F. Line and grease the bottom and sides of a deep 8-inch round cake pan. Sift the flour, baking powder and spices into a bowl. In another bowl, cream the butter or margarine and sugar with the lemon rind until it is light and fluffy, then beat in the eggs. Fold in the flour mixture, then the carrots, banana, raisins, chopped nuts and milk.

2 Spoon the mixture into the cake pan, level the top and bake for about 1 hour, until risen and the top is springy to touch. Turn the pan upside-down and let the cake cool in the pan for 30 minutes. Then turn out onto a wire rack. When cold, split the cake in half.

3 Cream the cheese with the confectioner's sugar, lemon juice and orange rind, then sandwich the two halves of the cake together with half of the frosting. Spread the rest of the frosting on top and decorate with walnut halves and sugar.

Caribbean Fruit and Rum Cake

Definitely a festive treat, this spicy cake contains both rum and sherry.

Makes one 10-inch round cake

2 cups currants	1¼ cups sherry, plus
2¾ cups raisins	more if needed
1 cup prunes, pitted	4 cups self-rising flour
¾ cup mixed candied peel	2 cups butter, softened
2⅔ cups dark brown	10 eggs, beaten
sugar	1 teaspoon vanilla
1 teaspoon mixed spice	extract
6 tablespoons rum, plus	
more if needed	

1 Finely chop the dried fruits and peel in a food processor or blender. Combine them in a bowl with generous ½ cup of the sugar, the mixed spice, rum and sherry. Cover and let stand for 2 weeks. Stir daily and add more alcohol if you wish.

2 Preheat the oven to 325°F. Grease and then line a 10-inch round cake pan with a double layer of wax paper.

3 Sift the flour, and set aside. Cream together the butter and remaining sugar and beat in the eggs until the mixture is smooth and creamy.

4 Add the fruit mixture, then gradually stir in the flour and vanilla extract. Mix well, adding more sherry if the mixture is too stiff; it should just fall off the back of the spoon.

5 Spoon the mixture into the prepared pan, cover loosely with foil and bake for about 2½ hours, until the cake is firm and springy. Let cool in the pan overnight.

Thai Rice Cake

A celebration gâteau made from fragrant Thai rice covered with a tangy cream icing and topped with fresh fruits.

Makes one 10-inch round cake

1¼ cups Thai fragrant	**For the topping**
rice	1¼ cups heavy cream
4½ cups milk	scant 1 cup quark
½ cup superfine sugar	1 teaspoon vanilla
6 cardamom pods,	extract
crushed open	grated rind of 1 lemon
2 bay leaves	scant ¼ cup superfine
1¼ cups whipping cream	sugar
6 eggs, separated	soft berry fruits and
	sliced star or kiwi
	fruit, to decorate

1 Grease and line a deep 10-inch round cake pan. Boil the rice in unsalted water for 3 minutes, then drain.

2 Return the rice to the pan with the milk, sugar, cardamom pods and bay leaves. Bring to a boil, then simmer for 20 minutes, stirring occasionally.

3 Let cool, then remove the bay leaves and any cardamom husks. Turn into a bowl. Beat in the cream and then the egg yolks. Preheat the oven to 350°F.

4 Whisk the egg whites until they form soft peaks and fold into the rice mixture. Spoon into the cake pan and bake for 45–50 minutes, until risen and golden brown. The center should be slightly wobbly – it will firm up as it cools.

5 Chill overnight in the pan. Turn out onto a large serving plate. Whip the cream until stiff, then mix in the quark, vanilla extract, lemon rind and sugar. Cover the top and sides of the cake with the cream, swirling it attractively. Decorate with soft berry fruits and sliced star or kiwi fruit.

Luxurious Chocolate Cake

This delicious chocolate cake contains no flour and has a light mousse-like texture.

Makes one 8-inch round cake

¾ cup butter, softened
⅔ cup superfine sugar
9 x 1-ounce squares
semisweet chocolate,
melted

2 cups ground almonds
4 eggs, separated
4 x 1-ounce squares
white chocolate,
melted, to decorate

1 Preheat the oven to 350°F. Grease and line the bottom of an 8-inch springform cake pan. Beat 8 tablespoons butter and all the sugar until light and fluffy. Add two-thirds of the semisweet chocolate, almonds and egg yolks and beat well.

2 Whisk the egg whites in another clean, dry bowl until stiff. Fold them into the chocolate mixture, then transfer to the pan and smooth the surface. Bake for 50–55 minutes or until a skewer inserted into the center comes out clean. Cool in the pan for 5 minutes, then remove from the pan and transfer to a wire rack. Remove the lining paper and cool completely.

3 Place the remaining butter and melted chocolate in a saucepan. Heat very gently, stirring constantly, until melted. Place a large sheet of wax paper under the wire rack to catch any drips. Pour the chocolate topping over the cake, allowing it to coat the top and sides. Let set for at least 1 hour.

4 To decorate, fill a paper icing bag with the melted white chocolate and snip the end. Drizzle the white chocolate around the edges. Use any remaining chocolate to make leaves. Let set, then place on top of the cake.

One-stage Chocolate Sponge

For family teas, quick-and-easy favorites like this chocolate cake are invaluable.

Makes one 7-inch round cake

¾ cup soft margarine, at
room temperature
½ cup superfine sugar
4 tablespoons maple
syrup
1½ cups self-rising flour,
sifted
3 tablespoons cocoa,
sifted

½ teaspoon salt
3 eggs, beaten
a little milk, as required
⅔ cup whipping cream
1–2 tablespoons fine
shred marmalade
confectioner's sugar, for
dusting

1 Preheat the oven to 350°F. Lightly grease or line two 7-inch sandwich cake pans. Place the margarine, sugar, syrup, flour, cocoa, salt and eggs in a large bowl, and cream together until well blended. If the mixture seems a little thick, stir in 1–2 tablespoons milk to get a soft dropping consistency.

2 Spoon the mixture into the prepared pans and bake for about 30 minutes, changing shelves if necessary after 15 minutes, until the tops are just firm and the cakes are springy to the touch.

3 Let the cakes cool for 5 minutes, then remove from the pans and let cool completely on a wire rack.

4 Whip the cream and fold in the marmalade, then use to sandwich the two cakes together. Sprinkle the top with sifted confectioner's sugar.

One-stage Victoria Sandwich

This versatile sponge recipe can be used for all sorts of cakes.

Makes one 7-inch round cake

1½ cups self-rising flour	**To finish**
pinch of salt	4–6 tablespoons
¾ cup butter, softened	raspberry jam
scant 1 cup superfine	superfine sugar or
sugar	confectioner's sugar
3 eggs	

1 Preheat the oven to 350°F. Grease two 7-inch sandwich cake pans, line the bottoms with wax paper and grease.

2 Whisk all the cake ingredients together until smooth and creamy. Divide the mixture between the cake pans and smooth the surfaces.

3 Bake for 25–30 minutes, or until a skewer inserted into the center of the cakes comes out clean. Turn out onto a wire rack, peel off the paper and let cool.

4 Place one of the cakes on a serving plate and spread with the raspberry jam. Place the other cake on top.

5 Cut out paper star shapes, place on the cake and dredge with sugar. Remove the paper to reveal the pattern.

Mocha Victoria Sponge

A light coffee- and cocoa-flavored sponge with a rich buttercream topping.

Makes one 7-inch round cake

¾ cup butter	**For the buttercream**
generous ¾ cup superfine	generous ½ cup butter
sugar	1 tablespoon coffee
3 eggs	extract or 2 teaspoons
1½ cups self-rising flour,	instant coffee powder
sifted	dissolved in
1 tablespoon strong black	1–2 tablespoons warm
coffee	milk
1 tablespoon cocoa mixed	2½ cups confectioner's
with 1–2 tablespoons	sugar
boiling water	

1 Preheat the oven to 350°F. Grease and line the bottoms of two 7-inch round sandwich cake pans. For the sponge, cream the butter and sugar until light and fluffy. Add the eggs, one at a time, beating well after each addition. Fold in the flour.

2 Divide the mixture into two bowls. Fold the coffee into one and the cocoa mixture into the other.

3 Place alternate spoonfuls of each mixture side by side in the cake pans. Bake for 25–30 minutes. Turn out onto a wire rack to cool.

4 For the buttercream, beat the butter until soft. Gradually beat in the remaining ingredients until smooth.

5 Sandwich the cakes, base-sides together, with a third of the buttercream. Cover the top and side with the rest.

Lemon and Apricot Cake

This cake is soaked in a tangy lemon syrup after baking to keep it really moist.

Makes one 9 x 5-inch loaf

¾ cup butter, softened
1½ cups self-rising flour
½ teaspoon baking powder
¾ cup superfine sugar
3 eggs, lightly beaten
finely grated rind of 1 lemon
1½ cups ready-to-eat dried apricots, finely chopped
¾ cup ground almonds

6 tablespoons pistachios, chopped
½ cup slivered almonds
2 tablespoons whole pistachios

For the syrup
3 tablespoons superfine sugar
freshly squeezed juice of 1 lemon

1 Preheat the oven to 350°F. Grease and line a 9 x 5-inch loaf pan with wax paper and grease the paper.

2 Place the butter in a mixing bowl. Sift over the flour and baking powder, then add the sugar, eggs and lemon rind. Beat for 1–2 minutes until smooth and glossy, then stir in the apricots, ground almonds and chopped pistachios.

3 Spoon the mixture into the loaf pan and smooth the surface. Sprinkle with the slivered almonds and the whole pistachios. Bake for 1¼ hours, or until a skewer inserted into the center of the cake comes out clean. Check the cake after 45 minutes and cover with a piece of foil when the top is nicely browned. Let the cake cool in the pan.

4 For the lemon syrup, gently dissolve the sugar in the lemon juice. Spoon the syrup over the cake. When the cake is completely cooled, turn it carefully out of the pan and peel off the lining paper.

Cherry Batter Cake

This colorful tray bake looks pretty cut into neat squares or fingers.

Makes one 13 x 9-inch cake

2 cups self-rising flour
1 teaspoon baking powder
6 tablespoons butter, softened
scant 1 cup light brown sugar
1 egg, lightly beaten
⅔ cup milk
confectioner's sugar, for dusting

whipped cream, to serve (optional)

For the topping
1½-pound bottle black cherries or black currants, drained
1 cup light brown sugar
½ cup self-rising flour
¼ cup butter, melted

1 Preheat the oven to 375°F. Grease and line a 13 x 9-inch jelly roll pan with wax paper and grease the paper.

2 To make the base, sift the flour and baking powder into a mixing bowl. Add the butter, sugar, egg and milk. Beat until the mixture becomes smooth, then turn into the prepared pan and smooth the surface.

3 Sprinkle the drained fruit evenly over the batter mixture.

4 Mix together the remaining topping ingredients and spoon evenly over the fruit. Bake for 40 minutes, or until golden brown and the center is firm to the touch.

5 Let cool, then dust with confectioner's sugar. Serve with whipped cream, if wished.

Fruit Salad Cake

You can use any combination of dried fruits in this rich, dark fruit cake.

Makes one 18cm/7in round cake

175g/6oz/1 cup roughly chopped mixed dried fruit, such as apples, apricots, prunes and peaches
250ml/8fl oz/1 cup hot tea
225g/8oz/2 cups wholemeal self-raising flour

5ml/1 tsp grated nutmeg
50g/2oz/⅓ cup dark muscovado sugar
45ml/3 tbsp sunflower oil
45ml/3 tbsp skimmed milk
demerara sugar, for sprinkling

1 Soak the dried fruits in the tea for several hours or overnight. Drain and reserve the liquid.

2 Preheat the oven to 180°C/350°F/Gas 4. Grease an 18cm/7in round cake tin and line the base with non-stick baking paper.

3 Sift the flour into a bowl with the nutmeg. Stir in the muscovado sugar, fruit and tea. Add the oil and milk, and mix well.

4 Spoon the mixture into the cake tin and sprinkle with demerara sugar. Bake for 50–55 minutes or until firm. Turn out on to a wire rack to cool.

Fairy Cakes with Blueberries

This luxurious treatment of fairy cakes means they will be as popular with adults as with children.

Makes 8–10

115g/4oz/½ cup soft margarine
115g/4oz/½ cup caster sugar
5ml/1 tsp grated lemon rind
pinch of salt
2 eggs, beaten

115g/4oz/1 cup self-raising flour, sifted
120ml/4fl oz/½ cup whipping cream
75–115g/3–4oz/¾– 1 cup blueberries
icing sugar, for dusting

1 Preheat the oven to 190°C/375°F/Gas 5. Cream the margarine, sugar, lemon rind and salt in a large bowl until pale and fluffy.

2 Gradually beat in the eggs, then fold in the flour until well mixed. Spoon the mixture into eight to ten paper cases on baking sheets and bake for 15–20 minutes, until just golden.

3 Leave the cakes to cool, then scoop out a circle of sponge from the top of each using the point of a small sharp knife, and set them aside.

4 Whip the cream and place a spoonful in each cake, plus a couple of blueberries. Replace the lids at an angle and sift over some icing sugar.

Jewel Cake

This pretty cake is excellent served as an afternoon treat.

Makes one 9 x 5-inch cake

½ cup mixed candied
    cherries, halved,
    washed and dried
4 tablespoons preserved
    ginger in syrup,
    chopped, washed and
    dried
5 tablespoons chopped
    mixed candied peel
1 cup self-rising flour
¼ cup all-purpose flour
3 tablespoons cornstarch
¾ cup butter
scant 1 cup superfine
    sugar

3 eggs
grated rind of 1 orange

To decorate
1½ cups confectioner's
    sugar, sifted
2–3 tablespoons freshly
    squeezed orange juice
¼ cup mixed candied
    cherries, chopped
2½ tablespoons mixed
    candied peel, chopped

1 Preheat the oven to 350°F. Grease and line a 9 x 5-inch loaf pan and grease the paper.

2 Place the cherries, ginger and candied peel in a plastic bag with 4 tablespoons of the self-rising flour and shake to coat evenly. Sift together the remaining flours and cornstarch.

3 Beat together the butter and sugar until light and fluffy. Beat in the eggs, one at a time. Fold in the sifted flours with the orange rind, then stir in the dried fruit.

4 Transfer the mixture to the prepared cake pan and bake for 1¼ hours, or until a skewer inserted into the center comes out clean. Let stand in the pan for 5 minutes, then cool on a wire rack.

5 For the decoration, mix the sugar with the orange juice until smooth. Drizzle the icing over the cake. Mix together the chopped cherries and peel, then use to decorate the cake. Let the icing set before serving.

Iced Paradise Cake

Makes one 9 x 5-inch cake

3 eggs
scant ½ cup superfine
    sugar
9 tablespoons all-purpose
    flour
1 tablespoon cornstarch
6 tablespoons dark rum
1½ cups semisweet
    chocolate chips
2 tablespoons maple
    syrup

2 tablespoons water
1¾ cups heavy cream
scant 1 cup dried
    coconut, toasted
2 tablespoons sweet
    butter
2 tablespoons light cream
5 tablespoons white
    chocolate chips, melted
coconut curls, to decorate
cocoa, for dusting

1 Preheat the oven to 400°F. Grease and flour two baking sheets. Line a 9 x 5-inch pan with plastic wrap.

2 Whisk the eggs and sugar in a heat proof bowl until blended. Place over a pan of simmering water and whisk until pale and thick. Whisk off the heat until cool. Sift over the flour and cornstarch and fold in. Pipe 30 x 3-inch sponge fingers onto the baking sheets. Bake for 8–10 minutes. Cool slightly on the sheets, then on a wire rack.

3 Line the bottom and sides of the loaf pan with sponge fingers. Brush with rum. Melt ½ cup chocolate chips, the syrup, water and 2 tablespoons rum in a bowl over simmering water.

4 Whip the heavy cream until it holds its shape, stir in the chocolate mixture and toasted coconut. Pour into the pan and top with the remaining sponge fingers. Brush over the remaining rum. Cover with plastic wrap and freeze until firm.

5 Melt the remaining chocolate, butter and cream as before, then cool slightly. Turn the cake out onto a wire rack. Pour over the icing to coat. Chill.

6 Drizzle the white chocolate in zigzags over the cake. Chill. Sprinkle with coconut curls and dust with cocoa.

Pound Cake with Red Fruit

This orange-scented cake is good for a snack, or served as a dessert with a fruit coulis.

Makes one 8 x 4-inch cake

*about 4 cups fresh
raspberries,
strawberries or pitted
cherries, or a
combination of any of
these*
*¾ cup superfine sugar,
plus 1–2 tablespoons,
plus extra for
sprinkling*

*1 tablespoon lemon juice
1½ cups all-purpose flour
2 teaspoons baking
powder
pinch of salt
¾ cup sweet butter,
softened
3 eggs
grated rind of 1 orange
1 tablespoon orange juice*

1 Reserve a few whole fruits for decorating. In a blender or food processor, process the fruit until smooth. Add 1–2 tablespoons sugar and the lemon juice, and process again. Strain the sauce and chill.

2 Grease the bottom and sides of an 8 x 4-inch loaf pan and line the bottom with nonstick parchment paper. Grease the paper. Sprinkle with sugar and turn out any excess. Preheat the oven to 350°F.

3 Sift together the flour, baking powder and salt. Beat the butter until creamy. Add the sugar and beat until light and fluffy. Add the eggs, one at a time, beating well after each addition. Beat in the orange rind and juice. Gently fold the flour mixture into the butter mixture in three batches, then spoon the mixture into the loaf pan and tap gently to release any air bubbles.

4 Bake for 35–40 minutes, until the top is golden and springy to the touch. Let the cake stand in its pan on a wire rack for 10 minutes, then remove the cake from the pan and cool for 30 minutes. Remove the paper and serve slices of cake with the fruit sauce, decorated with the reserved fruit.

Madeleine Cakes

These little tea cakes, baked in a special pan with shell-shape cups, are best eaten on the day they are made.

Makes 12

*generous 1¼ cups all-
purpose flour
1 teaspoon baking
powder
2 eggs
½ cup confectioner's
sugar, plus extra for
dusting*

*grated rind of 1 lemon or
orange
1 tablespoon lemon or
orange juice
6 tablespoons sweet
butter, melted and
slightly cooled*

1 Preheat the oven to 375°F. Grease a 12-cup madeleine cake pan. Sift together the flour and the baking powder.

2 Beat the eggs and confectioner's sugar until the mixture is thick and creamy and leaves ribbon trails. Gently fold in the lemon or orange rind and juice.

3 Beginning with the flour mixture, alternately fold in the flour and melted butter in four batches. Let stand for 10 minutes, then spoon into the pan. Tap gently to release any air bubbles.

4 Bake for 12–15 minutes, rotating the pan halfway through cooking, until a skewer inserted in the center comes out clean. Turn out onto a wire rack to cool completely and dust with confectioner's sugar before serving.

Chocolate-orange Battenburg Cake

A tasty variation on the traditional pink-and-white Battenburg cake.

Makes one 7-inch long rectangular cake

½ cup soft margarine
½ cup superfine sugar
2 eggs, beaten
few drops vanilla extract
1 tablespoon ground almonds
1 cup self-rising flour, sifted
grated rind and juice of ½ orange

2 tablespoons cocoa, sifted
2–3 tablespoons milk
1 jar chocolate and nut spread
8 ounces white almond paste

1 Preheat the oven to 350°F. Grease and line a 7-inch square cake pan. Put a double piece of foil across the middle of the pan, to divide it into two equal oblongs.

2 Cream the margarine and sugar. Beat in the eggs, vanilla and almonds. Divide the mixture into two halves. Fold half of the flour into one half, with the orange rind and enough juice to give a soft dropping consistency. Fold the rest of the flour and the cocoa into the other half, with enough milk to give a soft dropping consistency. Fill the pan with the two mixes and level the top.

3 Bake for 15 minutes, reduce the heat to 325°F and cook for 20–30 minutes more, until the top is just firm. Let cool in the pan for a few minutes. Turn out onto a board, cut each cake into two strips and trim evenly. Let cool.

4 Using the spread, sandwich the cakes together, Battenburg-style. Roll out the almond paste on a board lightly dusted with cornstarch to a rectangle 7-inch wide and long enough to wrap around the cake. Wrap the paste around the cake, putting the joint underneath. Press to seal.

Best-ever Chocolate Sandwich

A three-layered cake that would be ideal for a birthday party or a special tea.

Makes one 8-inch round cake

1 cup all-purpose flour
½ cup cocoa
1 teaspoon baking powder
pinch of salt
6 eggs
generous 1 cup superfine sugar
2 teaspoons vanilla extract

½ cup sweet butter, melted
8 ounces semisweet chocolate, chopped
6 tablespoons sweet butter
3 eggs, separated
1 cup whipping cream
3 tablespoons superfine sugar

1 Preheat the oven to 350°F. Line three 8-inch round pans with wax paper, grease the paper and dust with flour. Sift the flour, cocoa, baking powder and salt together three times.

2 Place the eggs and sugar in a heat proof bowl set over a pan of simmering water. Beat until doubled in volume, about 10 minutes. Add the vanilla. Fold in the flour mixture in three batches, then the butter.

3 Put the mixture in the pans. Bake until the cakes pull away from the pan sides, about 25 minutes. Transfer to a wire rack.

4 For the icing, melt the chocolate in the top of a double boiler. Remove from the heat and stir in the butter and egg yolks. Return to the heat and stir until thick.

5 Whip the cream until firm. In another bowl, beat the egg whites until stiff. Add the sugar and beat until glossy. Fold the cream, then the egg whites, into the chocolate mixture. Chill for about 20 minutes, then sandwich together and cover the cake with icing.

Chocolate Layer Cake

Makes one 9-inch cake

8-ounce can cooked whole
  beetroot, drained and
  juice reserved
½ cup sweet butter,
  softened
2½ cups light brown
  sugar
3 eggs
1 tablespoon vanilla
  extract
3 ounces bittersweet
  chocolate, melted
2 cups all-purpose flour

2 teaspoons baking
  powder
½ teaspoon salt
½ cup buttermilk
chocolate curls, to
  decorate (optional)

For the frosting
2 cups heavy cream
1 pound 2 ounces
  semisweet chocolate,
  chopped
1 tablespoon vanilla
  extract

1 Preheat the oven to 350°F. Grease two 9-inch cake pans and dust with cocoa. Grate the beetroot and add it to its juice. Beat the butter, brown sugar, eggs and vanilla until pale and fluffy. Beat in the chocolate.

2 Sift together the flour, baking powder and salt. With the mixer on low speed and beginning and ending with flour mixture, alternately beat in flour and buttermilk. Add the beetroot and juice and beat for 1 minute. Fill the pans and bake for 30–35 minutes, until a skewer inserted in the center comes out clean. Cool for 10 minutes, then unmold and cool.

3 To make the frosting, heat the cream until it just begins to boil, stirring occasionally to prevent scorching. Remove from the heat and stir in the chocolate, until melted and smooth. Stir in the vanilla. Strain into a bowl and chill, stirring every 10 minutes, for 1 hour.

4 Sandwich and cover the cake with frosting, and top with chocolate curls, if using. Let set for 20–30 minutes, then chill before serving.

Marbled Chocolate-peanut Cake

Serves 12–14

4 ounces bittersweet
  chocolate, chopped
1 cup sweet butter,
  softened
1 cup peanut butter
1 cup sugar
1 cup light brown sugar
5 eggs
2 cups all-purpose flour
2 teaspoons baking
  powder
½ teaspoon salt
½ cup milk
5 tablespoons chocolate
  chips

**For the chocolate-
peanut butter glaze**
2 tablespoons butter,
  diced
2 tablespoons smooth
  peanut butter
3 tablespoons maple
  syrup
1 teaspoon vanilla
  extract
6 ounces semisweet
  chocolate, broken into
  pieces

1 Preheat the oven to 350°F. Grease and flour a 12-cup tube pan or ring mold. In the top of a double boiler, melt the bittersweet chocolate.

2 Beat the butter, peanut butter and sugars until light and creamy. Add the eggs, one at a time, beating well after each addition. Sift together the flour, baking powder and salt. Add to the butter mixture alternately with the milk.

3 Pour half the batter into another bowl. Stir the melted chocolate into one half and stir the chocolate chips into the other half. Drop alternate large spoonfuls of the two batters into the pan or mold. Using a knife, pull through the batters to create a swirled marbled effect; do not let the knife touch the side or bottom of the pan. Bake for 50–60 minutes, until the top springs back when touched. Cool in the pan on a wire rack for 10 minutes. Then unmold onto the wire rack.

4 Combine the glaze ingredients and 1 tablespoon water in a small saucepan. Melt over low heat, stirring. Cool slightly, then drizzle over the cake, allowing it to run down the side.

Chocolate Fairy Cakes

Makes 24

4 ounces good-quality
    semisweet chocolate,
    cut into small pieces
1 tablespoon water
2½ cups all-purpose flour
1 teaspoon baking
    powder
½ teaspoon baking soda
pinch of salt
scant 1½ cups superfine
    sugar

¾ cup butter or
    margarine, at room
    temperature
⅔ cup milk
1 teaspoon vanilla
    extract
3 eggs
1 recipe quantity
    buttercream, flavored
    to taste

1 Preheat the oven to 350°F. Grease and flour 24 deep muffin pans, about 2¾-inch in diameter, or use paper muffin cases in the pans.

2 Put the chocolate and water in a bowl set over a pan of almost simmering water. Heat until melted and smooth, stirring. Remove from the heat and let cool.

3 Sift the flour, baking powder, baking soda, salt and sugar into a large bowl. Add the chocolate mixture, butter or margarine, milk and vanilla extract.

4 With an electric mixer on medium-low speed, beat until smoothly blended. Increase the speed to high and beat for 2 minutes. Add the eggs and beat for 2 minutes more.

5 Divide the mixture evenly among the prepared muffin pans and bake for 20–25 minutes, or until a skewer inserted into the center of a cake comes out clean. Cool in the pans for 10 minutes, then turn out to cool completely on a wire rack.

6 Ice the top of each cake with buttercream, swirling it into a peak in the center.

Chocolate Mint-filled Cupcakes

For extra mint flavor, chop eight thin mint cream-filled after-dinner mints and fold into the cake batter.

Makes 12

2 cups all-purpose flour
1 teaspoon baking soda
pinch of salt
½ cup cocoa
10 tablespoons sweet
    butter, softened
1½ cups superfine sugar
3 eggs
1 teaspoon peppermint
    extract
1 cup milk

For the filling
1¼ cups heavy or
    whipping cream
1 teaspoon peppermint
    extract

For the glaze
6 ounces semisweet
    chocolate
½ cup sweet butter
1 teaspoon peppermint
    extract

1 Preheat the oven to 350°F. Line a 12-cup muffin tray with paper cases. Sift together the flour, baking soda, salt and cocoa. In another bowl, beat the butter and sugar until light and creamy. Add the eggs, one at a time, beating well after each addition; beat in the peppermint. On low speed, beat in the flour mixture alternately with the milk, until just blended. Spoon into the paper cases.

2 Bake for 12–15 minutes, until a skewer inserted in the center of a cake comes out clean. Transfer to a wire rack to cool. When cool, remove the paper cases.

3 For the filling, whip the cream and peppermint until stiff. Spoon into an icing bag fitted with a small plain nozzle. Pipe about 1 tablespoon into each cake through the bottom.

4 For the glaze, melt the chocolate and butter, stirring until smooth. Remove from the heat and stir in the peppermint extract. Cool, then spread on top of each cake.

Rich Chocolate Nut Cake

Use walnuts or pecans for the cake sides, if you prefer.

Makes one 9-inch round cake

1 cup butter	**For the glaze**
8 ounces semisweet	4 tablespoons butter
chocolate	5 ounces bittersweet
1 cup cocoa	chocolate
1¼ cups superfine sugar	2 tablespoons milk
6 eggs	1 teaspoon vanilla
5 tablespoons brandy	extract
2 cups finely chopped	
hazelnuts	

1 Preheat the oven to 350°F. Line a 9 x 2-inch round pan with wax paper and grease the paper. Melt the butter and chocolate in the top of a double boiler. Let cool.

2 Sift the cocoa into a bowl. Add the sugar and eggs and stir until just combined. Pour in the chocolate mixture and brandy. Fold in three-quarters of the nuts, then pour the mixture into the cake pan.

3 Set the pan in a roasting pan and pour 1 inch hot water into the outer pan. Bake until the cake is firm to the touch, about 45 minutes. Let stand for 15 minutes, then unmold onto a wire rack. When cool, wrap in wax paper and chill for at least 6 hours.

4 For the glaze, melt the butter and chocolate with the milk and vanilla in the top of a double boiler.

5 Place the cake on a wire rack over a plate. Drizzle the glaze over, letting it drip down the sides. Cover the cake sides with the remaining nuts. Transfer to a serving plate when set.

Multi-layer Chocolate Cake

For a change, sandwich the cake layers with softened vanilla ice cream. Freeze before serving.

Makes one 8-inch round cake

4 ounces semisweet	1 cup chopped walnuts
chocolate	
¾ cup butter	**For the filling and**
2¼ cups superfine sugar	**topping**
3 eggs	1½ cups whipping cream
1 teaspoon vanilla	8 ounces semisweet
extract	chocolate
1½ cups all-purpose flour	1 tablespoon vegetable oil
1 teaspoon baking	
powder	

1 Preheat the oven to 350°F. Line two 8-inch round cake pans with wax paper and grease the paper.

2 Melt the chocolate and butter in the top of a double boiler. Transfer to a bowl and stir in the sugar. Add the eggs and vanilla and mix well. Sift over the flour and baking powder. Stir in the walnuts.

3 Pour the mixture into the cake pans. Bake until a skewer inserted in the center comes out clean, about 30 minutes. Let stand for 10 minutes, then unmold onto a wire rack to cool.

4 Whip the cream until firm. Slice the cakes in half horizontally. Sandwich them together and cover the cake with the cream. Chill.

5 To make the chocolate curls, melt the chocolate and oil in the top of a double boiler. Spread onto a non-porous surface. Just before it sets, hold the blade of a knife at an angle to the chocolate and scrape across the surface to make curls. Use to decorate the cake.

Chocolate Frosted Layer Cake

The contrast between the frosting and the sponge creates a dramatic effect when the cake is cut.

Makes one 8-inch round cake

*1 cup butter or
margarine, at room
temperature*
1½ cups sugar
4 eggs, separated
*2 teaspoons vanilla
extract*
3½ cups all-purpose flour
*2 teaspoons baking
powder*

¼ teaspoon salt
1 cup milk

For the frosting
*5 ounces semisweet
chocolate*
½ cup sour cream
¼ teaspoon salt

1 Preheat the oven to 350°F. Line two 8-inch round cake pans with wax paper and grease the paper. Dust the pans with flour. Tap to remove any excess.

2 Cream the butter or margarine until soft. Gradually add the sugar and beat until light and fluffy. Beat the egg yolks, then add to the butter mixture with the vanilla.

3 Sift the flour with the baking powder three times. Set aside. Beat the egg whites with the salt until they peak stiffly.

4 Fold the dry ingredients into the butter mixture in three batches, alternating with the milk. Add a dollop of the egg white and fold in to lighten the mixture. Fold in the rest until just blended.

5 Spoon into the cake pans and bake until the cakes pull away from the sides, about 30 minutes. Let stand in the pans for 5 minutes, then turn out onto a wire rack.

6 For the frosting, melt the chocolate in the top of a double boiler. When cool, stir in the sour cream and salt. Sandwich the layers with frosting, then spread on the top and side.

Devil's Food Cake with Orange

Makes one 9-inch round cake

½ cup cocoa
¾ cup boiling water
*¾ cup butter, at room
temperature*
2 cups dark brown sugar
3 eggs
2½ cups all-purpose flour
1½ teaspoons baking soda
*¼ teaspoon baking
powder*
½ cup sour cream
*blanched orange rind
shreds, to decorate*

For the frosting
1½ cups superfine sugar
2 egg whites
*4 tablespoons frozen
orange juice
concentrate*
1 tablespoon lemon juice
grated rind of 1 orange

1 Preheat the oven to 350°F. Line two 9-inch cake pans with wax paper and grease the paper. In a bowl, mix the cocoa and water until smooth.

2 Cream the butter and sugar until light and fluffy. Add the eggs, one at a time, beating well after each addition. When the cocoa mixture is lukewarm, add to the butter mixture.

3 Sift together the flour, soda and baking powder twice. Fold into the cocoa mixture in three batches, alternating with the sour cream. Pour into the pans and bake until the cakes pull away from the sides, 30–35 minutes. Let stand for 15 minutes, then turn out onto a wire rack.

4 For the frosting, place all the ingredients in the top of a double boiler. With an electric mixer, beat until the mixture holds soft peaks. Continue beating off the heat until thick enough to spread.

5 Sandwich the cake layers with frosting, then spread over the top and side. Decorate with orange rind shreds.

French Chocolate Cake

This is typical of a French homemade cake – dense, dark and delicious. Serve with cream or a fruit coulis.

Makes one 9-inch round cake

5 tablespoons superfine sugar
10 ounces semisweet chocolate, chopped
¾ cup sweet butter, cut into pieces
2 teaspoons vanilla extract
5 eggs, separated
¼ cup all-purpose flour, sifted
pinch of salt
confectioner's sugar, for dusting

1 Preheat the oven to 325°F. Grease a 9-inch springform pan, sprinkle with sugar and tap out the excess.

2 Set aside 3 tablespoons of the sugar. Place the chocolate, butter and remaining sugar in a heavy saucepan and cook over low heat until melted. Remove from the heat, stir in the vanilla extract and let cool slightly.

3 Beat the egg yolks, one at a time, into the chocolate mixture, then stir in the flour.

4 Beat the egg whites with the salt until soft peaks form. Sprinkle over the reserved sugar and beat until stiff and glossy. Beat a third of the whites into the chocolate mixture, then fold in the rest.

5 Pour the mixture into the pan and tap it gently to release any air bubbles.

6 Bake the cake for 35–45 minutes, until well risen and the top springs back when touched lightly. Transfer to a wire rack, remove the sides of the pan and let cool. Remove the pan bottom, dust the cake with confectioner's sugar and transfer to a serving plate.

Almond Cake

Serve this wonderfully nutty cake with coffee, or, for a treat, with a glass of almond liqueur.

Makes one 9-inch round cake

1⅓ cups blanched, toasted whole almonds
5 tablespoons confectioner's sugar
3 eggs
2 tablespoons butter, melted
½ teaspoon almond extract
4 tablespoons all-purpose flour
3 egg whites
1 tablespoon superfine sugar
toasted whole almonds, to decorate

1 Preheat the oven to 325°F. Line a 9-inch round cake pan with wax paper and grease the paper.

2 Coarsely chop the almonds and grind them with half the confectioner's sugar in a blender or food processor. Transfer to a mixing bowl.

3 Beat in the whole eggs and remaining confectioner's sugar until the mixture forms ribbon trails. Mix in the butter and almond extract. Sift over the flour and fold in.

4 Beat the egg whites until they peak softly. Add the superfine sugar and beat until stiff and glossy. Fold into the almond mixture in four batches.

5 Spoon the mixture into the cake pan and bake until golden brown, 15–20 minutes. Decorate with toasted almonds.

Caramel Layer Cake

Makes one 8-inch round cake

2½ cups all-purpose flour
1½ teaspoons baking
   powder
¾ cup butter, at room
   temperature
generous ⅔ cup superfine
   sugar
4 eggs, beaten
1 teaspoon vanilla
   extract
½ cup milk
whipped cream, to
   decorate

caramel threads, to
   decorate (optional)

For the frosting
1⅓ cups dark brown
   sugar
1 cup milk
2 tablespoons sweet
   butter
3–5 tablespoons
   whipping cream

1 Preheat the oven to 350°F. Line two 8-inch cake pans with wax paper and grease the paper. Sift the flour and baking powder together three times.

2 Cream the butter and sugar until light and fluffy. Slowly mix in the beaten eggs. Add the vanilla. Fold in the flour mixture, alternating with the milk. Divide the batter between the cake pans and spread evenly. Bake until the cakes pull away from the sides of the pan, about 30 minutes. Let stand in the pans for 5 minutes, then turn out and cool on a wire rack.

3 For the frosting, bring the brown sugar and milk to a boil, cover and cook for 2 minutes. Uncover and continue to boil, without stirring, until the mixture reaches 238°F (soft ball stage) on a sugar thermometer.

4 Remove the pan from the heat and add the butter, but do not stir it in. Let cool until lukewarm, then beat until the mixture is smooth. Stir in enough cream to obtain a spreadable consistency.

5 Sandwich the cake together with frosting and then cover the top and sides. Decorate with whipped cream, and caramel threads if liked.

Marbled Spice Cake

You could bake this cake in an 8-inch round pan if you do not have a kugelhopf.

Makes one ring cake

6 tablespoons butter,
   softened
generous ½ cup superfine
   sugar
2 eggs, lightly beaten
few drops vanilla extract
generous 1 cup all-
   purpose flour
1½ teaspoons baking
   powder

3 tablespoons milk
3 tablespoons molasses
1 teaspoon mixed spice
½ teaspoon ground
   ginger
1½ cups confectioner's
   sugar, sifted, to
   decorate

1 Preheat the oven to 350°F. Grease and flour a 2-pound kugelhopf or ring mold.

2 Cream together the butter and sugar until light and fluffy. Beat in the eggs and vanilla.

3 Sift together the flour and baking powder, then fold into the butter mixture, alternating with the milk.

4 Add the molasses and spices to a third of the mixture. Drop alternating spoonfuls of the two mixtures into the pan. Run a knife through them to give a marbled effect.

5 Bake for 50 minutes, or until a skewer inserted into the center comes out clean. Let stand in the pan for 10 minutes, then turn out onto a wire rack to cool.

6 To decorate, make a smooth icing with the confectioner's sugar and some warm water. Drizzle over the cake and let set.

Raspberry Meringue Gâteau

A rich hazelnut meringue filled with cream and raspberries makes a delicious combination of textures and tastes.

Serves 8

4 egg whites
1 cup superfine sugar
few drops vanilla extract
1 teaspoon malt vinegar
1 cup toasted chopped
   hazelnuts, ground
1¼ cups heavy cream
2 cups raspberries
confectioner's sugar, for
   dusting

raspberries and mint
   sprigs, to decorate

For the sauce
1⅓ cups raspberries
3 tablespoons
   confectioner's sugar
1 tablespoon orange
   liqueur

1 Preheat the oven to 350°F. Grease two 8-inch cake pans and line the bottoms with wax paper.

2 Whisk the egg whites in a large bowl until they hold stiff peaks, then gradually whisk in the superfine sugar a tablespoon at a time, whisking well after each addition.

3 Continue whisking the meringue mixture for a minute or two until very stiff, then fold in the vanilla, vinegar and the ground hazelnuts. Divide the meringue mixture between the prepared pans and spread level. Bake for 50–60 minutes, until crisp. Remove the meringues from the pans and let cool on a wire rack.

4 Meanwhile, make the sauce. Liquidize the raspberries with the confectioner's sugar and orange liqueur in a blender or food processor, then press it through a nylon strainer to remove any pips. Chill the sauce until ready to serve.

5 Whip the cream, then fold in the raspberries. Sandwich the meringue rounds with the raspberry cream. Dust with confectioner's sugar, decorate with fruit and mint and serve with the sauce.

Strawberry Mint Sponge

This combination of fruit, mint and ice cream will prove popular with everyone.

Makes one 8-inch round cake

6 – 10 fresh mint leaves,
   plus extra to decorate
¾ cup butter
¾ cup superfine sugar
1½ cups self-rising flour
3 eggs

5 cups strawberry ice
   cream, softened
2½ cups heavy cream
2 tablespoons mint
   liqueur
2 cups fresh strawberries

1 Tear the mint into pieces, mix with the sugar, and let stand overnight. (Remove the leaves from the sugar before use.)

2 Preheat the oven to 375°F. Grease and line an 8-inch deep springform cake pan. Cream the butter and sugar, add the flour, and then the eggs. Pour the mixture into the pan.

3 Bake for 20–25 minutes, or until a skewer inserted in the center comes out clean. Turn out onto a wire rack to cool. When cool, split into two layers.

4 Wash the cake pan and line with plastic wrap. Put the cake base back in the pan. Spread with the ice cream, then cover with the top half of the cake. Freeze for 3–4 hours.

5 Whip the cream with the liqueur. Turn the cake out onto a serving plate and quickly spread a layer of whipped cream all over it, leaving an uneven finish. Freeze until 10 minutes before serving. Decorate the cake with the strawberries and place fresh mint leaves around it.

Chestnut Cake

This rich, moist cake can be made up to 1 week in advance and kept, undecorated and wrapped, in an airtight pan.

Serves 8–10

1¼ cups all-purpose flour
pinch of salt
1 cup butter, softened
¾ cup superfine sugar
15-ounce can chestnut
   purée

9 eggs, separated
7 tablespoons dark rum
1¼ cups heavy cream
candied chestnuts and
   confectioner's sugar,
   to decorate

1 Preheat the oven to 350°F. Grease and line an 8-inch springform cake pan.

2 Sift the flour and salt and set aside. Beat the butter and sugar together until light and fluffy. Fold in two-thirds of the chestnut purée, with the egg yolks. Fold in the flour and salt.

3 Whisk the egg whites in a clean, dry bowl until stiff. Beat a little of the egg whites into the chestnut mixture, until evenly blended, then fold in the remainder. Transfer the cake mixture to the pan and smooth the surface. Bake in the center of the oven for about 1¼ hours, or until a skewer comes out clean. Let stand in the pan and place on a wire rack.

4 Using a skewer, pierce holes over the cake. Sprinkle with 4 tablespoons rum, then cool. Remove the cake from the pan, peel off the lining paper and cut horizontally into two layers. Place the bottom layer on a plate. Whisk the cream with the remaining rum, sugar and chestnut purée until smooth.

5 To assemble, spread two-thirds of the chestnut cream mixture over the bottom layer and place the other layer on top. Spread some chestnut cream over the top and sides of the cake, pipe the remainder in large swirls round the edge of the cake. Decorate with chopped candied chestnuts and confectioner's sugar.

Marbled Ring Cake

Glaze this cake with running icing if you prefer.

Makes one 10-inch ring cake

4 ounces semisweet
   chocolate
3 cups all-purpose flour
1 teaspoon baking
   powder
2 cups butter, at room
   temperature

3¾ cups superfine sugar
1 tablespoon vanilla
   extract
10 eggs, at room
   temperature
confectioner's sugar, for
   dusting

1 Preheat the oven to 350°F. Line a 10 x 4-inch ring mold with wax paper and grease the paper. Dust with flour. Melt the chocolate in the top of a double boiler, stirring occasionally. Set aside.

2 Sift together the flour and baking powder. In another bowl, cream the butter, sugar and vanilla extract until light and fluffy. Add the eggs, two at a time, then gradually blend in the flour mixture.

3 Spoon half of the mixture into the ring mold. Stir the chocolate into the remaining mixture, then spoon into the prepared ring mold. With a metal spatula, swirl the mixtures for a marbled effect.

4 Bake until a skewer inserted in the center comes out clean, about 1¾ hours. Cover with foil halfway through baking. Let stand for 15 minutes, then unmold and transfer to a wire rack. To serve, dust with confectioner's sugar.

Chocolate and Nut Gâteau

Hazelnuts give an interesting crunchy texture to this delicious iced dessert.

Serves 6–8

½ cup shelled hazelnuts
about 32 sponge fingers
¾ cup cold strong black
   coffee
2 tablespoons brandy
1¼ cups heavy cream

6 tablespoons
   confectioner's sugar,
   sifted
5 ounces semisweet
   chocolate
confectioner's sugar and
   cocoa, for dusting

1 Preheat the oven to 400°F. Spread out the hazelnuts on a baking sheet and toast them in the oven for 5 minutes until golden. Transfer the nuts to a clean dish towel and rub off the skins while still warm. Cool, then chop finely.

2 Line a 5-cup loaf pan with plastic wrap and cut enough sponge fingers to fit the bottom and sides. Reserve the remaining fingers.

3 Mix the coffee and brandy in a shallow dish. Dip the sponge fingers briefly into the coffee mixture and return to the pan, sugary-side down.

4 Whip the cream with the confectioner's sugar until it forms soft peaks. Coarsely chop 3 ounces of the chocolate, and fold into the cream with the hazelnuts. Melt the remaining chocolate in a bowl set over a pan of barely simmering water. Cool, then fold into the cream mixture. Spoon into the pan.

5 Moisten the remaining sponge fingers in the coffee mixture and lay over the filling. Wrap and freeze until firm.

6 Remove from the freezer 30 minutes before serving. Turn out onto a serving plate and dust with confectioner's sugar and cocoa.

Chocolate and Orange Angel Cake

This light-as-air sponge with its fluffy icing is the answer to a cake-lover's prayer.

Makes one 8-inch ring cake

¼ cup all-purpose flour
2 tablespoons cocoa
2 tablespoons cornstarch
pinch of salt
5 egg whites
½ teaspoon cream of
   tartar
scant ½ cup superfine
   sugar

blanched and shredded
   rind of 1 orange, to
   decorate

For the icing
1 cup superfine sugar
1 egg white

1 Preheat the oven to 350°F. Sift the flour, cocoa, cornstarch and salt together three times. Beat the egg whites in a large bowl until foamy. Add the cream of tartar, then whisk until soft peaks form.

2 Add the superfine sugar to the egg whites a spoonful at a time, whisking after each addition. Sift a third of the flour and cocoa mixture over the meringue and gently fold in. Repeat twice more.

3 Spoon the mixture into a nonstick 8-inch ring mold and level the top. Bake for 35 minutes, or until springy when lightly pressed. Turn upside-down onto a wire rack and let cool in the pan. Carefully ease out of the pan.

4 For the icing, put the sugar in a pan with 5 tablespoons cold water. Stir over low heat until dissolved. Boil until the syrup reaches soft ball stage (238°F on a sugar thermometer). Remove from the heat. Whisk the egg white until stiff. Add the syrup in a thin stream, whisking all the time, until the mixture is very thick and fluffy.

5 Spread the icing over the top and sides of the cooled cake. Sprinkle the orange rind over the top of the cake and serve.

Chocolate Date Cake

A stunning cake that tastes wonderful. Rich and gooey – it's a chocoholic's delight!

Serves 8
scant 1 cup ricotta cheese
scant 1 cup mascarpone
1 teaspoon vanilla
   extract, plus few extra
   drops
confectioner's sugar, to
   taste
4 egg whites

½ cup superfine sugar
7 ounces semisweet
   chocolate
scant 1 cup Medjool
   dates, pitted and
   chopped
1½ cups walnuts or
   pecans, chopped

1   Preheat the oven to 350°F. Grease and line the bottom of an 8-inch springform cake pan.

2   To make the frosting, mix together the ricotta cheese and mascarpone, add a few drops of vanilla extract and confectioner's sugar to taste, then set aside.

3   Whisk the egg whites until they form stiff peaks. Whisk in 2 tablespoons of the superfine sugar until the meringue is thick and glossy, then fold in the remainder.

4   Chop 6 ounces of the chocolate. Carefully fold into the meringue with the dates, nuts and 1 teaspoon of the vanilla extract. Pour into the prepared pan, spread level and bake for about 45 minutes, until risen around the edges.

5   Let cool in the pan for about 10 minutes, then unmold, peel off the lining paper and let stand until completely cold. Swirl the frosting over the top of the cake.

6   Melt the remaining chocolate in a bowl over hot water. Spoon into a small paper piping bag and drizzle the chocolate over the cake. Chill before serving.

Warm Lemon and Syrup Cake

This delicious cake is the perfect winter dessert for both kids and adults.

Serves 8
3 eggs
¾ cup butter, softened
¾ cup superfine sugar
1½ cups self-rising flour
½ cup ground almonds
¼ teaspoon freshly grated
   nutmeg
5 tablespoons candied
   lemon peel, finely
   chopped

grated rind of 1 lemon
2 tablespoons lemon juice
poached pears, to serve

For the syrup
¾ cup superfine sugar
juice of 3 lemons

1   Preheat the oven to 350°F. Grease and line the bottom of a deep, round 8-inch cake pan.

2   Place all the cake ingredients in a large bowl and beat well for 2–3 minutes, until light and fluffy.

3   Turn the mixture into the prepared pan, spread level and bake for 1 hour, or until golden and firm to the touch.

4   Meanwhile, make the syrup. Put the sugar, lemon juice and 5 tablespoons water in a saucepan. Heat gently, stirring, until the sugar has dissolved, then boil, without stirring, for 1–2 minutes more.

5   Turn out the cake onto a plate with a rim. Prick the surface of the cake all over with a fork, then pour over the hot syrup. Let soak for about 30 minutes. Serve the cake warm with thin wedges of poached pears.

Strawberry Shortcake Gâteau

A light cookie-textured sponge forms the base of this summertime dessert.

Makes one 8-inch round cake

2 cups fresh strawberries, hulled	3 tablespoons superfine sugar
2 tablespoons ruby port	1 egg, lightly beaten
2 cups self-rising flour	1–2 tablespoons milk
2 teaspoons baking powder	melted butter, for brushing
6 tablespoons sweet butter, diced	1 cup heavy cream confectioner's sugar, for dusting

1 Preheat the oven to 425°F. Grease and line the bottoms of two 8-inch round, loose-based cake pans. Reserve 5 strawberries, slice the rest and marinate in the port for 1–2 hours. Strain, reserving the port.

2 Sift the flour and baking powder into a bowl. Work in the butter until the mixture resembles fine bread crumbs and stir in the sugar. Work in the egg and 1 tablespoon of the milk to form a soft dough, adding more milk if needed.

3 Knead on a lightly floured surface and divide in two. Roll out each half, mark one half into eight wedges, and transfer to the cake pans. Brush with a little melted butter and bake for 15 minutes until risen and golden. Cool in the pans for 10 minutes, then transfer to a wire rack.

4 Cut the marked cake into wedges. Reserving a little cream for decoration, whip the rest until it holds its shape, and fold in the reserved port and strawberry slices. Spread over the cake. Place the wedges on top and dust with sugar.

5 Whip the remaining cream and use to pipe swirls on each wedge. Halve the reserved strawberries and use to decorate the cake.

Almond and Raspberry Swiss Roll

A light and airy sponge cake is rolled up with a fresh cream and raspberry filling for a decadent afternoon treat.

Makes one 9-inch long roll

3 eggs	1 cup heavy cream
⅓ cup superfine sugar	generous 1 cup fresh raspberries
½ cup all-purpose flour	16 slivered almonds, toasted, to decorate
2 tablespoons ground almonds	
superfine sugar, for dusting	

1 Preheat the oven to 400°F. Grease a 13 x 9-inch jelly roll pan, line with wax paper and grease the paper.

2 Whisk the eggs and sugar in a heat proof bowl until blended. Place over a pan of simmering water and whisk until thick and pale. Remove from the heat and whisk until cool. Sift over the flour and almonds and fold in gently.

3 Transfer to the prepared pan and bake for 10–12 minutes, until risen and springy to the touch. Invert the cake in its pan onto wax paper dusted with superfine sugar. Let cool, then remove the pan and lining paper.

4 Reserve a little cream, then whip the rest until it holds its shape. Fold in all but 8 raspberries and spread the mixture over the cooled cake, leaving a narrow border. Roll the cake up and sprinkle with superfine sugar.

5 Whip the reserved cream until it just holds its shape, and spoon along the cake center. Decorate with the reserved raspberries and toasted slivered almonds.

Orange and Walnut Jelly Roll

This unusual cake is tasty enough to serve alone, but you could also pour over some light cream.

Makes one 9½-inch long roll

4 eggs, separated
generous ½ cup superfine
  sugar
1 cup very finely chopped
  walnuts
pinch of cream of tartar
pinch of salt
confectioner's sugar, for
  dusting

For the filling
1¼ cups whipping cream
1 tablespoon superfine
  sugar
grated rind of 1 orange
1 tablespoon orange-
  flavor liqueur

1 Preheat the oven to 350°F. Line a 12 x 9½-inch jelly roll pan with wax paper and grease the paper.

2 Beat the egg yolks and sugar until thick. Stir in the walnuts. Beat the egg whites with the cream of tartar and salt until stiff peaks form. Fold into the walnut mixture.

3 Pour the mixture into the prepared pan and level. Bake for 15 minutes. Invert the cake onto wax paper dusted with confectioner's sugar. Peel off the lining paper. Roll up the cake with the sugared paper. Let cool.

4 For the filling, whip the cream until soft peaks form. Fold in the superfine sugar, orange rind and liqueur.

5 Unroll the cake. Spread with the filling, then re-roll. Chill. To serve, dust with confectioner's sugar.

Chocolate Jelly Roll

Makes one 13-inch long roll

8 ounces semisweet
  chocolate
3 tablespoons water
2 tablespoons rum,
  brandy or strong
  coffee
7 eggs, separated

scant 1 cup superfine
  sugar
¼ teaspoon salt
1½ cups whipping cream
confectioner's sugar, for
  dusting

1 Preheat the oven to 350°F. Line a 15 x 13-inch jelly roll pan with wax paper and grease.

2 Combine the chocolate, water and rum or other flavoring in the top of a double boiler, or in a heat proof bowl set over simmering water. Heat until melted. Set aside.

3 With an electric mixer, beat the egg yolks and sugar until thick. Stir in the melted chocolate.

4 In another bowl, beat the egg whites and salt until they hold stiff peaks. Fold a large dollop of egg whites into the yolk mixture to lighten it, then carefully fold in the rest of the egg whites.

5 Pour the mixture into the pan and smooth evenly with a metal spatula. Bake for 15 minutes. Remove from the oven, cover with wax paper and a damp cloth. Let stand for about 1–2 hours. With an electric mixer, whip the cream until stiff. Set aside.

6 Run a knife along the inside edge of the pan to loosen the cake, then invert the cake onto a sheet of wax paper that has been dusted with confectioner's sugar.

7 Peel off the lining paper. Spread with an even layer of whipped cream, then roll up the cake with the help of the sugared paper. Chill for several hours. Before serving, dust with an even layer of confectioner's sugar.

Apricot Brandy-snap Roll

A magnificent combination of soft and crisp textures, this cake looks impressive and is easy to prepare.

Makes one 13-inch long roll

4 eggs, separated
1½ teaspoons fresh
    orange juice
generous ½ cup superfine
    sugar
1½ cups ground almonds
4 brandy snaps, crushed,
    to decorate

For the filling
5 ounces canned apricots,
    drained
1¼ cups heavy cream
¼ cup confectioner's
    sugar

1 Preheat the oven to 375°F. Line a 13 x 9-inch jelly roll pan with wax paper and grease. Beat together the egg yolks, orange juice and sugar until thick and pale, about 10 minutes. Fold in the ground almonds.

2 Whisk the egg whites until they hold stiff peaks. Fold into the almond mixture, then transfer to the jelly roll pan and smooth the surface. Bake for 20 minutes, or until a skewer inserted into the center comes out clean. Let cool in the pan, covered with a just-damp dish towel.

3 For the filling, process the apricots in a blender or food processor until smooth. Whip the cream and confectioner's sugar until it holds soft peaks. Fold in the apricot purée.

4 Spread the crushed brandy snaps on a sheet of wax paper. Spread a third of the cream mixture over the cake, then invert onto the brandy snaps. Peel off the lining paper.

5 Use the remaining cream mixture to cover the whole cake, then roll up from a short end. Transfer to a serving dish.

Apricot and Orange Roll

This sophisticated dessert is very good served with a spoonful of strained yogurt or crème fraîche.

Makes one 13-inch long roll
For the roulade
4 egg whites
½ cup golden superfine
    sugar
½ cup all-purpose flour
finely grated rind of 1
    small orange
3 tablespoons orange
    juice

For the filling
½ cup ready-to-eat dried
    apricots
⅔ cup orange juice

To decorate
2 teaspoons
    confectioner's sugar
grated orange rind

1 Preheat the oven to 400°F. Line a 13 x 9-inch jelly roll pan with wax paper and grease.

2 To make the roll, place the egg whites in a large bowl and whisk until they hold soft peaks. Gradually add the sugar, whisking hard between each addition. Fold in the flour, orange rind and juice. Spoon the mixture into the pan and spread it evenly.

3 Bake for 15–18 minutes, or until the sponge is firm and light golden in color. Turn out onto a sheet of wax paper and roll it up loosely from one short side. Let cool.

4 Coarsely chop the apricots and place them in a saucepan with the orange juice. Cover and simmer until most of the liquid has been absorbed. Liquidize the apricots in a food processor or blender.

5 Unroll the cake and spread with the apricot mixture. Roll up, arrange strips of paper diagonally across the roll, sprinkle lightly with confectioner's sugar, remove the paper and sprinkle with orange rind.

Classic Cheesecake

Dust the top of the cheesecake with confectioner's sugar to decorate, if you wish.

Serves 8

⅔ cup digestive cookies, crushed

4 cups cream cheese, at room temperature

generous 1¼ cups sugar

grated rind of 1 lemon

3 tablespoons lemon juice

1 teaspoon vanilla extract

4 eggs

1 Preheat the oven to 325°F. Grease an 8-inch springform pan. Place on a 12-inch circle of foil. Press it up the sides to seal tightly. Press the cookies into the bottom of the pan.

2 Beat the cream cheese until smooth. Add the sugar, lemon rind and juice, and vanilla, and beat until blended. Beat in the eggs, one at a time.

3 Pour into the prepared pan. Set the pan in a larger baking tray and place in the oven. Pour enough hot water in the outer tray to come 1 inch up the side of the pan.

4 Bake until the top is golden brown, about 1½ hours. Cool in the pan.

5 Run a knife around the edge to loosen, then remove the rim of the pan. Chill for at least 4 hours before serving.

Chocolate Cheesecake

Substitute digestive cookies for the base to create a slightly different dessert.

Serves 10–12

10 ounces semisweet chocolate

5 cups cream cheese, at room temperature

1 cup sugar

2 teaspoons vanilla extract

4 eggs

1 tablespoon cocoa

¾ cup sour cream

For the base

2⅓ cups chocolate cookies, crushed

6 tablespoons butter, melted

½ teaspoon ground cinnamon

1 Preheat the oven to 350°F. Grease the bottom and sides of a 9 x 3-inch springform pan.

2 For the base, mix the cookies with the butter and cinnamon. Press into the bottom of the pan.

3 Melt the chocolate in the top of a double boiler. Set aside.

4 Beat the cream cheese until smooth, then beat in the sugar and vanilla. Add the eggs, one at a time.

5 Stir the cocoa into the sour cream. Add to the cream cheese mixture. Stir in the melted chocolate.

6 Pour over the crust. Bake for 1 hour. Cool in the pan, then remove the rim. Chill before serving.

Marbled Cheesecake

Serves 10

4 cups cream cheese, at
　room temperature
1 cup superfine sugar
4 eggs
1 teaspoon vanilla
　extract

½ cup cocoa, dissolved in
　5 tablespoons hot
　water
1 cup digestive cookies,
　crushed

1 Preheat the oven to 350°F. Grease and line the bottom of an
8 x 3-inch cake pan.

2 With an electric mixer, beat the cheese until smooth and
creamy. Add the sugar and beat to incorporate. Beat in the
eggs, one at a time. Do not overmix.

3 Divide the mixture between two bowls. Stir the vanilla
into one, then add the chocolate mixture to the other. Pour a
cupful of the vanilla mixture into the center of the pan to
make an even layer. Slowly pour over a cupful of chocolate
mixture in the center. Repeat, alternating cupfuls of the batter
in a circular pattern until both are used up.

4 Set the pan in a larger baking tray and pour in hot water to
come 1½ inches up the sides of the cake pan. Bake until the
top of the cake is golden, about 1½ hours. It will rise during
baking but will sink later. Let cool in the pan on a rack.

5 To turn out, run a knife around the inside edge. Place a flat
plate, bottom-side up, over the pan and invert onto the plate.

6 Sprinkle the crushed cookies evenly over the bottom,
gently place another plate over them, and invert again. Cover
and chill for at least 3 hours, or overnight. To serve, cut slices
with a sharp knife dipped in hot water.

Baked Cheesecake with Fresh Fruits

**Vary the fruit decoration to suit the season for this rich,
creamy dessert.**

Serves 12

2 cups digestive cookies,
　crushed
¼ cup sweet butter,
　melted
2 cups curd cheese
⅔ cup sour cream
generous ½ cup superfine
　sugar
3 eggs, separated
grated rind of 1 lemon
2 tablespoons Marsala

½ teaspoon almond
　extract
½ cup ground almonds
scant ½ cup golden
　raisins
1 pound prepared mixed
　fruits, such as figs,
　cherries, peaches and
　strawberries, to
　decorate

1 Preheat the oven to 350°F. Grease and line the sides of a
10-inch round springform pan. Combine the cookies and
butter and press into the bottom of the pan. Chill for
20 minutes.

2 For the cake mixture, beat together the cheese, cream,
sugar, egg yolks, lemon rind, Marsala and almond extract
until smooth and creamy.

3 Whisk the egg whites until stiff and fold into the cheese
mixture with all the remaining ingredients, except the fruit,
until evenly combined. Pour over the cookie base and bake
for 45 minutes, until risen and just set in the center.

4 Let stand in the pan until completely cold. Carefully
remove the pan and peel away the lining paper.

5 Chill the cheesecake for at least 1 hour before decorating
with the prepared fruits, just before serving.

151

Tofu Berry "Cheesecake"

Strictly speaking, this "cheesecake" is not a cheesecake at all, since it's based on tofu (beancurd)– but who would guess?

Serves 6

For the base
4 tablespoons margarine
2 tablespoons apple juice
1 cup bran flakes

For the filling
1½ cups tofu or low fat
   soft cheese
scant 1 cup plain yogurt
1 tablespoon/1 envelope
   powdered gelatin
4 tablespoons apple juice

For the topping
1½ cups mixed summer
   soft fruit, such as
   strawberries,
   raspberries, red
   currants, blackberries
2 tablespoons red currant
   jelly
2 tablespoons hot water

1 For the base, place the margarine and apple juice in a saucepan and heat gently until melted. Crush the cereal and stir it into the pan. Turn into a 9-inch round quiche pan and press down firmly. Let set.

2 For the filling, place the tofu or cheese and yogurt in a food processor or blender and process until smooth. Dissolve the gelatin in the apple juice and stir into the tofu mixture.

3 Spread the tofu mixture over the chilled base, smoothing it evenly. Chill until set.

4 Remove the quiche pan and place the "cheesecake" on a serving plate. Arrange the fruits over the top. Melt the red currant jelly with the hot water. Let it cool, and then spoon over the fruit to serve.

Baked Blackberry Cheesecake

This light cheesecake is best made with wild blackberries; if they're not available, use cultivated ones.

Serves 6

¾ cup cottage cheese
¾ cup plain yogurt
1 tablespoon whole wheat
   flour
2 tablespoons golden
   superfine sugar
1 egg

1 egg white
finely grated rind and
   juice of ½ lemon
scant 2 cups fresh or
   frozen and defrosted
   blackberries

1 Preheat the oven to 350°F. Lightly grease and line the bottom of a 7-inch sandwich cake pan.

2 Place the cottage cheese in a food processor or blender and process until smooth. Place in a bowl, then add the yogurt, flour, sugar, egg and egg white, and mix. Add the lemon rind, juice and blackberries, reserving a few.

3 Turn the mixture into the pan and bake for 30–35 minutes, or until just set. Turn off the oven and let the cake stand in it for 30 minutes more.

4 Run a knife around the edge of the cheesecake and turn it out. Remove the lining paper and place the cheesecake on a warm serving plate.

5 Decorate the cheesecake with the reserved blackberries and serve warm.

Coffee, Peach and Almond Daquoise

Makes one 9-inch cake

5 eggs, separated
scant 2 cups superfine
 sugar
1 tablespoon cornstarch
1½ cups ground
 almonds, toasted
generous ½ cup milk
1¼ cups sweet butter,
 diced
3–4 tablespoons coffee
 extract

2 x 14-ounce cans peach
 halves in juice,
 drained
generous ½ cup slivered
 almonds, toasted
confectioner's sugar, for
 dusting
few fresh mint leaves, to
 decorate

1 Preheat the oven to 300°F. Draw three 9-inch circles onto some wax paper and place on baking sheets.

2 Whisk the egg whites until stiff. Gradually whisk in scant 1½ cups of the sugar until thick and glossy. Fold in the cornstarch and almonds. Using a ½-inch plain piping nozzle, pipe circles of the mixture onto the paper. Bake for 2 hours. Turn onto wire racks to cool.

3 For the buttercream, beat together the egg yolks and remaining sugar until thick and pale. Heat the milk to boiling point and beat into the egg mixture. Return to the pan and heat until the mixture coats the back of a spoon. Strain into a large bowl and beat until lukewarm. Gradually beat in the butter until glossy. Beat in the coffee extract.

4 Trim the meringues and crush the trimmings. Reserve 3 peach halves, chop the rest and fold into half the buttercream with the crushed meringue. Use to sandwich the meringues together and place on a serving plate.

5 Ice the cake with the plain buttercream. Cover the top with slivered almonds and dust generously with confectioner's sugar. Thinly slice the reserved peaches and use to decorate the cake edge with some mint leaves.

Mocha Brazil Layer Torte

Makes one 8-inch round cake

For the meringue

3 egg whites
generous ½ cup superfine
 sugar
1 tablespoon coffee
 extract
¾ cup Brazil nuts,
 toasted and finely
 ground
8-inch chocolate sponge
 cake

For the icing

1 cup semisweet
 chocolate chips
2 tablespoons coffee
 extract
2 tablespoons water
2½ cups heavy cream,
 whipped

To decorate

12 chocolate-coated coffee
 beans
12 chocolate triangles

1 Preheat the oven to 300°F. Draw two 8-inch circles on wax paper and place on a baking sheet. Grease, line the bottom and flour an 8-inch round springform pan.

2 For the meringue, whisk the egg whites until stiff. Whisk in the sugar until glossy. Fold in the coffee extract and nuts. Using a ½-inch plain piping nozzle, pipe circles of the mixture onto the paper. Bake for 2 hours. Cool. Increase the oven temperature to 350°F.

3 For the icing, melt the chocolate chips, coffee extract and water in a bowl over a pan of simmering water. Remove from the heat and fold in the whipped cream.

4 Cut the cake into three equal layers. Trim meringue discs to the same size and assemble the cake with a layer of sponge, a little icing and a meringue disc, ending with sponge.

5 Reserve a little of the remaining icing, use the rest to cover the cake completely, forming a swirling pattern over the top. Using the reserved icing, and an icing bag with a star nozzle, pipe 24 small rosettes on top of the cake. Top alternately with the coffee beans and the chocolate triangles.

Fresh Fruit Genoese

This Italian classic can be made with any selection of seasonal fruits.

Serves 8–10

For the sponge
1½ cups all-purpose flour
pinch of salt
4 eggs
½ cup superfine sugar
6 tablespoons orange-
 flavored liqueur

For the filling and topping
4 tablespoons vanilla
 sugar
2½ cups heavy cream
1 pound mixed fresh
 fruits
1¼ cups pistachios,
 chopped
4 tablespoons apricot
 jam, warmed and
 strained

1 Preheat the oven to 350°F. Grease and line the bottom of an 8-inch springform cake pan.

2 Sift the flour and salt together three times, then set aside. Using an electric mixer, beat the eggs and sugar together for 10 minutes until thick and pale.

3 Fold the flour mixture gently into the egg and sugar mixture. Transfer the cake mixture to the prepared pan and bake for 30–35 minutes. Let the cake stand in the pan for 5 minutes, then transfer to a wire rack, remove the lining paper and cool.

4 Cut the cake horizontally in to two layers, place the bottom layer on a plate. Sprinkle both layers with liqueur.

5 Add the vanilla sugar to the cream and whisk until the cream holds peaks. Spread two-thirds of the cream over the bottom layer and top with half of the fruit. Top with the second layer and spread the top and sides with the remaining cream. Press the nuts around the sides, arrange the remaining fruit on top and brush with the apricot jam.

Fruit Gâteau with Heartsease

This gâteau would be lovely to serve as a dessert at a summer lunch party in the garden.

Makes one ring cake
½ cup soft margarine
scant ½ cup sugar
2 teaspoons honey
1¼ cups self-rising flour
½ teaspoon baking
 powder
2 tablespoons milk
2 eggs
1 tablespoon rose water
1 tablespoon Cointreau

To decorate
16 heartsease pansy
 flowers
1 egg white, lightly
 beaten
superfine sugar
confectioner's sugar
4 cups strawberries
strawberry leaves

1 Preheat the oven to 375°F. Grease and lightly flour a ring mold. Put the soft margarine, sugar, honey, flour, baking powder, milk and eggs into a mixing bowl and beat well for 1 minute. Add the rose water and the Cointreau and mix well.

2 Pour the mixture into the mold and bake for 40 minutes. Let stand for a few minutes, then turn onto a serving plate.

3 Crystalize the heartsease pansies by painting them with the lightly beaten egg white and sprinkling with superfine sugar. Let dry.

4 Sift confectioner's sugar over the cake. Fill the center of the ring with strawberries – if they will not all fit, place some around the edge. Decorate with the crystalized heartsease flowers and some strawberry leaves.

Nut and Apple Gâteau

Makes one 9-inch round cake

1 cup pecans or walnuts, toasted	3 eggs
½ cup all-purpose flour	scant 1¼ cups superfine sugar
2 teaspoons baking powder	1 teaspoon vanilla extract
¼ teaspoon salt	¾ cup whipping cream
2 large cooking apples	

1 Preheat the oven to 325°F. Line two 9-inch cake pans with wax paper and grease the paper.

2 Finely chop the nuts. Reserve 1½ tablespoons of them and place the rest in a mixing bowl. Sift over the flour, baking powder and salt and stir.

3 Peel and core the apples. Cut into ⅛-inch dice, then stir into the flour mixture.

4 Beat the eggs until frothy. Gradually add the sugar and vanilla and beat until ribbon trails form, about 8 minutes. Fold in the flour mixture.

5 Pour into the cake pans and bake until a skewer inserted in the center comes out clean, about 35 minutes. Let stand for 10 minutes, then turn out onto a wire rack to cool.

6 Whip the cream until firm. Use half for the filling. Pipe rosettes on the top and sprinkle over the reserved nuts.

Chocolate Pecan Torte

This torte uses finely ground nuts instead of flour. Toast, then cool the nuts before grinding finely in a processor.

Makes one 8-inch round cake

7 ounces semisweet chocolate, chopped	**For the chocolate honey glaze**
10 tablespoons sweet butter, cut into pieces	4 ounces semisweet chocolate, chopped
4 eggs	¼ cup sweet butter, cut into pieces
½ cup superfine sugar	
2 teaspoons vanilla extract	2 tablespoons honey
1 cup ground pecans	pinch of ground cinnamon
2 teaspoons ground cinnamon	
24 toasted pecan halves, to decorate (optional)	

1 Preheat the oven to 350°F. Grease an 8-inch springform pan, line with wax paper, then grease the paper. Wrap the pan with foil.

2 Melt the chocolate and butter over low heat, stirring until smooth. Set aside. Beat the eggs, sugar and vanilla until frothy. Stir in the melted chocolate and butter, ground nuts and cinnamon. Pour into the pan. Place in a large roasting pan and pour boiling water into the roasting pan, to come ¾ inch up the side of the springform pan. Bake for 25–30 minutes, until the edge of the cake is set, but the center soft. Remove the foil and set on a wire rack.

3 For the glaze, melt the chocolate, butter, honey and cinnamon, stirring until smooth. Remove from the heat. If using, dip toasted pecan halves halfway into the glaze and place on wax paper to set. Remove the cake from its pan and invert onto a wire rack. Remove the paper. Pour the glaze over the cake, tilting the rack to spread it. Use a metal spatula to smooth the sides. Arrange the nuts on top.

Coconut Lime Gâteau

Makes one 9-inch round cake

2 cups all-purpose flour
2½ teaspoons baking
   powder
¼ teaspoon salt
1 cup butter, at room
   temperature
generous 1 cup superfine
   sugar
grated rind of 2 limes
4 eggs

4 tablespoons fresh lime
   juice
1½ cups dried coconut

For the frosting

generous 2 cups sugar
4 tablespoons water
pinch of cream of tartar
1 egg white, whisked
   stiffly

1 Preheat the oven to 350°F. Grease and line the bottom of two 9-inch sandwich cake pans. Sift together the flour, baking powder and salt.

2 Beat the butter until soft. Add the sugar and lime rind and beat until pale and fluffy. Beat in the eggs, one at a time.

3 Gradually fold in the dry ingredients, alternating with the lime juice, then stir in two-thirds of the coconut.

4 Divide the mixture between the cake pans, even the tops and bake for 30–35 minutes. Cool in the pans on a wire rack for 10 minutes, then turn out and peel off the lining paper.

5 Bake the remaining coconut until golden brown, stirring occasionally. For the frosting, heat the sugar, water and cream of tartar until dissolved, stirring. Boil to reach 250°F on a sugar thermometer. Remove from the heat and, when the bubbles subside, whisk in the egg white until thick.

6 Sandwich and cover the cake with the frosting. Sprinkle over the toasted coconut. Let set.

Exotic Celebration Gâteau

Use any tropical fruits you can find to make a spectacular display of colors and tastes.

Makes one 8-inch ring gâteau

¾ cup butter, softened
scant 1 cup superfine
   sugar
3 eggs, beaten
2¼ cups self-rising flour
2–3 tablespoons milk
6–8 tablespoons light
   rum
scant 2 cups heavy cream
¼ cup confectioner's
   sugar, sifted

To decorate

1 pound mixed fresh
   exotic and soft fruits,
   such as figs, red
   currants, star fruit
   and kiwi fruit
6 tablespoons apricot
   jam, warmed and
   strained
2 tablespoons warm
   water
confectioner's sugar

1 Preheat the oven to 375°F. Grease and flour a deep 8-inch ring mold.

2 Beat together the butter and sugar until light and fluffy. Gradually beat in the eggs, then fold in the flour and milk.

3 Spoon the mixture into the ring mold. Bake the cake for 45 minutes, or until a skewer inserted into the center comes out clean. Turn out onto a wire rack and let cool.

4 Place the cake on a serving plate. Make holes randomly over the cake with a skewer. Drizzle over the rum and allow to soak in.

5 Beat together the cream and confectioner's sugar until the mixture holds soft peaks. Spread all over the cake. Arrange the fruits in the hollow center of the cake. Mix the apricot jam and water, then brush over the fruit. Sift over some confectioner's sugar.

Chocolate and Fresh Cherry Gâteau

Makes one 8-inch round cake

½ cup butter
⅔ cup superfine sugar
3 eggs, lightly beaten
1 cup semisweet
 chocolate chips, melted
4 tablespoons kirsch
1¼ cups self-rising flour
1 teaspoon ground
 cinnamon
½ teaspoon ground cloves
12 ounces fresh cherries,
 pitted and halved
3 tablespoons morello
 cherry jam, warmed
1 teaspoon lemon juice

For the frosting
⅔ cup semisweet
 chocolate chips
¼ cup sweet butter
4 tablespoons heavy
 cream

To decorate
½ cup white chocolate
 chips, melted
18 fresh cherries
few rose leaves, washed
 and dried

1 Preheat the oven to 325°F. Grease, line the bottom and flour an 8-inch round springform pan.

2 Cream the butter and ½ cup of the sugar until pale. Beat in the eggs. Stir in the chocolate and half the kirsch. Fold in the flour and spices. Put in the pan and bake for 55–60 minutes, or until a skewer inserted in the center comes out clean. Cool for 10 minutes then transfer to a wire rack.

3 For the filling, bring the cherries, remaining kirsch and sugar to a boil, cover, and simmer for 10 minutes. Uncover for 10 minutes more until syrupy. Let cool.

4 Halve the cake horizontally. Cut a ½-inch deep circle from the base, leaving a ½-inch edge. Crumble into the filling and stir to form a paste. Fill and cover the cake base.

5 Strain the jam and lemon juice. Brush all over the cake. For the frosting, melt all the ingredients. Cool, pour over the cake. Decorate with chocolate-dipped cherries and leaves.

Coffee Almond Flower Gâteau

This delicious cake can be made quite quickly. For a change, use coffee-flavored spongecakes instead of plain.

Makes one 8-inch round cake

2¼ cups coffee-flavor
 butter icing
2 x 8-inch round sponge
 cakes with chopped
 nuts

3 ounces semisweet
 chocolate
20 blanched almonds
4 chocolate-coated coffee
 beans

1 Reserve 4 tablespoons of the butter icing for piping and use the rest to sandwich the sponges together and cover the top and side of the cake. Smooth the top with a metal spatula and serrate the side with a scraper.

2 Melt the chocolate in a heat proof bowl over a pan of hot water. Remove from the heat, then dip in half of each almond at a slight angle. Let dry on wax paper. Return the chocolate to the pan of hot water (off the heat) so it does not set. Remove and let cool slightly.

3 Arrange the almonds on top of the cake to represent flowers. Place a chocolate-coated coffee bean in the flower centers. Spoon the remaining melted chocolate into a wax paper icing bag. Cut a small piece off the end in a straight line. Pipe the chocolate in wavy lines over the top of the cake and in small beads around the top edge.

4 Transfer the cake to a serving plate. Place the reserved buttercream in a fresh icing bag fitted with a No 2 writing nozzle. Pipe beads of icing all around the bottom of the cake, then top with small beads of chocolate.

Vegan Chocolate Gâteau

A rare treat for vegans, this gâteau tastes really delicious.

Makes one 8-inch gâteau

2½ cups self-rising whole
    wheat flour
½ cup cocoa
1 tablespoon baking
    powder
1¼ cups superfine sugar
few drops vanilla extract
9 tablespoons sunflower
    oil
1½ cups water

sifted cocoa, to decorate
¼ cup chopped nuts, to
    decorate

For the chocolate fudge

¼ cup soy margarine
3 tablespoons water
2¼ cups confectioner's
    sugar
2 tablespoons cocoa

1 Preheat the oven to 325°F. Grease and line the bottom of a deep 8-inch round cake pan, and grease the paper.

2 Sift the flour, cocoa and baking powder into a large mixing bowl. Add the sugar and vanilla, then gradually beat in the oil and water to make a smooth batter.

3 Pour the mixture into the cake pan and smooth the surface. Bake for 45 minutes, or until a skewer inserted into the center of the cake comes out clean. Let stand in the pan for 5 minutes, then turn out onto a wire rack and let cool. Cut the cake in half.

4 For the chocolate fudge, gently melt the margarine with the water. Remove from the heat, add the confectioner's sugar and cocoa, and beat until smooth and shiny. Let cool until firm enough to spread and pipe.

5 Place a layer of cake on a serving plate and spread over two-thirds of the chocolate fudge. Top with the other layer of cake. Using a star piping nozzle, pipe chocolate fudge stars over the cake. Sprinkle with cocoa and chopped nuts.

Black Forest Gâteau

A perfect gâteau for a special tea party, or for serving as a sumptuous dinner party dessert.

Makes one 8-inch gâteau

5 eggs
scant 1 cup superfine
    sugar
½ cup all-purpose flour
½ cup cocoa
6 tablespoons butter,
    melted

For the filling
5–6 tablespoons kirsch
2½ cups heavy cream

15-ounce can black
    cherries, drained,
    pitted and chopped

To decorate
chocolate curls
15–20 fresh cherries,
    preferably with stems
confectioner's sugar

1 Preheat the oven to 350°F. Line the bottom of two deep 8-inch round cake pans with wax paper and grease.

2 Beat together the eggs and sugar for 10 minutes, or until thick and pale. Sift over the flour and cocoa, and fold in gently. Trickle in the melted butter and fold in gently.

3 Transfer the mixture to the cake pans. Bake for 30 minutes, or until springy to the touch. Let stand in the pans for 5 minutes, then turn out onto a wire rack, peel off the lining paper and let cool. Cut each cake in half horizontally and sprinkle with the kirsch.

4 Whip the cream until soft peaks form. Combine two-thirds of the cream with the chopped cherries. Place a layer of cake on a serving plate and spread with one-third of the filling. Repeat twice, and top with a layer of cake. Use the reserved cream to cover the top and sides of the gâteau.

5 Decorate the gâteau with chocolate curls, fresh cherries and dredge with confectioner's sugar.

Walnut Coffee Gâteau

Serves 8–10

1¼ cups walnuts
generous ¾ cup superfine
   sugar
5 eggs, separated
scant 1 cup dry bread
   crumbs
1 tablespoon cocoa
1 tablespoon instant
   coffee
2 tablespoons rum or
   lemon juice

¼ teaspoon salt
6 tablespoons red currant
   jelly, warmed
chopped walnuts, for
   decorating

For the frosting
8 ounces semisweet
   chocolate
3 cups whipping cream

1 For the frosting, combine the chocolate and cream in the top of a double boiler until the chocolate melts. Cool, then cover and chill overnight, or until the mixture is firm.

2 Preheat the oven to 350°F. Line and grease 9 x 2-inch cake pan. Grind the nuts with 3 tablespoons of the sugar in a food processor, blender or coffee grinder.

3 With an electric mixer, beat the egg yolks and remaining sugar until thick and lemon-colored. Fold in the walnuts. Stir in the bread crumbs, cocoa, coffee and rum or lemon juice.

4 In another bowl, beat the egg whites with the salt until they hold stiff peaks. Fold carefully into the walnut mixture. Pour the meringue batter into the pan and bake until the top of the cake springs back when touched, about 45 minutes. Let the cake stand for 5 minutes, then turn out and cool, before slicing in half horizontally.

5 With an electric mixer, beat the chocolate frosting mixture on low speed until it becomes lighter, about 30 seconds. Brush some of the jelly over the cut cake layer. Spread with some of the chocolate frosting, then sandwich with the remaining cake layer. Brush the top of the cake with jelly, then cover the side and top with the remaining frosting. Make a starburst pattern with a knife and sprinkle chopped walnuts around the edge.

Sachertorte

A rich cake, ideal to serve as a treat for anyone who is a self-confessed chocoholic.

Makes one 9-inch round cake

4 ounces semisweet
   chocolate
⅓ cup sweet butter, at
   room temperature
¼ cup sugar
4 eggs, separated, plus 1
   egg white
¼ teaspoon salt
9 tablespoons all-purpose
   flour, sifted

For the topping
5 tablespoons apricot jam
1 cup water, plus 1
   tablespoon
1 tablespoon sweet butter
6 ounces semisweet
   chocolate
⅓ cup sugar
premade chocolate
   decorating icing

1 Preheat the oven to 325°F. Line and grease a 9-inch cake pan. Melt the chocolate in the top of a double boiler. Set aside.

2 Cream the butter and sugar until light and fluffy. Stir in the chocolate, then beat in the egg yolks, one at a time.

3 Beat the egg whites with the salt until stiff. Fold a dollop of whites into the chocolate mixture to lighten it. Fold in the remaining whites in three batches, alternating with the sifted flour. Pour into the pan and bake until a skewer comes out clean, about 45 minutes. Turn out onto a wire rack.

4 Meanwhile, melt the jam with 1 tablespoon of the water, then strain for a smooth consistency. For the frosting, melt the butter and chocolate in the top of a double boiler. In a heavy saucepan, dissolve the sugar in the remaining water, then boil until it reaches 225°F (thread stage) on a sugar thermometer. Plunge the bottom of the pan into cold water for 1 minute. Stir into the chocolate. Cool for a few minutes.

5 Brush the warm jam over the cake. Pour over the frosting and spread over the top and sides. Let set overnight. Decorate with chocolate icing.

Dundee Cake

This is the perfect recipe for a festive occasion when a lighter fruit cake is required.

Makes one 8-inch round cake

¾ cup butter
1 cup light brown sugar
3 eggs
2 cups all-purpose flour
2 teaspoon baking powder
1 teaspoons ground cinnamon
½ teaspoon ground cloves
¼ teaspoon grated nutmeg
generous 1½ cups golden raisins

generous 1 cup raisins
¾ cup candied cherries, halved
¾ cup chopped mixed candied peel
½ cup blanched almonds, chopped
grated rind of 1 lemon
2 tablespoons brandy
1 cup whole blanched almonds, to decorate

1 Preheat the oven to 325°F. Grease and line an 8-inch round deep cake pan. Cream the butter and sugar until pale and light. Add the eggs, 1 at a time, beating after each addition.

2 Sift together the flour, baking powder and spices. Fold into the egg mixture alternately with the remaining ingredients, until evenly combined. Transfer to the cake pan. Smooth the surface, then make a small dip in the center.

3 Decorate the top of the cake by pressing the blanched almonds in decreasing circles over the entire surface. Bake for 2–2¼ hours, until a skewer inserted in the center of the cake comes out clean.

4 Let cool in the pan for 30 minutes then transfer the cake to a wire rack.

Vegan Dundee Cake

As it contains neither eggs nor dairy products, this cake is suitable for vegans.

Makes one 8-inch square cake

scant 2½ cups whole wheat flour
1 teaspoon mixed spice
¾ cup soy margarine
1 cup dark muscovado sugar, plus 2 tablespoons
generous 1 cup golden raisins
1 cup currants
generous 1 cup raisins
½ cup chopped mixed candied peel
generous ½ cup candied cherries, halved
finely grated rind of 1 orange

2 tablespoons ground almonds
¼ cup blanched almonds, chopped
1 teaspoon baking soda
½ cup soy milk
⅓ cup sunflower oil
2 tablespoons malt vinegar

To decorate

mixed nuts, such as pistachios, pecans and macadamia nuts
candied cherries
angelica
4 tablespoons honey, warmed

1 Preheat the oven to 300°F. Grease and double-line a deep 8-inch square loose-based cake pan.

2 Sift together the flour and mixed spice. Work in the margarine. Stir in the sugar, dried fruits, peel, cherries, orange rind, ground almonds and blanched almonds.

3 Dissolve the baking soda in a little of the milk. Warm the remaining milk with the oil and vinegar and add the baking soda mixture. Stir into the flour mixture.

4 Spoon into the pan and smooth. Bake for 2½ hours. Let stand in the pan for 5 minutes, then cool on a rack. Decorate with the nuts, cherries and angelica and brush with the honey.

Panforte

This rich, spicy nougat-type cake is a Christmas speciality of Siena in Italy.

Makes one 8-inch round cake

1⅔ cups mixed chopped candied exotic peel, to include lemon orange, citron, papaya and pineapple
1 cup unblanched almonds
½ cup walnut halves
½ cup all-purpose flour
1 teaspoon ground cinnamon
¼ teaspoon each grated nutmeg, ground cloves and ground coriander
1 cup superfine sugar
4 tablespoons water
confectioner's sugar, for dusting

1   Preheat the oven to 350°F. Grease and line the bottom of an 8-inch round loose-based cake pan with rice paper. Put the mixed peel and nuts in a bowl. Sift in the flour and spices and mix well.

2   Dissolve the superfine sugar and water in a small saucepan, then boil until the mixture reaches 225°F on a sugar thermometer (thread stage). Pour onto the fruit mixture, stirring to coat well. Transfer to the cake pan, pressing into the sides with a metal spoon.

3   Bake for 25–30 minutes, until the mixture is bubbling. Cool in the pan for 5 minutes.

4   Use a lightly oiled metal spatula to work around the edges of the cake to loosen it. Remove the cake from the pan, leaving the base in place. Let it go cold, then remove the base and dust generously with confectioner's sugar.

Kulich

This Russian yeast cake is traditionally made at Easter.

Makes two cakes

1 tablespoon fast-rising dried yeast
6 tablespoons lukewarm milk
scant ½ cup superfine sugar
5 cups all-purpose flour
pinch of saffron strands
2 tablespoons dark rum
½ teaspoon ground cardamom seeds
½ teaspoon ground cumin
4 tablespoons sweet butter
2 eggs, plus 2 egg yolks
½ vanilla pod, finely chopped
2 tablespoons each candied ginger, mixed peel, almonds and currants, chopped

To decorate

¾ cup confectioner's sugar, sifted
1½–2 teaspoons warm water
drop of almond extract
2 candles
blanched almonds
mixed candied peel

1   Blend together the yeast, milk, 2 tablespoons sugar and ½ cup flour. Let stand in a warm place for 15 minutes, until frothy. Soak the saffron in the rum for 15 minutes.

2   Sift together the remaining flour and spices and work in the butter. Stir in the rest of the sugar. Add the yeast mixture, saffron liquid and remaining ingredients. Knead until smooth. Put in an oiled bowl, cover and let stand until doubled in size.

3   Preheat the oven to 375°F. Grease, line and flour two 1¼-pound coffee pans or 6-inch clay flowerpots.

4   Punch down the dough and form into two rounds. Press into the pans or pots, cover and let stand for 30 minutes. Bake for 35 minutes for the pots or 50 minutes for the pans. Cool.

5   Mix together the sugar, water and almond extract. Pour over the cakes. Decorate with the candles, nuts and peel.

Yule Log

This rich seasonal treat could provide an economic alternative to a traditional iced fruit cake.

Makes one 11-inch long roll

4 eggs, separated
¾ cup superfine sugar
1 teaspoon vanilla
    extract
pinch of cream of tartar
    (optional)
1 cup all-purpose flour,
    sifted

1 cup whipping cream
11 ounces semisweet
    chocolate, chopped
2 tablespoons rum or
    Cognac
confectioner's sugar, for
    dusting

1 Preheat the oven to 375°F. Grease, line and flour a 16 x 11-inch jelly roll pan.

2 Whisk the egg yolks with all but 2 tablespoons of the sugar until pale and thick. Add the vanilla extract.

3 Whisk the egg whites (with the cream of tartar if not using a copper bowl) until they form soft peaks. Add the reserved sugar and continue whisking until stiff and glossy.

4 Fold half the flour into the yolk mixture. Add a quarter of the egg whites and fold in to lighten the mixture. Fold in the remaining flour, then the remaining egg whites.

5 Spread the mixture in the pan. Bake for 15 minutes. Turn onto paper sprinkled with sugar. Roll up and let cool.

6 Bring the cream to a boil. Put the chocolate in a bowl and add the cream. Stir until the chocolate has melted, then beat until it is fluffy and has thickened to a spreading consistency. Mix a third of the chocolate cream with the rum or Cognac.

7 Unroll the cake and spread with the rum mixture. Re-roll and cut off about a quarter, at an angle. Arrange to form a branch. Spread the chocolate cream over the cake. Mark with a fork, add Christmas decorations and dust with sugar.

Chocolate Chestnut Roll

A traditional version of Bûche de Nôel, the delicious French Christmas gâteau.

Makes one 13-inch long roll

8 ounces semisweet
    chocolate
2 ounces white chocolate
4 eggs, separated
generous ½ cup superfine
    sugar

For the chestnut filling
⅔ cup heavy cream
8-ounce can chestnut
    purée
4–5 tablespoons
    confectioner's sugar,
    plus extra for dusting
1–2 tablespoons brandy

1 Preheat the oven to 350°F. Line a 9 x 13-inch jelly roll pan and grease it.

2 For the chocolate curls, melt 2 ounces of the semisweet and all of the white chocolate in separate bowls set over saucepans of hot water. When melted, spread on a non-porous surface and let set. Hold a long sharp knife at a 45-degree angle to the chocolate and push it along the chocolate, turning the knife in a circular motion. Put the curls on wax paper.

3 Melt the remaining semisweet chocolate. Beat the yolks and superfine sugar until thick and pale. Stir in the chocolate.

4 Whisk the whites until they form stiff peaks, then fold into the mixture. Turn into the pan and bake for 15–20 minutes. Cool, covered with a just-damp dish towel, on a wire rack.

5 Sprinkle a sheet of wax paper with superfine sugar. Turn the roll out onto it. Peel off the lining paper and trim the edges of the roll. Cover with the dish towel.

6 For the filling, whip the cream until softly peaking. Beat together the chestnut purée, sugar and brandy until smooth, then fold in the cream. Spread over the cake and roll it up. Top with chocolate curls and dust with confectioner's sugar.

Chocolate Christmas Cups

To crystalize cranberries for decoration, beat an egg white until frothy. Dip each berry in egg white then in sugar.

Makes about 35 cups

10 ounces semisweet
chocolate, broken
into pieces
70–80 foil or paper sweet
cases
6 ounces cooked, cold
Christmas pudding

⅓ cup brandy or whisky
chocolate leaves and a
few candied
cranberries, to
decorate

1 Place the chocolate in a bowl over a saucepan of hot water. Heat gently until the chocolate is melted, stirring until the chocolate is smooth.

2 Using a pastry brush, brush or coat the bottom and sides of about 35 sweet cases. Let set, then repeat, reheating the melted chocolate if necessary, and apply a second coat. Let cool and set completely, 4–5 hours or overnight. Reserve the remaining chocolate.

3 Crumble the Christmas pudding in a bowl, sprinkle with the brandy or whisky and let stand for 30–40 minutes, until the spirit is absorbed.

4 Spoon a little of the pudding mixture into each cup, smoothing the top. Reheat the remaining chocolate and spoon over the top of each cup to cover the surface of each cup to the edge. Let set.

5 When completely set, carefully peel off the cases and place in clean foil cases. Decorate with chocolate leaves and candied cranberries.

Eggless Christmas Cake

This simple cake contains a wealth of fruit and nuts to give it that traditional Christmas flavor.

Makes one 7-inch square cake

½ cup golden raisins
½ cup raisins
½ cup currants
scant ½ cup candied
cherries, halved
¼ cup mixed candied peel
1 cup apple juice
scant ¼ cup toasted
hazelnuts
2 tablespoons pumpkin
seeds
2 pieces preserved ginger
in syrup, chopped

finely grated rind of
1 lemon
½ cup milk
¼ cup sunflower oil
2 cups whole wheat self-
rising flour
2 teaspoons mixed spice
3 tablespoons brandy or
dark rum
apricot jam, for brushing
candied fruits, to
decorate

1 Soak the golden raisins, raisins, currants, cherries and mixed candied peel in the apple juice overnight.

2 Preheat the oven to 300°F. Grease and line a 7-inch square cake pan.

3 Add the hazelnuts, pumpkin seeds, ginger and lemon rind to the fruit. Stir in the milk and oil. Sift the flour and spice, then stir in with the brandy or rum.

4 Spoon into the cake pan and bake for about 1½ hours, or until the cake is golden brown and firm to the touch.

5 Turn out and cool on a wire rack. Brush with strained apricot jam and decorate with candied fruits.

Flourless Fruit Cake

This makes the perfect base for a birthday cake for anyone who needs to avoid eating flour.

Makes one 10-inch round cake

1⅓ cups mincemeat
2 cups dried mixed fruit
½ cup ready-to-eat dried apricots, chopped
⅔ cup ready-to-eat dried figs, chopped
½ cup candied cherries, halved
1 cup walnut pieces
8–10 cups cornflakes, crushed
4 eggs, lightly beaten
14½-ounce can evaporated milk
1 teaspoon mixed spice
1 teaspoon baking powder
mixed candied fruits, chopped, to decorate

1 Preheat the oven to 300°F. Grease a 10-inch round cake pan, line the bottom and sides with a double thickness of wax paper and grease the paper.

2 Put all the ingredients into a large mixing bowl. Beat together well.

3 Turn into the cake pan and smooth the surface.

4 Bake for about 1¾ hours or until a skewer inserted in the center of the cake comes out clean. Let the cake cool in the pan for 10 minutes, then turn out onto a wire rack, peel off the lining paper and let cool completely. Decorate with the chopped candied fruits.

Glazed Christmas Ring

Makes one 10-inch ring cake

generous 1½ cups golden raisins
generous 1 cup raisins
generous 1 cup currants
1 cup dried figs, chopped
6 tablespoons whiskey
3 tablespoons orange juice
1 cup butter
1 cup dark brown sugar
5 eggs
2¼ cups all-purpose flour
1 tablespoon baking powder
1 tablespoon mixed spice
⅔ cup candied cherries, chopped
1 cup brazil nuts, chopped
⅓ cup chopped mixed peel
½ cup ground almonds
grated rind and juice 1 orange
2 tablespoons thick-cut orange marmalade

To decorate

⅔ cup thick-cut orange marmalade
1 tablespoon orange juice
1 cup candied cherries
⅔ cup dried figs, halved
½ cup whole brazil nuts

1 Put the dried fruits in a bowl, pour over 4 tablespoons of the whiskey and all the orange juice and marinate overnight.

2 Preheat the oven to 325°F. Grease and line a 10-inch ring mold. Cream the butter and sugar. Beat in the eggs. Sift together the remaining flour, baking powder and mixed spice. Fold into the egg mixture, alternating with the rest of the ingredients, except the whiskey. Transfer to the pan and bake for 1 hour, then reduce the oven temperature to 300°F and bake for 1¾–2 hours more.

3 Prick the cake all over and pour over the reserved whiskey. Cool in the pan for 30 minutes, then transfer to a wire rack. Boil the marmalade and orange juice for 3 minutes. Stir in the fruit and nuts. Cool, then spoon over the cake and let set.

Noel Christmas Cake

If you like a traditional royal-iced cake, this is a simple design using only one icing and easy-to-pipe decorations.

Makes one 8-inch round cake

8-inch round rich fruit cake
2 tablespoons apricot jam, warmed and strained
5¼ cups marzipan
6 cups royal icing
red and green food coloring

Materials/equipment
9-inch round silver cake board
3 wax paper icing bags
No 1 writing nozzle
2 x No 0 writing nozzles
44 large gold dragées
2½ yards gold ribbon, ¾ inch wide
2½ yards red ribbon, ¼ inch wide

1 Brush the fruit cake with apricot jam, cover with the marzipan and place on the cake board.

2 Flat-ice the top of the cake with two layers of royal icing and let dry. Ice the sides of the cake and peak the royal icing, leaving a space around the center for the ribbon. Let dry. Reserve the remaining royal icing.

3 Pipe beads of icing around the top edge of the cake and place a gold dragée on alternate beads. Using a No 1 writing nozzle, write "NOEL" across the cake and pipe holly leaves, stems and berries around the top.

4 Secure the ribbons around the side of the cake. Tie a red bow and attach to the front of the cake. Use the remaining ribbon for the board. Let dry overnight.

5 Tint 2 tablespoons of the royal icing bright green and 1 tablespoon bright red. Using a No 0 writing nozzle, over-pipe "NOEL" in red, then the edging beads and berries. Over-pipe the holly in green. Let dry.

Christmas Tree Cake

No piping is involved in this bright and colorful cake, making it an easy choice.

Makes one 8-inch round cake

3 tablespoons apricot jam
8-inch round rich fruit cake
6 cups marzipan
green, red, yellow and purple food coloring

1½ cups royal icing
edible silver balls

Materials/equipment
10-inch round cake board

1 Warm, then strain the apricot jam and brush the cake with it. Color 4½ cups of the marzipan green. Use to cover the cake. Let dry overnight.

2 Secure the cake to the board with royal icing. Spread the icing halfway up the cake side. Press the flat side of a metal spatula into the icing, then pull away sharply to form peaks.

3 Make three different-size Christmas tree templates. Tint half the remaining marzipan a deeper green than the top. Using the templates, cut out three tree shapes and arrange them on the cake.

4 Divide the remaining marzipan into three and color red, yellow and purple. Use a little of each marzipan to make five 3-inch rolls. Loop them alternately around the top edge of the cake. Make small red balls and press onto the loop ends.

5 Use the remaining marzipan to make the tree decorations. Arrange on the trees, securing with water, if necessary. Finish the cake by adding silver balls to the Christmas trees.

Christmas Stocking Cake

A bright and happy cake that is sure to delight children at Christmas time.

Makes one 8-inch square cake

8-inch square rich fruit cake
3 tablespoons apricot jam, warmed and strained
6 cups marzipan
7½ cups fondant icing
1 tablespoon royal icing
red and green food coloring

Materials/equipment
10-inch square silver cake board
1½ yards red ribbon, ¾ inch wide
1 yard green ribbon, ¾ inch wide

1 Brush the cake with the apricot jam and place on the cake board. Cover with marzipan.

2 Set aside 1½ cups of the fondant icing. Cover the cake with the rest. Let dry. Secure the red ribbon around the board and the green ribbon around the cake with royal icing.

3 Divide the icing in half and roll out one half. Using a template, cut out two fondant stockings, one ¼ inch larger all around. Put the smaller one on top of the larger one.

4 Divide the other half of the fondant into two and tint one red and the other green. Roll out and cut each color into seven ½-inch strips. Alternate the strips on top of the stocking. Roll lightly to fuse and press the edges together. Let dry.

5 Shape the remaining white fondant into four packages. Trim with red and green fondant ribbons. Use the remaining red and green fondant to make thin strips to decorate the cake sides. Secure in place with royal icing. Stick small fondant balls over the joins. Arrange the stocking and packages on the cake top.

Marbled Cracker Cake

Here's a Christmas cake that's decorated in a most untraditional way!

Makes one 8-inch round cake

8-inch round rich fruit cake
3 tablespoons apricot jam, warmed and strained
4½ cups marzipan
5¼ cups fondant icing
red and green food coloring
edible gold balls

Materials /equipment
wooden toothpicks
10-inch round cake board
red, green and gold thin gift-wrapping ribbon
3 red and 3 green ribbon bows

1 Brush the cake with the jam. Roll out the marzipan and use to cover the cake. Let dry overnight.

2 Form a roll with 3¾ cups of the fondant icing. With a toothpick, dab a few drops of red coloring onto the icing. Repeat with the green. Knead lightly. Roll out the icing until marbled. Brush the marzipan with water and cover with the icing. Position the cake on the cake board.

3 Color half of the remaining fondant icing red and the rest green. Use half of each color to make five crackers, about 2½ inches long. Decorate each with a gold ball. Let dry on wax paper.

4 Roll out the remaining red and green icings, and cut into ½-inch wide strips. Then cut into 12 red and 12 green diamonds. Attach them alternately around the top and bottom of the cake with water.

5 Cut the ribbons into 4-inch lengths. Arrange them with the crackers on the cake top. Attach the bows with softened fondant icing, between the diamonds at the top cake edge.

Greek New Year Cake

A "good luck," foil-wrapped gold coin is traditionally baked into this cake.

Makes one 9-inch square cake

2½ cups all-purpose flour	4 eggs
2 teaspoons baking powder	⅔ cup fresh orange juice
½ cup ground almonds	½ cup blanched almonds
1 cup butter, softened	1 tablespoon sesame seeds
generous ¾ cup superfine sugar, plus extra for sprinkling	

1 Preheat the oven to 350°F. Grease a 9-inch square cake pan, line with wax paper and grease the paper.

2 Sift together the flour and baking powder and stir in the ground almonds.

3 Cream the butter and sugar until light and fluffy. Beat in the eggs, 1 at a time. Fold in the flour mixture, alternating with the orange juice.

4 Spoon the mixture into the cake pan. Arrange the blanched almonds on top, then sprinkle over the sesame seeds. Bake for 50 minutes, or until a skewer inserted in the center comes out clean.

5 Let stand in the pan for 5 minutes, then turn out onto a wire rack and peel off the lining paper. Sprinkle with superfine sugar before serving.

Starry New Year Cake

Makes one 9-inch round cake

9-inch round Madeira cake	**Materials/equipment**
3 cups butter icing	fine paintbrush
5¼ cups fondant icing	star-shape cutter
grape violet and mulberry food coloring	florist's wire, cut into short lengths
gold, lilac shimmer and primrose sparkle powdered food coloring	11-inch round cake board
	purple ribbon with gold stars

1 Cut the cake into three layers. Sandwich together with three-quarters of the butter icing. Spread the rest thinly over the top and sides of the cake.

2 Tint 3¼ cups of the fondant icing purple with the grape violet and mulberry food coloring. Roll out and use to cover the cake. Let dry overnight.

3 Place the cake on a sheet of wax paper. Water down some gold and lilac food coloring. Use a paintbrush to flick each color in turn over the cake. Let dry.

4 For the stars, divide the remaining fondant icing into three pieces. tint one portion purple with the grape violet food coloring, one with the lilac shimmer and one with the primrose sparkle. Roll out each color to ⅛ inch thick. Cut out ten stars in each color and highlight the stars by flicking on the watered-down gold and lilac colors.

5 While the icing is soft, push the florist's wire through the middle of 15 of the stars. Let dry overnight. Put the cake on the board. Arrange the stars on top. Secure the unwired ones with water. Secure the ribbon around the bottom.

Simnel Cake

This is a traditional cake to celebrate Easter but it is delicious at any time of the year.

Makes one 8-inch round cake

1 cup butter, softened
generous 1 cup superfine
* sugar*
4 eggs, beaten
3⅓ cups mixed dried
* fruit*
½ cup candied cherries
3 tablespoons sherry
* (optional)*

2½ cups all-purpose flour
1 tablespoon mixed spice
1 teaspoon baking
* powder*
4½ cups yellow marzipan
1 egg yolk, beaten
ribbons, sugared eggs
* and fondant animals,*
* to decorate*

1 Preheat the oven to 325°F. Grease a deep 8-inch round cake pan, line with a double thickness of wax paper and grease.

2 Beat together the butter and sugar until light and fluffy. Gradually beat in the eggs. Stir in the dried fruit, candied cherries and sherry, if using. Sift over the flour, mixed spice and baking powder, then fold in.

3 Roll out half the marzipan to an 8-inch round. Spoon half of the cake mixture into the cake pan and place the round of marzipan on top. Add the other half of the cake mixture and smooth the surface.

4 Bake for 2½ hours, or until golden and springy to the touch. Let stand in the pan for 15 minutes, then turn out onto a wire rack, peel off the lining paper and let cool.

5 Roll out the reserved marzipan to fit the cake. Brush the cake top with egg yolk and place the marzipan on top. Flute the edges and make a pattern on top with a fork. Brush with more egg yolk. Put the cake on a baking sheet and broil for 5 minutes to brown the top lightly. Cool before decorating.

Easter Sponge Cake

This light lemon quick-mix sponge cake is decorated with lemon butter icing and cut-out marzipan flowers.

Makes one 8-inch round cake

3-egg quantity lemon-
* flavor quick-mix*
* sponge cake*
3 cups lemon-flavor
* butter icing*
½ cup flaked almonds,
* toasted*

To decorate
5⅜ cup homemade or
* commercial white*
* marzipan*
green, orange and yellow
* food coloring*

1 Preheat the oven to 325°F. Bake the cakes in two lined and greased 8-inch round sandwich cake pans for 35–40 minutes until they are golden brown and spring back when lightly pressed in the center. Loosen the edges of the cakes with a metal spatula, turn out, remove the lining paper and cool on a wire rack.

2 Sandwich the cakes together with a quarter of the butter icing. Spread the side of the cake evenly with another-quarter of butter icing.

3 Press the almonds onto the sides to cover evenly. Spread the top of the cake evenly with another quarter of icing. Finish with a metal spatula dipped in hot water, spreading backward and forward to give an even lined effect.

4 Place the remaining icing into a nylon icing bag fitted with a medium-size gâteau nozzle and pipe a scroll edging.

5 Using the marzipan and food coloring, make six cut-out daffodils and ten green and eight orange cut-out marzipan flowers. Arrange them on the cake and let the icing set.

Easter Egg Nest Cake

Celebrate Easter with this colorfully adorned, fresh-tasting lemon sponge cake.

Makes one 8-inch ring cake

8-inch lemon sponge ring cake
1½ cups lemon-flavor butter icing
1½ cups marzipan
pink, green and purple food coloring

small foil-wrapped chocolate eggs

Materials/equipment
10-inch cake board

1 Cut the cake in half horizontally and sandwich together with a third of the butter icing. Place on the cake board. Use the remaining icing to cover the cake. Smooth the top and swirl the side with a metal spatula.

2 For the marzipan braids, divide the marzipan into three and tint pink, green and purple. Cut each portion in half. Using a half of each color, roll thin sausages long enough to go around the bottom. Pinch the ends together, then twist the strands into a rope. Pinch the other ends to seal.

3 Place the colored marzipan rope on the cake board around the cake.

4 For the nests, take the remaining portions of colored marzipan and divide each into five. Roll each piece into a 6½-inch rope. Take a rope of each color, pinch the ends together, twist to form a multi-colored rope and pinch the other ends. Form into a circle. Repeat to make five nests.

5 Space the nests evenly on the cake. Place small chocolate eggs in the nests.

Mother's Day Bouquet

A piped bouquet of flowers can bring as much pleasure as a fresh one for a Mother's Day treat.

Makes one 7-inch round cake

3 cups butter icing
7-inch round sponge cakes
green, blue, yellow and pink food coloring

Materials/equipment
serrated scraper
No 3 writing and petal nozzles
5 wax paper icing bags

1 Reserve a third of the butter icing for decorating. Sandwich together the two sponges with butter icing and place on a serving plate. Cover the top and side with the rest of the butter icing, smoothing the top with a metal spatula and serrating the side using a scraper.

2 Divide the remaining butter icing into four bowls. tint them green, blue, yellow and pink.

3 Decorate the top of the cake first. Use No 3 writing nozzles for the blue and green icing and petal nozzles for the yellow and pink. Pipe on the vase and flowers.

4 For the side decoration, spoon the remaining yellow icing into a fresh icing bag fitted with a No 3 writing nozzle. Pipe the stems, then the flowers and flower centers. Finish by piping green beads at the top and bottom edges of the cake.

Mother's Day Basket

Makes one 6-inch cake

1½ cups self-rising flour,
  sifted
scant 1 cup superfine
  sugar
¾ cup soft margarine
3 eggs
4 cups orange-flavor
  butter icing

Materials/equipment

thin 6-inch round silver
  cake board
wax paper icing bag
basketweave nozzle
foil
1 yard mauve ribbon,
  ½ inch wide
fresh flowers
½ yard spotted mauve
  ribbon, ⅛ inch wide

1 Preheat the oven to 325°F. Lightly grease and line the bottom of a 6-inch brioche mold. Place all the cake ingredients in a bowl, mix together, then beat for 1–2 minutes until smooth. Transfer to the prepared mold and bake for 1¼ hours, or until risen and golden.

2 Place the cooled cake upside-down on the board. Cover the sides with a third of the butter icing. Using a basketweave nozzle, pipe the sides with a basketweave pattern.

3 Invert the cake on the board and spread the top with butter icing. Pipe a shell edging with the basketweave nozzle. Pipe the basketweave pattern over the cake top, starting at the edge. Let set.

4 Fold a strip of foil several layers thick. Wrap the plain ribbon around the strip and bend up the ends to secure the ribbon. Form the foil into a handle and press into the icing.

5 Finish by tying a posy of fresh flowers with the spotted ribbon and making a mixed ribbon bow for the handle.

Basket Cake

This is a perfect cake for a retirement gathering or other special occasion.

Makes one basket-shaped cake

8-inch round
  Madeira cake
2 cups colored butter
  icing
chocolates or candies and
  ribbon for decoration

Materials/equipment

cardboard
pastillage (gum paste)
2 wax paper icing bags,
  fitted with a plain
  tube and a
  basketweave tube
powder food color

1 Cut a template from card to the same size as the top of the cake, fold it in half and cut along the fold. Roll out pastillage fairly thinly and cut out two pieces for the lid, using the templates as a guide. Leave to dry.

2 Coat the top of the cake with butter icing. Fill both icing bags with butter icing and on the side of the cake and about 1 inch onto the top of the cake, pipe a plain vertical line, then pipe short lengths of basketweave across the line. Pipe another plain line along the ends of the basketweave strips. Pipe the next row of basketweave strips in the spaces left between the existing strips and over the new plain line. Continue until the side of the cake and the area on the top is completely covered.

3 Brush the underside of the pastillage lid with powder food color, then pipe a basketweave on top of the lid.

4 Divide the top of the cake in half and pipe a line of basketweave along this central line. Use two or three pieces of pastillage to support each lid half in an open position on the cake. Fill the area under each lid half with chocolates or candies and decorate with ribbon

Valentine's Heart Cake

This cake could also be used to celebrate a special birthday or anniversary.

Makes one 8-inch square cake

8-inch square light fruit cake	**Materials/equipment**
8-inch square light fruit cake	10-inch square cake board
3 tablespoons apricot jam, warmed and strained	2- and 1-inch heart-shape cutter
6 cups marzipan	4 wax paper icing bags
9 cups royal icing	No 1 and No 2 writing
¾ cup fondant icing	and No 42 star
red food coloring	nozzles
	heart-patterned ribbon

1 Brush the cake with the apricot jam. Roll out the marzipan and use to cover the cake. Let dry overnight.

2 Secure the cake on the cake board with a little royal icing. Flat-ice the cake with three or four layers of smooth icing. Set aside some royal icing in an airtight container for piping.

3 Tint the fondant icing red. Roll it out and cut 12 hearts with the larger cutter. Stamp out the middles with the smaller cutter. Cut four extra small hearts. Dry on wax paper.

4 Using a No 1 writing nozzle, pipe wavy lines in royal icing around the four small hearts. Let dry. Using a fresh bag and a No 42 nozzle, pipe swirls around the top and bottom of the cake. Color 1 tablespoon of the remaining royal icing red and pipe red dots on top of each white swirl with the No 1 nozzle.

5 Secure the ribbon in place. Using a No 2 writing nozzle, pipe beads down each corner, avoiding the ribbon. Decorate the cake with the hearts, using royal icing to secure them.

Valentine's Box of Chocolates Cake

This cake would also make a wonderful surprise for Mother's Day.

Makes one 8-inch heart-shape cake

8-inch heart-shape chocolate sponge cake	**Materials/equipment**
8-inch heart-shape chocolate sponge cake	9-inch square piece of stiff cardboard
generous 2 cups marzipan	pencil and scissors
8 tablespoons apricot jam, warmed and strained	9-inch square cake board
	piece of string
6 cups fondant icing	small heart-shape cutter
red food coloring	length of ribbon and a pin
about 16–20 handmade chocolates	small paper sweet cases

1 Place the cake on the cardboard, draw around it and cut the heart shape out. It will be used to support the box lid. Cut through the cake horizontally just below the dome. Place the top section on the cardboard and the bottom on the board.

2 Use the string to measure around the outside of the bottom. Roll the marzipan into a long sausage to the measured length. Place on the cake around the outside edge. Brush both sections of the cake with jam. Tint the fondant icing red and cut off a third. Cut another 8-tablespoon portion from the larger piece. Set aside. Use the large piece to cover the bottom section of cake.

3 Stand the lid on a raised surface. Use the reserved third of fondant icing to cover the lid. Roll out the remaining piece of icing and stamp out small hearts with the cutter. Stick them around the edge of the lid with water. Tie the ribbon in a bow and secure on top of the lid with the pin.

4 Place the chocolates in the paper cases and arrange in the cake base. Position the lid slightly off-center, to reveal the chocolates. Remove the ribbon and pin before serving.

Double Heart Engagement Cake

For a celebratory engagement party, these sumptuous cakes make the perfect centerpiece.

Makes two 8-inch heart-shape cakes

12 ounces semisweet
   chocolate
2 x 8-inch heart-shape
   chocolate sponge cakes
3 cups coffee-flavor
   butter icing
confectioner's sugar, for
   dusting

fresh raspberries, to
   decorate

Materials/equipment
2 x 9-inch heart-shape
   cake boards

1 Melt the chocolate in a heat proof bowl over a saucepan of hot water. Pour the chocolate onto a smooth, non-porous surface and spread it out with a metal spatula. Let cool until just set, but not hard.

2 To make the chocolate curls, hold a large sharp knife at a 45-degree angle to the chocolate and push it along the chocolate in short sawing movements. Let set on wax paper.

3 Cut each cake in half horizontally. Use a third of the butter icing to sandwich the cakes together. Use the remaining icing to coat the tops and sides of the cakes.

4 Place the cakes on the cake boards. Generously cover the tops and sides of the cakes with the chocolate curls, pressing them gently into the butter icing.

5 Sift a little confectioner's sugar over the top of each cake and decorate with raspberries. Chill until ready to serve.

Sweetheart Cake

Makes one 8-inch heart-shape cake

8-inch heart-shape light
   fruit cake
2 tablespoons apricot
   jam, warmed and
   strained
6 cups marzipan
6 cups fondant icing
red food coloring
1½ cups royal icing

Materials/equipment
10-inch silver heart-
   shape cake board
large and medium heart-
   shape plunger cutters
1 yard red ribbon,
   1 inch wide
1 yard looped red ribbon,
   ½ inch wide
½ yard red ribbon,
   ¼ inch wide
wax paper icing bag
medium star nozzle
fresh red rosebud

1 Brush the cake with apricot jam, place on the cake board and cover with marzipan. Cover the cake and board with fondant icing. Let dry overnight.

2 Tint the fondant icing red. Cut 18 large and 21 medium-size hearts. Let dry on wax paper.

3 Secure the wide ribbon around the cake board. Secure a band of the looped ribbon around the side of the cake with a bead of icing. Tie a bow with long tails and attach to the side of the cake with a bead of icing.

4 Using the star nozzle, pipe a row of royal icing stars around the bottom of the cake and attach a medium-size heart to every third star. Pipe stars around the cake top, and arrange large red hearts on each one.

5 Tie a bow onto the rosebud stem and place on the cake top just before serving.

Cloth-of-Roses Cake

This cake simply says "congratulations." It is a very pretty cake that is bound to impress your guests.

Makes one 8-inch round cake

8-inch round light fruit cake

3 tablespoons apricot jam, warmed and strained

4½ cups marzipan

6 cups fondant icing yellow, orange and green food coloring

¾ cup royal icing

Materials/equipment

10-inch cake board

2¼-inch plain cutter

petal cutter

thin yellow ribbon

1 Brush the cake with apricot jam. Cover with marzipan and let dry overnight.

2 Cut off 4½ cups of the fondant icing and divide in half. Color pale yellow and pale orange.

3 Make a wax paper template for the orange icing by drawing a 10-inch circle around the cake board then, using the plain cutter, draw scallops around the circle.

4 Cover the cake side with yellow fondant icing. Place the cake on the board. Using the template, cut out the orange fondant icing. Place on the cake and bend the scallops slightly. Let dry overnight.

5 For the roses and leaves, cut off three-quarters of the remaining fondant icing and divide into four. Tint pale yellow, deep yellow, orange, and marbled yellow and orange. Make 18 roses. Tint the remaining icing green, then cut out 24 leaves with a petal cutter. Dry on wax paper.

6 Secure the leaves and roses with royal icing. Decorate the cake with the ribbon.

Rose Blossom Wedding Cake

Serves 80

9-inch square rich fruit cake

6-inch square rich fruit cake

5 tablespoons apricot jam, warmed and strained

10½ cups marzipan

10½ cups royal icing, to coat

4½ cups royal icing, to pipe

pink and green food coloring

Materials/equipment

11-inch square cake board

8-inch square cake board

No 1 writing and No 42 nozzles

wax paper icing bags

thin pink ribbon

8 pink bows

3–4 cake pillars

12 miniature roses

few fern sprigs

1 Brush the cakes with the jam and cover with marzipan. Let dry overnight, then secure to their boards with icing. Flat-ice the cakes with three or four layers, letting each dry overnight. Dry for several days.

2 For the sugar pieces, use the No 1 writing nozzle to pipe the double-triangle design in white icing on wax paper. You will need 40 pieces, but make extra. Tint some icing pale pink and some very pale green. Using No 1 writing nozzles, pipe pink dots on the corners of the top triangles and green on the corners of the lower triangles. Let dry.

3 Use a pin to mark out the triangles on the tops and sides of each cake. Using a No 1 writing nozzle, pipe double white lines over the pin marks, then pipe cornelli inside all the triangles. With a No 42 nozzle, pipe white shells around the top and bottom edges of each cake, between the triangles.

4 Using No 1 writing nozzles, pipe pink and green dots on the cake corners. Secure the sugar pieces to the cakes and boards with icing. Attach the ribbons and bows. Assemble the cake with the pillars and decorate with roses and fern sprigs.

Basketweave Wedding Cake

This wonderful wedding cake can be made in any flavor.

Serves 150
10-inch, 8-inch and
  6-inch square Madeira
  cakes
12 cups butter icing

Materials/equipment
12-inch square silver
  cake board
8-inch and 6-inch thin
  silver cake board
smooth scraper

12 small wax paper icing
  bags
No 4 writing and
  basketweave nozzles
1½ yards pale lilac
  ribbon, 1 inch wide
2½ yards deep lilac
  ribbon, ¼ inch wide
30 fresh lilac-colored
  freesias

1 Level the cake tops, then invert the cakes onto the boards and cover with butter icing. Use a smooth scraper on the sides and a metal spatula to smooth the top. Let set for 1 hour.

2 Pipe a line of icing with the No 4 writing nozzle onto the corner of the large cake, from the bottom to the top. Using the basketweave nozzle, pipe a basketweave pattern (see above photograph). Pipe all around the side of the cake and neaten the top edge with a shell border, using the basketweave nozzle. Repeat for the second cake.

3 To decorate the top of the small cake, start at the edge with a straight plain line, then pipe across with the basketweave nozzle, spacing the lines equally apart. When the top is complete, work the design around the sides, making sure the top and side designs align. Let the cakes set overnight.

4 Fit the wide and narrow lilac ribbons around the board. Use the remaining narrow ribbon to tie eight small bows with long tails. Trim off the flower stems.

5 Assemble the cakes. Decorate with the bows and flowers.

Chocolate-iced Anniversary Cake

This attractive cake is special enough to celebrate any wedding anniversary.

Makes one 8-inch round cake
8-inch round Madeira
  cake
2¼ cups chocolate-flavor
  butter icing

For the chocolate icing
6 ounces semisweet
  chocolate
⅔ cup light cream
½ teaspoon instant coffee
  powder

To decorate
chocolate buttons,
  quartered

selection of fresh fruits,
  such as kiwi fruit,
  nectarines, peaches,
  apricots and
  gooseberries, peeled
  and sliced as necessary

Materials/equipment
No 22 star nozzle
wax paper icing bag
gold ribbon, about
  ¼ inch wide
florist's wire

1 Cut the cake horizontally into three and sandwich together with three-quarters of the butter icing. Place on a wire rack over a baking sheet.

2 To make the satin chocolate icing, put all of the ingredients in a saucepan and melt over very low heat until smooth. Immediately pour over the cake to coat completely. Use a metal spatula, if necessary. Allow to set.

3 Transfer the cake to a serving plate. Using a No 22 star nozzle, pipe butter icing scrolls around the top edge. Decorate with chocolate button pieces and fruit.

4 Make seven ribbon decorations. For each one, make two small loops from ribbon and secure the ends with a twist of florist's wire . Cut the wire to the length you want and use to position the decoration in the fruit. Remove before serving.

Silver Wedding Cake

Makes one 10-inch round cake

10-inch round rich or light fruit cake	**Materials/equipment**
4 tablespoons apricot jam, warmed and strained	12-inch round silver cake board
7½ cups marzipan	1½ yards white ribbon, 1 inch wide
9 cups royal icing	2 yards silver ribbon, 1 inch wide
	club cocktail cutter
For the petal paste	tiny round cutter
2 teaspoons gelatin	wax paper icing bag
5 tablespoons cold water	No 1 writing nozzle
2 teaspoons liquid glucose	50 large silver dragées
2 teaspoons white vegetable shortening	1½ yards silver ribbon, ¼ inch wide
4 cups confectioner's sugar, sifted	7 silver leaves
1 teaspoon gum tragacanth, sifted	"25" silver cake decoration
1 egg white	

1 Brush the cake with apricot jam and cover with marzipan. Place on the board. Flat-ice the top and side of the cake with three or four layers of royal icing. Let dry overnight, then ice the board. Reserve the remaining royal icing. Secure the wider ribbons around the board and cake with icing.

2 For the petal paste, melt the first four ingredients in a bowl set over a pan of hot water. Mix the sugar, gum tragacanth, egg white and gelatin mixture to a paste and knead until smooth. Let stand for 2 hours, then re-knead. Make 65 cut-outs using the two cutters. Let dry overnight.

3 Arrange 25 cut-outs around the top and secure with icing beads piped with a No 1 writing nozzle. Repeat at the bottom. Pipe icing beads between and press a dragée in each. Let dry. Thread the thin ribbon through. Arrange seven cut-outs and seven dragées in the center. Position the leaves and "25."

Golden Wedding Heart Cake

Makes one 9-inch round cake

4 tablespoons apricot jam	pins
9-inch round rich fruit cake	small heart-shape plunger tool
6 cups marzipan	3-inch plain cutter
6 cups fondant icing	dual large and small blossom cutter
cream food coloring	stamens
¾ cup royal icing	frill cutter
	wooden toothpick
Materials/equipment	foil-wrapped chocolate hearts
11-inch round cake board	
crimping tool	

1 Warm, then strain the apricot jam and brush over the cake. Cover with marzipan and let dry overnight.

2 Tint 4½ cups of the fondant icing very pale cream and cover the cake. Put on the board. Crimp the top edge. With pins, mark eight equidistant points around the top edge. Crimp slanting lines to the bottom. Emboss the bottom edge with the plunger. Use the plain cutter to emboss a circle on top.

3 Divide the remaining fondant icing into two and tint cream and pale cream. Using half of each color, make flowers with the blossom cutter. Make pinholes in the large flowers. Let dry, then secure the stamens in the holes with royal icing.

4 Make eight frills with the rest of the fondant icing using the frill cutter, and a toothpick to trim and fill the edges. Attach the frills with water next to the crimped lines on the cake side. Crimp the edges of the deeper colored frills.

5 Secure the flowers on the top and sides of the cake with royal icing. Place the chocolate hearts in the center.

Marzipan Bell Cake

This cake can be easily adapted to make a christening cake if you leave out the holly decorations.

Makes one 7-inch round cake

7-inch round rich or light
fruit cake
2 tablespoons apricot
jam, warmed and
strained
6 cups marzipan
green, yellow and red
food coloring

Materials/equipment
8-inch round silver cake
board
crimping tool
bell and holly leaf cutter
1 yard red ribbon,
¾ inch wide
1 yard green ribbon,
¼ inch wide
¼ yard red ribbon,
¼ inch wide

1 Brush the cake with apricot jam and place on the cake board. Tint two-thirds of the marzipan pale green. Use to cover the cake. Crimp the top edge of the cake to make a scalloped pattern.

2 Tint a small piece of remaining marzipan bright yellow, another bright red and the rest bright green. Make two yellow bells and clappers, 11 green holly leaves (veins marked with the back of a knife), two green bell ropes, 16 red holly berries and two bell-rope ends. Let dry.

3 Secure the wide red and fine green ribbons around the side of the cake with a pin. Tie a double bow from red and green fine ribbon and attach to the side with a pin.

4 Arrange the bells, clappers, bell ropes, holly leaves and berries on top of the cake and secure with apricot jam.

Christening Sampler

Serves 30

8-inch square rich fruit
cake
3 tablespoons apricot
jam, warmed and
strained
3 cups marzipan
4½ cups fondant icing
brown, yellow, orange,
purple, cream, blue,
green and pink food
coloring

Materials/equipment
10-inch square cake
board
fine paintbrush
small heart-shape cookie
cutter

1 Brush the cake with apricot jam. Roll out the marzipan, cover the cake and let dry overnight. Roll out 1 cup of the fondant icing to fit the cake top. Brush the top with water and cover with the icing.

2 Color 2 cups of the icing brown and roll out four pieces to the length and about ½ inch wider than the cake sides. Brush the sides with water and cover with icing, folding over the extra width at the top and cutting the corners at an angle to make the picture frame. Place on a cake board. With a fine paintbrush, paint over the sides with watered-down brown food coloring to represent wood grain.

3 Take the remaining icing and color small amounts yellow, orange, brown, purple and cream and two shades of blue, green and pink. Leave some white. Use the colors to shape the ducks, teddy bear, bulrushes, water, branch and leaves. Cut out a pink heart and make the baby's initial from white icing.

4 Mix the white and pink icings together for the apple blossom flowers. Make the shapes for the border. Attach the decorations to the cake with a little water.

5 Use the leftover colors to make "threads." Arrange in loops around the bottom of the cake on the board.

Teddy Bear Christening Cake

To personalize the cake, make a simple plaque for the top and pipe on the name of the new baby.

Makes one 8-inch square cake

8-inch square light fruit
  cake
3 tablespoons apricot
  jam, warmed and
  strained
6 cups marzipan
5¼ cups fondant icing
peach, yellow, blue and
  brown food coloring
¾ cup royal icing

Materials/equipment
10-inch square cake
  board
crimping tool
cornstarch, for dipping
fine paintbrush
wooden toothpick
peach ribbon
small blue ribbon bow

1 Brush the cake with the apricot jam. Roll out the marzipan and use to cover the cake. Let dry overnight.

2 Color 3¾ cups of the fondant icing peach, then roll it out. Brush the marzipan with water and cover the cake with the icing. Place the cake on the board. Using a crimping tool dipped in cornstarch, crimp the top and bottom edges of the cake.

3 Divide the remaining fondant into three. Leave a third white and tint a third yellow. Divide the last third in two, tint one half peach and the other blue.

4 Make flowers from the peach and blue fondant. Let dry. Reserve the blue trimmings. Make a yellow teddy bear. Paint on its face with brown food coloring. Give it a blue button. Let dry. Make a blue blanket. Frill the white edge with a toothpick. Secure the frill to the blanket with water.

5 Decorate the cake with the ribbon, place the bear on top under its blanket, securing with royal icing. Secure the flowers and the bear's bow-tie in the same way.

Daisy Christening Cake

A ring of daisies sets off this pretty pink christening cake.

Makes one 8-inch round cake

8-inch round rich fruit
  cake
3 tablespoons apricot
  jam, warmed and
  strained
4½ cups marzipan
6 cups royal icing
¾ cup fondant icing
pink and yellow food
  coloring

Materials/equipment
10-inch round cake board
fine paintbrush
2-inch fluted cutter
wooden toothpick
2 wax paper icing bags
No 42 nozzle
pink and white ribbon

1 Brush the cake with the apricot jam. Roll out the marzipan and use to cover the cake. Let dry overnight.

2 Use a little royal icing to secure the cake to the board. Tint three-quarters of the royal icing pink. Flat-ice the cake with three or four layers, using white for the top and pink for the side. Let each layer dry overnight before applying the next. Set aside a little of both icings in airtight containers.

3 Make 28 daisies. For each daisy, shape a small piece of fondant icing to look like a golf tee. Snip the edges and curl them slightly. Dry on wax paper. Trim the stems and paint the edges pink and the centers yellow.

4 To make the plaque, roll out the remaining fondant icing and cut out a circle with the fluted cutter. Roll a toothpick around the edge until it frills. Dry on wax paper, then paint the name and the edges with pink food coloring.

5 Pipe twisted ropes around the top and bottom of the cake with the reserved white royal icing. Then pipe a row of stars around the top of the cake. Stick the plaque in the center with royal icing. Stick on the daisies and decorate with the ribbons.

Birthday Package

Serves 10

6-inch square Madeira
  cake
1⅓ cups orange-flavor
  butter icing
3 tablespoons apricot
  jam, warmed and
  strained
3 cups fondant icing
blue, orange and green
  food coloring

confectioner's sugar, for
  dusting

Materials/equipment
7–8-inch square cake
  board
small triangular and
  round cocktail cutters

1 Cut the cake in half horizontally and sandwich together with the butter icing. Brush the cake with apricot jam. Color three-quarters of the fondant icing blue. Divide the remaining fondant icing in half and color one half orange and the other half green. Wrap the orange and green fondant separately in plastic wrap and set aside. Roll out the blue icing on a work surface lightly dusted with confectioner's sugar and use it to cover the cake. Position on the cake board.

2 While the fondant covering is still soft, use the cocktail cutters to cut out triangles and circles from the blue icing, lifting out the shapes to expose the cake.

3 Roll out the orange and green icings and cut out circles and triangles to fill the exposed holes in the blue icing. Roll out the trimmings and cut three orange strips, ¾ inch wide and long enough to go over the corner of the cake, and three very thin green strips the same length as the orange ones. Place the strips next to each other to make three striped ribbons, and secure the pieces together with a little water.

4 Place one striped ribbon over one corner of the cake, securing with a little water. Place a second strip over the opposite corner. Cut the remaining ribbon in half. Bend each half to make loops and attach both to one corner of the cake with water to form a loose bow.

Chocolate Fruit Birthday Cake

The marzipan fruits on this moist chocolate Madeira cake make an eye-catching decoration.

Makes one 7-inch square cake

7-inch square deep
  chocolate Madeira
  cake
3 tablespoons apricot
  jam, warmed and
  strained
3 cups marzipan
2 cups chocolate fudge
  icing
red, yellow, orange, green
  and purple food
  coloring

whole cloves
angelica strips

Materials/equipment
8-inch square silver cake
  board
medium gâteau nozzle
nylon icing bag
¾ yard yellow ribbon,
  ½ inch wide

1 Level the cake top and invert. Brush with apricot jam.

2 Use two-thirds of the marzipan to cover the cake. Reserve the trimmings.

3 Place the cake on a wire rack over a tray and pour three-quarters of the chocolate fudge icing over, spreading with a metal spatula. Let stand for 10 minutes, then place on the cake board.

4 Using the reserved icing and a medium-size gâteau nozzle, pipe stars around the top edge and bottom of the cake. Let set.

5 Using the reserved marzipan, food coloring, cloves and angelica strips, model a selection of fruits.

6 Secure the ribbon around the sides of the cake. Decorate the top with the marzipan fruits.

Eighteenth Birthday Cake

A really striking cake for an eighteenth birthday. Change the shape if you cannot hire the pan.

Serves 80

13½ x 8-inch diamond-
  shape deep rich or
  light fruit cake
3 tablespoons apricot
  jam, warmed and
  strained
7½ cups marzipan
10½ cups fondant
black food coloring
2 tablespoons royal icing

Materials/equipment
15 x 9-inch diamond-
  shape cake board
"18" template
small wax paper icing
  bag
No 1 writing nozzle
2 yards white ribbon,
  1 inch wide
2 yards black ribbon,
  ⅛ inch wide

1   Make the cake using quantities for a 9-inch round cake. Brush with apricot jam. Cover in marzipan. Place on the cake board. Cover the cake using 7½ cups fondant icing. Knead the trimmings into the remaining fondant and tint black.

2   Use two-thirds of the black fondant to cover the board.

3   Use a quarter of the remaining fondant to cut out a number "18" using a template. Use the rest to cut out a variety of bow ties, wine glasses and music notes. Let dry on wax paper.

4   Tint the royal icing black. Using a No 1 writing nozzle, attach the cut-outs to the cake top and sides.

5   Tie four small bows with the black ribbon. Secure with icing to the top corners. Position and secure black ribbon around the cake bottom and white ribbon around the board.

Flickering Birthday Candle Cake

Flickering, stripy candles are ready to blow out on this birthday cake for all ages.

Makes one 8-inch square cake

8-inch square Madeira
  cake
1½ cups butter icing
3 tablespoons apricot
  jam, warmed and
  strained
5¼ cups fondant icing
pink, yellow, purple and
  jade food coloring
edible silver balls

Materials/equipment
9-inch square cake board
small round cutter
pink and purple food
  coloring pens
¼-inch wide jade-colored
  ribbon

1   Cut the cake into three layers. Sandwich together with the butter icing and brush the cake with the apricot jam. Roll out 3¾ cups of the fondant icing and use to cover the cake. Position on the cake board.

2   Divide the remaining fondant into four pieces and tint them pink, yellow, pale purple and jade.

3   Make the candles from jade and the flames from yellow icing. Press a silver ball into their bases. Position the candles and flames on the cake with a little water. Mold strips in yellow and purple icing to go around the candles. Secure with water. Cut small, wavy pieces from the pink and purple icing for smoke, and arrange them, using water, above the candles.

4   Cut out yellow circles with the cutter for the side decorations. Mold small pink balls and press a silver ball into their centers. Attach using water.

5   Using food coloring pens, draw wavy lines and dots coming from the purple and pink wavy icings. Decorate the sides of the cake board with the ribbon, securing at the back with a little softened fondant.

Flower Birthday Cake

A simple birthday cake decorated with piped yellow and white flowers and ribbons.

Makes one 7-inch round cake

7-inch round light fruit
cake
2 tablespoons apricot
jam, warmed and
strained
4½ cups marzipan
7½ cups royal icing
yellow and orange food
coloring

Materials/equipment
9-inch round silver cake
board
petal nozzle, Nos 1 and
2 writing nozzles, and
medium star nozzle
wax paper icing bags
1 yard white ribbon,
¾ inch wide
2 yards coral ribbon,
½ inch wide
10-inch coral ribbon,
¼ inch wide

1 Brush the cake with apricot jam and cover with marzipan. Place on the board.

2 Flat-ice the top and side of the cake with three layers of royal icing. Let dry, then ice the board. Reserve the remaining royal icing.

3 Tint one-third of the reserved royal icing yellow and 1 tablespoon of it orange. Using the petal nozzle for the petals and No 1 writing nozzle for the centers, make four white narcissi with yellow centers and nine yellow narcissi with orange centers. Make nine plain white flowers with a snipped icing bag with yellow centers. When dry, secure to the top.

4 Use the star nozzle to pipe shell edgings to the cake top and bottom. Pipe "Happy Birthday" using the No 2 writing nozzle. Overlay in orange using the No 1 writing nozzle.

5 Secure the ribbons around the board and cake side. Finish with a coral bow.

Jazzy Chocolate Gâteau

This cake is made with Father's Day in mind, though you can make it for anyone who loves chocolate.

Serves 12–15

2 x quantity chocolate-
flavor quick-mix
sponge cake mix
3 squares semisweet
chocolate
3 squares white chocolate
6 ounces fudge frosting
1 cup glacé icing
1 teaspoon weak coffee

8 tablespoons chocolate
hazelnut spread

Materials/equipment
2 x 8-inch round cake
pans
wax paper icing bag
No 1 writing nozzle

1 Preheat the oven to 325°F. Grease the cake pans, line the bottoms with wax paper and grease the paper. Divide the cake mixture evenly between the pans and smooth the surfaces. Bake in the center of the oven for 20–30 minutes, or until firm to the touch. Turn out onto a wire rack, peel off the lining paper and let cool.

2 Melt the chocolates in two separate bowls, pour onto parchment paper and spread evenly. As it begins to set, place another sheet of parchment paper on top and turn the chocolate "sandwich" over. When set, peel off the paper and turn the chocolate sheets over. Cut out haphazard shapes of chocolate and set aside.

3 Sandwich the two cakes together with fudge frosting. Place the cake on a plate. Color the glacé icing using the weak coffee and add enough water to form a spreading consistency. Spread the icing on top of the cake almost to the edges. Cover the side of the cake with chocolate hazelnut spread.

4 Press the chocolate pieces around the side of the cake and, using an icing bag fitted with a No 1 nozzle, decorate the top of the cake with "jazzy" lines over the glacé icing.

Petal Retirement Cake

Makes one 8-inch petal-shape cake

8-inch petal-shape deep
   light fruit cake
3 tablespoons apricot
   jam, warmed and
   strained
6 cups marzipan
mulberry and pink food
   coloring
6 cups fondant icing
10 ounces petal paste
1 tablespoon royal icing

Materials/equipment
9-inch petal-shape silver
   cake board

foam sponge
large and small blossom
   plunger cutters
2 yards white ribbon,
   ¾ inch wide
2 yards fuchsia ribbon,
   ½ inch wide
2 yards fuchsia ribbon,
   ⅛ inch wide
wax paper icing bag
No 1 writing nozzle
pink food coloring pen
fresh flowers

1   Brush the cake with jam and put on the board. Cover with marzipan. Knead mulberry coloring into the fondant icing. Use to cover the cake and board. Dry overnight.

2   Tint the petal paste with pink coloring. Roll and cut out a 2 x 1-inch rectangle. Fold in half and dry over a foam sponge to make the card. Make holes in the top edges of the fold for the ribbon. Cut out 30 large and four small plunger blossom flowers. Let dry.

3   Using the royal icing and a No 1 writing nozzle, secure the white and narrow fuchsia ribbons around the board and the medium ribbon around the cake bottom. Tie six small bows from the narrow ribbon for the base.

4   Attach the large flowers to the side of the cake with icing. Secure the small flowers to the board. Draw a design and write a message inside the card with the pen. Thread ribbon through the holes and tie a bow. Place on the cake top with the fresh flowers.

Pansy Retirement Cake

You can use other edible flowers such as nasturtiums, roses or tiny daffodils for this cake, if you prefer.

Makes one 8-inch round cake

8-inch round light fruit
   cake
3 tablespoons apricot
   jam, warmed and
   strained
4½ cups marzipan
7½ cups royal icing
orange food coloring
about 7 sugar-frosted
   pansies (orange and
   purple)

Materials/equipment
10-inch round cake board
2 wax paper icing bags
No 19 star and No 1
   writing nozzles
¾-inch wide purple
   ribbon
⅛-inch wide dark purple
   ribbon

1   Brush the cake with the apricot jam. Roll out the marzipan and use to cover the cake. Let dry overnight.

2   Secure the cake to the cake board with a little royal icing. Tint a quarter of the royal icing pale orange. Flat-ice the cake with three layers of smooth icing. Use the orange icing for the top and the white for the sides. Set aside a little of both icings in airtight containers for decoration.

3   Spoon the reserved white royal icing into a wax paper icing bag fitted with a No 19 star nozzle. Pipe a row of scrolls around the cake top. Pipe a second row directly underneath the first row in the reverse direction. Pipe another row of scrolls around the bottom of the cake.

4   Spoon the reserved orange icing into a fresh icing bag fitted with a No 1 writing nozzle. Pipe around the outline of the top of each scroll. Pipe a row of single orange dots below the lower row of reverse scrolls at the top and a double row of dots above the bottom row of scrolls. Arrange the pansies on top of the cake. Decorate the side with the ribbons.

Halloween Pumpkin Patch Cake

Celebrate Halloween with this fall-colored cake, colorfully decorated with fondant pumpkins.

Makes one 8-inch round cake

generous 1 cup fondant
   icing
brown and orange food
   coloring
2 x 8-inch round
   chocolate sponge cakes
3 cups orange-flavor
   butter icing
chocolate chips
angelica

Materials/equipment
wooden toothpick
fine paintbrush
9-inch round cake board
serrated scraper
No 7 writing nozzle
wax paper icing bag

1 For the pumpkins, tint a very small piece of the fondant icing brown, and the rest orange. Shape some balls of the orange icing the size of walnuts and some a bit smaller. Make ridges with a toothpick. Make stems from the brown icing and secure with water. Paint highlights on the pumpkins in orange. Let dry on wax paper.

2 Cut both cakes in half horizontally. Use a quarter of the butter icing to sandwich the cakes together. Place the cake on the board. Use two-thirds of the remaining icing to cover the cake. Texture the icing with a serrated scraper.

3 Using a No 7 writing nozzle, pipe a twisted rope pattern around the top and bottom edges of the cake with the remaining butter icing. Decorate with chocolate chips.

4 Cut the angelica into diamond shapes and arrange on the cake with the pumpkins.

Fudge-frosted Starry Roll

Whether it's for a birthday or another occasion, this sumptuous-looking cake is sure to please.

Makes one 13-inch long roll

9 x 13-inch jelly roll
   sponge
¾ cup chocolate butter
   icing
2 ounces white chocolate
2 ounces semisweet
   chocolate

3 cups confectioner's
   sugar, sifted
6 tablespoons butter or
   margarine
4½ tablespoons milk or
   light cream
1½ teaspoons vanilla
   extract

For the fudge frosting

3 ounces semisweet
   chocolate, broken into
   pieces

Materials/equipment
small star cutter
wax paper icing bags
No 19 star nozzle

1 Unroll the sponge and spread with the butter icing. Re-roll and set aside.

2 For the decorations, melt the white chocolate in a bowl set over a pan of hot water and spread onto a non-porous surface. Let firm, then cut out stars with the cutter. Let set on wax paper. To make lace curls, melt the semisweet chocolate and then cool slightly. Cover a rolling pin with wax paper. Pipe zigzags on the paper and let cool on the rolling pin.

3 For the frosting, stir all the ingredients over low heat until melted. Remove from the heat and beat frequently until cool and thick. Cover the cake with two-thirds of the frosting, swirling with a metal spatula.

4 With a No 19 star nozzle, use the remaining frosting to pipe diagonal lines on the cake.

5 Position the lace curls and stars. Transfer the cake to a serving plate and decorate with more stars.

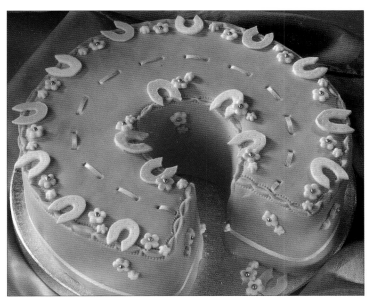

Lucky Horseshoe Cake

This horseshoe-shape cake, made to wish "good luck", is made from a round cake and the shape is then cut out.

Makes one 10-inch horseshoe cake

10-inch rich fruit cake
4 tablespoons apricot
  jam, warmed and
  strained
5¼ cups marzipan
6¾ cups fondant icing
peach and blue food
  coloring
edible silver balls
¾ cup royal icing

Materials/equipment
12-inch round cake board
crimping tool
pale blue ribbon, ⅛ inch
  wide
scalpel
large and small blossom
  cutters

1 Make a horseshoe template and use to shape the cake. Brush the cake with the apricot jam. Roll out 2¼ cups of the marzipan to a 10-inch circle. Using the template, cut out the shape and place on the cake. Measure the inside and outside of the cake. Cover with the remaining marzipan. Place the cake on the board and let stand overnight.

2 Tint 5¼ cups of the fondant icing peach. Cover the cake in the same way. Crimp the top edge.

3 Draw and measure the ribbon insertion on the template. Cut 13 pieces of ribbon fractionally longer than each slit. Make the slits through the template with a scalpel. Insert the ribbon with a painted tool. Let dry overnight.

4 Make a small horseshoe template. Tint half the remaining fondant icing pale blue. Using the template, cut out nine blue shapes. Mark each horseshoe with a sharp knife. Cut out 12 large and 15 small blossoms. Press a silver ball into the centers of the larger blossoms. Let dry. Repeat with the white icing. Decorate the cake and board with the ribbon, horseshoes and blossoms, securing with royal icing.

Bluebird Bon-voyage Cake

This cake is sure to see someone off on an exciting journey in a very special way.

Makes one 8-inch round cake

3 cups royal icing
blue food coloring
5¼ cups fondant icing
8-inch round Madeira
  cake
1½ cups butter icing
3 tablespoons apricot
  jam, warmed and
  strained
edible silver balls

Materials/equipment
No 1 writing nozzle
wax paper icing bags
10-inch round cake board
thin pale blue ribbon

1 Make two-thirds of the royal icing softer to use for the run-outs. Make the rest stiffer for the outlines and piping. Tint the softer icing bright blue. Cover and let stand overnight.

2 Make two bird templates in different sizes, and use to pipe the run-outs on wax paper. Using a No 1 writing nozzle, pipe the outlines, and then fill in. You need four large and five small birds. Let dry for at least 2 days.

3 Tint two-thirds of the fondant icing blue. Form all the icing into small rolls and place them alternately together on a work surface. Form into a round and lightly knead to marble.

4 Cut the cake horizontally into three and sandwich together with the butter icing. Place the cake on the board, flush with an edge, and brush with apricot jam. Roll out the marbled icing and use to cover the cake and board.

5 Using the No 1 writing nozzle and the stiffer royal icing, pipe a wavy line around the edge of the board. Position the balls evenly in the icing. Secure the birds to the cake with royal icing. Pipe beads of white icing for eyes and stick on a ball. Drape the ribbon between the beaks, securing with icing.

Ghost Cake

This children's cake is really simple to make yet very effective. It is ideal for a Hallowe'en party.

Serves 15–20
6 cups fondant icing
black food coloring
2 Madeira cakes, baked in a 7-inch square cake pan and a 1¼-cup ovenproof bowl

1½ cups butter icing

Materials/equipment
9-inch round cake board
fine paintbrush

1 Tint ¾ cup of the fondant icing dark gray and use to cover the cake board.

2 Cut two small corners off the large cake. Cut two larger wedges off the other two corners, then stand the cake on the board. Divide the larger trimmings in half and wedge around the bottom of the cake.

3 Secure the small cake to the top of the larger cake with butter icing. Completely cover both of the cakes with the remaining butter icing.

4 Roll out the remaining fondant icing to a 20 x 12-inch oval shape. Lay it over the cake, letting the icing fall into folds around the sides. Gently smooth the icing over the top half of the cake and trim off any excess.

5 Using black food coloring and a fine paintbrush, paint two oval eyes onto the head.

Cat-in-a-Basket Cake

Makes one 6-inch round cake
5¼ cups marzipan
red, green, yellow and brown food coloring
6-inch round deep sponge cake
2 tablespoons apricot jam, warmed and strained

4 tablespoons butter icing
4 tablespoons white fondant icing

Materials/equipment
8-inch round cake board
fine paintbrush

1 Tint 2 cups of the marzipan pink. Divide the rest in half and tint one half green and the other yellow. Brush the cake with the apricot jam and place it on the board.

2 Roll out the pink marzipan to a 6 x 10-inch rectangle. Cut five ½-inch wide strips, about 9½ inches long, keeping them attached to the rectangle at one end. Roll out the green marzipan and cut it into 3-inch lengths of the same width. Fold back alternate pink strips and lay a green strip across widthwise. Bring the pink strips over the green strip to form the weave. Keep repeating the process until the entire length is woven. Press lightly to join. Repeat with the rest of the rectangle and more strips of green marzipan.

3 Press the two pieces of basketweave onto the side of cake, joining them neatly. Model a yellow marzipan cat about 3 inches across. Let dry overnight.

4 Roll out the fondant icing and place on the center of the cake. Put the cat on top and arrange the icing in folds around it. Trim the edges neatly.

5 Make long ropes from any leftover pink and green marzipan. Twist together and press onto the top edge of the cake. Paint the cat's features in brown food coloring.

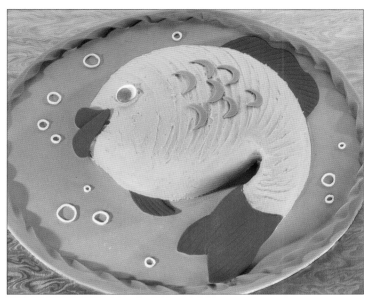

Fish-shaped Cake

A very easy, but colorful cake, perfect for a small child's birthday party.

Makes one fish-shape cake

3 cups fondant icing
blue, orange, red, mauve
  and green food
  coloring
sponge cake, baked in a
  15-cup ovenproof bowl
1½ cups butter icing
1 blue Smartie

Materials/equipment
large oval cake board
1-inch plain cookie cutter
wax paper icing bag

1 Tint two-thirds of the fondant icing blue, roll out very thinly and use to cover the dampened cake board.

2 Invert the cake and trim into the fish shape. Slope the sides. Place on the cake board.

3 Tint all but 1 tablespoon of the butter icing orange. Use to cover the cake, smoothing with a metal spatula. Score curved lines for scales, starting from the tail end.

4 Tint half the remaining fondant icing red. Shape and position two lips. Cut out the tail and fins. Mark with lines using a knife and position on the fish. Make the eye from white fondant and the blue Smartie.

5 Tint a little fondant mauve, cut out crescent-shape scales using a cookie cutter and place on the fish. Tint the remaining fondant green and cut into long thin strips. Twist each strip and arrange around the board.

6 To make the bubbles around the fish, place the reserved butter icing in an icing bag, snip off the end and pipe small circles onto the board.

Pink Monkey Cake

This cheeky little monkey could be made in any color icing you wish.

Makes one 8-inch cake

8-inch round sponge cake
½ cup butter icing
3 tablespoons apricot
  jam, warmed and
  strained
3 cups marzipan
scant 3¾ cups fondant
  icing

red, blue and black food
  coloring

Materials/equipment
10-inch round cake board
2 candles and holders

1 Trace the outline and paws of the monkey from the photograph. Enlarge to fit the cake and cut a template.

2 Split and fill the cake with butter icing. Place on the cake board and use the template to cut out the basic shape of the monkey. Use the trimmings to shape the nose and tummy. Brush with apricot jam and cover with a layer of marzipan.

3 Tint 3 cups of the fondant icing pale pink and use to cover the cake. Let dry overnight.

4 Mark the position of the face and paws. Tint a little of the fondant icing blue and use for the eyes. Tint a little icing black and cut out the pupils and tie.

5 Tint the remaining fondant icing dark pink and cut out the nose, mouth, ears and paws. Stick all the features in place with water. Roll the trimmings into balls and place on the board to hold the candles.

Porcupine Cake

Melt-in-the-mouth strips of chocolate flake give this porcupine its spiky coating.

Serves 15–20

2 chocolate sponge cakes,
  baked in a 5-cup and a
  2½-cup ovenproof
  bowl
2½ cups chocolate-flavor
  butter icing
cream, black, green,
  brown and red food
  coloring

5–6 chocolate flakes
⅓ cup white marzipan

Materials/equipment
14-inch long rectangular
  cake board
wooden toothpick
fine paintbrush

1 Use the smaller cake for the head and shape a pointed nose at one end. Reserve the trimmed wedges.

2 Place the cakes side-by-side on the board, inverted, and use the trimmings to fill in the sides and top where they meet. Secure with butter icing.

3 Cover the cake with the remaining butter icing and mark the nose with a toothpick.

4 Make the spikes by breaking the chocolate flakes into thin strips and sticking them into the butter icing all over the body part of the porcupine.

5 Reserve a small portion of marzipan. Divide the remainder into three, and tint cream, black and green. Tint a tiny portion of the reserved marzipan brown. Shape cream ears and feet, black-and-white eyes, and black claws and nose. Arrange all the features on the cake. Make green apples and highlight in red with a fine paintbrush. Make the stalks from the brown marzipan and push them into the apples.

Mouse-in-Bed Cake

This cake is suitable for almost any age. Make the mouse well in advance to give it time to dry.

Makes one 8 x 6-inch cake

8-inch square sponge
  cake
½ cup butter icing
3 tablespoons apricot
  jam, warmed and
  strained
3 cups marzipan
4½ cups fondant icing
blue and red food
  coloring

Materials/equipment
10-inch square cake
  board
flower cutter
blue and red food
  coloring pens

1 Cut 2 inches off one side of the cake. Split and fill the main cake with butter icing. Place on the cake board, brush with apricot jam and cover with a layer of marzipan. With the cake off-cut, shape a hollowed pillow, the torso and the legs of the mouse. Cover with marzipan and let dry overnight.

2 Cover the cake and pillow with white fondant icing. Lightly frill the edge of the pillow with a fork. To make the valance, roll out 2¼ cups of fondant icing and cut into four 3-inch wide strips. Attach to the bed with water. Arrange the pillow and mouse body on the cake.

3 For the quilt, tint ½ cup of fondant icing blue and roll out to a 7-inch square. Mark with a diamond pattern and the flower cutter. Cover the mouse with the quilt.

4 Cut a 1 x 7½-inch white fondant icing strip for the sheet, mark the edge and place over the quilt, tucking it under at the top edge.

5 Tint 2 tablespoons of marzipan pink and make the head and paws of the mouse. Put the head on the pillow, tucked under the sheet, and the paws over the edge of the sheet. Use food coloring pens to draw on the face of the mouse.

Teddy's Birthday

Party Teddy Bear Cake

After all the pieces have been assembled and stuck into the cake with a little water, an icing smoother is very useful to flatten the design.

The teddy on this cake is built up with royal icing and colored coconut.

Makes one 8-inch round cake

8-inch round cake	**Materials/equipment**
½ cup butter icing	10-inch round cake board
3 tablespoons apricot jam, warmed and strained	small wax paper icing bags
2 cups marzipan	No 7 shell and No 7 star nozzles
3 cups fondant icing brown, red, blue and black food coloring	1½ yards red ribbon
¾ cup royal icing	2 candles and holders
edible silver balls	

Makes one 8-inch square cake

8-inch square sponge cake	**Materials/equipment**
½ cup butter icing	10-inch square cake board
3 tablespoons apricot jam, warmed and strained	2 small wax paper icing bags
3 cups marzipan	small red bow
2 cups white fondant icing	No 7 shell nozzle
½ cup dried coconut	1½ yards red ribbon
blue and black food coloring	6 candles and holders
¾ cup royal icing	

1 Split and fill the cake with butter icing. Place on the cake board and brush with apricot jam. Cover with a layer of marzipan then a layer of fondant icing. Using a template, mark the design on top of the cake.

2 Color a third of the remaining fondant icing pale brown. Color a piece pink, a piece red, some blue and a tiny piece black. Using the template, cut out the pieces and place in position on the cake. Stick down by lifting the edges carefully and brushing the undersides with a little water. Roll small ovals for the eyes and stick in place with the nose and eyebrows. Cut out a mouth and press flat.

3 Tie the ribbon around the cake. Color the royal icing blue and pipe the border around the bottom of the cake with the shell nozzle and tiny stars around the small cake with the star nozzle, inserting silver balls. Put the candles on the cake.

1 Cut the cake in half and sandwich together with butter icing. Place on the cake board and brush with apricot jam. Cover with a thin layer of marzipan and then white fondant icing. Let dry overnight. Using a template, carefully mark the position of the teddy onto the cake.

2 Put the coconut into a bowl and mix in a drop of blue coloring to color it pale blue. Spread a thin layer of royal icing within the outline of the teddy. Before the icing dries, sprinkle on some pale blue coconut and press it down lightly.

3 Roll out the fondant trimmings and cut out a nose, ears and paws. Stick in place with a little royal icing. Tint some royal icing black and pipe on the eyes, nose and mouth. Use the bow as a tie and stick it in place. Pipe a white royal icing border around the bottom of the cake, tie the ribbon around the cake and position the candles on top.

Iced Fancies

These cakes are ideal for a children's tea party. Premade cake decorating products may be used instead, if preferred.

Makes 16

½ cup butter, at room
    temperature
generous 1 cup superfine
    sugar
2 eggs, at room
    temperature
1½ cups all-purpose flour
¼ teaspoon salt
1½ teaspoons baking
    powder
½ cup milk
1 teaspoon vanilla
    extract

For the icing
2 large egg whites
3½ cups sifted
    confectioner's sugar
1–2 drops glycerine
juice of 1 lemon
food colorings
colored vermicelli, to
    decorate
candied lemon and
    orange slices, to
    decorate

1   Preheat the oven to 375°F. Line a 16-cup muffin tray with paper cases.

2   Cream the butter and sugar until light and fluffy. Add the eggs, 1 at a time, beating well after each addition. Sift over and stir in the flour, salt and baking powder, alternating with the milk. Add the vanilla extract.

3   Half-fill the cups and bake for about 20 minutes, or until the tops spring back when touched. Stand in the tray to cool for 5 minutes, then unmold onto a wire rack.

4   For the icing, beat the egg whites until stiff. Gradually add the sugar, glycerine and lemon juice, and beat for 1 minute.

5   Tint the icing with different food colorings. Ice the cakes.

6   Decorate the cakes with colored vermicelli and candied lemon and orange slices. Make freehand decorations using a paper icing bag.

Fairy Castle Cake

If the icing on this cake dries too quickly, dip a metal spatula into hot water to help smooth the surface.

Makes one castle-shape cake

8-inch round sponge cake
½ cup butter icing
3 tablespoons apricot
    jam, warmed and
    strained
4½ cups marzipan
8 mini jelly rolls
4½ cups royal icing
red, blue and green food
    coloring

jelly diamonds
4 ice cream cones
2 ice cream wafers
1 cup dried coconut
8 marshmallows

Materials/equipment
12-inch square cake
    board
wooden toothpick

1   Split and fill the cake with butter icing, place in the center of the board and brush with apricot jam. Cover with a layer of marzipan. Cover each of the jelly rolls with marzipan. Stick four of them around the cake and cut the other four in half.

2   Tint two-thirds of the royal icing pale pink and cover the cake. Ice the extra pieces of jelly roll and stick them around the top of the cake. Use a toothpick to score the walls with a brick pattern. Make windows on the corner towers from jelly diamonds. Cut the ice cream cones to make the tower spires and stick them in place. Let dry overnight.

3   Tint half the remaining royal icing pale blue and cover the cones. Use a fork to pattern the icing. Shape the wafers for the gates, stick to the cake and cover with blue icing. Use the back of a knife to mark planks.

4   Tint the coconut with a few drops of green coloring. Spread the board with the remaining royal icing and sprinkle over the coconut. Stick on the marshmallows with a little royal icing to make the small turrets.

Sailing Boat

For chocoholics, make this cake using chocolate sponge.

Makes one boat-shape cake

8-inch square sponge cake	**Materials/equipment**
1 cup butter icing	10-inch square cake board
1 tablespoon cocoa	rice paper
4 large chocolate flakes	blue and red powder tints
¾ cup royal icing	paintbrush
blue food coloring	plastic drinking straw
	wooden toothpick
	2 small cake ornaments

1 Split and fill the cake with half of the butter icing. Cut 2¾ inches from one side of the cake. Shape the larger piece to resemble the hull of a boat. Place diagonally across the cake board. Mix the cocoa into the remaining butter icing and spread evenly over the top and sides of the boat.

2 Make the rudder and tiller from short lengths of flake and place them at the stern of the boat. Split the rest of the flakes lengthwise and press onto the sides of the boat, horizontally, to resemble planks of wood. Sprinkle the crumbs over the top.

3 Cut two rice paper rectangles, one 5¾ x 6½ inches and the other 6 x 3 inches. Cut the bigger one in a gentle curve to make the large sail and the smaller one into a triangle. Brush a circle of blue powder tint onto the large sail. Wet the edges of the sails and stick onto the straw. Make a hole for the straw 3 inches from the bow of the boat and push into the cake.

4 Cut a rice paper flag and brush with red powder tint. Stick the flag onto a toothpick and insert into the top of the straw. Tint the royal icing blue and spread on the board in waves. Place the small ornaments on the boat.

Spiders' Web Cake

A spooky cake for any occasion, fancy dress or otherwise.

Makes one 2-pound cake

2-pound dome-shape lemon sponge cake	cocoa, for dusting
¾ cup lemon-flavor glacé icing	chocolate vermicelli
black and yellow food coloring	2–3 liquorice wheels, candy centers removed
	2 tablespoons fondant icing

For the spiders

4 ounces semisweet chocolate, broken into pieces	**Materials/equipment**
⅔ cup heavy cream	wax paper
3 tablespoons ground almonds	small wax paper icing bag
	wooden skewer
	8-inch cake board

1 Place the cake on wax paper. Tint 3 tablespoons of the glacé icing black. Tint the rest yellow and pour it over the cake, letting it run down the sides.

2 Fill an icing bag with the black icing and, starting at the center top, drizzle it around the cake in an evenly-spaced spiral. Finish the web by drawing downward through the icing with a skewer. When set, place on the cake board.

3 For the spiders, gently melt the chocolate with the cream, stirring frequently. Transfer to a bowl, let cool, then beat the mixture for 10 minutes, or until thick and pale. Stir in the ground almonds, then chill until firm enough to handle. Dust your hands with a little cocoa, then make walnut-size balls with the mixture. Roll the balls in chocolate vermicelli.

4 For the legs, cut the liquorice into 1½-inch lengths. Make holes in the sides of the spiders and insert the legs. For the spiders' eyes, tint a piece of fondant icing black and form into tiny balls. Make larger balls with white icing. Stick on using water. Arrange the spiders on and around the cake.

Toy Telephone Cake

The child's name could be piped in a contrasting color of icing, if you wish.

Makes one telephone-shaped cake

6-inch square sponge
  cake
¼ cup butter icing
2 tablespoons apricot
  jam, warmed and
  strained
2 cups marzipan
2 cups fondant icing
yellow, blue, red and
  black food coloring

liquorice strips
¾ cup royal icing

Materials/equipment
8-inch square cake board
piping nozzle
small wax paper icing
  bag
No 1 writing nozzle

1 Split and fill the cake with butter icing. Trim to the shape of a telephone. Round off the edges and cut a shallow groove where the receiver rests on the telephone. Place the cake on the board and brush with apricot jam.

2 Cover the cake with marzipan then fondant icing. Tint half the remaining fondant icing yellow, a small piece blue and the rest of the icing red. To make the dial, cut out a 3½-inch diameter circle in yellow and a 1½-inch diameter circle in blue. Stamp out 12 red discs for the numbers with the end of a piping nozzle and cut out a red receiver. Position on the cake with water.

3 Twist the liquorice around to form a curly cord and use royal icing to stick one end to the telephone and the other end to the receiver. Tint the royal icing black and pipe the numbers on the discs and the child's name on the telephone.

Bumble Bee Cake

The edible sugar flowers that are used to decorate this cake were bought premade.

Makes one bee-shape cake

8-inch round sponge cake
½ cup butter icing
3 tablespoons apricot
  jam, warmed and
  strained
2¼ cups marzipan
3¾ cups fondant icing
yellow, black, blue and
  red food coloring

¾ cup royal icing
1 cup dried coconut

Materials/equipment
10-inch square cake
  board
6 fondant daisies
1 paper doily
sticky tape
1 pipe cleaner

1 Split and fill the cake with butter icing. Cut in half to make semicircles, sandwich the halves together and stand upright on the cake board. Trim the ends to shape the head and tail. Brush with apricot jam and cover with a layer of marzipan. Tint 2¼ cups of the fondant icing yellow and cover the cake.

2 Tint ¾ cup of the fondant icing black. Roll out and cut three stripes, each 1 x 10 inches. Space evenly on the cake and stick on with water. Use the remaining icing to make the eyes and mouth, tinting the icing blue for the pupils and pink for the mouth. Stick on with water.

3 Tint the coconut with a drop of yellow coloring. Cover the cake board with royal icing then sprinkle with coconut. Place the daisies on the board.

4 To make the wings, cut the doily in half, wrap each half into a cone shape and stick together with sticky tape. Cut the pipe cleaner in half and stick the pieces into the cake, just behind the head. Place the wings over the pipe cleaners.

Toy Car Cake

You can add a personalized number plate with the child's name and age to the back of this car.

Makes one car-shape cake

8-inch round sponge cake	**Materials/equipment**
½ cup butter icing	10-inch round cake board
3 tablespoons apricot	wooden toothpick
jam, warmed and	cutters, 1½ inches and
strained	1 inch
3 cups marzipan	small wax paper icing
3¾ cups fondant icing	bag
yellow, red and black food	No 1 writing nozzle
coloring	2 candles and holders
2 tablespoons royal icing	
red and green candies	

1 Split and fill the cake with the butter icing. Cut in half and sandwich the halves together. Stand upright and slice off pieces to create the windscreen and bonnet. Place on the cake board and brush with apricot jam.

2 Cut a strip of marzipan to cover the top of the cake to level the joins. Then cover the cake all over with marzipan. Tint 3 cups of the fondant icing yellow and use to cover the cake. Let dry overnight.

3 Mark the outlines of the doors and windows onto the car with a toothpick.

4 Tint the remaining fondant icing red. Cut out four wheels with the larger cutter. Stick in place with water. Mark the hubs in the center of each wheel with the smaller cutter.

5 Tint the royal icing black and pipe over the outline marks of the doors and windows. Stick on candies for headlights with royal icing. Press the candles into candies and stick to the board with royal icing.

Fire Engine Cake

This jolly fire engine is simplicity itself as the decorations are mainly bought candies and novelties.

Makes one 8 x 4-inch cake

8-inch square sponge	4 tablespoons royal icing
cake	candies
½ cup butter icing	1 cup dried coconut
3 tablespoons apricot	
jam, warmed and	**Materials/equipment**
strained	10-inch round cake board
2¼ cups marzipan	small wax paper icing
3 cups fondant icing	bag
red, black and green food	No 2 plain nozzle
coloring	2 silver bells
liquorice strips	3 candles and holders

1 Split and fill the cake with the butter icing. Cut in half and sandwich one half on top of the other. Place on the cake board and brush with apricot jam.

2 Trim a thin wedge off the front edge to make a sloping windscreen. Cover with marzipan. Tint 2¼ cups of the fondant icing red and use to cover the cake.

3 For the ladder, cut the liquorice into two strips and some short pieces for the rungs. Tint half the royal icing black and use some to stick the ladder to the top of the cake. Roll out the remaining fondant icing, cut out windows and stick them on with a little water.

4 Pipe around the windows in black royal icing. Stick candies in place for headlights, lamps and wheels and stick the silver bells on the roof. Tint the coconut green, spread a little royal icing over the cake board and sprinkle with the coconut. Stick candies to the board with royal icing and press the candles into the candies.

Sandcastle Cake

Crushed digestive cookies make convincing-looking sand when used to cover this fun cake.

Makes one 6-inch round cake

2 x 6-inch round sponge
  cakes
½ cup butter icing
3 tablespoons apricot
  jam, warmed and
  strained
¾ cup digestive cookies
¾ cup royal icing
blue food coloring

shrimp-shape candies

Materials/equipment
10-inch square cake
  board
rice paper
plastic drinking straw
4 candles and holders

1 Split both of the cakes, then sandwich all the layers together with the butter icing. Place in the center of the cake board. Cut 1¼ inches off the top just above the filling and set aside. Shape the rest of the cake with slightly sloping sides.

2 Cut four 1¼-inch cubes from the reserved piece of cake. Stick on the cubes for the turrets and brush with apricot jam.

3 Crush the cookies and press through a sifter to make the "sand." Press some crushed cookies onto the cake, using a metal spatula to get a smooth finish.

4 Color some royal icing blue and spread on the board around the sandcastle to make a moat. Spread a little royal icing on the board around the outside edge of the moat and sprinkle on some crushed cookie.

5 To make the flag, cut a small rectangle of rice paper and stick onto half a straw with water. Push the end of the straw into the cake. Stick candles into each turret and arrange the shrimp-shape candies on the board.

Clown Face Cake

Kids love this happy clown whose frilly collar is surprisingly simple to make.

Makes one 8-inch cake

8-inch round sponge cake
½ cup butter icing
3 tablespoons apricot
  jam, warmed and
  strained
3 cups marzipan
3 cups fondant icing
¾ cup royal icing
edible silver balls
red, green, blue and black
  food coloring

Materials/equipment
10-inch round cake board
small wax paper icing
  bag
No 8 star nozzle
wooden toothpick
cotton wool
two candles and holders

1 Split and fill the cake with butter icing. Place on the cake board and brush with apricot jam. Cover with a thin layer of marzipan then with white fondant icing. Mark the position of the features. Pipe stars around the bottom of the cake with some royal icing, placing silver balls as you work, and let dry overnight.

2 Make a template for the face and features. Tint half the remaining fondant icing pink and cut out the face base. Tint and cut out all the features, rolling a sausage to make the mouth. Cut thin strands for the hair. Stick all the features and hair in place with a little water.

3 Tint the remaining fondant icing green. Cut three strips 1½ inches wide. Give each a scalloped edge and stretch by rolling a toothpick along it to make the frill. Stick on with water and arrange the frills, holding them in place with cotton wool until dry. Place the candles at the top of the head.

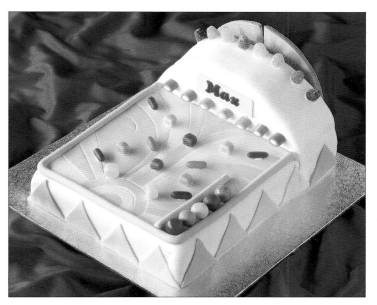

Pinball Machine

Serves 8–10

10-inch square sponge
   cake
1½ cups butter icing
3 tablespoons apricot
   jam, warmed and
   strained
3 cups marzipan
¾ cup royal icing
3 cups fondant icing
yellow, blue, green and
   red food coloring

candies
2 ice cream fan wafers

Materials/equipment
8-inch round cake tin
12-inch square cake
   board
small wax paper icing
   bag
No 1 writing nozzle

1 Split and fill the sponge cake with butter icing. Cut off a 2-inch strip from one side and reserve. Cut a thin wedge off the top of the cake, diagonally along its length, to end just above the halfway mark. This will give a sloping table.

2 Using the cake pan as a guide, cut the reserved strip of cake to make a rounded back for the pinball table. Brush the back and table with apricot jam, then cover separately with marzipan and place on the board. Stick them together with royal icing. Let dry overnight.

3 Cover with a layer of fondant icing and let dry. Use a template to mark out the pinball design on the top of the cake. Color the remaining fondant icing yellow, blue, green and pink. Roll out the colors and cut to fit the design. Stick on the pieces with water and smooth the joins carefully.

4 Using royal icing, stick candies on the cake as buffers, flippers, lights and knobs. Roll some blue fondant icing into a long sausage and edge the pinball table and divider. Cut zigzags for the sides and a screen for the back. Stick on with water. Stick the ice cream fans at the back of the screen. Load the pinball candies. Add the child's name on the screen with run-out letters or piping.

Pirate's Hat

If you prefer, buy premade black fondant icing rather than tinting it yourself.

Serves 8–10

10-inch round sponge
   cake
1 cup butter icing
3 tablespoons apricot
   jam, warmed and
   strained
3 cups marzipan
3¾ cups fondant icing
black and gold food
   coloring

chocolate money
jewel candies

Materials/equipment
12-inch square cake
   board
fine paint brush

1 Split and fill the cake with butter icing. Cut in half and sandwich the halves together. Stand upright diagonally across the cake board and cut shallow dips from each end to create the brim of the hat. Brush with apricot jam.

2 Cut a strip of marzipan to lay over the top of the cake. Then cover the whole of the cake with a layer of marzipan. Tint 3 cups of the fondant icing black. Use to cover the cake.

3 Roll out the remaining fondant icing and cut some ½-inch strips. Stick the strips in place with a little water around the brim of the pirate's hat and mark with the prongs of a fork to make a braid.

4 Make a skull and crossbones template and mark onto the hat. Cut the shapes out of the white fondant icing and stick in place with water. Paint the braid strip gold and arrange the chocolate money and jewel candies on the board.

Noah's Ark Cake

This charming cake is decorated with small animals, about 1½ inches high, available from cake decorating stores.

Makes one 8 x 5-inch cake

8-inch square sponge
  cake
½ cup butter icing
3 tablespoons apricot
  jam, warmed and
  strained
3 cups marzipan
3 cups fondant icing
brown, yellow and blue
  food coloring

¾ cup royal icing
chocolate mint stick

Materials/equipment
10-inch square cake
  board
skewer
rice paper flag
small animal cake
  ornaments

1 Split and fill the cake with butter icing. Cut off and set aside a 3-inch strip. Shape the remaining piece of cake to form the hull of the boat. Place diagonally on the cake board.

2 Cut a 4 x 2½-inch rectangle for the cabin from the set aside piece of cake and a triangular piece for the roof. Sandwich together with butter icing or apricot jam.

3 Cover the three pieces with a layer of marzipan. Tint the fondant icing brown and use most of it to cover the hull and cabin. Use the remaining brown icing to make a long sausage. Stick around the edge of the hull with water. Mark planks with the back of a knife. Let dry overnight.

4 Tint a third of the royal icing yellow and spread it over the cabin roof with a metal spatula. Roughen it with a skewer to create a thatch effect.

5 Tint the remaining royal icing blue and spread over the cake board, making rough waves. Stick a rice paper flag onto the chocolate mint stick and press on the back of the boat. Stick the small animals onto the boat with a dab of icing.

Balloons Cake

This is a simple yet effective cake design that can be adapted to suit any age.

Makes one 8-inch round cake

8-inch round cake
½ cup butter icing
3 tablespoons apricot
  jam, warmed and
  strained
3 cups marzipan
3 cups fondant icing
red, blue, green and
  yellow food coloring
¾ cup royal icing

Materials/equipment
10-inch round cake board
2 small wax paper icing
  bags
No 2 plain and No 7 star
  nozzles
1½ yards blue ribbon
3 candles and holders

1 Split and fill the cake with butter icing. Place on the cake board and brush with apricot jam. Cover with a layer of marzipan then fondant icing.

2 Divide the remaining fondant icing into three pieces and tint pink, blue and green. Make a balloon template, roll out the colored fondant and cut out one balloon from each color. Stick onto the cake with water and rub the edges gently to round them off.

3 Tint the royal icing yellow. With a plain nozzle, pipe on the balloon strings and a number on each balloon. Using the star nozzle, pipe a border around the bottom of the cake.

4 Tie the ribbon around the cake and place the candles on the top.

Horse Stencil Cake

Use a fairly dry brush when painting the design on this cake and allow each color to dry before adding the next.

Makes one 8-inch round cake

8-inch round sponge cake
½ cup butter icing
3 tablespoons apricot
    jam, warmed and
    strained
3 cups marzipan
3 cups fondant icing
yellow, brown, black, red,
    orange and blue food
    coloring

Materials/equipment
10-inch round cake board
spoon with decorative
    handle
fine paintbrush
horse and letter stencils
1½ yards blue ribbon
7 candles and holders

1   Split and fill the cake with butter icing. Place on the cake board and brush with apricot jam. Cover with a layer of marzipan. Tint the fondant icing yellow, roll out and use to cover the cake. Roll the trimmings into two thin ropes, long enough to go halfway around the cake. Brush water in a thin band around the bottom of the cake, lay on the ropes and press together. Pattern the border with the decorative spoon handle. Let dry overnight.

2   If you do not have a stencil, make one by tracing a simple design onto a thin piece of cardboard and cutting out the shape with a craft knife. Place the horse stencil in the center of the cake. With a fairly dry brush, gently paint over the parts you want to color first. Let these dry completely before adding another color, otherwise the colors will run into each other. Clean the stencil between colors.

3   When the horse picture is finished, carefully paint on the lettering. Tie the ribbon around the side of the cake and place the candles on top.

Doll's House Cake

Serves 8–10

10-inch square sponge
    cake
1 cup butter icing
3 tablespoons apricot
    jam, warmed and
    strained
3 cups marzipan
3 cups fondant icing
red, yellow, blue, black,
    green and gold food
    coloring
¾ cup royal icing

Materials/equipment
12-inch square cake
    board
pastry wheel
large and fine
    paintbrushes
wooden toothpick
small wax paper icing
    bags
No 2 writing nozzle
flower decorations

1   Split and fill the cake with butter icing. Cut triangles off two corners and use the pieces to make a chimney. Place on the cake board and brush with apricot jam. Cover with a layer of marzipan then fondant icing.

2   Mark the roof with a pastry wheel and the chimney with the back of a knife. Paint the chimney red and the roof yellow.

3   Tint 2 tablespoons of fondant icing red and cut out a 3 x 4½-inch door. Tint enough fondant icing blue to make a fanlight. Stick to the cake with water. Mark 2½-inch square windows with a toothpick. Paint on curtains with blue food coloring. Tint half the royal icing black and pipe around the windows and the door.

4   Tint the remaining royal icing green. Pipe the flower stems and leaves under the windows and the climber up onto the roof. Stick the flowers in place with a little icing and pipe green flower centers. Pipe the house number or child's age, the knocker and handle on the door. Let dry for 1 hour, then paint with gold food coloring.

Treasure Chest Cake

Allow yourself a few days before the party to make this cake as the lock and handles need to dry for 48 hours.

Makes one 8 x 4-inch cake

8-inch square sponge
   cake
½ cup butter icing
3 tablespoons apricot
   jam, warmed and
   strained
2 cups marzipan
2½ cups fondant icing
brown and green food
   coloring

1 cup dried coconut
¾ cup royal icing
edible gold dusting
   powder
edible silver balls
chocolate money

Materials/equipment
12-inch round cake board
fine paintbrush

1 Split and fill the cake with butter icing. Cut the cake in half and sandwich the halves on top of each other with butter icing. Place on the cake board.

2 Shape the top into a rounded lid and brush with apricot jam. Cover with a layer of marzipan. Tint 2¼ cups of the fondant icing brown and use to cover the cake.

3 Use the brown fondant trimmings to make strips. Stick onto the chest with water. Mark the lid with a sharp knife.

4 Tint the coconut with a few drops of green coloring. Spread a little royal icing over the cake board and press the green coconut lightly into it to make the grass.

5 From the remaining fondant icing, cut out the padlock and handles. Cut a keyhole shape from the padlock and shape the handles over a small box. Let dry. Stick the padlock and handles in place with royal icing and paint them gold. Stick silver balls on to look like nails. Arrange the chocolate money on the board.

Lion Cake

For an animal lover or a celebration cake for a Leo horoscope sign, this cake is ideal.

Makes one 11 x 9-inch oval cake

10 x 12-inch sponge cake
1½ cups orange-flavor
   butter icing
orange and red food
   coloring
4½ cups yellow marzipan
generous 4 tablespoons
   fondant icing
red and orange liquorice
   bootlaces

long and round
   marshmallows

Materials/equipment
12-inch square cake
   board
cheese grater
small heart-shape cutter

1 With the flat side of the cake uppermost, cut it to make an oval shape with an uneven scallop design around the edge. Turn the cake over and trim the top level.

2 Place the cake on the cake board. Tint the butter icing orange and use it to cover the cake.

3 Roll ¾ cup of marzipan to a 6-inch square. Place in the center of the cake for the lion's face.

4 Grate the remaining marzipan and use to cover the sides and the top of the cake up to the face panel.

5 Tint the fondant icing red. Use the heart-shape cutter to stamp out the lion's nose and position on the cake with water. Roll the remaining red icing into two thin, short strands to make the lion's mouth, and stick on with water.

6 Cut the liquorice into graduated lengths, and place on the cake for the whiskers. Use two flattened round marshmallows for the eyes and two snipped long ones for the eyebrows.

Train Cake

This cake is made in a train-shape pan, so all you need to do is decorate it.

Makes one train-shape cake

train-shape sponge cake, about 14 inches long	**Materials/equipment**
3 cups butter icing	*10 x 15-inch cake board*
yellow food coloring	*2 fabric icing bags*
red liquorice bootlaces	*small round and small*
6–8 tablespoons colored vermicelli	*star nozzles*
4 liquorice wheels	*pink and white cotton wool balls*

1 Slice off the top surface of the cake to make it flat. Place it diagonally on the cake board.

2 Tint the butter icing yellow. Use half of it to cover the cake.

3 Using a round nozzle and a quarter of the remaining butter icing, pipe a straight double border around the top edge of the cake.

4 Place the red liquorice bootlaces on the piped border. Cut the bootlaces around the curves on the train.

5 Using a small star nozzle and the remaining butter icing, pipe small stars over the top of the cake. Add extra liquorice and piping, if you like. Use a metal spatula to press on the colored vermicelli all around the sides of the cake.

6 Pull a couple of balls of cotton wool apart for the steam and stick them onto the cake board with butter icing. Press the liquorice wheels in place for the wheels.

Number 7 Cake

Any combination of colors will work well for this cake with its marble effect.

Makes one 12-inch long cake

9 x 12-inch sponge cake	*blue and green food coloring*
1½ cups orange-flavour butter icing	*rice paper candies*
4 tablespoons apricot jam, warmed and strained	**Materials /equipment**
4½ cups fondant icing	*10 x 13-inch cake board*
	small "7" cutter

1 Place the cake flat-side up and cut out the number seven. Slice the cake horizontally, sandwich together with the butter icing and place on the board.

2 Brush the cake evenly with apricot jam. Divide the fondant icing into three and tint one of the pieces blue and another green. Set aside scant ½ cup from each of the colored icings. Knead together the large pieces of blue and green icing with the third piece of white icing to marble. Cover the cake.

3 Immediately after covering, use the cutter to remove fondant shapes in a random pattern from the covered cake.

4 Roll out the reserved blue and green fondant icing and stamp out shapes with the same cutter. Use these to fill the stamped-out shapes from the cake. Decorate the board with some rice paper candies.

Musical Cake

Creating a sheet of music on a cake requires very delicate piping work, so it is best to practice first.

Makes one 8 x 10-inch cake

10-inch square sponge cake	**Materials/equipment**
1 cup butter icing	*10 x 12-inch cake board*
3 tablespoons apricot jam, warmed and strained	*wooden toothpick*
	2 small wax paper icing bags
3 cups marzipan	*No 0 writing and No 7 shell nozzles*
3 cups fondant icing	*1½ yards red ribbon*
¾ cup royal icing	
black food coloring	

1 Split and fill the cake with a little butter icing. Cut a 2-inch strip off one side of the cake. Place the cake on the cake board and brush with apricot jam. Cover with a layer of marzipan then fondant icing. Let dry overnight.

2 Make a template and mark out the sheet of music and child's name with a toothpick.

3 Using white royal icing and a No 0 nozzle, begin by piping the lines and bars. Let dry.

4 Tint the remaining icing black and pipe the clefs, name and notes. With the shell nozzle, pipe a royal icing border around the bottom of the cake. Tie a ribbon around the side.

Magic Rabbit Cake

Makes one 6-inch tall round cake

2 x 6-inch round cakes	*edible silver balls*
1 cup butter icing	
¾ cup royal icing	
3 tablespoons apricot jam, warmed and strained	**Materials/equipment**
	10-inch square cake board
4½ cups marzipan	*2 small wax paper icing bags*
4½ cups fondant icing	
black and pink food coloring	*star nozzle*
	1½ yards pink ribbon

1 Split and fill the cakes with butter icing, then sandwich them one on top of the other. Stick on the center of the cake board with a little royal icing. Brush with apricot jam. Use 3 cups of the marzipan to cover the cake.

2 Tint the fondant icing gray. Use about two-thirds of it to cover the cake. Roll out the rest to an 8-inch round. Cut a 6-inch circle from its center. Lower the brim over the cake. Shape the brim sides over wooden spoon handles until dry.

3 Cut a cross in the 6-inch gray circle and place on the hat. Curl the triangles over a wooden spoon handle to shape. Smooth the join at the top and sides of the hat.

4 Tint the remaining marzipan pink and make the rabbit's head, about 2 inches wide with a pointed face. Mark the position of the eyes, nose and mouth. Let dry overnight.

5 Stick the rabbit in the center of the hat with a little royal icing. Pipe a border of royal icing around the top and bottom of the hat and decorate with silver balls while still wet. Tint the remaining royal icing black and pipe the rabbit's eyes and mouth. Tie the ribbon around the hat.

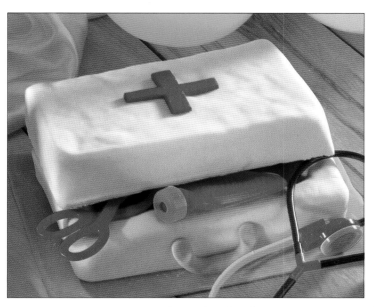

Nurse's Kit Cake

The box is easy to make and is simply filled with toy kit.

Makes one 8 x 6½-inch cake

14 x 8-inch chocolate
    sponge cake
½ cup apricot jam,
    warmed and strained
4½ cups fondant icing
red food coloring

Materials/equipment
10-inch square cake
    board
selection of toy medical
    equipment

1   Place the cake dome-side down and cut in half widthwise.

2   To make the bottom of the nurse's box, turn one cake half dome-side up and hollow out the center to a depth of ½ inch, leaving a ½-inch border on the three uncut edges. Brush the tops and sides of both halves with jam.

3   Tint generous ½ cup fondant icing deep pink. Use a little to make a small handle for the box. Wrap in plastic wrap and set aside. Cover the cake board with the rest of the pink icing. Tint 2 tablespoons of the fondant icing red. Cover with plastic wrap and set aside.

4   Tint the remaining icing light pink and divide into two portions, one slightly bigger than the other. Roll out the bigger portion and use to cover the bottom of the box, easing it into the hollow and along the edges. Trim, then position the bottom on the cake board.

5   Roll out the other portion and use to cover the lid of the box. Trim, then place on top of the bottom at a slight angle.

6   Stick the handle to the bottom of the box using water. Cut a small cross out of red icing and stick it on the lid. Place a few toy items under the lid, protruding slightly. Arrange some more items around the board and cake.

Ballerina Cake

Use flower cutters with ejectors to make the tiny flowers.

Makes one 8-inch round cake

8-inch round sponge cake
½ cup butter icing
3 tablespoons apricot
    jam, warmed and
    strained
3 cups marzipan
3 cups fondant icing
pink, yellow, blue and
    green food coloring
¾ cup royal icing

Materials/equipment
10-inch round cake board
small flower cutter
small circle cutter
wooden toothpick
cotton wool
fine paintbrush
3 small wax paper icing
    bags
No 7 shell nozzle
1½ yards pink ribbon

1   Split and fill the cake with butter icing. Place on the board and brush with apricot jam. Cover with marzipan then fondant icing. Let dry overnight. Divide the rest of the fondant into three. Tint flesh tone, light pink and dark pink. Stamp out 15 pale pink flowers. Let dry.

2   Make a template of the ballerina. Mark her position on the cake. Cut out a flesh-tone body and dark pink bodice. Stick on with water, rounding off the edges.

3   Cut two dark pink underskirts, a pale pink top skirt and a dark pink bodice extension to make the tutu. Stamp out hollow, fluted circles, divide the circles into four and frill the fluted edges with a toothpick. Stick the tutu in place, supported with cotton wool. Cut out and stick on pale pink shoes. Let dry overnight.

4   Paint the ballerina's face and hair. Position 12 hoop and three headdress flowers. Tint some royal icing green and dark pink to complete the flowers and ballet shoes. Pipe a border around the bottom with the shell nozzle. Tie the ribbon on.

Monsters on the Moon

A great cake for little monsters! This cake is best eaten on the day of making.

Serves 12–15

1 quantity quick-mix
    sponge cake
3¾ cups fondant icing
1½ cups marzipan
black food coloring
edible silver glitter
    powder (optional)
¾ cups superfine sugar
2 egg whites
4 tablespoons water

Materials/equipment
ovenproof wok
various sizes of plain
    round and star cutters
12-inch round cake board
small monster toys

1 Preheat the oven to 350°F. Grease and line the wok. Spoon in the cake mixture and smooth the surface. Bake in the center of the oven for 35–40 minutes. Let stand for 5 minutes, then turn out onto a wire rack and peel off the paper.

2 With the cake dome-side up, use the round cutters to cut out craters. Press in the cutters to about 1 inch deep, then remove and cut the craters out of the cake with a knife.

3 Use ¾ cup of the fondant icing to cover the cake, pulling off small pieces and pressing them in uneven strips around the edges of the craters. Tint the remaining fondant icing black. Roll out and cover the board. Stamp out stars and replace with marzipan stars of the same size. Dust with glitter powder, if using, and place on the board.

4 Put the sugar, egg whites and water in a heat proof bowl over a pan of simmering water. Beat until thick and peaks form. Spoon the icing over the cake, swirling it into the craters and peaking it unevenly. Sprinkle over the silver glitter powder, if using, then position the monsters on the cake.

Circus Cake

This colorful design is easy to achieve and is sure to delight young children.

Makes one 8-inch cake

8-inch round sponge cake
½ cup butter icing
3 tablespoons apricot
    jam, warmed and
    strained
3 cups marzipan
3 cups fondant icing
red and blue food
    coloring
¾ cup royal icing

edible silver balls
3 digestive cookies

Materials/equipment
10-inch round cake board
small wax paper icing
    bag
No 5 star nozzle
2-inch plastic circus
    ornaments

1 Split and fill the cake with butter icing. Place on the cake board and brush with apricot jam. Cover with a layer of marzipan then fondant icing.

2 Tint ¾ cup fondant icing pink, then roll into a rope and stick around the top edge of the cake with a little water.

3 Tint half the remaining fondant icing red and half blue. Roll out each color and cut into twelve 1-inch squares. Stick the squares alternately at an angle around the side of the cake with a little water. Pipe stars around the bottom of the cake with royal icing and stick in the edible silver balls.

4 Crush the cookies by pressing through a sifter to make the "sand" for the circus ring. Sprinkle over the top of the cake and place small circus ornaments on top.

Frog Prince Cake

Serves 8–10

8-inch round sponge cake
½ cup butter icing
3 tablespoons apricot
  jam, warmed and
  strained
3 cups marzipan
cornstarch, for dusting
3¾ cups fondant icing
¾ cup royal icing

green, red, black and gold
  food coloring

Materials/equipment
10-inch square cake
  board
glass
fine paintbrush

1 Split and fill the cake with butter icing. Cut in half and sandwich the halves together with apricot jam. Stand upright diagonally across the cake board. Brush the cake with apricot jam and cover with marzipan.

2 Tint 3 cups of the fondant icing green and cover the cake. Roll the remaining green fondant icing into ½-inch diameter sausages. You will need two folded 8-inch lengths for the back legs and 14 x 4-inch lengths for the front legs and feet. Stick in place with a little royal icing. Roll balls for the eyes and stick in place.

3 Roll out the reserved icing and cut a 2 x 7½-inch strip. Cut out triangles along one edge to make the crown shape. Wrap around a glass dusted with cornstarch and moisten the edges to join. Let dry.

4 Cut a 4-inch circle for the white shirt. Stick in place and trim the bottom edge. Cut white circles and stick to the eyes. Tint a little fondant pink, roll into a sausage and stick on for the mouth. Tint the rest black and use for the pupils and the bow tie. Stick in place.

5 Paint the crown with gold food coloring. Let dry, then stick into position with royal icing.

Ladybird Cake

Children will love this colorful and appealing ladybird, and it is very simple to make.

Serves 10–12

3-egg quantity quick-mix
  sponge cake
¾ cup butter icing
4 tablespoons lemon
  curd, warmed
confectioner's sugar, for
  dusting
7 cups fondant icing

food colorings
5 marshmallows
4 tablespoons marzipan

Materials/equipment
wooden skewer
garlic crusher
2 pipe cleaners

1 Cut the cake in half crosswise and sandwich together with the butter icing. Cut vertically through the cake, about a third of the way in. Brush both pieces with the lemon curd.

2 Color 1 pound of the fondant icing red. Dust a work surface with confectioner's sugar and roll out the icing to about ¼ inch thick. Use to cover the larger piece of cake for the body. Using a wooden skewer, make an indentation down the center for the wings.

3 Color 1½ cups of fondant icing black, roll out three-quarters and use to cover the smaller piece of cake for the head. Place both cakes on a cakeboard, press together.

4 Roll out 2 ounces fondant icing and cut out two 2-inch circles for the eyes, and stick to the head with water. Roll out the remaining black icing and cut out eight 1½-inch circles. Use two of these for the eyes and stick the others onto the body.

5 Color some icing green and squeeze through a garlic crusher to make grass. Flatten the marshmallows and stick a marzipan in the center of each. Color pipe cleaners black and press a ball of black icing onto the end of each. Arrange the grass around the cake with the ladybird and decorations.

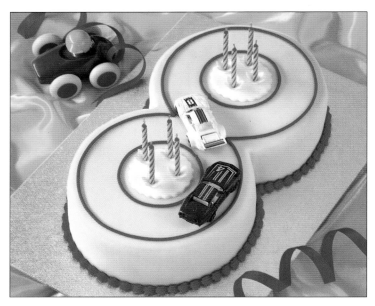

Spaceship Cake

Serves 10–12

10-inch square sponge
   cake
1 cup butter icing
4 tablespoons apricot
   jam, warmed and
   strained
2¼ cups marzipan
3 cups fondant icing
blue, red and black food
   coloring

Materials/equipment

12-inch square cake
   board
4 silver candles and
   holders
gold paper stars

1 Split and fill the sponge cake with butter icing. Cut a 4-inch wide piece diagonally across the middle of the cake, about 10 inches long. Shape the nose end and straighten the other end.

2 From the off-cuts make three 3-inch triangles for the wings and top of the ship. Cut two smaller triangles for the booster jets. Position the main body, wings and top of the cake diagonally across the board. Add extra pieces of cake in front of the top triangle. Brush the cake and booster jets with apricot jam, then cover with a layer of marzipan and fondant icing.

3 Divide the remaining fondant icing into three. Tint blue, pink and black. Roll out the blue icing and cut it into ½-inch strips. Stick around the bottom of the cake with water and outline the boosters. Cut a 1-inch strip and stick down the center of the spaceship.

4 Roll out the pink and black fondant icing separately and cut shapes, numbers and the child's name to finish the design. When complete, position the boosters.

5 Make small cubes with the off-cuts of fondant icing and use to stick the candles to the cake board. Decorate the board with gold stars.

Racing Track Cake

This cake will delight eight-year-old racing car enthusiasts.

Serves 10–12

2 x 6-inch round sponge
   cakes
½ cup butter icing
4 tablespoons apricot
   jam, warmed and
   strained
3 cups marzipan
3¾ cups fondant icing
blue and red food
   coloring
¾ cup royal icing

Materials/equipment

10 x 14-inch cake board
2-inch fluted cutter
2 small wax paper icing
   bags
No 8 star and No 2 plain
   nozzles
8 candles and holders
2 small racing cars

1 Split and fill the cakes with a little butter icing. Cut off a ½-inch piece from the side of each cake and place the cakes on the cake board, cut edges together.

2 Brush the cake with apricot jam and cover with a layer of marzipan. Tint 3 cups of the fondant icing pale blue and use to cover the cake.

3 Mark a 2-inch circle in the center of each cake. Roll out the remaining white fondant icing and cut out two fluted 2-inch circles and stick them in the marked spaces.

4 Tint the royal icing red. Pipe a shell border around the bottom of the cake using the star nozzle. Pipe a track for the cars on the cake using the plain nozzle and stick the candles into the two white circles. Place the cars on the track.

Floating Balloons Cake

Makes one 8-inch round cake

8-inch round sponge or
fruit cake, covered
with 5½ cups
marzipan, if liked
6 cups fondant icing
red, green and yellow
food coloring
3 eggs
2 egg whites
4 cups confectioner's
sugar

Materials/equipment
10-inch round cake board
3 bamboo skewers, 10,
9½ and 9 inches long
small star cutter
wax paper icing bags
fine writing nozzle
1 yard fine colored ribbon
8 candles

1 Place the cake on the board. Tint scant ½ cup of the fondant icing red, scant ½ cup green and 1 cup yellow. Cover the cake with the remaining icing. Use just under half the yellow icing to cover the board.

2 Using a skewer, pierce the eggs and carefully empty the contents. Wash and dry the shells. Cover them carefully with the tinted fondant and insert a bamboo skewer in each. Use the trimmings to stamp out a star shape of each color. Thread onto the skewers for the balloon knots.

3 Trace 16 balloon shapes onto parchment paper. Beat the egg whites with the confectioner's sugar until smooth and divide among four bowls. Leave one white and tint the others red, green and yellow. With the fine writing nozzle and white icing, trace around the balloon shapes. Thin the tinted icings with water. Fill the run-outs using cut icing bags. Let dry overnight.

4 Stick the run-outs around the side of the cake with icing. Pipe white balloon strings. Push the large balloons into the center and decorate with the ribbon. Push the candles into the icing around the edge.

Number 6 Cake

Use the round cake pan as a guide to cut the square cake to fit neatly around the round cake.

Serves 10–12

6-inch round and 6-inch
square sponge cakes
½ cup butter icing
4 tablespoons apricot
jam, warmed and
strained
3 cups marzipan
3¾ cups fondant icing
yellow and green food
coloring
¾ cup royal icing

Materials/equipment
10 x 14-inch cake board
2 small wax paper icing
bags
3-inch fluted cutter
No 1 plain and No 8 star
nozzles
plastic train set with 6
candles

1 Split and fill the cakes with butter icing. Cut the square cake in half and cut, using the round cake pan as a guide, a rounded end from one rectangle to fit around the round cake. Trim the cakes to the same depth and assemble the number on the cake board. Brush with apricot jam and cover with a thin layer of marzipan.

2 Tint 3 cups of the fondant icing yellow and the rest green. Cover the cake with the yellow icing. With the cutter, mark a circle in the center of the round cake. Cut out a green fondant icing circle. Stick in place with water and let dry overnight.

3 Mark a track the width of the train on the top of the cake. Tint the royal icing yellow and pipe the track with the plain nozzle. Use the star nozzle to pipe a border around the bottom and top of the cake. Pipe the name on the green circle and attach the train and candles with royal icing.

Spider's Web Cake

Make the marzipan spider several days before you need the cake to give it time to dry.

Makes one 8-inch round cake

8-inch round deep sponge
  cake
1 cup butter icing
3 tablespoons apricot
  jam, warmed and
  strained
2 tablespoons cocoa
  chocolate vermicelli
4 tablespoons marzipan
yellow, red, black and
  brown food coloring

1½ cups confectioner's
  sugar
1–2 tablespoons water

Materials/equipment
10-inch round cake board
2 small wax paper icing
  bags
wooden toothpick
star nozzle
8 candles and holders

1 Split and fill the cake with half the butter icing. Brush the sides with apricot jam, add the cocoa to the remaining butter icing then smooth a little over the sides of the cake. Roll the sides of the cake in chocolate vermicelli. Place on the board.

2 For the spider, tint the marzipan yellow. Roll half of it into two balls for the head and body. Tint a small piece red and make three balls and a mouth. Tint a tiny piece black for the eyes. Roll the rest of the marzipan into eight legs and two smaller feelers. Stick together.

3 Gently heat the confectioner's sugar and water over a saucepan of hot water. Use two-thirds of the glacé icing to cover the cake top.

4 Tint the remaining glacé icing brown and use it to pipe concentric circles onto the cake. Divide the web into eighths by drawing lines across with a toothpick. Let set.

5 Put the rest of the chocolate butter icing into an icing bag fitted with a star nozzle and pipe a border around the web. Put candles around the border and the spider in the center.

Dart Board

Makes one 10-inch round cake

10-inch round sponge
  cake
¾ cup butter icing
3 tablespoons apricot
  jam, warmed and
  strained
3 cups marzipan
3 cups fondant icing
¾ cup royal icing
black, red, yellow and
  silver food coloring

Materials/equipment
12-inch round cake board
icing smoother
½-inch plain circle cutter
small wax paper icing
  bag
No 1 writing nozzle
3 candles and holders

1 Split and fill the cake with butter icing and put onto the board. Brush with jam and cover with marzipan. Color some of the fondant icing black, a small piece red and the remaining yellow. Cover the cake with black fondant icing. Cut an 8-inch circular template out of wax paper. Fold it in quarters, then divide each quarter into fifths.

2 Using the template, mark the center and wedges on the top of the cake with a sharp knife. Cut out ten wedges from the yellow fondant, using the template as a guide. Place on alternate sections but do not stick in place yet. Repeat with the black fondant. Cut ⅛ inch off each wedge and swop the colors. Mark a 5-inch circle in the center of the board and cut out ⅛-inch pieces to swop with adjoining colors. Stick in place and use an icing smoother to flatten.

3 Use the cutter to remove the center for the bull's eye. Replace with a circle of red fondant, cut with the same cutter. Surround it with a strip of black fondant. Roll the remaining black fondant into a long sausage to fit around the bottom of the cake and stick in place with a little water. Mark numbers on the board and pipe on with royal icing. Let dry, then paint with silver food coloring. Stick candles in at an angle to resemble darts.

Camping Tent Cake

Makes one 8 x 4-inch cake

8-inch square sponge
  cake
½ cup butter icing
3 tablespoons apricot
  jam, warmed and
  strained
3 cups marzipan
3¾ cups fondant icing
brown, orange, green, red
  and blue food coloring
¾ cup royal icing
1 cup dried coconut
chocolate mint sticks

Materials/equipment
10-inch square cake
  board
wooden toothpicks
fine paintbrush
4 small wax paper icing
  bags
No 1 basketweave and
  plain nozzles

1 Split and fill the cake with butter icing. Cut the cake in half. Cut one half in two diagonally from the top right edge to the bottom left edge to form the roof of the tent. Stick the two wedges, back-to-back, on top of the rectangle with jam. Trim to 4 inches high and use the trimmings on the bottom. Place the cake diagonally on the board and brush with jam.

2 Cover with marzipan, reserving some for modeling. Tint scant ½ cup of the fondant icing brown and cover one end of the tent. Tint the rest orange and cover the rest of the cake. Cut a semicircle for the tent opening and a central 3-inch slit. Lay over the brown end. Secure the flaps with royal icing. Put halved toothpicks in the corners and ridge.

3 Tint the coconut green. Spread the board with a thin layer of royal icing and sprinkle with the coconut.

4 Tint the reserved marzipan flesh-color and use to make a model of a child. Paint on a blue T-shirt and let dry. Tint some royal icing brown and pipe on the hair with a basketweave nozzle. Tint the icing and pipe on the mouth and eyes. Make a bonfire with broken chocolate mint sticks.

Army Tank Cake

Create an authentic camouflaged tank by combining green and brown fondant icing.

Makes one 10 x 6-inch cake

10-inch square sponge
  cake
1 cup butter icing
3 tablespoons apricot
  jam, warmed and
  strained
3 cups marzipan
3 cups fondant icing
brown, green and black
  food coloring

chocolate flake
liquorice strips
4 tablespoons royal icing
round cookies
candies

Materials/equipment
10 x 14-inch cake board

1 Split and fill the sponge cake with butter icing. Cut off a 4-inch strip from one side of the cake. Use the off-cut to make a 6 x 3-inch rectangle, and stick on the top.

2 Shape the sloping top and cut a 1-inch piece from both ends between the tracks. Shape the rounded ends for the wheels and tracks. Place on the cake board and brush with apricot jam. Cover with a layer of marzipan.

3 Tint a quarter of the fondant icing brown and the rest green. Roll out the green to a 10-inch square. Break small pieces of brown icing and place all over the green. Flatten and roll out together to give a camouflage effect. Turn the icing over and repeat.

4 Continue to roll out until the icing is ⅛ inch thick. Lay it over the cake and gently press to fit. Cut away the excess. Cut a piece into a 2½-inch disc and stick on the top with a little water. Cut a small hole in it for the gun and insert the chocolate flake. Stick liquorice on for the tracks, using a little black royal icing. Stick on cookies for the wheels and candies for the lights and portholes.

Computer Game Cake

Making a cake look like a computer is easier than you think. This cake is ideal for a computer game fan.

Makes one 5½ x 5-inch cake

*6-inch square sponge
    cake*
½ cup butter icing
*3 tablespoons apricot
    jam, warmed and
    strained*
1½ cups marzipan
*scant 2 cups fondant
    icing*
*black, blue, red and
    yellow food coloring*

royal icing, to decorate

Materials/equipment
*8-inch square cake board
wooden toothpick
fine paintbrush
small wax paper icing
    bag*

1 Split and fill the cake with a little butter icing. Cut 1 inch off one side of the cake and ½ inch off the other side. Round the corners slightly. Place on the cake board and brush with apricot jam. Cover with a layer of marzipan.

2 Tint 1½ cups of the fondant black. Use to cover the cake. Reserve the trimmings. With a toothpick, mark the speaker holes and position of the screen and knobs.

3 Tint half the remaining fondant pale blue, roll and cut out a 2½-inch square for the screen. Stick in the center of the game with a little water. Tint a small piece of fondant red and the remainder yellow. Use to cut out the switch and controls. Stick them in position with water. Roll the reserved black fondant icing into a long, thin sausage and edge the screen and bottom of the cake.

4 With a fine paintbrush, draw the game onto the screen with a little blue coloring. Pipe letters onto the buttons with royal icing.

Chessboard Cake

To make this cake look most effective, make sure that the squares have very sharp edges.

Makes one 10-inch square cake

*10-inch square sponge
    cake*
1 cup butter icing
*4 tablespoons apricot
    jam, warmed and
    strained*
5¼ cups marzipan
3¾ cups fondant icing
*black and red food
    coloring*

edible silver balls
¾ cup royal icing

Materials/equipment
*12-inch square cake
    board
small wax paper icing
    bag
No 8 star nozzle*

1 Split and fill the cake with butter icing. Place on the board and brush with jam. Roll out 3 cups of marzipan and use to cover the cake. Then cover with 3 cups of the fondant icing. Let dry overnight.

2 Divide the remaining marzipan into two, and tint black and red. To shape the chess pieces, roll 4 tablespoons of each color into a sausage and cut into eight equal pieces. Shape into pawns.

3 Divide generous 4 tablespoons of each color into six equal pieces and use to shape into two castles, two knights and two bishops.

4 Divide 2 tablespoons of each color marzipan in half and shape a queen and a king. Decorate with silver balls. Let dry overnight.

5 Cut ½-inch black strips of marzipan to edge the board, and stick in place with water. Pipe a border around the bottom of the cake with royal icing. Place the chess pieces in position.

Kite Cake

The happy face on this cheerful kite is a great favorite with kids of all ages.

Serves 10–12

10-inch square sponge cake
1 cup butter icing
3 tablespoons apricot jam, warmed and strained
4½ cups fondant icing yellow, red, green, blue and black food coloring
3 cups marzipan
¾ cup royal icing

Materials/equipment
12-inch square cake board
wooden toothpick
small wax paper icing bag
No 8 star nozzle
6 candles and holders

1 Trim the cake into a kite shape, then split and fill with butter icing. Place diagonally on the cake board and brush with apricot jam. Cover with a layer of marzipan

2 Tint 1½ cups of the fondant icing pale yellow and cover the cake. Make a template of the face, tie and buttons and mark onto the cake with a toothpick. Divide the rest of the fondant icing into four and tint red, green, blue and black. Cut out the features and stick on with water.

3 Pipe a royal icing border around the bottom of the cake.

4 For the kite's tail, roll out each color separately and cut two 1½ x ½-inch lengths in blue, red and green. Pinch each length to shape into a bow.

5 Roll the yellow into a long rope and lay it on the board in a wavy line from the narrow end of the kite. Stick the bows in place with water. Roll balls of yellow fondant, stick onto the board with a little royal icing and press in the candles.

Hotdog Cake

Makes one 9-inch long cake

9 x 13-inch jelly roll sponge
¾ cup coffee-flavor butter icing
6 tablespoons apricot jam, warmed and strained
3 cups fondant icing brown and red food coloring
1–2 tablespoons toasted sesame seeds
¾ cup glacé icing

Filling
6 ounces sponge cake pieces
¼ cup dark brown sugar
3 tablespoons orange juice
5 tablespoons honey

Materials/equipment
fine paintbrush
2 small wax paper icing bags
napkin, plate, knife and fork

1 Unroll the jelly roll, spread with butter icing, then roll up again. Slice the jelly roll along the center lengthwise, almost to the bottom and ease the two halves apart.

2 Mix all the filling ingredients in a food processor or blender until smooth. Shape the mixture with your hands to a 9-inch sausage shape.

3 Tint all the fondant icing brown. Set aside scant ½ cup and use the remainder to cover the cake.

4 Paint the top of the "bun" with diluted brown food coloring to give a toasted effect. Position the "sausage."

5 Divide the glacé icing in half. Tint one half brown and the other red. Pipe red icing along the sausage, then overlay with brown icing. Sprinkle the sesame seeds over the bun.

6 Cut the reserved brown fondant icing into thin strips. Place on the cake with the joins under the sausage. Place the cake on a napkin on a serving plate, with a knife and fork.

Drum Cake

This is a colorful cake for very young children. It even come complete with drumsticks.

Makes one 6-inch round cake

6-inch round sponge cake
4 tablespoons butter
    icing
3 tablespoons apricot
    jam, warmed and
    strained
2 cups marzipan

3 cups fondant icing
red, blue and yellow food
    coloring
royal icing, for sticking

Materials/equipment
8-inch round cake board

1 Split and fill the cake with a little butter icing. Place on the cake board and brush with apricot jam. Cover with a layer of marzipan and let dry overnight.

2 Tint half of the fondant icing red and roll it out to a rectangle 10 x 12 inches. Cut in half and stick to the side of the cake with water.

3 Roll out a circle of white fondant icing to fit the top of the cake and divide the rest in half. Tint one half blue and the other yellow. Divide the blue into four pieces and roll into sausages long enough to go halfway around the cake. Stick around the bottom and top of the cake with a little water.

4 Mark the cake into six around the top and bottom. Roll the yellow fondant icing into 12 strands long enough to cross diagonally from top to bottom to form the drum strings. Roll the rest of the yellow icing into 12 small balls and stick where the strings join the drum.

5 Knead together the red and white fondant icing until streaky, then roll two balls and sticks 6 inches long. Let dry overnight. Stick together with royal icing to make the drumsticks and place on top of the cake.

Ice Cream Cones

Individual cakes make a change for a party. Put a candle in the special person's one.

Makes 9

¾ cup marzipan
9 ice cream cones
9 sponge fairy cakes
1½ cups butter icing
red, green and brown
    food coloring
colored and chocolate
    vermicelli, wafers and
    chocolate sticks

candies

Materials/equipment
3 x 12-egg egg boxes
foil

1 Make the stands for the cakes by turning the egg boxes upside down and pressing three balls of marzipan into evenly spaced holes in each box. Wrap the boxes in foil. Pierce the foil above the marzipan balls and insert the cones, pressing them in gently.

2 Gently push a fairy cake into each cone. If the bottoms of the cakes are too large, trim them down with a small, sharp knife. The cakes should be quite secure in the cones.

3 Divide the butter icing into three bowls and tint them pale red, green and brown.

4 Using a small metal spatula, spread each cake with some of one of the icings, making sure that the finish on the icing is a little textured so it looks like ice cream.

5 To insert a wafer or chocolate stick into an ice cream, use a small, sharp knife to make a hole through the icing and into the cake, then insert the wafer or stick. Add the finishing touches to the cakes by sprinkling over some colored and chocolate vermicelli. Arrange candies around the cones.

Treasure Map

Makes one 8 x 10-inch cake

10-inch square sponge
  cake
1½ cups butter icing
3 tablespoons apricot
  jam, warmed and
  strained
3 cups marzipan
4½ cups fondant icing
yellow, brown, paprika,
  green, black and red
  food coloring
¾ cup royal icing

Materials/equipment
10 x 14-inch cake board
fine paintbrush
paper towels
4 small wax paper icing
  bags
No 7 shell and No 1
  writing nozzles
6 candles and holders

1 Split and fill the cake with butter icing, cut it into a
8 x 10-inch rectangle and place on the cake board. Brush with
apricot jam. Cover with a layer of marzipan then with 3 cups
fondant icing.

2 Color the remaining fondant icing yellow and cut out with
an uneven outline. Stick onto the cake with water and let dry
overnight. Mark the island, river, lake, mountains and trees
on the map.

3 With brown and paprika colors and a fine paintbrush,
paint the edges of the map to look old, smudging the colors
together with paper towels. Paint the island pale green and
the water around the island, the river and the lake pale blue.
Dry overnight before painting on the other details, otherwise
the colors will run.

4 Pipe a border of royal icing around the bottom of the cake
with a shell nozzle. Color a little royal icing red and pipe the
path to the treasure, marked with an "X." Color some icing
green and pipe on grass and trees. Finally color some icing
black and pipe on a North sign with the writing nozzle.

Royal Crown Cake

This regal cake is sure to delight any prince or princess.

Serves 16–20

8-inch and 6-inch round
  sponge cake
¾ cup butter icing
3 tablespoons apricot
  jam, warmed and
  strained
3 cups marzipan
3¾ cups fondant icing
red food coloring
3 cups royal icing

small black jelly candies
4 ice cream fan wafers
edible silver balls
jewel candies

Materials/equipment
12-inch square cake
  board
wooden toothpicks

1 Split and fill the cakes with butter icing. Sandwich one on
top of the other and place on the board. Shape the top cake
into a dome.

2 Brush the cake with apricot jam and cover with marzipan.
Set aside ¾ cup of the fondant icing and use the remainder to
cover the cake.

3 Tint the reserved fondant icing red, and use to cover the
dome of the cake. Trim away the excess.

4 Spoon uneven mounds of royal icing around the bottom of
the cake and stick a black jelly candy on each mound.

5 Cut the ice cream wafers in half. Spread both sides of the
wafers with royal icing and stick to the cake, smoothing the
icing level with the sides of the cake.

6 Use toothpicks to support the wafers until they are dry.
Put silver balls on top of each point and stick jewel candies
around the side of the crown with a little royal icing.

Box of Chocolates Cake

This sophisticated cake is perfect for an adult's birthday and will delight chocolate lovers.

Makes one 6-inch square cake

6-inch square sponge
cake
4 tablespoons butter
icing
2 tablespoons apricot
jam, warmed and
strained
2¼ cups marzipan
2¼ cups fondant icing

red food coloring
wrapped chocolates

Materials/equipment
8-inch square cake board
small paper sweet cases
1½ yards x 1½-inch wide
gold and red ribbon

1 Split and fill the cake with butter icing. Cut a shallow square from the top of the cake, leaving a ¼-inch border around the edge. Place on the cake board and brush with apricot jam. Cover with a layer of marzipan.

2 Roll out the fondant icing and cut a 7-inch square. Ease it into the hollow dip and trim. Tint the remaining fondant icing red and use to cover the sides.

3 Put the chocolates into paper cases and arrange in the box. Tie the ribbon around the sides and tie a big bow.

Strawberry Cake

Makes one 2-pound cake

scant 4½ cups marzipan
green, red and yellow
food coloring
2 tablespoons apricot
jam, warmed and
strained
2-pound heart-shape
sponge cake

superfine sugar, for
dusting

Materials/equipment
12-inch round cake board
icing smoother
teaspoon

1 Tint generous 1 cup of the marzipan green. Brush the cake board with apricot jam, roll out the green marzipan and use to cover the board. Trim the edges. Use an icing smoother to flatten and smooth the marzipan.

2 Brush the remaining apricot jam over the top and sides of the cake. Position the cake on the cake board. Tint scant 2 cups of the remaining marzipan red. Roll it out to ¼ inch thick and use to cover the cake, smoothing down the sides. Trim the edges. Use the handle of a teaspoon to indent the "strawberry" evenly and lightly all over.

3 For the stalk, tint generous 1 cup of the marzipan bright green. Cut it in half and roll out one portion into a 4 x 6-inch rectangle. Cut "V" shapes out of the rectangle, leaving a 1-inch border across the top, to form the calyx. Position on the cake, curling the "V" shapes to make them look realistic.

4 Roll the rest of the green marzipan into a sausage shape 5 inches long. Bend it slightly, then position it on the board to form the stalk.

5 For the strawberry pips, tint the remaining marzipan yellow. Pull off tiny pieces and roll them into tear-shape pips. Place them in the indentations all over the strawberry. Dust the cake and board with sifted sugar.

Gift-wrapped Package

If you don't have a tiny flower cutter for the "wrapping paper" design, then press a small decorative button into the icing while still soft to create a pattern.

Makes one 6-inch square cake

6-inch square cake
4 tablespoons butter
  icing
3 tablespoons apricot
  jam, warmed and
  strained
3 cups marzipan
2¼ cups pale lemon
  yellow fondant icing

red and green food
  coloring
2 tablespoons royal icing

Materials/equipment
8-inch square cake board
small flower cutter
  (optional)

1 Split and fill the cake with butter icing. Place on the cake board and brush with jam. Cover with half the marzipan, then yellow fondant and mark with a small flower cutter.

2 Divide the remaining marzipan in half, color one half pink and the other pale green. Roll out the pink marzipan and cut into four 1 x 7-inch strips. Roll out the green marzipan and cut into four ½-inch strips the same length. Center the green strips on top of the pink strips and stick onto the cake with a little water. Cut two 2-inch strips from each color and cut a "V" from the ends to form the ends of the ribbon. Stick in place and let dry overnight.

3 Cut the rest of the green into four 1 x 3-inch lengths and the pink into four ½ x 3-inch lengths. Center the pink on top of the green, fold in half, stick the ends together and slip over the handle of a wooden spoon, dusted with cornstarch. Let dry overnight.

4 Cut the ends in "V" shapes to fit neatly together on the cake. Cut two pieces for the join in the center. Remove the bows from the spoon and stick in position with royal icing.

Sweetheart Cake

The heart-shape run-outs can be made a week before the cake is made to make sure that they are completely dry.

Makes one 8-inch round cake

8-inch round sponge cake
½ cup butter icing
3 tablespoons apricot
  jam, warmed and
  strained
3 cups marzipan
4½ cups fondant icing
red food coloring
¾ cup royal icing

Materials/equipment
10-inch round cake board
spoon with decorative
  handle
small wax paper icing
  bag
No 1 writing nozzle
8 candles and holders
1½ yards x 1-inch wide
  ribbon

1 Split and fill the cake with butter icing. Place on the cake board and brush with apricot jam. Cover with a layer of marzipan. Tint the fondant icing pale pink and cover the cake and board. Mark the edge with the decorative handle of a spoon.

2 Tint the royal icing dark pink. Make a heart-shape template and use to pipe the run-outs on wax paper. Using a No 1 writing nozzle, pipe the outlines in a continuous line. Then fill in until the hearts are rounded. You will need eight for the cake top. Let dry for at least 2 days.

3 Arrange the hearts on top of the cake and place the candles in the center. Tie the ribbon around the cake.

Rosette Cake

This cake is quick to decorate and looks truly professional.

Makes one 8-inch square cake

8-inch square sponge cake	**Materials/equipment**
2 cups butter icing	10-inch square cake board
4 tablespoons apricot jam, warmed and strained	serrated scraper
	icing bag
mulberry red food coloring	No 8 star nozzle
candied violets	4 candles and holders

1 Split and fill the cake with a little butter icing. Place in the center of the cake board and brush with apricot jam. Tint the remaining butter icing dark pink. Spread the top and sides with butter icing.

2 Using the serrated scraper, hold it against the cake and move it from side to side across the top to make waves. Hold the scraper against the side of the cake, resting the flat edge on the board and draw it along to give straight ridges along each side.

3 Put the rest of the butter icing into an icing bag fitted with a No 8 star nozzle. Mark a 6-inch circle on the top of the cake and pipe stars around it and around the bottom of the cake. Place the candles and violets in the corners.

Number 10 Cake

This is a very simple cake to decorate. If you can't master the shell edge, pipe stars instead.

Makes one 8-inch tall round cake

8-inch and 6-inch round sponge cakes	**Materials/equipment**
2 cups butter icing	10-inch round cake board
5 tablespoons apricot jam, warmed and strained	wooden toothpick
	plastic "10" cake decoration
colored vermicelli	small wax paper icing bag
cream food coloring	No 7 shell and No 7 star nozzles
	10 candles and holders

1 Split and fill both cakes with a little butter icing. Brush the sides with apricot jam. When cold, spread a layer of butter icing on the sides then roll in colored vermicelli to cover.

2 Tint the rest of the icing cream, spread over the top of each cake. Place the small cake on top of the large cake. Using a toothpick, make a pattern in the icing on top of the cake.

3 Using the remaining icing, pipe around the bottom of the cakes and around the edge. Stick the "10" decoration in the center of the top tier and two candles on either side. Arrange the other candles evenly around the bottom cake.

Shirt and Tie Cake

Makes one 7½ x 10½-inch cake

coffee sponge cake, baked
  in a 7½ x 5-inch loaf
  pan
1½ cups coffee-flavor
  butter icing
6 tablespoons apricot
  jam, warmed and
  strained
generous 7 cups fondant
  icing
blue food coloring
1 cup confectioner's
  sugar, sifted

3–4 tablespoons water

Materials/equipment
15½ x 12-inch cake board
steel ruler
small wax paper icing
  bag
small round nozzle
cardboard collar template
"Happy Birthday"
  decoration
tissue paper (optional)

1 Cut the cake in half horizontally and sandwich together with the butter icing. Brush the cake with apricot jam. Color 4½ cups fondant icing light blue and roll out to about ¼ inch thick. Use to cover the whole cake. Trim away any excess icing. Place the cake on the cake board.

2 Using a steel ruler, make grooves down the length and sides of the cake, about 1 inch apart. Mix the confectioner's sugar and water to make an icing to pipe into the grooves.

3 To make the collar, roll out 1½ cups fondant icing to a 16½ x 4-inch rectangle. Lay the piece of cardboard for the collar on top. Brush water around the edges, then carefully lift one edge over the cardboard to encase it completely. Trim the two short ends to match the angles of the cardboard. Lift the collar and gently bend it around and position on the cake.

4 Color 1 cup fondant icing dark blue. Cut off one-third and shape into a tie knot. Position the knot. Roll out the rest to about ½ inch thick. Cut out a tie piece to fit under the knot and long enough to hang over the edge of the cake. Position the tie piece, tucking it under the knot and securing in place with a little water. Finish the cake with the "Happy Birthday" decoration and tissue paper, if using.

Mobile Phone Cake

Makes one 9 x 5-inch cake

sponge cake, baked in a
  9 x 5-inch loaf pan
2 tablespoons apricot
  jam, warmed and
  strained
2¼ cups fondant icing
black food coloring
10 small square candies
2 striped liquorice sweets
2–3 tablespoons
  confectioner's sugar

½–1 teaspoon water

Materials/equipment
10 x 7-inch cake board
diamond-shaped cookie
  cutter
small piece of foil
small wax paper icing
  bag
small, round nozzle

1 Turn the cake upside-down. Make a 1-inch diagonal cut 1 inch from one end. Cut down vertically to remove the wedge. Remove the middle of the cake to the wedge depth up to 1½ inches from the other end.

2 Place the cake on the board and brush with apricot jam. Tint 1¼ cups of the fondant icing black. Use to cover the cake, smoothing it over the carved shape. Reserve the trimmings.

3 Tint ½ cup of the fondant icing gray. Cut a piece to fit the hollowed center, leaving a ½-inch border, and another piece 1-inch square. Stamp out the center of the square with the cutter. Secure all the pieces on the cake with water.

4 Position the candies and the foil for the display pad. For the glacé icing, mix the confectioner's sugar with the water and tint black. With the small, round nozzle, pipe border lines around the edges of the phone, including the gray pieces of fondant. Pipe the numbers on the keys.

5 Roll a sausage shape from the reserved black fondant for the aerial. Indent one side of the top with a knife and secure the aerial with water.

Heart Cake

Makes one 8-inch heart-shape cake

3 egg whites
1¾ cups superfine sugar
2 tablespoons cold water
2 tablespoons fresh
   lemon juice
¼ teaspoon cream of
   tartar
red food coloring
8-inch heart-shape
   sponge cake

¾–1 cup confectioner's
   sugar

Materials/equipment
12-inch square cake
   board
small wax paper icing
   bag
small nozzle

1 Make the icing by combining 2 of the egg whites, the superfine sugar, water, lemon juice and cream of tartar in the top of a double boiler or in a bowl set over simmering water. With an electric mixer, beat until thick and holding soft peaks, about 7 minutes. Remove from the heat and continue beating until the mixture is thick enough to spread. Color the icing pale pink.

2 Put the cake on the cake board and spread the icing evenly on the cake. Smooth the top and sides. Let set for 3–4 hours, or overnight.

3 Place 1 tablespoon of the remaining egg white in a bowl and whisk until frothy. Gradually beat in enough confectioner's sugar to make a stiff mixture suitable for piping.

4 Spoon the white icing into an icing bag and pipe the decorations on the top and sides of the cake as shown in the photograph above.

Bowl-of-Strawberries Cake

The strawberry theme of the painting is carried on into the molded decorations on this summery birthday cake.

Makes one 8-inch petal-shape cake

1½ cups butter icing
red, yellow, green and
   claret food coloring
8-inch petal-shape
   Madeira cake
3 tablespoons apricot
   jam, warmed and
   strained
4½ cups fondant icing
yellow powder tint

Materials/equipment
10-inch petal-shape cake
   board
paint palette or small
   saucers
fine paintbrushes
thin red and green
   ribbons

1 Tint the butter icing pink. Cut the cake horizontally into three. Sandwich together with the butter icing. Brush the cake with apricot jam. Use 3¾ cups of the fondant icing to cover the cake. Place on the cake board and let dry overnight.

2 For the strawberries, tint three-quarters of the remaining fondant icing red, and equal portions of the rest yellow and green. Make the strawberries, securing with water, if necessary. Let dry on wax paper.

3 Put the red, green, yellow and claret food coloring in a palette and water them down slightly. Paint the bowl and strawberries, using yellow powder tint to highlight the bowl.

4 Decorate the cake with the ribbons. Secure two strawberries to the top of the cake, and arrange the others around the bottom.

Barley Twist Cake

Makes one 8-inch round cake

8-inch round sponge cake
½ cup butter icing
3 tablespoons apricot
　jam, warmed and
　strained
3 cups marzipan
3 cups pale yellow
　fondant icing
¾ cup white fondant
　icing
¾ cup royal icing
blue food coloring
pink dusting powder

Materials/equipment

10-inch round cake board
wooden toothpick
fine paintbrush
No 1 plain nozzle
small wax paper icing
　bags
6 small blue bows

1 Split and fill the cake with butter icing. Place on the board and brush with jam. Cover with marzipan, then yellow fondant icing, extending it over the board. Mark six equidistant points around the cake with a toothpick.

2 Color 1 tablespoon of white fondant icing pale blue and roll out thinly. Moisten a paintbrush with water and brush lightly over it. Roll out the same quantity of white icing, lay on top and press together. Roll out to an 8-inch square.

3 Cut ¼-inch strips, carefully twist each one, moisten the six marked points around the cake with water and drape each barley twist into place, pressing lightly to stick to the cake.

4 Cut out a sweater shape from white icing and stick on with water. Roll some icing into a ball and color a small amount dark blue. Roll into two tapering 3-inch needles with a small ball at the end. Let dry overnight. Stick the needles and ball in position. Using royal icing and a No 1 nozzle, pipe the stitches and wool in position. Pipe a white border around the bottom of the cake. Stick small bows around the edge of the cake with a little royal icing and carefully brush the knitting with red powder tint.

Tablecloth Cake

Makes one 8-inch round cake

8-inch round sponge cake
½ cup butter icing
3 tablespoons apricot
　jam, warmed and
　strained
3 cups marzipan
4½ cups fondant icing
¾ cup royal icing
red food coloring

Materials/equipment

10-inch round cake board
spoon with decorative
　handle
8 wooden toothpicks
sharp needle
skewer
8 red ribbon bows
small wax paper icing
　bags
No 2 and No 0 plain
　nozzles

1 Split and fill the cake with butter icing. Place on the board and brush with apricot jam. Cover with a layer of marzipan. Tint 3 cups of the fondant icing red and cover the cake and board. Roll the rest of the red fondant into a thin rope long enough to go around the cake. Stick around the bottom of the cake with water. Mark with the decorative handle of a spoon. Let dry overnight.

2 Roll out the remaining icing to a 10-inch circle and trim. Lay this icing over the cake and drape the "cloth" over the wooden toothpicks set at equidistant points.

3 Mark a 4-inch circle in the center of the cake. Make a template of the flower design and transfer to the cake with a needle. Use a skewer to make the flowers; the red color should show through.

4 Remove the toothpicks and stick on the bows with royal icing. With a No 2 plain nozzle and white royal icing, pipe around the circle in the center. With a No 0 plain nozzle, pipe small dots around the edge of the cloth. Color some royal icing red and pipe a name in the center.

Pizza Cake

Quick-and-easy, this really is a definite winner for pizza fans everywhere.

Makes one 9-inch round cake

9-inch shallow sponge
cake
1½ cups butter icing
red and green food
coloring
generous 1 cup yellow
marzipan
4 tablespoons fondant
icing

1 tablespoon dried
coconut

Materials/equipment
10-inch pizza plate
cheese grater
leaf cutter

1 Place the cake on the pizza plate. Tint the butter icing red and spread evenly over the cake, leaving a ½-inch border.

2 Knead the marzipan for a few minutes, to soften slightly, then grate it like cheese, and sprinkle all over the top of the red butter icing.

3 Tint the fondant icing green. Use the leaf cutter to cut out two leaf shapes. Mark the veins with the back of a knife and place on the pizza cake.

4 For the chopped herbs, tint the dried coconut dark green. Then sprinkle over the pizza cake.

Flowerpot Cake

Makes one round cake

Madeira cake, baked in a
5-cup ovenproof bowl
½ cup jam
¾ cup butter icing
2 tablespoons apricot
jam, warmed and
strained
4¼ cups fondant icing
¾ cup royal icing
dark orange-red, red,
silver, green, purple
and yellow food
coloring

2 chocolate flakes,
coarsely crushed

Materials/equipment
fine paintbrush
wooden spoon

1 Slice the cake into three layers and stick together again with jam and butter icing. Cut out a shallow circle from the cake top, leaving a ½-inch rim. Brush the outside of the cake and rim with apricot jam. Tint 2¼ cups of the fondant orange-red and cover the cake, molding it over the rim. Reserve the trimmings. Let dry.

2 Use the trimmings to make decorations and handles for the flowerpot. Let dry on wax paper. Sprinkle the chocolate flakes into the pot for soil.

3 Tint a small piece of fondant very pale orange-red. Use to make a seed bag. When dry, paint on a pattern in food coloring. Tint two small pieces of icing red and silver. Make a trowel and dry over a wooden spoon handle.

4 Tint the remaining icing green, purple and a small piece yellow. Use to make the flowers and leaves, attaching together with royal icing. Score leaf veins with the back of a knife. Let dry on wax paper.

5 Attach all the decorations to the flowerpot and arrange the plant, seed bag and trowel with soil, seeds and grass made from leftover tinted fondant.

Glittering Star Cake

With a quick flick of a paintbrush you can give a sparkling effect to this glittering cake.

Makes one 8-inch round cake

8-inch round rich fruit
  cake
2½ tablespoons apricot
  jam, warmed and
  strained
4½ cups marzipan
4 cups fondant icing
¾ cup royal icing

silver, gold, lilac-
  shimmer, red-sparkle,
  glitter-green and
  primrose-sparkle food
  coloring and powder
  tints

Materials/equipment
paintbrush
10-inch round cake board

1 Brush the cake with the apricot jam. Use two-thirds of the marzipan to cover the cake. Let dry overnight.

2 Cover the cake with the fondant icing. Let dry.

3 Place the cake on a large sheet of wax paper. Dilute a little powdered silver food coloring and, using a loaded paintbrush, flick it all over the cake to give a spattered effect. Let dry.

4 Make templates of two different-size moon shapes and three irregular star shapes. Divide the remaining marzipan into six pieces and tint silver, gold, lilac, pink, green and yellow. Cut into stars and moons using the templates as a guide, cutting some of the stars in half.

5 Place the cut-outs on wax paper and brush each with its own color powder tint. Let dry.

6 Secure the cake on the board with royal icing. Arrange the stars and moons at different angles all over the cake, attaching with royal icing, and position the halved stars upright as though coming out of the cake. Let set.

Racing Ring Cake

Serves 12

ring mold sponge cake
1½ cups butter icing
4⅛ cups fondant icing
¾ cup royal icing, for
  fixing
black, blue, yellow, green,
  orange, red, purple
  food coloring
selection of liquorice
  candies, dolly
  mixtures and teddy
  bears

4½-ounce package
  liquorice Catherine
  wheels

Materials/equipment
10-inch round cake board
wooden kebab skewer
fine paintbrush

1 Cut the cake in half horizontally and fill with some butter icing. Cover the outside with the remaining butter icing.

2 Use 2¼ cups of fondant icing to coat the top and inside of the cake. Use the trimmings to roll an oblong for the flag. Cut the skewer to 15 inches and fold one end of the flag around it, securing with water. Paint on the pattern with black food coloring. Color a ball of icing black, and stick on top of the skewer. Make a few folds and let dry.

3 Color the remaining fondant icing blue, yellow, green, orange, red and a very small amount purple. Shape each car in two pieces, attaching in the center with royal icing where the seat joins the body of the car. Add decorations and headlights and attach dolly mixture wheels with royal icing. Place a teddy bear in each car and Let set.

4 Unwind the Catherine wheels and remove the center sweets. Fix them to the top of the cake with royal icing. Secure one strip round the bottom. Cut some of the liquorice into small strips and attach round the middle of the outside of the cake with royal icing. Arrange small liquorice sweets around the bottom of the cake. Position the cars on top of the cake on the tracks and attach the flag to the outside with royal icing.

Artist's Cake

Making cakes is an art in itself, and this cake proves it!

Makes one 8-inch square cake

*8-inch square rich fruit
cake
3 tablespoons apricot
jam, warmed and
strained
3 cups marzipan
5¼ cups fondant icing
¾ cup royal icing
chestnut, yellow, blue,
black, silver, paprika,
green and mulberry
food coloring*

Materials/equipment
*10-inch square cake
board
fine paintbrush*

1 Brush the cake with the apricot jam. Cover in marzipan and let dry overnight.

2 Make a template of a painter's palette that will fit the cake top. Tint generous 1 cup of the fondant very pale chestnut. Cut out the palette shape, place on wax paper and let dry overnight.

3 Tint 3 cups of the fondant icing dark chestnut, cover the cake and secure it to the board with royal icing. Let dry.

4 Divide half the remaining fondant icing into seven equal parts and tint yellow, blue, black, silver, paprika, green and mulberry. Make all the decorative pieces for the box and palette, using the remaining white fondant for the paint tubes. Let dry on wax paper.

5 Paint black markings on the paint tubes and chestnut wood markings on the box.

6 Position all the fondant pieces on the cake and board using royal icing. Let dry.

Liquorice Candy Cake

Makes one 8-inch square cake

*8-inch and 6-inch square
Madeira cakes
3 cups butter icing
3 tablespoons apricot
jam, warmed and
strained
2¼ cups marzipan
5¼ cups fondant icing*

*egg-yellow, black, blue
and mulberry food
coloring*

Materials/equipment
*10-inch square cake
board
1¾-inch round cutter*

1 Cut both cakes horizontally into three. Fill with butter icing, reserving a little to coat the smaller cake. Wrap and set aside the smaller cake. Brush the larger cake with apricot jam. Cover with marzipan and secure on the cake board with butter icing. Let dry overnight.

2 Tint 2¼ cups of the fondant icing yellow. Take ¾ cup of the fondant icing and tint half black and leave the other half white. Cover the top and a third of the sides of the cake with yellow fondant icing.

3 Use the white icing to cover the lower third of the sides of the cake. Use the black icing to fill the central third.

4 Cut the smaller cake into three equal strips. Divide two of the strips into three squares each. Cut out two circles from the third strip, using a cutter as a guide.

5 Tint ¾ cup of the remaining fondant black. Divide the rest into four equal portions, leave one white and tint the others blue, pink and yellow.

6 Coat the outsides of the cake cut-outs with the reserved butter icing. Use the tinted and white fondant to cover the pieces to resemble candies. Make small rolls from the trimmings. Arrange on and around the cake.

Sun Cake

Makes one 8-inch star-shaped cake

2 8 x 2-inch sponge cakes
2 tablespoons sweet
    butter
4 cups sifted
    confectioner's sugar
½ cup apricot jam
2 tablespoons water
2 large egg whites
1–2 drops glycerine

juice of 1 lemon
yellow and orange food
    coloring

Materials/equipment
16-inch square cake
    board
fabric icing bag
small star nozzle

1 Cut one of the cakes into eight wedges. Trim the outsides to fit around the other cake. Make butter icing with the butter and 2 tablespoons of the confectioner's sugar. Place the whole cake on the board and attach the sunbeams with butter icing.

2 Melt the jam with the water and brush over the cake.

3 For the icing, beat the egg whites until stiff. Gradually add the confectioner's sugar, glycerine and lemon juice, and beat for 1 minute. Tint yellow and spread over the cake. Tint the remaining icing bright yellow and orange. Pipe the details onto the cake.

Strawberry Basket Cake

Makes one small rectangular cake

sponge cake baked in a
    3-cup loaf pan
3 tablespoons apricot
    jam, warmed and
    strained
4½ cups marzipan
1½ cups chocolate-flavor
    butter icing
red food coloring
4 tablespoons superfine
    sugar

Materials/equipment
small star nozzle
small wax paper icing
    bag
10 plastic strawberry
    stalks
12 x 3-inch strip foil
12 inches thin red ribbon

1 Level the top of the cake and make it perfectly flat. Score a ¼-inch border around the edge and scoop out the inside to make a shallow hollow.

2 Brush the sides and border edges of the cake with apricot jam. Roll out scant 2 cups of the marzipan, cut into rectangles and use to cover the sides of the cake, overlapping the borders. Press the edges together to seal.

3 Using the star nozzle, pipe vertical lines 1 inch apart all around the sides of the cake. Pipe short horizontal lines of butter icing alternately crossing over and then stopping at the vertical lines to give a basketweave effect. Pipe a decorative line of icing around the top edge of the basket to finish.

4 Tint the remaining marzipan red and mold it into ten strawberry shapes. Roll in the superfine sugar and press a plastic stalk into each top. Arrange in the "basket."

5 For the basket handle, fold the foil into a thin strip and wind the ribbon around it to cover. Bend up the ends and then bend into a curve. Push the ends into the sides of the cake. Decorate with bows made from the ribbon.

Banana Gingerbread Slices

Bananas make this spicy bake delightfully moist. The flavor develops on keeping, so store the gingerbread for a few days before cutting, if possible.

Makes 20 slices

2¹/₂ cups all-purpose
   flour
4 teaspoons ground
   ginger
2 teaspoons mixed spice
1 teaspoon baking soda
¹/₂ cup light brown sugar
4 tablespoons corn oil
2 tablespoons molasses

2 tablespoons malt
   extract
2 eggs, beaten
4 tablespoons orange
   juice
3 ripe bananas
scant 1 cup raisins or
   golden raisins

1 Preheat the oven to 350°F. Line and grease a 11 x 7-inch baking pan.

2 Sift the flour, spices and baking soda into a mixing bowl. Spoon some of the mixture back into the sifter, add the brown sugar and sift the mixture back into the bowl.

3 Make a well in the center of the dry ingredients and add the oil, molasses, malt extract, eggs, and orange juice. Mix together thoroughly.

4 Mash the bananas in a bowl. Add to the gingerbread mixture with the raisins or golden raisins. Mix well.

5 Scrape the mixture into the prepared pan. Bake for 35–40 minutes or until the center springs back when the surface of the cake is lightly pressed.

6 Let the gingerbread stand in the pan to cool for 5 minutes, then turn onto a wire rack, remove the lining paper and let cool completely. Cut into 20 slices to serve.

Banana and Apricot Chelsea Buns

Old favorites get a new twist with a delectable filling.

Serves 9

2 cups bread flour
2 teaspoons mixed spice
¹/₂ teaspoon salt
2 tablespoons soft
   margarine
1¹/₂ teaspoons fast-rising
   dried yeast
¹/₄ cup superfine sugar
6 tablespoons hand-hot
   milk
1 egg, beaten

For the filling
1 large, ripe banana
1 cup ready-to-eat dried
   apricots
2 tablespoons light
   brown sugar

For the glaze
2 tablespoons superfine
   sugar
2 tablespoons water

1 Grease a 7-inch square cake pan. Prepare the filling. Mash the banana in a bowl. Using kitchen scissors, cut in the apricots, then stir in the brown sugar. Mix well.

2 Sift the flour, spice and salt into a mixing bowl. Work in the margarine, then stir in the yeast and sugar. Make a well in the center and pour in the milk and the egg. Mix to a soft dough, adding a little extra milk, if necessary.

3 Turn the dough onto a floured surface and knead for 5 minutes until smooth and elastic. Roll out to a 12 x 9-inch rectangle. Spread the filling over the dough and roll up lengthwise like a jelly roll, with the join underneath. Cut into nine pieces and place cut-side downward in the pan. Cover and let stand in a warm place until doubled in size.

4 Preheat the oven to 400°F. Bake the Chelsea buns for 20–25 minutes until golden brown. Meanwhile make the glaze: mix the superfine sugar and water in a small saucepan. Heat, stirring, until dissolved, then boil for 2 minutes. Brush the glaze over the buns while still hot, then remove from the tin and cool on a wire rack.

Lemon Sponge Fingers

These sponge fingers are perfect for serving with fruit salads or light, creamy desserts.

Makes about 20
2 eggs
6 tablespoons superfine sugar
grated rind of 1 lemon

¹/₂ cup all-purpose flour, sifted
superfine sugar, for sprinkling

1 Preheat the oven to 375°F. Line two baking sheets with nonstick parchment paper. Whisk the eggs, sugar and lemon rind together with a hand-held electric whisk until thick and mousse-like: when the whisk is lifted, a trail should remain on the surface of the mixture for at least 30 seconds.

2 Carefully fold in the flour with a large, metal spoon using a figure-of-eight action.

3 Place the mixture in an icing bag fitted with a ¹/₂-inch plain nozzle. Pipe into finger lengths on the prepared baking sheets, leaving room for spreading.

4 Sprinkle the fingers with superfine sugar. Bake for about 6–8 minutes until golden brown, then remove to a wire rack to cool completely.

Variation
To make Hazelnut Fingers, omit the lemon rind and fold in ¹/₄ cup toasted ground hazelnuts and 1 teaspoon mixed spice with the flour.

Apricot and Almond Fingers

These delicious almond fingers will stay moist for several days, thanks to the addition of apricots.

Makes 18
2 cups self-rising flour
¹/₂ cup light brown sugar
¹/₃ cup semolina
1 cup ready-to-eat dried apricots, chopped
2 tablespoons honey
2 tablespoons malt extract

2 eggs, beaten
4 tablespoons skim milk
4 tablespoons sunflower oil
few drops of almond extract
2 tablespoons slivered almonds

1 Preheat the oven to 325°F. Grease and line an 11 x 7-inch baking pan. Sift the flour into a bowl and stir in the sugar, semolina and apricots. Make a well in the center and add the honey, malt extract, eggs, milk, oil and almond extract. Mix well until combined.

2 Turn the mixture into the prepared pan, spread to the edges and sprinkle with the slivered almonds.

3 Bake for 30–35 minutes, or until the center springs back when lightly pressed. Invert the cake on a wire rack to cool. Remove the lining paper, if necessary, and cut into 18 slices with a sharp knife.

Cook's Tip
If you cannot find ready-to-eat dried apricots, soak chopped, dried apricots in boiling water for 1 hour, then drain them and add to the mixture. This works well with other dried fruit too. Try ready-to-eat dried pears or peaches for a change.

Raspberry Muffins

These muffins are beautifully light and spongy.

Makes 10–12
2¹/₂ cups all-purpose flour	1 egg
1 tablespoon baking powder	1 cup buttermilk
	4 tablespoons sunflower oil
¹/₂ cup superfine sugar	1 cup raspberries

1 Preheat the oven to 400°F. Arrange 12 paper cases in a deep muffin pan. Sift the flour and baking powder into a mixing bowl, stir in the sugar, then make a well in the center.

2 Mix the egg, buttermilk and oil together in a pitcher, pour into the bowl and mix quickly until just combined.

3 Add the raspberries and lightly fold in with a metal spoon. Spoon into the paper cases to within a third of the top.

4 Bake the muffins for 20–25 minutes until golden brown and firm in the middle. Remove to a wire rack and serve while still warm.

Cook's Tip
This is a fairly moist mixture which should only be lightly mixed. Over-mixing toughens the muffins and breaks up the fruit. Use blackberries, blueberries or black currants instead of raspberries, if you prefer.

Date and Apple Muffins

These tasty muffins are delicious with morning coffee or breakfast. You'll only need one or two per person as they are very filling.

Makes 12
1¹/₄ cups self-rising whole wheat flour	6 tablespoons light brown sugar
1¹/₄ cups self-rising white flour	1 cup apple juice
1 teaspoon ground cinnamon	2 tablespoons pear and apple spread
1 teaspoon baking powder	1 egg, lightly beaten
2 tablespoons soft margarine	1 eating apple
	¹/₂ cup chopped dates
	1 tablespoon chopped pecans

1 Preheat the oven to 400°F. Arrange 12 paper cases in a deep muffin pan. Put the whole wheat flour in a mixing bowl. Sift in the white flour with the cinnamon and baking powder. Work in the margarine until the mixture resembles bread crumbs, then stir in the brown sugar.

2 In a bowl, stir a little of the apple juice with the pear and apple spread until smooth. Add the remaining juice, mix well, then add to the flour mixture with the egg. Peel and core the apple, chop the flesh finely and add it to the bowl with the dates. Mix quickly until just combined.

3 Divide the mixture among the muffin cases. Sprinkle with the chopped pecans.

4 Bake the muffins for 20–25 minutes until golden brown and firm in the middle. Turn onto a wire rack and serve while still warm.

Filo and Apricot Purses

Filo pastry is very easy to use and is low in fat. Always keep a package in the freezer ready for rustling up a speedy afternoon treat.

Makes 12
1 cup ready-to-eat dried
   apricots
3 tablespoons apricot
   compote
3 amaretti cookies,
   crushed

3 sheets filo pastry
4 teaspoons soft
   margarine, melted
confectioner's sugar, for
   dusting

1 Preheat the oven to 350°F. Grease two baking sheets. Chop the apricots, put them in a bowl and stir in the apricot compote. Mix in the amaretti cookies.

2 Cut the filo pastry into 24 x 5-inch squares, pile the squares on top of each other and cover with a clean dish towel to prevent the pastry from drying out.

3 Lay one pastry square on a flat surface, brush lightly with melted margarine and lay another square diagonally on top. Brush the top square with melted margarine. Spoon a small mound of apricot mixture in the center of the pastry, bring up the edges and pinch together in a money-bag shape. The margarine will help to make the pastry stick.

4 Repeat with the remaining filo squares and filling to make 12 purses in all. Arrange on the prepared baking sheets and bake for 5–8 minutes until golden brown. Dust with confectioner's sugar and serve warm.

Cook's Tip
The easiest way to crush the amaretti cookies is to put them in a plastic bag and roll with a rolling pin.

Filo Scrunchies

Quick-and-easy to make, these are an ideal afternoon snack. Eat them warm or they will lose their crispness.

Makes 6
5 apricots or plums
4 sheets filo pastry
4 teaspoons soft
   margarine, melted
¼ cup raw sugar

2 tablespoons slivered
   almonds
confectioner's sugar, for
   dusting

1 Preheat the oven to 375°F. Cut the apricots or plums in half, remove the pits and slice the fruit thinly.

2 Cut the filo pastry into 12 x 7-inch squares. Pile the squares on top of each other and cover with a clean dish towel to prevent the pastry from drying out. Remove one square and brush it with melted margarine. Lay a second filo square on top, then, using your fingers, mold the pastry into neat folds.

3 Lay the scrunched filo square on a baking sheet. Make five more scrunchies in the same way, working quickly so that the pastry does not dry out. Arrange a few slices of fruit in the folds of each scrunchie, then sprinkle generously with raw sugar and almonds.

4 Bake the scrunchies for 8–10 minutes until golden brown, then loosen from the baking sheet with a metal spatula. Place on a plate, dust with confectioner's sugar and serve immediately.

Cook's Tip
Filo pastry dries out very quickly. Keep it covered as much as possible with plastic wrap or a dry cloth to limit exposure to the air, or it will become too brittle to use.

Coffee Sponge Drops

These light cookies are delicious on their own, but taste even better with a filling made by mixing low-fat cream cheese with chopped preserved ginger.

Makes about 24

¹⁄₂ cup all-purpose flour	**For the filling (optional)**
1 tablespoon instant coffee powder	¹⁄₂ cup low fat cream cheese
2 eggs	¹⁄₄ cup chopped preserved ginger
6 tablespoons superfine sugar	

1 Preheat the oven to 375°F. Line two baking sheets with nonstick parchment paper. Sift the flour and instant coffee powder together.

2 Combine the eggs and superfine sugar in a heat proof bowl. Place over a saucepan of simmering water. Beat with a hand-held electric whisk until thick and mousse-like: when the whisk is lifted a trail should remain on the surface of the mixture for at least 30 seconds.

3 Carefully fold in the sifted flour mixture with a large metal spoon, being careful not to knock out any air.

4 Spoon the mixture into an icing bag fitted with a ¹⁄₂-inch plain nozzle and pipe 1¹⁄₂-inch rounds on the prepared baking sheets. Bake for 12 minutes. Cool on a wire rack. Sandwich together in pairs with a ginger-cheese filling (above) or a coffee icing, if you like.

Variation
To make Chocolate Sponge Drops, replace the coffee with 2 tablespoons reduced-fat cocoa.

Oaty Crisps

These cookies are very crisp and crunchy – ideal to serve with morning coffee.

Makes 18

1¹⁄₂ cups rolled oats	4 tablespoons sunflower oil
6 tablespoons light brown sugar	2 tablespoons malt extract
1 egg	

1 Preheat the oven to 375°F. Grease two baking sheets. Mix the oats and brown sugar in a bowl, breaking up any lumps in the sugar.

2 Add the egg, oil and malt extract, mix well, then let soak for 15 minutes.

3 Using a teaspoon, place small heaps of the mixture on the prepared baking sheets, leaving room for spreading. Press into 3-inch rounds with a dampened fork.

4 Bake the cookies for 10–15 minutes until golden brown. Let cool for 1 minute, then remove with a metal spatula and cool on a wire rack.

Variation
Add ¹⁄₂ cup chopped almonds or hazelnuts to the mixture. You can also add some jumbo oats to give a coarser texture.

Snowballs

These light and airy morsels make a good accompaniment to yogurt ice cream.

Makes about 20
2 egg whites
$^{1}/_{2}$ cup superfine sugar
1 tablespoon cornstarch, sifted
1 teaspoon white wine vinegar
$^{1}/_{4}$ teaspoon vanilla extract

1 Preheat the oven to 300°F and line two baking sheets with nonstick parchment paper. Whisk the egg whites in a clean bowl, using a hand-held electric whisk, until very stiff.

2 Add the superfine sugar, a little at a time, whisking until the meringue is very stiff. Whisk in the cornstarch, vinegar and vanilla extract.

3 Using a teaspoon, mound the mixture into snowballs on the prepared baking sheets. Bake for 30 minutes.

4 Cool on the baking sheets, then remove the snowballs from the paper with a metal spatula.

Variation
Make Pineapple Snowballs by lightly folding about $^{1}/_{3}$ cup finely chopped semi-dried pineapple into the meringue.

Caramel Meringues

Muscovado sugar gives these meringues a marvelous caramel flavor. Take care not to overcook them, so that they stay chewy in the middle.

Makes about 20
$^{1}/_{2}$ cup muscovado sugar
2 egg whites
1 teaspoon finely chopped walnuts

1 Preheat the oven to 325°F. Line two baking sheets with nonstick parchment paper. Press the sugar through a metal sifter into a bowl. Whisk the egg whites in a clean bowl until very stiff and dry, then add the sifted brown sugar, about 1 tablespoon at a time, whisking it into the meringue until it is thick and glossy.

2 Spoon small mounds of the mixture onto the prepared baking sheets. Sprinkle with the walnuts.

3 Bake for 30 minutes, then let cool for 5 minutes on the baking sheets. Transfer the meringues to a wire rack to cool completely.

Cook's Tip
For an easy, sophisticated filling, mix $^{1}/_{2}$ cup low-fat cream cheese with 1 tablespoon confectioner's sugar. Chop 2 slices of fresh pineapple and add to the mixture. Sandwich the meringues together in pairs.

Chocolate Banana Cake

A delicious sticky chocolate cake, moist enough to eat without the icing if you want to cut down on the calories.

Serves 8

2 cups self-rising flour
3 tablespoons fat-reduced cocoa
½ cup light brown sugar
2 tablespoons malt extract
2 tablespoons maple syrup
2 eggs, beaten
4 tablespoons skim milk

4 tablespoons sunflower oil
2 large ripe bananas

For the icing
1½ cups confectioner's sugar, sifted
2 tablespoons fat-reduced cocoa, sifted
1–2 tablespoons warm water

1 Preheat the oven to 325°F. Line and grease a deep 8-inch round cake pan. Sift the flour into a mixing bowl with the cocoa. Stir in the sugar.

2 Make a well in the center and add the malt extract, syrup, eggs, milk and oil. Mix well. Mash the bananas thoroughly and stir them into the mixture until thoroughly combined.

3 Spoon the mixture into the prepared pan and bake for 1–1¼ hours or until the center of the cake springs back when lightly pressed. Remove the cake from the pan and turn onto a wire rack to cool.

4 Make the icing: put the confectioner's sugar and cocoa in a mixing bowl and gradually add enough water to make a mixture thick enough to coat the back of a wooden spoon. Pour over the top of the cake and ease to the edges, allowing the icing to dribble down the sides.

Spiced Apple Cake

Grated apple and dates give this cake a natural sweetness. It may not be necessary to add all the sugar.

Serves 8

2 cups self-rising whole wheat flour
1 teaspoon baking powder
2 teaspoons ground cinnamon
1 cup chopped dates
scant ½ cup light brown sugar

1 tablespoon pear and apple spread
½ cup apple juice
2 eggs, beaten
6 tablespoons sunflower oil
2 eating apples, cored and grated
1 tablespoon chopped walnuts

1 Preheat the oven to 350°F. Line and grease an 8-inch deep round cake pan. Sift the flour, baking powder and cinnamon into a mixing bowl, then mix in the dates and make a well in the center.

2 Mix the sugar with the pear and apple spread in a small bowl. Gradually stir in the apple juice. Add to the dry ingredients with the eggs, oil and apples. Mix thoroughly.

3 Spoon into the prepared cake pan, sprinkle with the walnuts and bake for 60–65 minutes or until a skewer inserted into the center of the cake comes out clean. Invert onto a wire rack, remove the lining paper and let cool.

Cook's Tip
It is not necessary to peel the apples – the skin adds extra fiber and softens on cooking.

Irish Whiskey Cake

This moist, rich fruit cake is drizzled with whiskey as soon as it comes out of the oven.

Serves 10

scant 1 cup golden raisins	1¼ cups cold tea
scant 1 cup raisins	1 egg, beaten
½ cup currants	2½ cups self-rising flour, sifted
½ cup candied cherries	3 tablespoons Irish whiskey
1 cup light brown sugar	

1 Mix the dried fruit, cherries, sugar and tea in a large bowl. Let soak overnight until the tea has been absorbed.

2 Preheat the oven to 350°F. Line and grease a 2¼-pound loaf pan. Add the egg and flour to the fruit mixture and beat thoroughly until well mixed.

3 Pour into the prepared pan and bake for 1½ hours or until a skewer inserted into the center comes out clean.

4 Prick the top of the cake with a skewer and drizzle over the whiskey while still hot. Let stand for 5 minutes, then remove from the pan and cool on a wire rack.

Cook's Tip
If time is short, use hot tea and soak the fruit for 2 hours instead of overnight.

Fruit and Nut Cake

A rich fruit cake that matures with keeping.

Serves 12–14

1½ cups self-rising whole wheat flour	6 tablespoons sunflower oil
1½ cups self-rising white flour	¾ cup orange juice
2 teaspoons mixed spice	2 eggs, beaten
1 tablespoon apple and apricot spread	4 cups luxury mixed fruit
3 tablespoons honey	½ cup candied cherries, halved
1 tablespoon molasses	3 tablespoons split almonds

1 Preheat the oven to 325°F. Line and grease a deep 8-inch cake pan. Tie a band of newspaper around the outside of the pan and stand it on a pad of newspaper on a baking sheet.

2 Combine the flours in a mixing bowl. Stir in the mixed spice and make a well in the center.

3 Put the apple and apricot spread in a small bowl. Gradually stir in the honey and molasses. Add to the bowl with the oil, orange juice, eggs and mixed fruit. Stir with a wooden spoon to mix thoroughly.

4 Scrape the mixture into the prepared pan and smooth the surface. Arrange the cherries and almonds in a decorative pattern over the top. Bake for 2 hours or until a skewer inserted into the center of the cake comes out clean. Turn onto a wire rack to cool, then remove the lining paper.

Cook's Tip
For a less elaborate cake, omit the cherries, chop the almonds coarsely and sprinkle them over the top.

Angel Cake

Served with ricotta cheese and fresh raspberries, this makes a light dessert.

Serves 10
scant ½ cup cornstarch
scant ½ cup all-purpose
  flour
8 egg whites
1 cup superfine sugar,
  plus extra for
  sprinkling

1 teaspoon vanilla
  extract
confectioner's sugar, for
  dusting

1 Preheat the oven to 350°F. Sift both flours into a bowl.

2 Whisk the egg whites in a large, clean bowl until very stiff, then gradually add the sugar and vanilla extract, whisking until the mixture is thick and glossy.

3 Fold in the flour mixture with a large, metal spoon. Spoon into an ungreased 10-inch angel cake pan, smooth the surface and bake for 40–45 minutes.

4 Sprinkle a piece of wax paper with superfine sugar and set an egg cup in the center. Invert the cake pan over the paper, balancing it carefully on the egg cup. When cold, the cake will drop out of the pan. Transfer it to a plate, dust generously with confectioner's sugar and serve.

Variation
Make a lemon icing by mixing 1½ cups confectioner's sugar with 1–2 tablespoons lemon juice. Drizzle the icing over the cake and decorate with lemon slices and mint sprigs or physalis.

Peach Jelly Roll

This is the perfect cake for a summer afternoon snack in the garden.

Serves 6–8
3 eggs
½ cup superfine sugar
¾ cup all-purpose flour,
  sifted
1 tablespoon boiling
  water

6 tablespoons peach jam
confectioner's sugar, for
  dusting (optional)

1 Preheat the oven to 400°F. Line and grease a 12 x 8-inch jelly roll pan. Combine the eggs and sugar in a bowl. Beat with a hand-held electric whisk until thick and mousse-like: when the whisk is lifted a trail should remain on the surface of the mixture for at least 30 seconds.

2 Carefully fold in the flour with a large, metal spoon, then add the boiling water in the same way.

3 Spoon into the prepared pan, spread evenly to the edges and bake for 10–12 minutes until the cake springs back when lightly pressed.

4 Spread a sheet of wax paper on a flat surface, sprinkle it with superfine sugar, then invert the cake on top. Peel off the lining paper.

5 Make a neat cut two-thirds of the way through the cake, about ½ inch from the short edge nearest you – this will make it easier to roll. Trim the remaining edges.

6 Spread the cake with the peach jam and roll up quickly from the partially-cut end. Hold in position for a minute, making sure the join is underneath. Cool on a wire rack. Dust with confectioner's sugar before serving, if you like.

Pear and Golden Raisin Teabread

This is an ideal teabread to make when pears are plentiful. There's no better use for windfalls.

Serves 6–8

3 cups rolled oats
¼ cup light brown sugar
2 tablespoons pear or apple juice
2 tablespoons sunflower oil
1 large or 2 small pears
1 cup self-rising flour
scant 1 cup golden raisins
½ teaspoon baking powder
2 teaspoons mixed spice
1 egg

1 Preheat the oven to 350°F. Line a 1-pound loaf pan with nonstick parchment paper. Put the oats in a bowl with the sugar, pour over the pear or apple juice and oil, mix well and let stand for 15 minutes.

2 Quarter, core and grate the pear(s). Add to the bowl with the flour, golden raisins, baking powder, spice and egg. Using a wooden spoon, mix thoroughly.

3 Spoon the teabread mixture into the prepared loaf pan. Bake for 55–60 minutes or until a skewer inserted into the center comes out clean.

4 Invert the teabread onto a wire rack and remove the lining paper. Let cool.

Cook's Tip
Health-food stores sell concentrated pear juice, ready for diluting as required.

Banana and Ginger Teabread

The bland creaminess of banana is given a delightful lift with chunks of preserved ginger in this tasty teabread. If you like a strong ginger flavor add 1 teaspoon ground ginger with the flour.

Serves 6–8

1½ cups self-rising flour
1 teaspoon baking powder
3 tablespoons soft margarine
¼ cup light brown sugar
⅓ cup drained preserved ginger, chopped
4 tablespoons skim milk
2 ripe bananas, mashed

1 Preheat the oven to 350°F. Line and grease a 1-pound loaf pan. Sift the flour and baking powder into a mixing bowl.

2 Work in the margarine until the mixture resembles bread crumbs, then stir in the sugar.

3 Add the ginger, milk and mashed bananas and mix to a soft dough.

4 Spoon into the prepared pan and bake for 40–45 minutes. Run a metal spatula around the edges to loosen them, turn the teabread onto a wire rack and let cool.

Variation
To make Banana and Walnut Teabread, add 1 teaspoon mixed spice and omit the chopped preserved ginger. Stir in ½ cup chopped walnuts and add scant ½ cup golden raisins.

Olive and Oregano Bread

This is an excellent accompaniment to all salads and is very good with broiled goat cheese.

Serves 8 – 10

1 tablespoon olive oil
1 onion, chopped
4 cups bread flour
2 teaspoons fast-rising
dried yeast
1 teaspoon salt
¹/₄ teaspoon black pepper
¹/₃ cup pitted black olives,
coarsely chopped

1 tablespoon black olive
paste
1 tablespoon chopped
fresh oregano
1 tablespoon chopped
fresh parsley
1¹/₄ cups hand-hot water

1 Lightly oil a baking sheet. Heat the olive oil in a frying pan and fry the onion until golden brown.

2 Sift the flour into a mixing bowl. Add the yeast, salt and pepper. Make a well in the center. Add the fried onion (with the oil), the olives, olive paste, herbs and water. Gradually incorporate the flour and mix to a soft dough, adding a little extra water, if necessary.

3 Turn the dough onto a floured surface and knead for 5 minutes until it is smooth and elastic. Shape into an 8-inch round and place on the prepared baking sheet. Using a sharp knife, make crisscross cuts over the top, cover and let stand in a warm place until doubled in size. Preheat the oven to 425°F.

4 Bake the loaf for 10 minutes, then lower the oven temperature to 400°F. Bake for 20 minutes more, or until the loaf sounds hollow when tapped underneath. Let cool on a wire rack.

Sun-dried Tomato Braid

This makes a marvelous centerpiece for a summer buffet.

Serves 8 – 10

2 cups whole wheat flour
2 cups bread flour
1 teaspoon salt
¹/₄ teaspoon black pepper
2 teaspoons fast-rising
dried yeast
pinch of sugar
1¹/₄ cups hand-hot water

³/₄ cup drained sun-dried
tomatoes in oil,
chopped, plus
1 tablespoon oil from
the jar
¹/₄ cup freshly grated
Parmesan cheese
2 tablespoons red pesto
¹/₂ teaspoon coarse
sea salt

1 Lightly oil a baking sheet. Put the whole wheat flour in a mixing bowl. Sift in the bread flour, salt and pepper. Add the yeast and sugar. Make a well in the center and add the water, sun-dried tomatoes, oil, Parmesan and pesto. Gradually incorporate the flour and mix to a soft dough, adding a little extra water, if necessary.

2 Turn the dough onto a floured surface and knead for 5 minutes until it is smooth and elastic. Shape into three 13-inch long sausages.

3 Dampen the ends of the three sausages. Press them together at one end, braid them loosely, then press them together at the other end. Place on the baking sheet, cover and let stand in a warm place until doubled in size. Preheat the oven to 425°F.

4 Sprinkle the braid with coarse sea salt. Bake in the oven for 10 minutes, then lower the temperature to 400°F and bake for 15–20 minutes more, or until the loaf sounds hollow when tapped underneath. Let cool on a wire rack.

Cheese and Onion Herb Stick

An extremely tasty bread that is very good with soup or salads. Use a strong cheese to give plenty of flavor.

Makes 2 sticks, each serving 4–6

1 tablespoon sunflower oil
1 red onion, chopped
4 cups bread flour
1 teaspoon salt
1 teaspoon mustard powder
2 teaspoons fast-rising dried yeast

3 tablespoons chopped fresh herbs, such as thyme, parsley, marjoram or sage
¾ cup grated reduced-fat Cheddar cheese
1¼ cups hand-hot water

1 Lightly oil two baking sheets. Heat the oil in a frying pan and fry the onion until well browned.

2 Sift the flour, salt and mustard powder into a mixing bowl. Stir in the yeast and herbs. Set aside 2 tablespoons of the cheese. Add the rest to the flour mixture and make a well in the center. Add the water with the fried onions and oil; gradually incorporate the flour and mix to a soft dough, adding a little extra water, if necessary.

3 Turn the dough onto a floured surface and knead for 5 minutes until it is smooth and elastic. Divide the mixture in half and roll each piece into a stick 12 inches in length.

4 Place each stick on a baking sheet, make diagonal cuts along the top and sprinkle with the reserved cheese. Cover and let stand until doubled in size. Preheat the oven to 425°F.

5 Bake the loaves for 25 minutes or until the bread sounds hollow when tapped underneath.

Focaccia

This Italian flatbread is best served warm. It makes a delicious snack with olives and feta cheese.

Serves 8

3 cups bread flour
1 teaspoon salt
¼ teaspoon freshly ground black pepper
2 teaspoons fast-rising dried yeast
1¼ cups hand-hot water
pinch of sugar
1 tablespoon pesto

⅔ cup pitted black olives, chopped
3 tablespoons drained sun-dried tomatoes in oil, chopped, plus 1 tablespoon oil from the jar
1 teaspoon coarse sea salt
1 teaspoon chopped fresh rosemary

1 Lightly oil a 12 x 8-inch jelly roll pan. Sift the flour, salt and pepper into a bowl. Add the yeast and sugar and make a well in the center.

2 Add the water with the pesto, olives and sun-dried tomatoes (reserve the oil). Mix to a soft dough, adding a little extra water, if necessary.

3 Turn the dough onto a floured surface and knead for 5 minutes until it is smooth and elastic. Roll into a rectangle measuring 13 x 9 inches. Place over the rolling pin and place in the prepared pan. Let rise until doubled in size. Preheat the oven to 425°F.

4 Using your fingertips, make indentations all over the dough. Brush with the oil from the sun-dried tomatoes, then sprinkle with salt and rosemary. Bake for 20–25 minutes until golden. Transfer to a wire rack and serve warm.

Spinach and Bacon Bread

This bread is so good that it is a good idea to make double the quantity and freeze one of the loaves.

Makes 2 loaves, each serving 8

1 tablespoon olive oil
1 onion, chopped
4 ounces rindless smoked bacon rashers, chopped
6 cups all-purpose flour
1¹/₂ teaspoon salt
¹/₂ teaspoon grated nutmeg

1 envelope fast-rising dried yeast
2 cups hand-hot water
8 ounces chopped spinach, defrosted if frozen
¹/₄ cup grated reduced-fat Cheddar cheese

1 Lightly oil two 9-inch cake pans. Heat the oil and fry the onion and bacon for 10 minutes until golden brown.

2 Sift the flour, salt and nutmeg into a mixing bowl, add the yeast and make a well in the center. Add the water, the fried bacon and onion, with the oil, then add the drained spinach. Gradually incorporate the flour and mix to a soft dough.

3 Turn the dough onto a floured surface and knead for 5 minutes until it is smooth and elastic. Divide the mixture in half. Shape each half into a ball, flatten slightly and place in a pan, pressing the dough so that it extends to the edges.

4 Mark each loaf into six wedges and sprinkle with the cheese. Cover loosely with a plastic bag and let stand in a warm place until each loaf has doubled in size. Preheat the oven to 400°F.

5 Bake the loaves for 25–30 minutes, or until they sound hollow when tapped underneath. Let cool on a wire rack.

Parma Ham and Parmesan Bread

This nourishing bread can be made very quickly, and is a meal in itself when served with a tomato and feta salad.

Serves 8

2 cups self-rising whole wheat flour
2 cups self-rising all-purpose flour
1 teaspoon salt
1 teaspoon freshly ground black pepper
3 ounces Parma ham, chopped

2 tablespoons chopped fresh parsley
2 tablespoons freshly grated Parmesan cheese
3 tablespoons Meaux mustard
1¹/₂ cups buttermilk
skim milk, to glaze

1 Preheat the oven to 400°F. Flour a baking sheet. Put the whole wheat flour in a bowl and sift in the all-purpose flour, salt and pepper. Stir in the ham and parsley. Set aside about half of the grated Parmesan and add the rest to the flour mixture. Make a well in the center.

2 Mix the mustard and buttermilk in a pitcher, pour into the bowl and quickly mix to a soft dough.

3 Turn onto a well-floured surface and knead very briefly. Shape into an oval loaf and place on the baking sheet.

4 Brush the loaf with milk, sprinkle with the reserved Parmesan and bake for 25–30 minutes until golden brown. Cool on a wire rack.

Cook's Tip
When chopping the ham, sprinkle it with flour so that it does not stick together. Do not knead the mixture as for a yeast dough, or it will become tough. It should be mixed quickly and kneaded very briefly before shaping.

Austrian Three-Grain Bread

A mixture of grains gives this close-textured bread a delightful nutty flavor.

Makes 1 large loaf

2 cups bread flour
1¹/₂ teaspoons salt
2 cups malted brown
   flour
2 cups rye flour
¹/₂ cup medium oatmeal
1 envelope fast-rising
   dried yeast

3 tablespoons sunflower
   seeds
2 tablespoons linseeds
2 cups hand-hot water
2 tablespoons malt
   extract

1 Sift the all-purpose flour and salt into a mixing bowl and add the remaining flours, oatmeal, yeast and sunflower seeds. Set aside 1 teaspoon of the linseeds and add the rest to the flour mixture. Make a well in the center.

2 Add the water to the bowl with the malt extract. Gradually incorporate the flour and mix to a soft dough, adding extra water, if necessary.

3 Flour a baking sheet. Turn the dough onto a floured surface and knead for 5 minutes until it is smooth and elastic. Divide it in half. Roll each half into a sausage, about 12 inches in length. Twist the two pieces together, dampen each end and press together firmly.

4 Lift the loaf onto the prepared baking sheet. Brush with water, sprinkle with the remaining linseeds and cover loosely with a large plastic bag (balloon it to trap the air inside). Let stand in a warm place until doubled in size. Preheat the oven to 425°F.

5 Bake the bread for 10 minutes, then lower the oven temperature to 400°F and cook for 20 minutes more, or until the loaf sounds hollow when tapped underneath. Let cool on a wire rack.

Rye Bread

Rye bread is popular in Northern Europe and makes an excellent base for open sandwiches.

Makes 2 loaves, each serving 10

3 cups whole wheat flour
2 cups rye flour
1 cup bread flour
1¹/₂ teaspoons salt
1 envelope fast-rising
   dried yeast

2 tablespoons caraway
   seeds
2 cups hand-hot water
2 tablespoons molasses
2 tablespoons sunflower
   oil

1 Grease a baking sheet. Put the flours in a bowl with the salt and yeast. Set aside 1 teaspoon of the caraway seeds and add the rest to the bowl. Mix, then make a well in the center.

2 Add the water to the bowl with the molasses and oil. Gradually incorporate the flour and mix to a soft dough, adding a little extra water, if necessary.

3 Turn the dough onto a floured surface and knead for 5 minutes until it is smooth and elastic. Divide the dough in half and shape into two 9-inch long oval loaves.

4 Flatten the loaves slightly and place them on the baking sheet. Brush them with water and sprinkle with the remaining caraway seeds. Cover and let stand in a warm place until doubled in size. Preheat the oven to 425°F.

5 Bake the loaves for 30 minutes until they sound hollow when tapped underneath. Let cool on a wire rack.

Soda Bread

Finding the bread bin empty need never be a problem when your repertoire includes a recipe for soda bread. It takes only a few minutes to make and needs no rising or proving. If possible, eat soda bread warm from the oven as it does not keep well.

Serves 8
4 cups all-purpose flour
1 teaspoon salt
1 teaspoon baking soda
1 teaspoon cream of
  tartar
1¹/₂ cups buttermilk

1 Preheat the oven to 425°F. Flour a baking sheet. Sift the dry ingredients into a mixing bowl and make a well in the center.

2 Add the buttermilk and mix quickly to a soft dough. Turn onto a floured surface and knead lightly. Shape into a round about 7 inches in diameter; place on the baking sheet.

3 Cut a deep cross on top of the loaf and sprinkle with a little flour. Bake for 25–30 minutes, then transfer to a wire rack to cool.

Cook's Tip
Soda bread needs a light hand. The ingredients should be bound together quickly in the bowl and kneaded very briefly. The aim is just to get rid of the largest cracks, as the dough becomes tough if handled for too long.

Malt Loaf

This is a rich and sticky loaf. If it lasts long enough to go stale, try toasting it for a delicious afternoon treat.

Serves 8
3 cups all-purpose flour
¹/₄ teaspoon salt
1 teaspoon fast-rising
  dried yeast
pinch of superfine sugar
2 tablespoons light
  brown sugar
generous 1 cup golden
  raisins
²/₃ cup hand-hot skim
  milk

1 tablespoon sunflower
  oil
3 tablespoons malt
  extract

To glaze
2 tablespoons superfine
  sugar
2 tablespoons water

1 Sift the flour and salt into a mixing bowl, stir in the yeast, pinch of sugar, brown sugar and golden raisins, and make a well in the center. Add the hot milk with the oil and malt extract. Gradually incorporate the flour and mix to a soft dough, adding a little extra milk, if necessary.

2 Turn onto a floured surface and knead for about 5 minutes until it is smooth and elastic. Lightly oil a 1-pound loaf pan.

3 Shape the dough and place it in the prepared pan. Cover with a damp dish cloth and let stand in a warm place until doubled in size. Preheat the oven to 375°F.

4 Bake the loaf for 30–35 minutes, or until it sounds hollow when tapped underneath.

5 Meanwhile make the glaze by dissolving the sugar in the water in a small saucepan. Bring to a boil, stirring, then lower the heat and simmer for 1 minute. Brush the loaf while hot, then transfer it to a wire rack to cool.

Banana and Cardamom Bread

The combination of banana and cardamom is delicious in this soft-textured moist loaf.

Serves 6

10 cardamom pods
3½ cups bread flour
1 teaspoon salt
1 teaspoon fast-rising
  dried yeast
⅔ cup hand-hot water
2 tablespoons malt
  extract
2 ripe bananas, mashed
1 teaspoon sesame seeds

1 Grease a 1-pound loaf pan. Split the cardamom pods. Remove the seeds and chop the pods finely.

2 Sift the flour and salt into a mixing bowl, add the yeast and make a well in the center. Add the water with the malt extract, chopped cardamom pods and bananas. Gradually incorporate the flour and mix to a soft dough, adding a little extra water, if necessary.

3 Turn the dough onto a floured surface and knead for 5 minutes until it is smooth and elastic. Shape into a braid and place in the prepared pan. Cover loosely with a plastic bag (ballooning it to trap the air) and let stand in a warm place until well risen. Preheat the oven to 425°F.

4 Brush the braid lightly with water and sprinkle with the sesame seeds. Bake for 10 minutes, then lower the oven temperature to 400°F. Cook for 15 minutes more, or until the loaf sounds hollow when tapped underneath. Transfer to a wire rack to cool.

Swedish Golden Raisin Bread

A lightly sweetened bread that goes very well with the cheeseboard and is also excellent toasted as a teabread.

Serves 10

2 cups whole wheat flour
2 cups bread flour
1 teaspoon fast-rising
  dried yeast
1 teaspoon salt
scant 1 cup golden
  raisins
½ cup walnuts, chopped
1 tablespoon honey
⅔ cup hand-hot water
¾ cup hand-hot skim
  milk, plus extra for
  glazing

1 Grease a baking sheet. Put the flours in a bowl with the yeast, salt and golden raisins. Set aside 1 tablespoon of the walnuts and add the rest to the bowl. Mix lightly and make a well in the center.

2 Dissolve the honey in the water and add it to the bowl with the milk. Gradually incorporate the flour, mixing to a soft dough and adding a little extra water, if necessary.

3 Turn the dough onto a floured surface and knead for 5 minutes until smooth and elastic. Shape into an 11-inch long sausage shape. Place on the prepared baking sheet.

4 Make diagonal cuts down the length of the loaf, brush with milk, sprinkle with the remaining walnuts and let stand in a warm place until doubled in size. Preheat the oven to 425°F.

5 Bake the loaf for 10 minutes, then lower the temperature to 400°F and bake for 20 minutes more, or until the loaf sounds hollow when tapped underneath. Transfer to a wire rack and let cool.

Poppy Seed Rolls

Pile these soft rolls in a basket and serve them for breakfast or with dinner.

Makes 12

4 cups bread flour
1 teaspoon salt
1 teaspoon fast-rising
   dried yeast
1¼ cups hand-hot skim
   milk

1 egg, beaten

For the topping
1 egg, beaten
poppy seeds

1 Lightly grease two baking sheets. Sift the flour and salt into a mixing bowl. Add the yeast. Make a well in the center and pour in the milk and the egg. Gradually incorporate the flour and mix to a soft dough.

2 Turn the dough onto a floured surface and knead for 5 minutes until it is smooth and elastic. Cut into 12 pieces and shape into rolls.

3 Place the rolls on the prepared baking sheets, cover loosely with a large plastic bag (ballooning it to trap the air inside) and let stand in a warm place until the rolls have doubled in size. Preheat the oven to 425°F.

4 Glaze the rolls with beaten egg, sprinkle with poppy seeds and bake for 12–15 minutes until golden brown.

Variations
Vary the toppings. Linseed, sesame and caraway seeds all look good; try adding caraway seeds to the dough, too, for extra flavor.

Granary Baps

These make excellent picnic fare and are also good buns for hamburgers.

Makes 8

4 cups malted brown
   flour
1 teaspoon salt
2 teaspoons fast-rising
   dried yeast

1 tablespoon malt extract
1¼ cups hand-hot water
1 tablespoon rolled oats

1 Lightly oil a large baking sheet. Put the malted flour, salt and yeast in a mixing bowl and make a well in the center. Dissolve the malt extract in the water and add it to the well. Gradually incorporate the flour and mix to a soft dough.

2 Turn the dough onto a floured surface and knead for 5 minutes until it is smooth and elastic. Divide it into eight pieces. Shape into balls and flatten with the palm of your hand to make 4-inch rounds.

3 Place the rounds on the prepared baking sheet, cover loosely with a large plastic bag (ballooning it to trap the air inside), and let stand in a warm place until the baps have doubled in size. Preheat the oven to 425°F.

4 Brush the baps with water, sprinkle with the oats and bake for 20–25 minutes or until they sound hollow when tapped underneath. Cool on a wire rack.

Variation
To make a large loaf, shape the dough into a round, flatten it slightly and bake for 30–40 minutes. Test by tapping the bottom of the loaf – if it sounds hollow, it is cooked.

Whole Wheat Herb Triangles

These make a good lunchtime snack when stuffed with ham and salad and also taste good when served with soup.

Makes 8
2 cups whole wheat flour
1 cup bread flour
1 teaspoon salt
¹/₂ teaspoon baking soda
1 teaspoon cream of tartar
¹/₂ teaspoon chili powder
¹/₄ cup soft margarine
1 cup skim milk
4 tablespoons chopped mixed fresh herbs
1 tablespoon sesame seeds

1 Preheat the oven to 425°F. Flour a baking sheet. Put the whole wheat flour in a bowl. Sift in the other dry ingredients, including the chili powder. Work in the margarine.

2 Add the milk and herbs and mix quickly to a soft dough. Turn onto a lightly floured surface. Knead very briefly or the dough will become tough.

3 Roll out to a 9-inch circle and place on the baking sheet. Brush lightly with water and sprinkle with the sesame seeds.

4 Cut the dough round into eight wedges, separate slightly and bake for 15–20 minutes. Transfer the triangles to a wire rack to cool. Serve warm or cold.

Variation
Sun-dried Tomato Triangles: replace the mixed herbs with 2 tablespoons chopped, drained sun-dried tomatoes in oil, and add 1 tablespoon mild paprika, 1 tablespoon chopped fresh parsley and 1 tablespoon chopped fresh marjoram.

Caraway Breadsticks

Ideal to eat with drinks, these can be made in many flavors, including cumin seed, poppy seed and celery seed, as well as the coriander and sesame variation given below.

Makes about 20
2 cups all-purpose flour
¹/₂ teaspoon salt
¹/₂ teaspoon fast-rising dried yeast
2 teaspoons caraway seeds
²/₃ cup hand-hot water
pinch of sugar

1 Grease two baking sheets. Sift the flour, salt, yeast and sugar into a mixing bowl, stir in the caraway seeds and make a well in the center. Add the water and gradually mix the flour to make a soft dough, adding a little extra water, if necessary.

2 Turn the dough onto a lightly floured surface and knead for 5 minutes until it is smooth and elastic. Divide the mixture into 20 pieces and roll each one into a 12-inch stick.

3 Arrange the breadsticks on the baking sheets, leaving room to allow for rising. Let stand for 30 minutes until well risen. Meanwhile, preheat the oven to 425°F.

4 Bake the breadsticks for 10–12 minutes until golden brown. Cool on the baking sheets.

Variation
Coriander and Sesame Sticks: replace the caraway seeds with 1 tablespoon crushed coriander seeds. Dampen the breadsticks lightly and sprinkle them with sesame seeds before baking.

Curry Crackers

These spicy, crisp little crackers are ideal for serving with drinks or cheese.

Makes 12
¹/₂ cup all-purpose flour
1 teaspoon curry powder
¹/₄ teaspoon chili powder
¹/₄ teaspoon salt
1 tablespoon chopped
  fresh cilantro
2 tablespoons water

1 Preheat the oven to 350°F. Sift the flour, curry powder, chili powder and salt into a mixing bowl and make a well in the center. Add the chopped cilantro and water. Gradually incorporate the flour and mix to a fine dough.

2 Turn the dough onto a lightly floured surface, knead until it is smooth, then let rest for 5 minutes.

3 Cut the dough into 12 pieces and knead into small balls. Roll each ball out very thinly to a 4-inch round.

4 Arrange the rounds on two ungreased baking sheets. Bake for 15 minutes, turning over once during cooking.

Variations
These can be flavored in many different ways. Omit the curry and chili powders and add 1 tablespoon caraway, fennel or mustard seeds. Any of the stronger spices such as nutmeg, cloves or ginger will give a good flavor but you will only need to add 1 teaspoon.

Oatcakes

These are traditionally served with cheese, but are also delicious topped with thick honey for breakfast.

Makes 8
1 cup medium oatmeal,
  plus extra for
  sprinkling
pinch of baking soda
¹/₂ teaspoon salt
1 tablespoon butter
5 tablespoons water

1 Preheat the oven to 300°F. Grease a baking sheet. Put the oatmeal, baking soda and salt in a mixing bowl.

2 Melt the butter with the water in a small saucepan. Bring to a boil, then add to the oatmeal and mix to a moist dough.

3 Turn onto a surface sprinkled with oatmeal and knead to a smooth ball. Turn a large baking sheet upside down, sprinkle it lightly with oatmeal and place the ball of dough on top. Dust with oatmeal; roll out thinly to a 10-inch round.

4 Cut the round into eight sections, ease apart slightly and bake for 50–60 minutes until crisp. Let cool on the baking sheet, then remove the oatcakes with a metal spatula.

Cook's Tip
To get a neat circle, place a 10-inch cake board or plate on top of the oatcake. Cut away any excess dough with a metal spatula, then remove the board or plate.

Chive and Potato Biscuits

These little biscuits should be fairly thin, soft and crisp. They are delicious served for breakfast.

Makes 20
1 pound potatoes
1 cup all-purpose flour, sifted
2 tablespoons olive oil
2 tablespoons chopped chives
salt and freshly ground black pepper
low-fat spread, for topping

1 Cook the potatoes in a saucepan of boiling salted water for 20 minutes, then drain thoroughly. Return the potatoes to the clean pan and mash them. Preheat a griddle or heavy-bottomed frying pan over low heat.

2 Tip the hot mashed potato into a bowl. Add the flour, oil and chives, with a little salt and pepper. Mix to a soft dough.

3 Roll out the dough on a well-floured surface to a thickness of ¼ inch and stamp out rounds with a 2-inch biscuit cutter, re-rolling and cutting the trimmings.

4 Cook the biscuits, in batches, on the hot griddle or frying pan for about 10 minutes until they are golden brown. Keep the heat low and turn the biscuits once. Spread with a little low-fat spread and serve immediately.

Cook's Tip
Use floury potatoes such as King Edwards. The potatoes must be freshly cooked and mashed and should not be allowed to cool before mixing. Cook the biscuits over low heat so that the outside does not burn before the inside is cooked.

Ham and Tomato Biscuits

These make an ideal accompaniment for soup. If you have any left over the next day, halve them, sprinkle with cheese, and toast under the broiler.

Makes 12
2 cups self-rising flour
1 teaspoon mustard powder
1 teaspoon paprika, plus extra for topping
½ teaspoon salt
2 tablespoons soft margarine
2 ounces Black Forest ham, chopped
1 tablespoon chopped fresh basil
⅓ cup drained sun-dried tomatoes in oil, chopped
⅓–½ cup skim milk, plus extra for brushing

1 Preheat the oven to 400°F. Flour a large baking sheet. Sift the flour, mustard, paprika and salt into a bowl. Work in the margarine until the mixture resembles bread crumbs.

2 Stir in the ham, basil and sun-dried tomatoes and mix lightly. Pour in enough milk to mix to a soft dough.

3 Turn the dough onto a lightly floured surface, knead lightly and roll out to a 8 x 6-inch rectangle. Cut into 2-inch squares and arrange on the baking sheet.

4 Brush sparingly with milk, sprinkle with paprika and bake for 12–15 minutes. Transfer to a wire rack to cool.

Cook's Tip
Biscuit dough should be soft and moist and mixed for just long enough to bind the ingredients together. Too much kneading makes the biscuits tough.

Drop Pancakes

Children love making – and eating – these little pancakes.

Makes 18
2 cups self-rising flour
1/2 teaspoon salt
1 tablespoon superfine
* sugar*
1 egg, beaten
1¹/4 cups skim milk
oil, for brushing

1 Preheat a griddle, heavy-bottomed frying pan or an electric frying pan. Sift the flour and salt into a mixing bowl. Stir in the sugar and make a well in the center.

2 Add the egg and half the milk and gradually incorporate the surrounding flour to make a smooth batter. Beat in the remaining milk.

3 Lightly grease the griddle or pan. Drop tablespoons of the batter onto the surface, letting them bubble and the bubbles begin to burst.

4 Turn the drop pancakes with a metal spatula and cook until the underside is golden brown. Keep the cooked pancakes warm and moist by wrapping them in a clean napkin while cooking successive batches. Serve with jam.

Variation
For a savory version of these tasty pancakes, add 2 chopped scallions and 1 tablespoon freshly grated Parmesan cheese to the batter. Serve with cottage cheese.

Pineapple and Spice Drop Pancakes

Making the batter with pineapple or orange juice instead of milk cuts down on fat and adds to the taste. Semi-dried pineapple has an intense flavor that makes it ideal to use in baking.

Makes 24
1 cup self-rising whole
* wheat flour*
1 cup self-rising white
* flour*
1 teaspoon ground
* cinnamon*
1 tablespoon superfine
* sugar*
1 egg, beaten
1¹/4 cups pineapple juice
¹/2 cup semi-dried
* pineapple, chopped*
oil, for greasing

1 Preheat a griddle, heavy-bottomed frying pan or an electric frying pan. Put the whole wheat flour in a mixing bowl. Sift in the white flour, ground cinnamon and sugar and make a well in the center.

2 Add the egg with half the pineapple juice and gradually incorporate the surrounding flour to make a smooth batter. Beat in the remaining juice with the chopped pineapple.

3 Lightly grease the griddle or pan. Drop tablespoons of the batter onto the surface, letting them bubble and the bubbles begin to burst.

4 Turn the drop pancakes with a metal spatula and cook until the underside is golden brown. Keep the cooked pancakes warm and moist by wrapping them in a clean napkin while cooking successive batches.

Cook's Tip
Drop pancakes do not keep well and are best eaten freshly cooked. These taste good with cottage cheese.

Peach and Amaretto Cake

Try this delicious cake for dessert, with reduced-fat ricotta cheese, or serve it solo as an afternoon snack.

Serves 8

3 eggs, separated
¾ cup superfine sugar
grated rind and juice of
  1 lemon
⅓ cup semolina
scant ½ cup ground
  almonds
¼ cup all-purpose flour

For the syrup

6 tablespoons superfine
  sugar
6 tablespoons water
2 tablespoons Amaretto
  liqueur
2 peaches or nectarines,
  halved and pitted
4 tablespoons apricot
  jam, strained, to glaze

1 Preheat the oven to 350°F. Grease an 8-inch round loose-bottomed cake pan. Whisk the egg yolks, sugar, lemon rind and juice in a bowl until thick, pale and creamy, then fold in the semolina, almonds and flour until smooth.

2 Whisk the egg whites in a clean bowl until fairly stiff. Using a metal spoon, stir a generous spoonful of the whites into the semolina mixture to lighten it, then fold in the remaining egg whites. Spoon into the prepared cake pan.

3 Bake for 30–35 minutes, then remove the cake from the oven and carefully loosen the edges. Prick the top with a skewer and let cool slightly in the pan.

4 Meanwhile, make the syrup. Heat the sugar and water in a small saucepan, stirring until dissolved, then boil without stirring for 2 minutes. Add the Amaretto liqueur and drizzle slowly over the cake.

5 Remove the cake from the pan and transfer it to a serving plate. Slice the peaches or nectarines, arrange them in concentric circles over the top and brush with the glaze.

Chestnut and Orange Roll

A very moist roll – ideal to serve as a dessert.

Serves 8

3 eggs, separated
½ cup superfine sugar
15½-ounce can
  unsweetened chestnut
  purée
grated rind and juice of
  1 orange
confectioner's sugar, for
  dusting

For the filling

1 cup low-fat cream
  cheese
1 tablespoon honey
1 orange

1 Preheat the oven to 350°F. Line and grease a 12 x 8-inch jelly roll pan. Whisk the egg yolks and sugar in a mixing bowl until thick and creamy. Put the chestnut purée in a separate bowl. Whisk the orange rind and juice into the purée, then whisk into the egg mixture.

2 Whisk the egg whites until fairly stiff. Stir a generous spoonful of the whites into the chestnut mixture to lighten it, then fold in the remaining egg whites. Spoon the mixture into the prepared pan and bake for 30 minutes until firm. Cool for 5 minutes, then cover with a clean damp dish cloth and let stand until cold.

3 Meanwhile, make the filling. Put the cream cheese in a bowl with the honey. Finely grate the orange rind and add to the bowl. Peel away all the pith from the orange, cut the fruit into segments, chop coarsely and set aside. Add any juice to the bowl, then beat until smooth. Mix in the orange segments.

4 Sprinkle a sheet of wax paper with confectioner's sugar. Turn the cake out onto the paper and peel off the lining paper. Spread the filling over the cake and roll up like a jelly roll. Transfer to a plate and dust with confectioner's sugar.

Cinnamon and Apple Gâteau

Make this lovely gâteau for a fall teatime treat.

Serves 8
3 eggs
½ cup superfine sugar
¾ cup all-purpose flour
1 teaspoon ground
   cinnamon

For the filling and topping
4 large eating apples
1 tablespoon water
4 tablespoons honey
½ cup golden raisins
½ teaspoon ground
   cinnamon
1½ cups low-fat cream
   cheese
4 tablespoons reduced-fat
   ricotta cheese
2 teaspoons lemon juice

1 Preheat the oven to 375°F. Line and grease a 9-inch sandwich cake pan. Whisk the eggs and sugar until thick, then sift the flour and cinnamon over the surface and carefully fold in with a large, metal spoon.

2 Pour into the prepared pan and bake for 25–30 minutes, or until the cake springs back when lightly pressed. Let cool on a wire rack.

3 To make the filling, peel, core and slice three of the apples and cook them in a covered pan with the water and half the honey until softened. Add the golden raisins and cinnamon, stir well, replace the lid and let cool.

4 Put the cream cheese in a bowl with the ricotta cheese, the remaining honey and half the lemon juice and beat until smooth. Split the sponge cake in half, place the bottom half on a plate and drizzle over any liquid from the apples. Spread with two-thirds of the cheese mixture, then top with the apple filling. Fit the top of the cake in place.

5 Swirl the remaining filling over the top of the sponge. Quarter, core and slice the remaining apple, dip the slices in the remaining lemon juice and use to decorate the edges.

Lemon Chiffon Cake

Lemon mousse makes a tangy and delicious sponge filling.

Serves 8
1 lemon sponge cake mix
lemon glacé icing
shreds of blanched
   lemon rind

For the filling
2 eggs, separated
6 tablespoons superfine
   sugar
grated rind and juice of
   1 small lemon
4 teaspoons water
2 teaspoons gelatin
½ cup reduced-fat ricotta
   cheese

1 Preheat the oven to 350°F. Line and grease an 8-inch loose-bottomed cake pan, add the sponge mixture and bake for 20–25 minutes until firm and golden. Cool on a wire rack, then split in half. Return the lower half of the cake to the clean cake pan and set aside.

2 Make the filling. Whisk the egg yolks, sugar, lemon rind and juice in a bowl until thick, pale and creamy. In a clean bowl, whisk the egg whites to soft peaks.

3 Sprinkle the gelatin over the water in a bowl. When spongy, dissolve over simmering water. Cool slightly, then whisk into the yolk mixture. Fold in the ricotta cheese. When the mixture begins to set, fold in a generous spoonful of the egg whites to lighten it, then fold in the remaining whites.

4 Spoon the lemon mousse over the sponge in the cake pan. Set the second layer of sponge on top and chill until set.

5 Carefully transfer the cake to a serving plate. Pour the glacé icing over the cake and spread it evenly to the edges. Decorate with the lemon shreds.

Strawberry Gâteau

It is difficult to believe that a cake that tastes so delicious can be low fat.

Serves 6

2 eggs
6 tablespoons superfine sugar
grated rind of ¹/₂ orange
¹/₂ cup all-purpose flour

2 tablespoons superfine sugar
4 tablespoons reduced-fat ricotta cheese
8 ounces strawberries, halved and chopped
¹/₄ cup chopped almonds, toasted

For the filling

1¹/₄ cups low-fat cream cheese
grated rind of ¹/₂ orange

1 Preheat the oven to 375°F. Line an 8-inch jelly roll pan with nonstick parchment paper.

2 In a bowl, whisk the eggs, sugar and orange rind until thick and mousse-like, then fold in the flour lightly. Turn the mixture into the prepared pan. Bake for 15–20 minutes, or until firm and golden. Let cool on a wire rack, removing the lining paper.

3 Meanwhile make the filling. In a bowl, mix the cream cheese with the orange rind, sugar and ricotta cheese until smooth. Divide between two bowls. Add half the strawberries to one bowl. Cut the sponge widthwise into three equal pieces and sandwich together with the strawberry filling. Place on a serving plate.

4 Spread the plain filling over the top and sides of the cake. Press the toasted almonds over the sides and decorate the top with the remaining strawberry halves.

Tia Maria Gâteau

A feather-light coffee sponge with a creamy liqueur-flavored filling spiked with preserved ginger.

Serves 8

³/₄ cup all-purpose flour
2 tablespoons instant coffee powder
3 eggs
¹/₂ cup superfine sugar

¹/₃ cup preserved ginger, chopped

For the icing

2 cups confectioner's sugar, sifted
2 teaspoons coffee extract
1 teaspoon fat-reduced cocoa
coffee beans (optional)

For the filling

³/₄ cup low-fat cream cheese
1 tablespoon honey
1 tablespoon Tia Maria

1 Preheat the oven to 375°F. Line and grease an 8-inch round cake pan. Sift the flour and coffee powder together.

2 Whisk the eggs and sugar in a bowl until thick and mousse-like, then fold in the flour mixture lightly. Turn the mixture into the prepared pan. Bake for 30–35 minutes or until firm and golden. Let cool on a wire rack.

3 Make the filling. Mix the cream cheese with the honey in a bowl. Beat until smooth, then stir in the Tia Maria and ginger. Split the cake in half horizontally and sandwich together with the Tia Maria filling.

4 Make the icing. In a bowl, mix the confectioner's sugar and coffee extract with enough water to make an icing which will coat the back of a wooden spoon. Pour three-quarters of the icing over the cake. Stir the cocoa into the remaining icing, spoon it into an icing bag fitted with a writing nozzle and drizzle the mocha icing over the coffee icing. Decorate with coffee beans, if desired.

Quick-mix Sponge Cake

Choose either chocolate or lemon flavoring for this light and versatile sponge cake, or leave it plain.

Makes 1 x 8-inch round cake

1 cup self-rising flour
1 teaspoon baking powder
½ cup soft margarine
½ cup superfine sugar
2 eggs

For the flavourings
Chocolate: 1 tablespoon cocoa blended with 1 tablespoon boiling water
Lemon: 2 teaspoons grated lemon rind

1 Preheat the oven to 325°F. Grease an 8-inch round cake pan, line the bottom with wax paper and grease the paper.

2 Sift the flour and baking powder into a bowl. Add the margarine, sugar and eggs with the chosen flavorings, if using.

3 Beat with a wooden spoon for 2–3 minutes. The mixture should be pale in color and slightly glossy.

4 Spoon the mixture into the cake pan and smooth the surface. Bake in the center of the oven for 30–40 minutes, or until a skewer inserted into the center of the cake comes out clean. Turn out onto a wire rack, remove the lining paper and let cool completely.

Genoese Sponge Cake

This sponge cake has a firm texture due to the addition of butter and is suitable for cutting into layers for gâteaux.

Makes 1 x 8-inch round cake

4 eggs
½ cup superfine sugar
6 tablespoons sweet butter, melted and cooled slightly
¾ cup all-purpose flour

For the flavourings
Citrus: 2 teaspoons grated orange, lemon or lime rind
Chocolate: 2 ounces bittersweet chocolate, melted
Coffee: 2 teaspoons coffee granules, dissolved 1 teaspoon boiling water

1 Preheat the oven to 350°F. Grease an 8-inch round cake pan, line the bottom with wax paper and grease the paper.

2 Whisk the eggs and sugar together in a heat proof bowl until thoroughly blended. Place the bowl over a saucepan of simmering water and continue to whisk the mixture until thick and pale.

3 Remove the bowl from the saucepan and continue to whisk until the mixture is cool and leaves a thick trail on the surface when beaters are lifted.

4 Pour the butter carefully into the mixture, leaving any sediment behind.

5 Sift the flour over the surface. Using a plastic spatula, carefully fold the flour, butter and any flavorings into the mixture until smooth and evenly blended. Scrape the mixture into the prepared pan, tilt to level and bake for 30–40 minutes, until firm to the touch and golden. Cool on a wire rack.

Madeira Cake

Enjoy this cake in the traditional way with a large glass of Madeira or a schooner of sherry.

Serves 6–8

2 cups all-purpose flour
1 teaspoon baking
  powder
1 cup butter or
  margarine, at room
  temperature
1 cup superfine sugar
grated rind of 1 lemon
1 teaspoon vanilla
  extract
4 eggs

1 Preheat the oven to 325°F. Grease a 9 x 5-inch loaf pan, line the bottom with wax paper and grease the paper.

2 Sift the flour and baking powder into a bowl. Set the mixture aside.

3 Cream the butter or margarine, adding the superfine sugar about 2 tablespoons at a time, until light and fluffy. Stir in the lemon rind and vanilla. Add the eggs one at a time, beating for 1 minute after each addition. Add the flour mixture and stir until just combined.

4 Pour the cake mixture into the prepared pan and tap lightly to level. Bake for about 1¼ hours, or until a metal skewer inserted in the center comes out clean.

5 Cool in the pan on a wire rack for 10 minutes, then turn the cake out onto a wire rack and let cool completely.

Jelly Roll

Vary the flavor of the jelly roll by adding a little grated orange, lime or lemon rind to the mixture.

Serves 6–8

4 eggs, separated
½ cup superfine sugar
1 cup all-purpose flour
1 teaspoon baking
  powder

For a chocolate flavoring
Replace 1½ tablespoons
  of the flour with
  1½ tablespoons cocoa

1 Preheat the oven to 350°F. Grease a 13 x 9-inch jelly roll pan, line the bottom with wax paper and grease the paper. Whisk the egg whites until stiff. Beat in 2 tablespoons of the superfine sugar.

2 Beat the egg yolks with the remaining superfine sugar and 1 tablespoon water for about 2 minutes until the mixture is pale and leaves a thick ribbon trail.

3 Sift together the flour and baking powder. Carefully fold the beaten egg yolks into the egg whites, then fold in the flour mixture.

4 Pour the mixture into the prepared pan and gently smooth the surface. Bake in the center of the oven for 12–15 minutes, or until the cake starts to come away from the edges of the pan.

5 Turn out onto a piece of wax paper lightly sprinkled with superfine sugar. Peel off the lining paper and cut off any crisp edges. Spread with jam, if wished, and roll up, using the wax paper as a guide. Let cool completely on a wire rack.

Rich Fruit Cake

Make this cake a few weeks before icing, wrap well and store in an airtight container to mature.

Makes 1 x 8-inch round or 7-inch square cake

1¾ cups currants
scant 2 cups golden raisins
1 cup raisins
scant ½ cup candied cherries, halved
scant 1 cup almonds, chopped
scant ½ cup mixed candied peel
grated rind of 1 lemon
2½ tablespoons brandy
2¼ cups all-purpose flour, sifted

1¼ teaspoons mixed spice
½ teaspoon grated nutmeg
generous ½ cup ground almonds
scant 1 cup soft margarine or butter
1¼ cups brown sugar
1 tablespoon molasses
5 eggs, beaten

1 Preheat the oven to 275°F. Grease a deep 8-inch round or 7-inch square cake pan, line the bottom and sides with a double thickness of wax paper and grease the paper.

2 Combine the ingredients in a large mixing bowl. Beat with a wooden spoon for 5 minutes until well mixed.

3 Spoon the mixture into the prepared cake pan. Make a slight depression in the center.

4 Bake in the center of the oven for 3–3½ hours. Test the cake after 3 hours. If it is ready it will feel firm and a skewer inserted in the center will come out clean. Cover the top loosely with foil if it starts to brown too quickly.

5 Let the cake cool completely in the pan. Then turn out. The lining paper can be left on to help keep the cake moist.

Light Fruit Cake

For those who prefer a slightly less dense fruit cake, here is one that is still ideal for marzipanning and icing.

Makes 1 x 8-inch round or 7-inch square cake

1 cup soft margarine or butter
1 cup superfine sugar
grated rind of 1 orange
5 eggs, beaten
2¾ cups all-purpose flour
½ teaspoon baking powder
2 teaspoons mixed spice

¾ cup currants
generous 1 cup raisins
generous 1 cup golden raisins
⅓ cup dried, ready-to-eat apricots
⅔ cup mixed candied peel

1 Preheat the oven to 300°F. Grease a deep 8-inch round or 7-inch square cake pan, line the bottom and sides with a double thickness of wax paper and grease the paper.

2 Combine all the ingredients in a large mixing bowl, cutting the apricots in strips, using kitchen scissors. Beat thoroughly with a wooden spoon for 3–4 minutes until thoroughly mixed.

3 Spoon the mixture into the cake pan. Make a slight depression in the center. Bake in the center of the oven for 2½–3¼ hours. Test the cake after 2½ hours. If it is ready it will feel firm and a skewer inserted in the center will come out clean. Test at intervals if necessary. Cover the top loosely with foil if it starts to brown too quickly.

4 Let the cake cool completely in the pan. Then turn out. The lining paper can be left on to help keep the cake moist.

Marzipan

Marzipan can be used on its own, under an icing or for modeling.

Makes 3 cups

2 cups ground almonds
½ cup superfine sugar
1 cup confectioner's
    sugar, sifted
1 teaspoon lemon juice

a few drops of almond
    extract
1 small egg, or 1 large
    egg white

1 Stir the ground almonds and sugars together in a bowl until evenly mixed. Make a well in the center and add the lemon juice, almond extract and enough egg or egg white to mix to a soft but firm dough, using a wooden spoon.

2 Form the marzipan into a ball. Lightly dust a surface with confectioner's sugar and knead the marzipan until smooth. Wrap in plastic wrap or store in a polythene bag until needed. Tint with food coloring if required.

Fondant Icing

Fondant icing is wonderfully pliable and can be colored, molded and shaped in imaginative ways.

Makes 2¼ cups

1 egg white
1 tablespoon liquid
    glucose, warmed

3 cups confectioner's
    sugar, sifted

1 Put the egg white and glucose in a mixing bowl. Stir them together to break up the egg white.

2 Add the confectioner's sugar and mix together with a metal spatula, using a chopping action, until well blended and the icing begins to bind together. Knead the mixture with your fingertips until it forms a ball.

3 Knead the fondant on a work surface lightly dusted with confectioner's sugar for several minutes until smooth, soft and pliable. If the icing is too soft, knead in some more sifted sugar until it reaches the right consistency.

Marzipan Roses

To decorate a cake, shape the roses in a variety of colors and sizes, then arrange on top.

Form a small ball of colored marzipan into a cone shape. This forms the central core which supports the petals. To make the petals, take a piece of marzipan about the size of a large pea, and make a petal shape which is thicker at the base. Wrap the petal around the cone, pressing the petal to the cone to secure. Bend back the ends of the petal to curl. Repeat with more petals, each overlapping. Make some petals bigger until the required size is achieved.

Royal Icing

Royal icing gives a professional finish. This recipe makes enough icing to cover the top and sides of a 7-inch cake.

Makes 4½ cups

3 egg whites
about 6 cups
  confectioner's sugar,
  sifted

1½ teaspoons glycerine
few drops of lemon juice
food coloring (optional)

1   Put the egg whites in a bowl and stir lightly with a fork to break them up.

2   Add the confectioner's sugar gradually, beating well with a wooden spoon after each addition. Add enough sugar to make a smooth, shiny icing that has the consistency of very stiff meringue.

3   Beat in the glycerine, lemon juice and food coloring, if using. Let stand for 1 hour before using, covered with damp plastic warp, then stir to burst any air bubbles.

Storing
The icing will keep for up to three days, stored in a plastic container with a tight-fitting lid in a fridge.

Icing consistencies
This recipe is for an icing consistency suitable for flat icing a marzipan-covered rich fruit cake. When the spoon is lifted, the icing should form a sharp point, with a slight curve at the end, known as "soft peak." For piping, the icing needs to be slightly stiffer. It should form a fine sharp peak when the spoon is lifted.

Butter Icing

The creamy, rich flavor and silky smoothness of butter icing is popular with both children and adults.

Makes 1½ cups

6 tablespoons soft
  margarine or butter,
  softened
2 cups confectioner's
  sugar, sifted
1 teaspoon vanilla
  extract
2–3 teaspoons milk

For the flavorings
*Chocolate: blend
  1 tablespoon cocoa
  with 1 tablespoon hot
  water and let cool
  before beating into the
  icing.*

*Coffee: blend 2 teaspoons
  coffee powder with
  1 tablespoon boiling
  water, omit the milk
  and let cool before
  beating into the icing.*

*Lemon, orange or lime:
  substitute the vanilla
  extract and milk for
  lemon, orange or lime
  juice and 2 teaspoons
  of finely grated citrus
  rind. Omit the rind if
  using the icing for
  piping. Lightly tint
  the icing with food
  coloring, if wished.*

1   Put the margarine or butter, confectioner's sugar, vanilla extract and 1 teaspoon of the milk in a bowl.

2   Beat with a wooden spoon or an electric mixer, adding sufficient extra milk to give a light, smooth and fluffy consistency. For flavored butter icing, follow the instructions above for the flavor of your choice.

Storing
The icing will keep for up to three days in an airtight container stored in a fridge.

Fudge Frosting

A darkly delicious frosting, this can transform a simple sponge cake into one worthy of a very special occasion. Spread fudge frosting smoothly over the cake or swirl it. Or be even more elaborate with a little piping – it really is very versatile. This recipe makes enough to fill and coat the top and sides of a 8-inch or 9-inch round sponge cake.

Makes 1½ cups

2 ounces semisweet chocolate
2 cups confectioner's sugar, sifted
4 tablespoons butter
3 tablespoons milk or light cream
1 teaspoon vanilla extract

1 Break or chop the chocolate into small pieces. Put the chocolate, confectioner's sugar, butter, milk or cream and vanilla extract in a heavy-bottomed saucepan.

2 Stir over very low heat until both the chocolate and the butter have melted. Remove the mixture from the heat and stir until evenly blended.

3 Beat the icing frequently as it cools until it thickens sufficiently to use for spreading or piping. Use the icing immediately and work quickly once it has reached the right consistency.

Storing
This icing should be used straightaway.

Crème au Beurre

The rich, smooth, light texture of this icing makes it ideal for spreading, filling or piping onto cakes and gâteaux for all occasions.

Makes 1½ cups

4 tablespoons water
6 tablespoons superfine sugar
2 egg yolks
generous ½ cup sweet butter, softened

Chocolate: add 2 ounces semisweet chocolate, melted
Coffee: add 2 teaspoons instant coffee granules, dissolved in 1 teaspoon boiling water, cooled

For the flavorings
Citrus: replace water with orange, lemon or lime juice and 2 teaspoons grated rind

1 Bring the water to a boil, remove from the heat and stir in the sugar. Heat gently, stirring, until the sugar has dissolved. Then boil rapidly until the mixture becomes syrupy, or reaches the "thread" stage. To test, place a little syrup on the back of a dry teaspoon. Press a second teaspoon onto the syrup and gently pull apart. The syrup should form a fine thread. If not, return to the heat, boil rapidly and re-test a minute later.

2 Whisk the egg yolks together in a bowl. Continue to whisk while slowly adding the sugar syrup. Whisk until thick, pale and cool.

3 Beat the butter until light and fluffy. Add the egg mixture gradually, beating well after each addition, until thick and fluffy. For Chocolate or Coffee Crème au Beurre, fold in the flavoring at the end. If you prefer a citrus flavor, follow the instructions above.

American Frosting

A light marshmallow icing which crisps on the outside when left to dry – swirl or peak it into a soft coating.

Makes 1½ cups

1 egg white
2 tablespoons water
1 tablespoon maple syrup
1 teaspoon cream of tartar

1½ cups confectioner's sugar, sifted

1 Place the egg white with the water, syrup and cream of tartar in a heat proof bowl. Whisk together until blended.

2 Stir the confectioner's sugar into the mixture and place the bowl over a saucepan of simmering water. Whisk until the mixture becomes thick and white.

3 Remove the bowl from the saucepan and continue to whisk the frosting until cool and thick, and the mixture stands up in soft peaks. Use immediately to fill or cover cakes.

Glacé Icing

An instant icing for finishing large or small cakes.

Makes 1½ cups

2 cups confectioner's sugar
2–3 tablespoons hot water
food coloring (optional)

For the flavorings
Citrus: replace the water with orange, lemon or lime juice
Chocolate: sift 2 teaspoons cocoa with the confectioner's
Coffee: replace water with strong coffee

1 Sift the confectioner's sugar into a bowl. Using a wooden spoon, gradually stir in enough water to obtain the consistency of thick cream.

2 Beat until white and smooth, and the icing thickly coats the back of the spoon. Tint with a few drops of food coloring, if desired, or flavor the icing as suggested above. Use immediately to cover the top of the cake.

Simple Piped Flowers

Bouquets of iced blossoms, such as roses, pansies and bright summer flowers make colorful cake decorations.

For a rose, make a fairly firm icing. Color the icing. Fit a petal nozzle into a paper icing bag, half-fill with icing and fold over top to seal. Hold the icing bag so the wider end is pointing at what will be the bottom of the rose and hold a toothpick in the other hand. Pipe a small cone shape around the tip of the toothpick, pipe a petal half way around the cone, lifting it so it is at an angle and curling outward, turning the toothpick at the same time. Repeat with more petals so they overlap. Remove from the toothpick and let dry.

Butterscotch Frosting

Makes 3 cups

6 tablespoons sweet
    butter
3 tablespoons milk
2 tablespoons light
    brown sugar
1 tablespoon molasses
3 cups confectioner's
    sugar, sifted

For the flavorings

Chocolate: sift
    1 tablespoon cocoa
    with the confectioner's
    sugar

Citrus: replace the
    molasses with maple
    syrup and add
    2 teaspoons finely
    grated orange, lemon
    or lime rind
Coffee: replace the
    molasses with
    1 tablespoon coffee
    granules

1 Place the butter, milk, sugar and molasses in a bowl over a pan of simmering water. Stir until the butter and sugar melt.

2 Remove the bowl and stir in the confectioner's sugar. Beat until smooth and glossy. For flavoring, follow instructions above. Pour over the cake, or cool for a thicker consistency.

Chocolate Fudge Icing

A rich, glossy icing which sets like chocolate fudge, this is versatile enough to smoothly coat, swirl or pipe, depending on the temperature of the icing when it is used.

Makes 2 cups

4 ounces semisweet
    chocolate, in squares
¼ cup sweet butter

1 egg, beaten
1½ cups confectioner's
    sugar, sifted

1 Place the chocolate and butter in a heat proof bowl over a saucepan of hot water.

2 Stir occasionally with a wooden spoon until both the chocolate and butter are melted. Add the egg and beat well.

3 Remove the bowl from the saucepan and stir in the confectioner's sugar, then beat until smooth and glossy.

4 Pour immediately over the cake for a smooth finish, or let cool for a thicker spreading or piping consistency.

Making Caramel

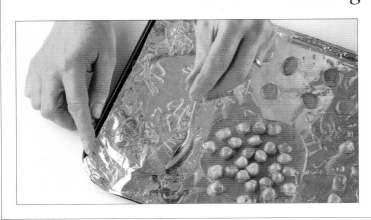

Caramel has endless uses – for dipping fruits and nuts, crushing for cake coating, or drizzling into shapes.

Place ⅔ cup water in a saucepan. Bring to a boil, remove from the heat and stir in ¾ cup superfine sugar. Heat gently until the sugar has dissolved. Bring the syrup to a boil, boil rapidly until the bubbles begin to subside and the syrup begins to turn a pale golden brown. For praline, add ¾ cup toasted almonds to the caramel, shake to mix, then pour onto a sheet of oiled foil on a baking sheet. Cool, then crush with a rolling pin, or process in a food processor or blender until finely ground.

Apricot Glaze

It is a good idea to make a large quantity of apricot glaze, especially when making celebration cakes.

Makes 1½ cups
1½ cups apricot jam
3 tablespoons water

1 Place the jam and water in a saucepan. Heat gently, stirring occasionally until melted. Boil rapidly for 1 minute, then rub through a strainer, pressing the fruit against the sides of the strainer with the back of a wooden spoon. Discard the skins left in the strainer. Use the warmed glaze to brush cakes before applying marzipan, or use for glazing fruits on gâteaux and cakes.

Glossy Chocolate Icing

A rich, smooth glossy icing, this can be made with semi-sweet or milk chocolate.

Makes 1¼ cups
6 ounces semisweet
 chocolate
⅔ cup light cream

1 Break up the chocolate into small pieces and place it in a saucepan with the cream.

2 Heat gently, stirring occasionally, until the chocolate has melted and the mixture is smooth.

3 Let the icing cool until it is thick enough to coat the back of a wooden spoon. Use it at this stage for a smooth glossy icing, or allow it to thicken to obtain an icing which can be swirled or patterned with a cake decorating scraper.

Sugar-frosting Flowers

Choose edible flowers such as pansies, primroses, violets, roses, freesias, tiny daffodils or nasturtiums.

Lightly beat an egg white in a small bowl and sprinkle some superfine sugar on a plate. Wash the flowers then dry on paper towels. If possible, leave some stem attached. Evenly brush both sides of the petals with the egg white. Hold the flower by its stem over a plate lined with paper towels, sprinkle it evenly with the sugar, then shake off any excess. Place on a flat board or wire rack covered with paper towels and let dry in a warm place. Use to decorate a cake.

Petal Paste

Makes 1¼ pound

2 teaspoons gelatin
1½ teaspoons cold water
2 teaspoons liquid
   glucose
2 teaspoons white
   vegetable fat

4 cups confectioner's
   sugar, sifted
1 teaspoon gum
   tragacanth
1 egg white

1 Place the gelatin, water, liquid glucose and white fat in a heat proof bowl over a saucepan of hot water until melted, stirring occasionally. Remove the bowl from the heat.

2 Sift the sugar and gum tragacanth into a bowl. Make a well in the center and add the egg white and the gelatin mixture. Mix together to form a soft, malleable white paste.

3 Knead on a surface dusted with confectioner's sugar until smooth, white and free from cracks. Place in a plastic bag or plastic wrap, sealing well to exclude all the air. Let stand for two hours before use, then knead again and use small pieces at a time, leaving the remaining petal paste well sealed.

Meringue Frosting

Makes 1½ cups

2 egg whites
1 cup confectioner's
   sugar, sifted
⅔ cup butter, softened

For the flavorings
Chocolate: 2 ounces
   semisweet chocolate

Citrus: 2 teaspoons finely
   grated orange, lemon
   or lime rind.
Coffee: 2 teaspoons coffee
   granules, blended with
   1 teaspoon boiling
   water, cooled

1 Whisk the egg whites in a clean, heat proof bowl, add the sugar and gently whisk to mix well. Place the bowl over a saucepan of simmering water and whisk until thick and white. Remove the bowl from the saucepan and continue to whisk until cool and the meringue stands up in soft peaks.

2 Beat the butter in a separate bowl until light and fluffy. Add the meringue gradually, beating well after each addition, until thick and fluffy. Fold in the chosen flavoring, using a metal spatula, until evenly blended. Use immediately for coating, filling and piping onto cakes.

Marbling

Fondant, lends itself to tinting in all shades and marbling is a good way to color the paste.

Using a toothpick, add a few drops of the chosen edible food color to some fondant icing. Do not knead the food coloring fully into the icing.

When the fondant is rolled out, the color disperses in such a way that it gives a marbled appearance.

Marbled fondant icing can be used to cover novelty cakes. Several colors can be used in the same icing to give an interesting multi-colored effect.

Almond paste, see Marzipan
Almonds: almond and raspberry
    jelly roll, 147
  almond cake, 141
  almond mincemeat tartlets, 98
  almond syrup tart, 104
  almond tile cookies, 18
  chocolate amaretti, 23
  chocolate macaroons, 16
  chocolate nut tart, 93
  crunchy apple and almond
    flan, 90
  Italian almond biscotti, 12
  marzipan, 247
  nut lace wafers, 29
  peach tart with almond
    cream, 106
  pear and almond tart, 107
Alsatian plum tart, 97
American frosting, 250
Angel cake, 118, 228
  chocolate and orange, 145
Apples: apple and cranberry
    lattice, 86
  apple & cranberry muffins, 60
  apple cake, 122
  apple crumble cake, 115
  apple loaf, 50
  apple strudel, 96
  cinnamon and apple
    gâteau, 242
  cranberry and apple ring, 126
  crunchy apple and almond
    flan, 90
  date and apple muffins, 222
  Dorset apple cake, 112
  festive apple pie, 91
  nut and apple gâteau, 155
  open apple pie, 86
  pear and apple pie, 100
  spiced apple cake, 226
  sticky date and apple bars, 36
Apricots: apricot & almond
    fingers, 221
  apricot and orange roll, 149
  apricot brandy-snap roll, 149
  apricot glaze, 252
  apricot nut loaf, 41
  apricot specials, 14
  apricot yogurt cookies, 9
  banana and apricot buns, 220
  filo and apricot purses, 223
  filo scrunchies, 223
  lemon and apricot cake, 132
  oat and apricot clusters, 9
  pineapple & apricot cake, 123
Army tank cake, 205
Artist's cake, 218
Austrian three-grain bread, 233

Bacon: spinach and bacon
    bread, 232
Ballerina cake, 199
Balloons cake, 194
Bananas: banana and apricot
    Chelsea buns, 220
  banana and cardamom
    bread, 235
  banana & ginger teabread, 229
  banana and nut buns, 56
  banana bread, 52
  banana chocolate brownies, 32

banana coconut cake, 121
banana ginger parkin, 113
banana gingerbread slices, 220
banana nut loaf, 41
banana orange loaf, 52
chocolate banana cake, 226
creamy banana pie, 89
fruit and nut teabread, 51
glazed banana spiced loaf, 51
passion cake, 128
Baps, granary, 236
Barley twist, 215
Basket cake, 170
Basketweave wedding cake, 174
Battenburg cake,
    chocolate-orange, 136
Best chocolate sandwich, 136
Bilberry teabread, 42
Birthday cakes, 178-80
Birthday package, 178
Biscuits, 63-7, 239-40
Black bottom pie, 92
Black Forest gâteau, 158
Blackberry cheesecake, 152
Blueberries: blueberry fairy
    cakes, 133
  blueberry muffins, 60
  blueberry pie, 88
  blueberry streusel slice, 36
Bluebird bon-voyage cake, 183
Bowl-of-strawberries cake,
    210, 214
Box-of-chox cake, 210
Braided loaf, 69
Brandy snaps, 14
Bread, 68-85, 230-7
Breadsticks, 81
Brioches, individual, 75
Brittany butter cookies, 18
Brownies: banana chocolate
    brownies, 32
  chocolate chip brownies, 31
  chocolate fudge brownies, 34
  fudge-glazed brownies, 34
  maple-pecan brownies, 33
  marbled brownies, 31
  oatmeal and date brownies, 32
  raisin brownies, 30
  white chocolate brownies, 33
Bumble bee cake, 190
Buns, 54-9
Butter icing, 248
Buttermilk biscuits, 66
Butterscotch frosting, 251

Camping tent cake, 205
Candied fruit pie, 99
Caramel: caramel layer cake, 142
  caramel meringues, 225
  making caramel, 251
Caraway breadsticks, 237
Cardamom: banana and
    cardamom bread, 235
  cardamom and saffron loaf, 44
  pear and cardamom spice
    cake, 127
Caribbean fruit & rum cake, 129
Carrots: and zucchini cake, 120
  carrot buns, 57
  carrot cake with geranium
    cheese, 120
  Clare's American carrot

cake, 128
  passion cake, 128
Cat-in-a-basket cake, 184
Cheese: and chive biscuits, 65
  cheese and marjoram
    biscuits, 67
  cheese & onion herb stick, 231
  cheese bread, 72
  cheese popovers, 47
  Parma ham and Parmesan
    bread, 232
  zucchini crown bread, 83
Cheese, cream: carrot cake with
    geranium cheese, 120
  cream cheese spirals, 11
  red berry tart with lemon
    cream, 106
Cheesecakes: baked
    blackberry, 152
  baked cheesecake with fresh
    fruits, 151
  chocolate, 150
  chocolate cheesecake tart, 103
  classic, 150
  marbled, 151
  tofu berry "cheesecake," 152
Chelsea buns, 58
  banana and apricot, 220
Cherries: Black Forest
    gâteau, 158
  cherry batter bake, 132
  cherry marmalade muffins, 53
  cherry strudel, 96
  chocolate and fresh cherry
    gâteau, 157
  dried cherry buns, 57
  rhubarb and cherry pie, 91
Chessboard cake, 206
Chestnuts: chestnut and orange
    roll, 241
  chestnut cake, 144
  chocolate chestnut roll, 162
Chiffon pie, chocolate, 99
Children's party cakes, 184-209
Chive and potato biscuits, 239
Chocolate: banana chocolate
    brownies, 32
  best-ever chocolate
    sandwich, 136
  black bottom pie, 92
  Black Forest gâteau, 158
  chewy chocolate cookies, 22
  choc and coconut slices, 28
  chocolate amaretti, 23
  chocolate amaretto
    marquise, 122
  chocolate and cherry
    gâteau, 157
  chocolate and nut gâteau, 145
  chocolate and orange angel
    cake, 145
  chocolate banana cake, 226
  chocolate cake, luxurious, 130
  chocolate cheesecake, 150
  chocolate cheesecake tart, 103
  chocolate chestnut roll, 162
  chocolate chiffon pie, 99
  chocolate chip brownies, 31
  chocolate chip cookies, 17
  chocolate chip oat cookies, 28
  chocolate crackle-tops, 27
  chocolate date cake, 146

chocolate delights, 26
chocolate fairy cakes, 138
chocolate fruit cake, 178
chocolate fudge brownies, 34
chocolate fudge icing, 251
chocolate-iced anniversary
    cake, 174
chocolate layer cake, 137, 140
chocolate lemon tart, 101
chocolate macaroons, 16
chocolate mint-filled cakes, 138
chocolate nut tart, 93
chocolate-orange Battenburg
    cake, 136
chocolate-orange drops, 16
chocolate-peanut cake, 137
chocolate pear tart, 100
chocolate pecan torte, 155
chocolate pretzels, 15
chocolate raspberry macaroon
    bars, 35
chocolate jelly roll, 148
chocolate walnut bars, 39
chunky chocolate drops, 27
Devil's cake with orange, 140
French chocolate cake, 141
fudge-glazed chocolate
    brownies, 34
ginger florentines, 19
glossy chocolate icing, 228
jazzy chocolate gâteau, 180
maple-pecan brownies, 33
marbled brownies, 31
mocha Brazil layer torte, 153
mocha Victoria sponge, 131
multi-layer chocolate cake, 139
nutty chocolate squares, 30
oatmeal and date brownies, 32
one-stage chocolate
    sponge, 130
raisin brownies, 30
rich chocolate nut cake, 139
rich chocolate pie, 105
Sachertorte, 159
truffle filo tarts, 95
Valentine's box of chocolates
    cake, 171
vegan chocolate gâteau, 158
velvety mocha tart, 109
white chocolate brownies, 33
Christening cakes, 176-7
Christening sampler, 176
Christmas cakes: Christmas
    stocking cake, 166
  Christmas tree cake, 165
  eggless, 163
  glazed Christmas ring, 164
  marbled cracker cake, 166
  moist and rich, 163
  Noel Christmas cake, 165
  Yule log, 162
Christmas cookies, 13
Christmas shapes, 19
Cinnamon: cinnamon and apple
    gâteau, 242
  cinnamon-coated cookies, 10
  cinnamon treats, 26
  Mexican cinnamon cookies, 21
Circus cake, 200
Clare's American carrot cake, 128
Cloth-of-roses cake, 173
Clover leaf rolls, 73

Clown face cake, 192
Coconut: banana coconut
    cake, 121
   choc and coconut slices, 28
   coconut bread, 84
   coconut cream tart, 109
   coconut lime gâteau, 156
   coconut macaroons, 16
   lemon coconut layer cake, 119
   oaty coconut cookies, 10
Coffee: coffee almond gâteau, 157
   coffee, peach and almond
    daquoise, 153
   coffee sponge drops, 224
   mocha Brazil layer torte, 153
   mocha Victoria sponge, 131
   velvety mocha tart, 109
Computer game, 206
Cookies, 8-29, 224, 238
Corn: cornsticks, 46
   savory bread, 46
   spicy corn bread, 43
Country bread, 70
Crackers, curry, 238
Cranberries: apple and cranberry
    lattice, 86
   apple & cranberry muffins, 60
   cranberry and apple ring, 126
Cream cheese spirals, 11
Crème au beurre, 249
Creole Christmas cake, 117
Croissants, 74
Crumble cakes, 124
Crunchy jumbles, 10
Crunchy-topped sponge loaf, 114
Cupcakes, mint-filled, 138
Curry crackers, 238

Daisy christening cake, 177
Danish wreath, 85
Dart board, 204
Dates: chocolate date cake, 146
   date and apple muffins, 222
   date and nut malt loaf, 49
   date and pecan loaf, 40
   date oven biscuits, 66
   oatmeal and date brownies, 32
   spiced date and walnut
    cake, 54
   sticky date and apple bars, 36
Devil's cake with orange, 140
Dill: dill and potato cakes, 67
   dill bread, 76
Dinner milk rolls, 75
Doll's house cake, 195
Dorset apple cake, 112
Double heart cake, 172
Dried fruit: dried fruit loaf, 42
   fruit salad cake, 133
   see also Fruit cakes
Drop pancakes, 63, 240
Drum cake, 208
Dundee cake, 160

Easter cookies, 24
Easter egg nest cake, 169
Easter sponge cake, 168
Eggless Christmas cake, 163
Eighteenth birthday cake, 179
Engagement cake, 172
Exotic celebration gâteau, 156
Fairy cakes, 133, 138

Fairy castle cake, 188
Fall dessert cake, 115
Farmhouse cookies, 8
Festive apple pie, 91
Figgy bars, 37
Filo and apricot purses, 223
Filo scrunchies, 223
Filo tarts, truffle, 95
Fire engine cake, 191
Fish-shaped cake, 185
Flapjacks, 25
Flickering candle cake, 179
Floating balloons cake, 203
Florentines, 15
   ginger florentines, 19
Flourless fruit cake, 164
Flower birthday cake, 180
Flowerpot cake, 216
Flowers, sugar-frosting, 252
Focaccia, 78, 231
Fondant icing, 247
French bread, 74
French chocolate cake, 141
Fresh fruit genoese, 154
Frog prince cake, 201
Frostings, see Icings
Fruit: baked cheesecake with
    fresh fruits, 151
   exotic celebration gâteau, 156
   fruit tartlets, 102
   lattice berry pie, 111
   pound cake with red fruit, 135
   red berry sponge tart, 89
   red berry tart with lemon
    cream, 106
   surprise fruit tarts, 95
   tofu berry "cheesecake," 152
Fruit and Brazil nut teabread, 51
Fruit and cinnamon buns, 56
Fruit and nut cake, 227
Fruit cakes, 116-17, 129, 160,
   163-6, 168, 246, 227
Fruit salad cake, 133
Fruity teabread, 40
Fudge-frosted starry roll, 182
Fudge frosting, 249
Fudge-glazed brownies, 34
Fudge icing, chocolate, 251

Gâteaux, 145, 147, 153-9
Genoese sponge cake, 244
Geranium cheese, carrot cake
   with, 120
Ghost cake, 184
Gift wrapped package, 211
Ginger: banana and ginger
    teabread, 229
   banana ginger parkin, 113
   banana gingerbread slices, 220
   ginger cookies, 11
   ginger shapes, 15
   ginger florentines, 19
   spice cake with ginger, 118
   upside-down pear and ginger
    cake, 125
Glacé icing, 250
Glaze, apricot, 228
Glazed Christmas ring, 164
Glittering star cake, 217
Golden wedding heart cake, 175
Golden raisins: golden raisin
    cornmeal cookies, 21

Swedish golden raisin
   bread, 235
Gooseberry cake, 113
Granary baps, 236
Granola: chewy fruit slice, 35
   crunchy granola muffins, 62
Greek honey and lemon
   cake, 126
Greek New Year cake, 167

Halloween pumpkin cake, 182
Ham: and tomato biscuits, 239
   Parma ham and Parmesan
    bread, 232
Hazelnuts: chocolate and nut
    gâteau, 145
   hazelnut squares, 39
   pear and hazelnut flan, 94
   raspberry hazelnut
    meringue, 143
   rich chocolate nut cake, 139
Heart cake, 214
Herbs: herb popovers, 47
   spiral herb bread, 76
Honey: Greek honey and lemon
   cake, 126
   spiced honey nut cake, 127
Horse stencil cake, 195
Hotdog cake, 207

Ice cream cones, 208
Iced fancies, 188
Iced paradise cake, 134
Icings: American frosting, 250
   butter icing, 248
   butterscotch frosting, 251
   chocolate fudge icing, 251
   crème au beurre, 249
   fondant, 247
   fudge frosting, 249
   glacé icing, 250
   glossy chocolate icing, 228
   meringue frosting, 253
   royal icing, 248,
   simple piped flowers, 250
Irish soda bread, 80
Irish whiskey cake, 114, 227
Italian almond biscotti, 12

Jazzy chocolate gâteau, 180
Jelly roll, 149, 162, 245
   almond and raspberry, 147
   chestnut and orange, 241
   chocolate, 148
   orange and walnut, 148
   peach, 228
Jewel cake, 134

Kite cake, 207
Kiwi ricotta tart, 101
Kugelhopf, 85
Kulich, 161

Ladybird cake, 201
Lattice berry pie, 111
Latticed peaches, 94
Lavender cookies, 23
Lemon: chocolate lemon tart, 101
   Greek honey and lemon
    cake, 126
   lemon and apricot cake, 132
   lemon and walnut teabread, 48

lemon bars, 37
lemon chiffon cake, 242
lemon coconut layer cake, 119
lemon meringue pie, 88
lemon sponge fingers, 221
lemon tart, 107
lemon yogurt ring, 119
red berry tart with lemon
   cream, 106
tangy lemon cake, 123
warm lemon syrup cake, 146
Light fruit cake, 116, 246
Light jeweled fruit cake, 117
Lime: coconut lime gâteau, 156
   lime tart, 102
Lion cake, 196
Liquorice candy cake, 218
Low fat drop pancakes, 240
Lucky horseshoe cake, 183

Macaroons: chocolate
   macaroons, 16
   chocolate macaroon bars, 35
   coconut macaroons, 16
Madeira cake, 245
Madeleine cakes, 135
Magic rabbit cake, 198
Malt loaf, 244
   date and nut, 49
Mangoes: and amaretti strudel, 40
   mango teabread, 45
Maple syrup: maple-pecan
   brownies, 33
   maple walnut tart, 108
Marbled brownies, 31
Marbled cheesecake, 151
Marbled chocolate-nut cake, 137
Marbled cracker cake, 166
Marbled ring cake, 144
Marbled spice cake, 142
Marbling, 253
Marmalade: cherry muffins, 53
   marmalade teabread, 53
Marsala cookies, 21
Marzipan, 247
   chocolate fruit cake, 178
   chocolate-orange cake, 136
   marzipan bell cake, 176
Melting moments, 24
Meringue frosting, 253
Meringues, 22
   caramel meringues, 225
   coffee, peach and almond
    daquoise, 153
   forgotten gâteau, 154
   lemon meringue pie, 88
   mocha Brazil layer torte, 153
   raspberry meringue
    gâteau, 143
   raspberry vacherin, 40
   snowballs, 225
   toasted oat meringues, 22
   toffee meringue bars, 38
Mexican cinnamon cookies, 21
Mincemeat: almond tartlets, 98
   deluxe mincemeat tart, 90
   mince pies with orange
    pastry, 98
Mobile phone cake, 213
Mocha Brazil layer torte, 153
Mocha tart, velvety, 109
Mocha Victoria sponge, 131

Monsters on the moon, 200
Mother's Day basket, 170
Mother's Day bouquet, 169
Mouse-in-bed cake, 186
Muffins: apple and cranberry, 60
    blueberry, 60
    cherry marmalade, 53
    crunchy granola, 62
    date and apple, 222
    prune, 61
    raspberry, 62, 222
    yogurt and honey, 61
Multi-grain bread, 68
Musical cake, 198

New Year cakes, 167
Noah's ark cake, 194
Noel Christmas cake, 165
Novelty cakes, 210-19
Number 6 cake, 203
Number 7 cake, 197
Number 10 cake, 212
Nurse's kit cake, 199
Nut lace wafers, 29
Nutty chocolate squares, 30

Oats: banana ginger parkin, 113
    chocolate chip oat cookies, 28
    crunchy oatmeal cookies, 8
    flapjacks, 25
    oat and apricot clusters, 9
    oatcakes, 238
    oatmeal and date brownies, 32
    oatmeal bread, 69
    oatmeal buttermilk muffins, 59
    oatmeal lace rounds, 29
    oaty coconut cookies, 10
    oaty crisps, 224
    parkin, 112, 122
    toasted oat meringues, 22
Olive and oregano bread, 230
One-stage chocolate sponge, 130
One-stage Victoria sandwich, 131
Orange: apricot and orange
    roll, 149
    banana orange loaf, 52
    chestnut and orange roll, 241
    chocolate-orange drops, 16
    orange and honey teabread, 50
    orange and raisin biscuits, 64
    orange and walnut roll, 148
    orange cookies, 12
    orange tart, 110
    orange wheat loaf, 49

Panforte, 161
Pansy retirement cake, 181
Parkin, 112, 122
    banana ginger parkin, 113
Parma ham and Parmesan
    bread, 232
Party teddy bear cake, 187
Passion cake, 128
Peaches: coffee, peach and
    almond daquoise, 153
    latticed peaches, 94
    peach and Amaretto cake, 241
    peach jelly roll, 228
    peach leaf pie, 87
    peach tart with almond, 106
Peanut butter: marbled
    chocolate-peanut cake, 137

peanut butter cookies, 17
Pears: chocolate pear tart, 100
    pear and almond tart, 107
    pear and apple crumble
        pie, 100
    pear and cardamom cake, 127
    pear and golden raisin
        teabread, 229
    pear and hazelnut flan, 94
    upside-down pear and ginger
        cake, 125
    walnut and pear lattice pie, 87
Pecans: chocolate torte, 155
    date and pecan loaf, 40
    maple-pecan brownies, 33
    nut and apple gâteau, 155
    nutty chocolate squares, 30
    pecan rye bread, 82
    pecan tart, 108
    pecan tartlets, 93
    sticky nut buns, 58
Pepper cookies, 20
Petal retirement cake, 181
Pies, 86-9, 91, 111
Pinball machine, 193
Pineapple: pineapple and apricot
        cake, 123
    pineapple and cinnamon drop
        pancakes, 240
    upside-down cake, 125
Pink monkey cake, 185
Pirate's hat, 193
Pistachios: spiced cake, 127
Pizza cake, 216
Pleated rolls, 72
Plums: Alsatian plum tart, 97
    autumn dessert cake, 115
    plum crumble cake, 124
    plum pie, 111
Popovers, 47
Poppy seed knots, 73
Poppy seed rolls, 236
Porcupine, 186
Potatoes: chive and potato
        biscuits, 239
    dill and potato cakes, 67
    potato bread, 79
Pound cake with red fruit, 135
Pretzels, chocolate, 15
Prunes: braided prune bread, 83
    prune and peel buns, 54
    prune muffins, 61
Pumpkin: pumpkin muffins, 59
    pumpkin pie, 92

Quick-mix sponge cake, 244

Racing ring, 217
Racing track cake, 202
Raisins: raisin bran buns, 55
    raisin bread, 84
    raisin brownies, 30
    spiced raisin bars, 38
Raspberries: almond and
        raspberry jelly roll, 147
    raspberry crumble buns, 55
    raspberry meringue,
        gâteau, 143
    raspberry cookies, 13
    raspberry muffins, 62, 222
    raspberry tart, 110
    raspberry vacherin, 40

Red berry sponge tart, 89
Red berry tart with lemon, 106
Retirement cakes, 181
Rhubarb and cherry pie, 91
Rice cake, Thai, 129
Rich fruit cake, 116, 246
Rolls: clover leaf rolls, 73
    dinner milk rolls, 75
    pleated rolls, 72
    poppy seed knots, 73
    poppy seed rolls, 236
    whole wheat rolls, 70
Rose blossom wedding cake, 173
Rosemary: rosemary bread, 79
    rosemary focaccia, 78
Rosette cake, 212
Royal crown cake, 209
Royal icing, 248,
Rye bread, 77, 233
    pecan rye bread, 82

St Clement's cake, 121
Sachertorte, 159
Saffron: cardamom and saffron
        tea loaf, 44
    saffron focaccia, 78
Sage soda bread, 80
Sailing boat, 189
Sand castle cake, 192
Sesame seed bread, 77
Shirt and tie cake, 213
Shortbread, 25
Shortcake gâteau, 147
Silver wedding cake, 175
Simnel cake, 168
Snowballs, 225
Soda bread, 80, 244
Sour cream crumble cake, 124
Space ship cake, 202
Spice cake with ginger, 118
Spicy corn bread, 43
Spicy pepper cookies, 20
Spider's web cake, 189, 204
Spinach and bacon bread, 232
Spiral herb bread, 76
Sponge cakes, 130-1, 244
Sponge fingers, 221
Starry New Year cake, 167
Sticky nut buns, 58
Strawberries: strawberry tart, 103
    gâteau with heartsease, 154
    strawberry basket cake, 219
    strawberry cake, 210
    strawberry gâteau, 243
    strawberry mint sponge, 143
    strawberry gâteau, 147
    strawberry tart, 97
Strudel: apple, 96
    cherry, 96
    mango and amaretti, 40
Sugar cookies, 20
Sun cake, 219
Sun-dried tomato braid, 230
Sunflower golden raisin
        biscuits, 65
Surprise fruit tarts, 95
Swedish golden raisin
        bread, 235
Sweetheart cake, 172, 211
Sweet potato and raisin bread, 48
Sweet sesame loaf, 44
Syrup tart, almond, 104

Tablecloth cake, 215
Tarte Tatin, 105
Tarts, 89-90, 92-5, 97-110
Teabreads, 40-54, 229
Teddy bear christening cake, 177
Teddy's birthday, 187
Thai rice cake, 129
Tia Maria gâteau, 243
Toffee meringue bars, 38
Tofu berry "cheesecake," 152
Tomatoes: ham and tomato
        biscuits, 239
    sun-dried tomato braid, 230
    tomato breadsticks, 81
Toy car cake, 191
Toy telephone cake, 190
Traditional sugar cookies, 20
Train cake, 197
Treacle tart, 104
Treasure chest cake, 196
Treasure map, 209
Truffle filo tarts, 95
Two-tone bread, 71

Upside-down cakes, 125

Vacherin, raspberry, 40
Valentine's box of chocolates
        cake, 171
Valentine's heart cake, 171
Vegan chocolate gâteau, 158
Vegan Dundee cake, 160
Velvety mocha tart, 109
Victoria sandwich, one-stage, 131
Victoria sponge, mocha, 131

Walnuts: apricot nut loaf, 41
    chocolate walnut bars, 39
    chocolate walnut buns, 59
    lemon and walnut teabread, 48
    maple walnut tart, 108
    orange and walnut jelly
        roll, 148
    prune bread, 84
    sour cream crumble cake, 124
    walnut and pear lattice pie, 87
    walnut bread, 82
    walnut coffee gâteau, 159
Wedding cakes: basketweave, 174
    rose blossom, 173
Whiskey cake, Irish, 114, 227
White bread, 68
Whole wheat banana nut loaf, 41
Whole wheat biscuits, 64
Whole wheat bread, 71
Whole wheat herb triangles, 237
Whole wheat rolls, 70

Yogurt: apricot yogurt cookies, 9
    lemon yogurt ring, 119
    yogurt and honey muffins, 61
Yule log, 162

Zucchini: carrot and zucchini
        cake, 120
    zucchini crown bread, 83
    zucchini teabread, 45